Southern Crossroads

Religion in the South

John B. Boles, Series Editor

All According to God's Plan: Southern Baptist Missions and Race, 1945–1970
Alan Scot Willis

Can Somebody Shout Amen! Inside the Tents and Tabernacles of American Revivalists
Patsy Sims

A Coat of Many Colors: Religion and Society along the Cape Fear River of North Carolina
Walter H. Conser Jr.

Episcopalians and Race: Civil War to Civil Rights
Gardiner H. Shattuck Jr.

A Genealogy of Dissent: Southern Baptist Protest in the Twentieth Century
David Stricklin

God's Rascal: J. Frank Norris and the Beginnings of Southern Fundamentalism
Barry Hankins

The Great Revival: Beginnings of the Bible Belt
John B. Boles

*Liquor in the Land of the Lost Cause:
Southern White Evangelicals and the Prohibition Movement*
Joe L. Coker

Politics and Religion in the White South
Edited by Glenn Feldman

Raccoon John Smith: Frontier Kentucky's Most Famous Preacher
Elder John Sparks

The Roots of Appalachian Christianity: The Life and Legacy of Elder Shubal Stearns
Elder John Sparks

Serving Two Masters: Moravian Brethren in Germany and North Carolina
Elisabeth W. Sommer

*When Slavery Was Called Freedom:
Evangelicalism, Proslavery, and the Causes of the Civil War*
John Patrick Daly

William Louis Poteat: A Leader in the Progressive-Era South
Randal L. Hall

CROSSROADS

Perspectives on
Religion and Culture

SOUTHERN

Edited by
Walter H. Conser Jr.
and Rodger M. Payne

THE UNIVERSITY PRESS OF KENTUCKY

 # 181601266

The University Press of Kentucky

Scholarly publisher for the Commonwealth,
serving Bellarmine University, Berea College, Centre College of Kentucky,
Eastern Kentucky University, The Filson Historical Society, Georgetown
College, Kentucky Historical Society, Kentucky State University, Morehead
State University, Murray State University, Northern Kentucky University,
Transylvania University, University of Kentucky, University of Louisville,
and Western Kentucky University.
All rights reserved.

Editorial and Sales Offices: The University Press of Kentucky
663 South Limestone Street, Lexington, Kentucky 40508-4008
www.kentuckypress.com

12 11 10 09 08   5 4 3 2 1

Library of Congress Cataloging-in-Publication Data

Southern crossroads : perspectives on religion and culture / edited by Walter H.
Conser, Jr. and Rodger M. Payne.
    p. cm. — (Religion in the south)
  Includes bibliographical references and index.
  ISBN 978-0-8131-2494-0 (hardcover : alk. paper)
  1. Christianity and culture—Southern States. 2. United States—Church
history. I. Conser, Walter H. II. Payne, Rodger M. (Rodger Milton)
  BR535.S68 2008
  200.975—dc22   2007052576

This book is printed on acid-free recycled paper meeting the requirements of the
American National Standard for Permanence in Paper for Printed Library Materials.

Manufactured in the United States of America.

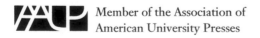   Member of the Association of
American University Presses

To Sam Hill and Don Mathews,
  two gurus of southern religion

Contents

Introduction

Walter H. Conser Jr. and Rodger M. Payne

Crossroads are places of power and transformation. The traveler at a crossroads may suddenly change directions or transgress established boundaries; at the crossroads, different worlds come into contact, and perhaps conflict, with one another. In some religions, such as the African diasporic religion of Vodun, the guardian of the crossroads must always be first addressed and propitiated before the beneficence of the supernatural world may be accessed. Similarly, in Christianity, the cross is a powerful symbol that connects the mundane human world with the realm of the divine; but this dynamic can, however, move equally well in the opposite direction. According to a famous southern folktale, at a crossroads in the Mississippi Delta's Bible Belt, Robert Johnson sold his soul to the devil for the ability to play the blues guitar like no other.

Never static, the crossroads is a place of energy and movement, of potency and potential. It can represent a crisis, an epiphany, or a time of decision when one is faced with the need to make a choice about which road to follow. Crossroads are also places of exchange. At the crossroads, trajectories of influence can extend outward from the center to the periphery, while new energies flow inward.

The title of this volume invokes this metaphor of crossroads to suggest the motion and potentiality contained in the study of southern religion. As a field of study, it is less than fifty years old. It emerged at a time marked by change, and the field itself has remained fluid over the years. The first scholars to focus on southern religion—as opposed to congregational or denominational histories from within the region—wrote at a time when the old order of Jim Crow segregation was dissolving with the emergence of the civil rights movement. Their concerns were often as theological as they were academic: for example, how should the "churches" respond to the rapidly changing society? Samuel S. Hill's *Southern Churches in*

Crisis (1966) captured this perspective with its expressed desire to "provide the church with a richer and more authentic vision of itself and its mission."[1] Probing the impact (both constructive and negative) of evangelical Protestantism in the region's history, this book served as a charter document for the field.

Subsequent scholars, writing after Jim Crow had been defeated, if not entirely vanquished, were less concerned with theology and the call for social justice and more focused on religion and cultural values as these were expressed in an identifiable mythology, ritual, and organization. Charles Reagan Wilson's *Baptized in Blood: The Religion of the Lost Cause, 1865–1920* (1980) continued to interrogate the place of religion in the formation of southern identity.[2] Cultural identity replaced political identity for white southerners, and religion, Wilson suggested, was at the very center of that identity, providing familiar theological tropes such as the "chosen people," the "spirituality of the church," and a providential interpretation of history. Occasions such as Confederate Memorial Day made the slight etymological shift from holiday to holy day, as southern ministers led their congregations in religious commemorations and took up positions of leadership in emerging organizations dedicated to perpetuating the Lost Cause. Wilson's approach was paralleled by other monographs of the period as well as an encyclopedia and a bibliography dedicated to exploring southern religion.[3]

Wilson's volume was significant in other ways. By incorporating insights and methods drawn from sociology and anthropology, *Baptized in Blood* signaled a departure in the study of southern religious history, a phenomenon that would become more pronounced through the 1980s and 1990s. Books such as Rhys Isaac's *The Transformation of Virginia, 1740–1790* and Ted Ownby's *Subduing Satan: Religion, Recreation, and Manhood in the Rural South, 1865–1920* made use of theorists such as Clifford Geertz and Victor Turner to supplement their historical analyses.[4] More specifically ethnographic approaches, such as *Diversities of Gifts: Field Studies in Southern Religion*, began to appear.[5] Thomas A. Tweed's award-winning *Our Lady of the Exile* both presented a model ethnography of Cuban immigrant Catholicism in Miami and indicated that the older boundaries of what constituted the study of southern religion had been breached for good.[6]

Responding to these new interdisciplinary approaches, the *Jour-*

nal of Southern Religion (*JSR*) began publication in 1998. As a fully peer-reviewed academic journal reflecting the best traditions of scholarship in the study of religion, *JSR* has garnered contributions by some of the leading scholars in the field. As demonstrated in the essays from the journal selected for inclusion in this volume, this new direction in the field of southern religion now incorporates cultural and ritual studies, geography, sociology, and anthropology as partners to the examinations of systems of thought, doctrine, and belief found in traditional historical, philosophical, and literary analyses of religion. Recently, *JSR* has expanded its reach even further by including interviews with documentary filmmakers and prominent southerners, as well as presenting critical forums by scholars that are designed to comment on the developing "canon" of southern religious studies and reflect upon the current status of classic texts. While the journal has stimulated new research, the potential benefits offered to the study of religion—to say nothing of the study of the South—by electronic publication has yet to be realized in full, and will continue to develop as scholars learn how to use the World Wide Web to its fullest advantage.

At the same time as those within the field of southern religion embraced an interdisciplinary approach, scholars in the broader field of American religious history began giving renewed attention to studies with a regional focus. The background to this shift in the scholarly literature was increasing suspicion about the continued utility of a master narrative for American religious history. How much longer could the story of that history be told as the story of Puritan theology and its vicissitudes, or as the consensus model of mainline Protestantism, or even as the rise of religious liberty? Regional identity provided a matrix for understanding important aspects of American religious history and furnished grounds for analysis of salient comparisons and contrasts in the examination of the Pacific Slope, the upper Midwest, New England, and the Great Basin as well as the South. Though it may not be the only identifiable region in the United States, clearly the South is considered by most observers to be a uniquely distinctive area. Born of politics and economics, slavery and secession, perduring religious habits and recent commercial advances, the South has been an obvious choice for regional analysis.

Finally, together with the move away from grand narratives to more regional ones has come the shift from theology to the lived experience of religious believers. On the one hand, this has meant a new interest in the kaleidoscopic religious diversity of the American experience, even in places, such as the American South, where one least expected to find it. Thus *Religion in the American South* carried the subtitle "Protestants and Others in History and Culture."[7] Similarly, *Religion in the Contemporary South: Changes, Continuities, and Context* included chapters dealing with Latinos, Hindus, Jews, and Muslims.[8] On the other hand, attention to lived experiences also highlighted the variety to be found within that experience and reinforced the interdisciplinary inclination of the field.

Thus *Southern Crossroads* showcases the fusion of interdisciplinary research, with exploration into such domains as food, music, art, vernacular folkways, and literature; it examines the intersection of southern religion with violence, ritual, and gender. At the crossroads, one can gain fresh insights by looking at the familiar with new questions as well as by looking at unfamiliar conjunctions with new understanding. Beyond that, one can see—for example, through the everyday experience of food, understood out of a religious past and projected into an equally religious future—the establishment of boundaries and their observance and occasional transgression. And one can watch as those same conventions move out to other regions and maintain the old or evolve into something new. Indeed, whether it is the diaspora of southern Baptists throughout the United States or the nation's familiarity with white and black southern gospel music traditions, southern religion has moved out and beyond over the crossroads. But other influences, such as Buddhism and Afro-Cuban Santeria or Jewish and Scottish heritage, have likewise come *into* the South, and the dynamic of exchange continues unabated.

In this volume, one sees the shift in the study of southern religiosity away from churches and denominations and toward religious life as it encounters disparate cultural elements. Rather than adopt a discipline-specific definition of culture, the editors employ a rather elastic understanding of the category of culture, which includes symbolic representations, material artifacts, ideological formulations, and aesthetic sensibilities. The essays canvass popular through elite forms of cultural experience as well as attend to material embodiments of religion. Consequently, in some essays congregations or denominations provide the sites for engagement with issues of authority and power, worship style and musical tradition, or syncretism and resistance, while other pieces move entirely outside the traditional focus on the church.

Three themes shape this book and thus the rubrics of its organization. The first set of contributions addresses the religious aspects of southern cultural components such as music, art, vernacular folkways and material culture, suburban experience, and literature. Not surprisingly, religious contexts help to shape the contours and meanings of these domains of human experience in a variety of ways. Through a wealth of previous associations, present understandings, and anticipated connections, religion infuses these forms of life, sometimes even in unexpected fashions. The essays in the second section explore the interactions of local, immigrant, and folk religions with other groups. Here issues of achieving recognition in the eyes of others and accomplishment for oneself come front and center. How do categories of *refugee* or *immigrant* change into those of *neighbor* or *resident*? Can a region noted for its heritage of religious self-consciousness reach beyond exclusivity to become more authentically inclusive? And, ironically, how have some groups sought to use religiously derived borders and heritages to preserve their own individuality and push against pressure for conformity from the dominant culture? The last collection of essays investigates religion and markers of identity such as gender, violence, ritual, and politics. Sometimes constraining, often contested, always present, these dimensions of human life engage the religious situation at the deepest levels. Their horizons of meaning include boundary formation and transgression, compositions of hopes fulfilled or ambushed, and patterns of behavior at times ecstatic and at times familiar. Their structures bristle with energy and evidence transformative power. From our location at the crossroads, the complexity of identity becomes more intelligible.

Finally, race is a major trope in any discussion of the South, including its religious heritage and experience. Readers will find that race threads through many of the essays, sometimes directly, sometimes obliquely. The violence that underlines the experience of race in the South is well known, though it remains disturbing. Yet in several essays readers will also discover areas of interaction, partnership, and engagement between white and black religious believers.

Standing thus at the crossroads, our readers—not only scholars and college students but all those interested in southern religion—will understand the recent trajectories undertaken and glimpse what still lies ahead.

NOTES

1. Samuel S. Hill, *Southern Churches in Crisis* (Boston: Beacon, 1966), xii.

2. Charles Reagan Wilson, *Baptized in Blood: The Religion of the Lost Cause, 1865–1920* (Athens: University of Georgia Press, 1980).

3. Samuel S. Hill, ed., *Encyclopedia of Religion in the South* (Macon, Ga.: Mercer University Press, 1984); Charles H. Lippy, ed., *Bibliography of Religion in the South* (Macon, Ga.: Mercer University Press, 1985).

4. Rhys Isaac, *The Transformation of Virginia, 1740–1790* (Chapel Hill: University of North Carolina Press, 1982); Ted Ownby, *Subduing Satan: Religion, Recreation, and Manhood in the Rural South, 1865–1920* (Chapel Hill: University of North Carolina Press, 1990).

5. Ruel W. Tyson, James L. Peacock, and Daniel W. Patterson, eds., *Diversities of Gifts: Field Studies in Southern Religion* (Urbana: University of Illinois Press, 1988).

6. Thomas A. Tweed, *Our Lady of the Exile* (New York: Oxford University Press, 1997).

7. Beth Barton Schweiger and Donald G. Mathews, eds., *Religion in the American South: Protestants and Others in History and Culture* (Chapel Hill: University of North Carolina Press, 2004).

8. Corrie E. Norman and Don S. Armentrout, eds., *Religion in the Contemporary South: Changes, Continuities, and Context* (Knoxville: University of Tennessee Press, 2005).

RELIGIOUS ASPECTS
OF SOUTHERN CULTURE

"JUST A LITTLE TALK WITH JESUS"

Elvis Presley, Religious Music, and Southern Spirituality

CHARLES REAGAN WILSON

Popular religious music, such as that sung by gospel quartets and country music bands, is a powerful expression of southern religious life. Nurtured in Nashville and Memphis, in local congregations and regional songfests, this music sometimes transgressed boundaries, though often it confirmed them. Using the person of Elvis Presley as a window to explore southern religious practice and belief, Charles Reagan Wilson identifies a distinctive southern spirituality that is often overlooked in studies of the South. Wilson finds that Elvis's journey from the Spirit-filled Pentecostal faith of his youth to the experimental spirituality of the 1960s mirrors changes in American as well as southern culture. Moreover, Wilson investigates the ethos of Protestant evangelicalism, with its dynamic of individualism and personal piety, a theme that is also examined by others in this volume.

In December 1956 Elvis Presley dropped in at Sun Studios in Memphis, just as a Carl Perkins recording session was ending. Presley was now a national star, having transcended earlier that year his previous status as a regional rockabilly performer. That special day became known as the Million Dollar Session because of the supposed "million dollars" worth of talent that included Presley, Perkins, Jerry Lee Lewis, and, briefly, Johnny Cash. An open microphone recorded a lively jam session. For the student of southern religious music,

9

it was an especially revealing moment. In addition to improvising with country, blues, and early rock songs, the group sang from the common body of southern religious songs, some of them gospel tunes that dated from nineteenth-century revivals, others African American spirituals, others popular gospel-quartet numbers. All of these young performers who had grown up in the countryside near Memphis knew the songs, and when one started singing, the others easily fell into supporting lines. They had all come out of church backgrounds and would have been familiar with "Farther Along," "When God Dips His Love in My Heart," "Blessed Jesus (Hold My Hand)," and "As We Travel Along on the Jericho Road." Elvis sang "Peace in the Valley," an old classic written by black composer Thomas A. Dorsey and the song he sang on the "Ed Sullivan Show" to defuse public concerns that he was an immoral renegade destroying America's youth. Between songs the boys talked about the white gospel quartets that were so active around Memphis, an epicenter of white and black gospel traditions.[1]

"Just a Little Talk with Jesus" was an especially revealing song of southern spirituality that day in Sun Studios, two years after the 1954 Brown decision and one year before the Soviet satellite Sputnik, during a decade that launched extraordinary cultural changes in the South. Elvis knew the song profoundly, singing a lively version and then slowing down the pace to fit the mood of the lyrics. The song's narrator tells the essential evangelical story of one "lost in sin" but not without hope because "Jesus took me in." When that happened, "a little light from heaven" filled his soul. Redemption is seen in the next lines, which say God "made my heart in love and He wrote my name above." Despite "doubts and fears" and even though "your eyes be filled with tears," "my Jesus is a friend who watches day and night." In the end, "just a little talk with Jesus gonna make it right."[2]

The Million Dollar Session is an appropriate introduction to the importance of Elvis Presley in understanding the role that music played in defining a distinctive southern spirituality and the impact on that relationship of the dramatic changes in the South over the roughly two decades between that day in Sun Studios in 1956 and Presley's death in Memphis in 1977. Charles Wolfe, Peter Guralnick, and other historians and journalists have written about Presley's relationship to the gospel music tradition, but the broader question of how Presley can help open up the unexplored issue of southern spirituality has not been explored.

Studies of "American spirituality" that stress the distinction between "religion" and "spirituality" have recently appeared. Robert Wuthnow, a leading student of American spirituality, concludes that this new scholarly work reflects increasing popular interest in spirituality. People see spirituality as "somehow more authentic, more personally compelling, an expression of their search for the sacred," whereas religion suggests a "social arrangement that seems arbitrary, limiting or at best convenient."[3] Despite the new popular and scholarly interest in American spirituality, none of the scholarly works even mentions the South or southerners, and certainly none addresses a regional expression of spirituality that comes out of the white working-class culture of the South. Neither the *Encyclopedia of Religion in the South* nor the *Encyclopedia of Southern Culture* include entries on "spirituality," and a survey of classic works by historians Samuel Hill, David Edwin Harrell, Wayne Flynt, and others suggest they have seldom dealt directly with "spirituality" in the context of a southern regional religious tradition.

Historian Samuel Weber's recent article, "Spirituality in the South," prepared for *The New Encyclopedia of Southern Culture*, has intentionally opened up the topic for analysis, but the essay stresses that "one can see as many 'spiritualities' . . . as there are individual seekers."[4] While undoubtedly true, Elvis Presley's inherited and changing spirituality does relate to predominant regional patterns. While young Presley can easily be seen as a representative southerner of his time and place, it is hard to make that argument for the last two decades of his life, dominated as they were by the extraordinary success and celebrity that moved him beyond regional to national and international contexts. Nonetheless, his relationship to religious music and southern spirituality makes him a revealing and perhaps even an emblematic figure in southern culture.

The scholarly discussion of spirituality originally came more out of Catholic tradition than the Protestant one that has dominated the American South. *The Oxford Dictionary of the Christian Church* defines the term "spirituality" as referring to "people's subjective practice and experience of their religion, or to the spiritual exercises and beliefs which individuals or groups have with regard to their personal experience with God." This might include prayer, meditation, contemplation, and mysticism. It notes that certain groups have "a characteristic set of spiritual practices and beliefs" such that "they may be regarded as constituting a 'school of spirituality,'" such as Cistercian spirituality, Carmelite spirituality, or Jesuit spirituality. Reflecting recent changes, the dictionary notes that this usage is now more generalized, "so that there is an increasing interest in 'lay spirituality,' 'married spirituality,' etc."[5] In this context, religious music should be seen as the essence of a distinctive southern school of spirituality, rooted in particular spiritual exercises and devotional practices.

Consideration of spirituality in a regional context deepens the understanding that religiosity has infused southern culture far beyond the church doors. Presley's spirituality reflected the significance of the role of spiritual practice. Robert Wuthnow makes a useful distinction between "spirituality," which he defines as "a transcendent state of being or an aspect of reality," and the related idea of "spiritual practice," which he sees as "a more active or intentional form of behavior."[6] Few studies have examined ways in which spiritual practices change during people's lives and even fewer give attention to ways that American cultural changes affect the meaning of spiritual practices. Spirituality is socially constructed, and Elvis Presley's evolving spirituality, based in distinctive southern spiritual practices, provides a revealing focus for examining a virtually unexplored area of southern religiosity over several decades in the mid-twentieth century.

OLD-TIME MUSIC—ELVIS'S SPIRITUAL INHERITANCE

Gladys Presley's favorite singing group was the Louvin Brothers, the harmonizing country-music duo steeped in the South's religious music, and their experience shows something of a traditional, southern white school of spirituality based in religious music, which Elvis inherited. Born in the 1920s, the Louvins grew up at Sand Mountain, an isolated area in northern Alabama less than two hundred miles from Presley's Tupelo and part of the same hill-country, predominantly white folk culture. Music was an essential part of individual, family, and community life. In addition to dances and fiddling contests, such specifically religious gatherings as all-day church singings and Sacred Harp singings characterized the culture of the area. Their grandfather was a traditional banjo picker, and their mother sang old, unaccompanied folk ballads, like "Knoxville Girl," with roots in the British Isles. Their mother's family in general were active in Sacred Harp singing, a tradition based on songs from a popular songbook of that name from the 1840s that used shape notes, rather than position on the musical staff, to determine pitch. Once popular in New England and other areas of the United States, by the twentieth century shape-note singing came to be associated mostly with southern rural communities. Churches moved beyond its forms as worship music, but periodic singings, often in church buildings, created a "second church" experience as people renewed a traditional Calvinist-inspired faith by singing the old songs the old way. Sacred Harp singing helped to perpetuate a strong strain of Calvinism in the rural South, even as churches themselves softened Calvinism's rigors through a theology of redemption.

As well as growing up singing Sacred Harp songs, the Louvins participated in other activities that gave structure to this southern school of spirituality. Rural singing schools taught by traveling teachers who would instruct students in religious and other music, for example, became pervasive in the hill-country South. The singing convention also anchored southern spirituality. It gathered together those who wanted to sing new songs, published in small, paperback religious songbooks—which became an important devotional factor—and made accessible older and newer religious songs. Companies in the Tennessee towns of Lawrenceburg and Chattanooga, not far from either the Louvins or the Presleys, used modern, aggressive sales practices to promote their books, including sponsoring professional gospel quartets who sang from the new songbooks. These institutions and practices provided a structure for a southern spirituality rooted in religious music.[7]

The Louvins lived through the modernization of southern religious music, and the publishing companies were one example of that. The coming of radio in the 1920s and rural electrification of much of the rural South in the 1930s made religious music even more accessible and important to a changing culture. The Louvins heard Sunday morning preaching and everyday hymn singing on their radios. Phonograph records as well became an important source for the Louvins and other southerners in the evolving culture of spirituality in the decades between world wars. When their father visited Knoxville, he would go to the music store and bring home a dozen or so albums, which the family would listen to long into the night, including the mournful ballads of the Carter Family and the up-tempo religious songs of the Chuck Wagon Gang, both enormously popular, early southern recording artists who drew from the traditional musical culture and defined it for a new generation of listeners. Once they started performing, the Louvins themselves became a force in this school of southern spirituality. "We were always running into people who said that Louvin Brothers music caused them to live in a Christian home," remembered Charlie Louvin. "I run into people constantly that make you feel like you're a preacher."[8] Listening devoutly to Louvin Brothers records became a regular practice for those seeking not only entertainment but spiritual enlightenment rooted in the old ways of southern religion.

Music-based southern spirituality had, in fact, several expressions. Hank Williams, who grew up in central Alabama, not far south of the Louvin Brothers' home on Sand Mountain, was an immediate predecessor to Elvis as reigning musical giant in the South, and his experiences reveal much as well about southern spirituality. Hank's mother, Lillie, played organ at the Mount Olive West Baptist Church, and Hank sat beside her and sang "louder 'n' anybody else," as he put it. Lillie wanted him to "shout for the Lord," so she scraped together the money to send him to a shape-note singing school in Avant, Alabama. He learned hymns and gospel songs there that music critic Colin Escott says influenced Williams's approach to music in general more than anything else.[9] With Hank Williams we encounter a version of southern spirituality that is different from what Presley's would be. Williams's is a dark spirituality, based not on the Spirit-filled religion of Holiness-Pentecostalism that influenced Presley. Rather, Williams grew up in the Baptist church, inheriting a strong feeling of Calvinist sinfulness reinforced by the temptations he faced in his life as a working-class entertainer. His favorite song was "Death Is Only a Dream," filled with morbid images and supernaturalism:

> Sadly we sing with tremulous breath
> As we stand by the mystical stream,
> In the valley and by the dark river of death
> And yet 'tis no more than a dream.

His moralistic spirituality appeared in his narrative recordings as the fictitious singer Luke the Drifter, which included titles such as "Pictures from Life's Other Side," "Too Many Parties and Too Many Pals," "The Funeral," and "I've Been Down That Road Before." He bragged that "Men with Broken Hearts," which he wrote, was "the awfulest, morbidest song you ever heard in your life." The song on the charts at the time of his death was "You'll Never Get out of This World Alive." Hank Williams came out of a hard-scrabble, working-class world, and he came out of a hard-shell religious world as well. The broken bodies and broken hearts of this poor South nurtured a demanding, rigorous faith realized in a morbid, otherworldly, and unforgiving religious music. An important aspect of southern spirituality in its time and place, religious music was pervasive and articulated the frustrated spiritual strivings and spiritual dislocations of white working-class southerners moving from a world of sharecropping into that of a modern South.[10]

Elvis Presley grew up in the Assemblies of God church, a Pentecostal denomination that resembled Hank Williams's Baptist church in its fundamentalist theology and rigorous expectations about moral behavior, but Pentecostals also sought the gifts of the Spirit that could bring a transcendent spiritual ecstasy to people who often suffered life's vale of tears. Gladys took young Elvis to church in east Tupelo, and she reported the singing and the service left her feeling "renewed and restored."[11] When Presley was two years old, he jumped out of her lap at church and ran down to the front to sing with the choir, foreshadowing his musical preoccupations and his attraction to religious music. As a child he listened to the country gospel records his mother favored—the Louvin Brothers, the Bailes Brothers, and James and Martha Carson, for example. Charles Wolfe describes the formative recorded religious music Elvis heard as "urgent, passionate, straining harmonies born in the Pentecostal church."[12] His spirituality took shape not only through these recordings but also by hearing the same songs at church revivals and Friday night gospel singings in Tupelo, regularly attended by Elvis and his parents. Such listening to "urgent, passionate, straining harmonies," along with attendance at communal singings and the everyday singing of religious music by his mother, provided a family devotional context for Elvis's developing spirituality akin to that of countless white southerners before and after him.

Elvis was thirteen when his family moved to Memphis, a musically vibrant community particularly rich in gospel singing. Sunday afternoon singings in church were typical, and gospel quartets often held song battles to gain fame and respect. In 1950 the Mississippi-born Blackwood Brothers, the most famous white gospel quartet in the nation, moved to Memphis, presiding over two daily shows on WMPS, developing their own record label, and initiating concerts at Ellis Auditorium, the mother church of Memphis gospel music. A new institution of the school of southern musical spirituality developed in the 1940s when promoter Wally Fowler popularized packaged all-night gospel singings that soon spread across the region, including Memphis. Elvis heard dignified older groups like the Speers and the Chuck Wagon Gang, whose songs grew out of shape-note influences, and he heard the soaring harmonies of the Blackwood Brothers, who adapted songs from black quartets such as the Soul Stirrers and the Golden Gate Quartet. While extending the centrality of music to southern spirituality, these singings were commercial and performance events of popular culture with a new flashy showmanship. As Charles Wolfe notes, "It was the hottest and most exciting fad in gospel music at the time: the dynamic young quartets, clicked up in their white coats, bow ties, and pencil-thin mustaches, backed up by a pumping piano player that owed as much to Art Tatum as to Liberace, framed by sky-high tenors and booming bass voices, throwing the old stand-up mikes back and forth like batons." He adds that "it was a different kind of spirituality, but spirituality nonetheless," with a new vigor of movement.[13] It represented show business to Elvis and others at the all-night singings, but these performances reinforced the function of religious music in teaching about such tenets of predominant southern evangelical culture as a familiarity with biblical characters and stories, moralistic expectations seen in song lyrics, and the peculiar dynamic of sin and salvation at work in evangelical faith. The increasingly slick world of modern gospel music nonetheless reinforced older, familiar messages for religious southerners.

Presley was also able to experience black religious music in Memphis, making it a formative part of his developing spirituality. He listened to daily radio shows over WDIA, which dominated the black gospel scene with disc jockey Theo "Bless My Bones" Wade daily broadcasting nationally known black gospel groups and local groups like the Spirit of Memphis, the Brewsteraires, and the Dixie Nightingales. The radio station sponsored Goodwill Revues at Ellis Auditorium.[14] Presley went to East Trigg Baptist Church to hear the preaching and singing of the Reverend William Herbert Brewster, one of the greatest of African American gospel songwriters, and his lead soloist, Queen C. Anderson. Presley later remembered that he enjoyed Brewster's frequent preaching on the idea that a better day was coming, one in which all men could walk together as brothers.[15] Brewster recalled when Elvis and other young whites came to the church not only to worship but to sing. "I knew that it wasn't going to hurt when I said 'Must Jesus Bear the Cross Alone,' whether I say it with one beat or two or high or low. I told them to come in here and put your stuff together. They came in here and it was a glorious experience and Elvis was in that group."[16]

The Elvis before Sun Studios continued developing an identifiable religiosity. In 1954 he began attending an Assemblies of God church in south Memphis, whose preacher denounced films and dancing and encouraged "ecstatic demonstrations of faith," such as speaking in tongues. He attended a Bible study group on Sunday mornings; yes, he was one of the Christ Ambassadors (a youthful group that sought to bring people to church). The Blackwood Brothers were also members of this congregation, and Presley grew increasingly involved in attending their gospel singings and became a frequent presence backstage. Soon, quartet singing became, as Peter Guralnick says, "the center of his musical universe. Gospel music combined the spiritual force that he felt in all music with this sense of physical release and exaltation for which, it seemed, he was casting about."[17] As a teenager, then, religious music came particularly to embody a "spiritual force," which was linked with the exaltation he must have first felt when singing religious music with his family and at Spirit-filled Pentecostal services.

When Presley entered the national stage of early rock success, he faced criticism from ministers about his lewd performances, and a friend at the time said he cried when he read a newspaper story that claimed he was ignoring his religion. In an interview he admitted that his travel schedule did not permit his attending church, but he avowed, "I believe in God. I believe in Him with all my heart. I believe all good things come from God. . . . And the way I feel about it, being religious means that you love God and are real grateful for all He's given, and want to work for Him. I feel deep in my heart that I'm doing all this." He was defensive about the Assemblies of God and charges that his energetic performance style came from the church. He objected with uncharacteristic vehemence to the label "holy rollers," a derogatory term applied to Pentecostal groups such as the Assemblies of God. He labeled his denomination a holiness church but insisted, "I have never used the expression Holy Roller." He also declared that he "always attended church where people sang, stood up, and sang in the choir and worshiped God." In a separate interview a reporter asked him about his "unique style," and he admitted that he had "landed upon it accidentally. More or less I am a pretty close follower of religious quartets, and they do a lot of rockin' spirituals." When a story then appeared that, in Presley's words, "I got the jumping around from my religion," he denied it. "My religion has nothin' to do with what I do now," he said, adding that "the type stuff I do now is not religious music." For Presley, religious music remained in a different category from rock, one that expressed his spiritual strivings above and beyond the material success he attained. Despite his enormous success with rock 'n' roll, he insisted on recording his first gospel album, *Peace in the Valley*, in 1957, early in his national career.[18]

Into the New—1960s and Beyond

Through the coming decades, religious music remained an anchor for him, despite the successes and temptations of such places as Hollywood and Las Vegas and frequent touring in the last years of his life. Like the South itself in the 1960s and early 1970s, Presley experienced enormous changes that took him far beyond the spirituality that a Spirit-filled Pentecostal faith and the power of gospel music embodied. By the mid-1960s, for example, Presley was using LSD at Graceland and reading about Timothy Leary, although, as one scholar has noted, he did so in typically Presley fashion—turning on the television and ordering a pizza to go with his LSD. Larry Geller was Elvis's hair dresser, but he became his spiritual guru, directing Presley into much new spiritual reading and practice. It began with Presley's reading of Joseph Benner's *The Impersonal Life*, a 1917 volume teaching that God was in each human. That message was one that Presley responded to immediately, having long before embraced the belief that his extraordinary success was a gift from God with some purpose to it he had yet to discover. He later read *Autobiography of a Yogi*, by Indian holy man Paramahansa Yogananda, and he read New Thought treatises by Madame Blavatsky and Krishnamurti. This was, to be sure, an extraordinary change for the unlettered Presley, and one that disrupted his life. His buddy Joe Esposito recalled that Presley would get up in the morning, "and he's sitting there reading a book and asking questions about religion. Hey, what about the football game that happened last weekend? We used to sit and watch football games. All that stuff was gone." In March 1965 Presley had a profound religious experience in the desert near Flagstaff, Arizona, where he said he saw the face of God in the clouds. He began visiting the Self-Realization Fellowship Lake Shrine Retreat in California and told one friend he wanted to become a monk. He found a new serenity through the leader of the Self-Realization Fellowship, Sri Daya Mata. She recalled later that "he wanted to be a great spiritual influence on all these young people— that was at the basis of his desire." Presley told her that he wanted "to awaken in all these young people a closer relationship to God."[19]

What can one make of this increasingly experimental spirituality that Presley embraced in the mid-1960s? For purposes of considering southern spirituality, it obviously is a wild departure from the norms with which he had grown up, reflecting perhaps his struggles to come to terms with fame and its demands upon him. Part of him surely became unmoored from formerly reliable anchors. In moving from traditional evangelical-based spirituality into new forms of popular religion, Presley was getting caught up in larger changing patterns of American spirituality and should not be seen as entirely idiosyncratic. He joined countless other southerners and other Americans as participants in new forms of popular spirituality. Asian religions, for example, developed a new influence in the 1960s, and transcendental meditation in particular became prominent in popular religion. Like so many other southerners, Presley now had access to these ideas through television, the movies, inexpensive paperback books, popular magazines, and especially tabloids that told of psychic phenomena, communicating with the dead, UFOs, Ravi Shankar's spiritual influence on the Beatles, and other phenomena that would appear outrageously unorthodox to the traditional evangelical denominations.[20]

At the same time, those traditional denominations continued to dominate the southern religious scene in these years, becoming even more powerful forces in politics, whether for liberal civil rights causes or conservative New Right issues, and gaining in economic clout as the region's economy boomed in the years of the Sunbelt. Similarly, despite his early New Age instincts, Presley at the same time held fast to religious music as his anchor amid other changes in both his material and spiritual life. Gospel music continued to represent the legacy of the southern spirituality that he had grown up with and which now saw him through the transitions of his life in the 1960s and 1970s. Back in Memphis in the mid-1960s, after an extended stay in California, Presley visited his mother's grave weekly and sent flowers three times a week. His mother symbolized his earlier faith, and his return to Memphis seemed to trigger a new concern for his traditional spirituality. He told a reporter that he wanted to start going to church again, recalling that church had been "our way of life since I can remember." He admitted that the last time he had attended church services "there was so much confusion, and autograph seeking, that out of respect I've stayed away." Still, he felt continuing religious needs and believed his music best expressed his faith. "I've been working on religious songs for an album. I feel God and His goodness, and I believe I can express His love for us in music."[21]

Spirituality is, by definition, about the interior life and the spiritual exercises to cultivate it, but Presley saw his spirituality as also having a public dimension, that of reaching countless people through his music. In addition to his first gospel album, *Peace in the Valley*, Presley recorded three other gospel albums, and the songs and arrangements he selected reveal much about his spirituality in the 1960s and 1970s. His second gospel album, *His Hand in Mine*, recorded in the fall of 1960, included seven songs by the Statesmen, the white gospel group that influenced him so much in general. Among the songs were "Milky White Way," a black gospel standard, with the arrangement modeled on the Trumpeteers, a Baltimore quartet of the 1940s; "Mansion over the Hilltop," a country gospel number based on an old preacher's story; "Swing Down Sweet Chariot," a quartet number recorded by one of Presley's favorite black gospel groups, the Golden Gate Quartet, but with an arrangement from the Blackwood Brothers; and "If We Never

Meet Again," written by one of the great white gospel songwriters, Albert Brumley. His third gospel album, *How Great Thou Art*, was not a tribute to classic gospel quartet singing as much as it was a collection of "church specials," numbers popular in revivals and the churches themselves. Again, it was a mix of songs popularized by black and white gospel groups. Among the songs on the album were "Farther Along," a country gospel classic that first appeared in the Stamps-Baxter songbook in 1937; "Where Could I Go but to the Lord," another songbook tune that a Mississippi singing-school teacher had written; "Run On," which had been popularized by the Golden Gate Quartet; and "Stand By Me," which Charles Albert Tindley, another prolific African American songwriter, published in 1905.[22]

Presley's fourth gospel album appeared in 1971 and reflected changes in gospel music and the evolution of his spirituality. California-centered Jesus music, exultant praise music, and the beginnings of Christian rock were well represented, moving beyond the southern origins of gospel. New gospel songwriters such as Andrae Crouch and Ralph Carmichael had songs on the album. As a California-based songwriter who added strings and large orchestras to his gospel compositions, Carmichael was particularly significant in terms of changes. One sacred song on the album stood out even more than the others. "Miracle of the Rosary" explored a more Catholic sensibility than anything Presley had ever done, again suggesting that his spiritual journeying in music was not just in new spiritualities of the 1960s but in a traditional Catholic one that now resonated with him.[23]

Presley's public spirituality included an active promotion of religious music. He incorporated gospel songs into his movie soundtracks, as when he included "Swing Down Sweet Chariot" in *Trouble with Girls*. He introduced gospel music to Las Vegas—no mean feat—including religious numbers in his performances there. He showcased the Jordanaires, the Stamps Quartet, and other gospel groups wherever he performed in the 1970s. Such promotion conveyed his personal spirituality to audiences that were not expecting such open religiosity in an entertainment venue, even if they were often receptive to it. He saw his actions as essential parts of his growing efforts to witness his faith through religious music. The mix of private and public spirituality appears on the tape of a 1970s concert, when Presley asks the audience to listen to the Stamps Quartet singing "Sweet, Sweet Spirit." Presley lets them sing, while he appears transported by listening to the music, his eyes closed, his head gently shaking, and then smiling along with a certain line and musical notes—the image of his private spirituality written on his public stage.[24]

In his use of music to convey a religious message, Presley reflected the abiding evangelical impulse toward conversion as the essence of religious faith, which Samuel Hill has called the central theme of southern religion.[25] Despite the importance of theology, doctrine, ritual, and morality for southern evangelicals, the experience of God's saving grace is essential. Presley's personal life in the mid-1970s became increasingly tortured, with abuse of prescription drugs the best symbol of a life that strayed far from the notably ascetic demands of his early Pentecostalism. Presley used religious music as a counterweight in nurturing his private spirituality as well as a tool to influence his fans to appreciate God's goodness. J. D. Sumner, the legendary gospel singer who became his close friend, has said that he thought that Presley, in the last five years of his life, was returning to his roots in music, to the gospel music that even preceded his rockabilly classics. Sumner suggested that if Presley had lived another six months, he would have become a full-time gospel singer.[26]

Even before then, one can see the centrality of religious music for Presley's spirituality in these last years of his life in the informal jam session caught on film in March 1972 for the documentary *Elvis on Tour.* Like the Million Dollar Session in 1956, this spontaneous sing-along was spirited and relaxed, showing the ease with which Presley sang gospel music in private. This filmed session reflected others that had long been typical of his quest for quiet moments with the music. Early in his career, while performing on the road with the Louvin Brothers, he sat at the piano and began playing gospel songs, saying, "This is really my favorite kind of music." When he performed on stage, he said, "I do what they want to hear; when I'm back here, I do what I want to do."[27] In his last years of performing, he always wanted the Stamps Quartet to come to his suite after his shows so he could relax by singing gospel music with them all night. At the 1972 jam, he joined in singing old quartet numbers, spirituals, "Nearer My God to Thee" (which goes back to the 1840s), and a

1922 hymn, "Turn Your Eyes upon Jesus." As he said in an interview for the film, gospel music "more or less puts your mind to rest. At least it does mine, since I was two."[28]

Presley's spirituality was also a witness to racial reconciliation. With every gospel album he recorded and with his wide and deep appreciation of black, as well as white, southern gospel music, he extended the biracial musical interaction that had been so obvious in his appreciation of blues and rhythm and blues early in his career. Toward the end of his career, this biracialism became even more pronounced, at least publicly, as he incorporated black gospel singers into his inner circle of backup performers, who increasingly served as his friends and surrogate family, as well as his fellow performers. When Sherman Andrus became the first African American member of the white gospel group the Imperials, which was Presley's backup group during the 1970s, Andrus also became the first black member of a white southern gospel group in general. He recalls warnings to Presley from promoters at a concert in Houston not to have Andrus on stage. Presley's response was not only to include Andrus but to showcase his talents. Andrus recalls Presley's knowledge of black gospel was even greater than his own.[29] Presley also prominently included the Sweet Inspirations, a female black backup group, in his 1970s performances. By the end of his career, Presley was using music to challenge inherited divisions in the national spirit. His signature concert song of the 1970s was "An American Trilogy," and it evoked a national cultural memory, a civil religion, drawing from and attempting to transcend sentiments rooted in biracial southern antecedents going back to the Civil War. The song combined a mournful, haunting arrangement of the southern Civil War song "Dixie," the slave spiritual "Hush, Little Baby, Don't You Cry," and the Union army anthem, "The Battle Hymn of the Republic," the latter the background music to William T. Sherman's march through the South. The spirituality here uses the concert stage to challenge listeners to go beyond divisive ideologies and cultural memories. As theologian Tex Sample has noted of his own experience listening to the song, "I am by now struggling with the question of my own identity as a southerner, an American, and a Christian."[30]

Religious music has been a traditional spiritual exercise in the South, one that individuals cultivated privately, at church singings, and in a variety of institutions such as Sacred Harp singings, singing schools, singing conventions, and all-night gospel singings. Preferences in spirituality—including preferences in religious music—need to be seen in relationship to social conditions. As Robert Wuthnow notes, region, race, gender, age, level of education, and religious background can all shape people's embrace of differing spiritual practices, and the spirituality of the South cannot be fully understood outside these contexts.[31] In particular, Elvis Presley's spiritual life, as distinct from his limited role in religious organizations, suggests a rich, white working-class southern spirituality. Presley's experience showed the changes in spirituality in the South as the region modernized and its religious and musical institutions used the technology and promotional techniques of the modern entertainment industry to extend the old-time message of evangelical spirituality.

Samuel Weber's article on spirituality in the South in *The New Encyclopedia of Southern Culture* concludes that in the past three decades, "for many, 'spirituality' has become synonymous with 'finding the true self' and 'unleashing the potential for truth and love,' as well as terms such as 'serenity' and 'peace of heart.'"[32] This describes Presley's spiritual questing perfectly. His attraction to the Self-Realization Fellowship in the 1960s represents a new expression of a long journeying that grew out of the intensity of his Pentecostal background and was expressed in his religious music. His embrace of a civil religiosity represented a very public plea for harmony despite the racial and national bitterness growing out of the past. His traditional southern spirituality rested on the hope of redemption, even for a sinner, stemming from a personal relationship with the divine. Elvis's Aunt Lorene recalled that when Elvis was a young boy he disappeared one day, only to return in tears, saying that "he had been talking to Jesus."[33] As the lyric to one of his favorite songs says, Elvis appears to have continued to believe, as his native region did in his lifetime, that "Just a Little Talk with Jesus Gonna Make It Right."

READ MORE ABOUT IT

For background on southern gospel music, see James R. Goff Jr., *Close Harmony: A History of Southern Gospel* (Chapel Hill: University of North Carolina Press, 2002).

For background on black gospel, see Kip Lornell, *Happy in the Service of the Lord: Afro-American Gospel Quartets in Memphis* (Urbana: University of Illinois Press, 1988).

On Presley and gospel music, see especially Charles Wolfe, "Presley and the Gospel Tradition," *Southern Quarterly* 18 (1979): 135–50; and Cheryl Thurber, "Elvis and Gospel Music," *Rejoice* 1 (1988): 6.

On American spirituality, see Amanda Porterfield, *The Transformation of American Religion: The Story of a Late Twentieth-Century Awakening* (Oxford: Oxford University Press, 2001); Leigh Eric Schmidt, *Restless Souls: The Making of American Spirituality* (New York: HarperCollins, 2005); and Robert Wuthnow, *After Heaven: Spirituality in America since the 1950s* (Berkeley: University of California Press, 1998).

NOTES

This essay was originally a paper delivered at the Organization of American Historians meeting in April 2004. The author thanks the commentators at that session, Charles Joyner and Joel Williamson, for their suggestions.

1. Colin Escott, liner notes, *Million Dollar Quartet* (RCA Records, 1990), 1–3. Peter Guralnick discussed the Million Dollar Session in *Last Train to Memphis: The Rise of Elvis Presley* (Boston: Little Brown, 1994), 365–68.

2. Escott, *Million Dollar Quartet*, 1–3.

3. Robert Wuthnow, "Spirituality and Spiritual Practice," in *The Blackwell Companion to Sociology of Religion*, ed. Richard K. Fenn (Oxford and Malden, Mass.: Blackwell, 2001), 306.

4. Samuel F. Weber, "Spirituality in the South," in *The New Encyclopedia of Southern Culture*, vol. 1, ed. Charles Reagan Wilson (Chapel Hill: University of North Carolina Press, 2006), 143. See also Bill Leonard, "Spirituality in America: Signs of the Times," *Religion and American Culture* 9 (1999): 152–57.

5. "Spirituality," in *The Oxford Dictionary of the Christian Church*, 3rd ed., ed. F. L. Cross (Oxford: Oxford University Press, 1997), 1532. See also Gerald O'Collins and Edward G. Farragia, *A Concise Dictionary of Theology* (New York: Paulist, 2000).

6. Wuthnow, "Spirituality and Spiritual Practice."

7. Charles Wolfe, *In Close Harmony: The Story of the Louvin Brothers* (Jackson: University Press of Mississippi, 1996), 3–23.

8. Ibid., 65.

9. Colin Escott, liner notes, Hank Williams (as Luke the Drifter): *Beyond the Sunset* (Mercury Records, 2001), 2.

10. See Colin Escott, *Hank Williams: The Biography* (Boston: Little, Brown, 1994), 6–9; and Roger M. Williams, *Sing a Sad Song* (Urbana: University of Illinois Press, 1981).

11. Elaine Dundes, *Gladys and Elvis* (New York: Macmillan, 1985), 82.

12. Charles Wolfe, liner notes, Elvis Presley: *Amazing Grace: His Greatest Sacred Performances* (RCA Records, 1994), 10. For the importance of the Assemblies of God to Presley, see Van K. Brock, "Assemblies of God: Elvis and Pentecostalism," *Bulletin of the Center for the Study of Southern Culture and Religion* (1979).

13. Wolfe, liner notes, Elvis Presley: *Amazing Grace*, 10. For the Memphis music context in the 1950s, see Michael T. Bertrand, *Race, Rock, and Elvis* (Urbana: University of Illinois Press, 2000).

14. Wolfe, liner notes, Elvis Presley: *Amazing Grace*, 11–12.

15. Guralnick, *Last Train to Memphis*, 75.

16. *He Touched Me: The Gospel Music of Elvis Presley* (Coming Home Music, 1999), video.

17. Guralnick, *Last Train to Memphis*, 47.

18. Jerry Osbourne, *Elvis: Word for Word* (New York: Harmony, 2002), 30, 52–53, 70.

19. Peter Guralnick, *Careless Love: The Unmaking of Elvis Presley* (Boston: Little, Brown, 1999), 175–77, 195–96, 209, 363.

20. See Charles H. Lippy, *Being Religious, American Style: A History of Popular Religiosity in the United States* (Westport, Conn.: Praeger, 1994), 210–17.

21. Guralnick, *Careless Love*, 222–23. For the idea of Presley as a liminal figure in southern popular religion, see Charles Reagan Wilson, *Judgment and Grace in Dixie: Southern Faiths from Faulkner to Elvis* (Athens: University of Georgia Press, 1996), 136. Wolfe, liner notes, Elvis Presley: *Amazing Grace*, 16–23.

22. Wolfe, liner notes, Elvis Presley: *Amazing Grace*, 16–23.

23. Ibid., 24–26.

24. *He Touched Me.*

25. Samuel S. Hill Jr., *Southern Churches in Crisis* (Boston: Beacon, 1966).

26. Charles Wolfe, "Presley and the Gospel Tradition," *Southern Quarterly* 18 (1979): 148.

27. Wolfe, *In Close Harmony*, 81.

28. *He Touched Me.* See also Wolfe, liner notes, Elvis Presley: *Amazing Grace*, 26–28.

29. *He Touched Me.* See also Bertrand, *Race, Rock, and Elvis.*

30. Tex Sample, *The Spectacle of Worship in a Wired World: Electronic Culture and the Gathered People of God* (Nashville: Abingdon, 1998), 103.

31. Wuthnow, "Spirituality and Spiritual Practice," 318.

32. Weber, "Spirituality in the South," 143.

33. Vester Presley, as told to Deda Bonura, *A Presley Speaks* (Memphis: Wimmer Brothers, 1978), 117.

Miami's Little Havana

Yard Shrines, Cult Religion, and Landscape

James R. Curtis

Sacred space is a concept well known in the history of religions. It is also familiar in southern religious experience. Whether hallowed by human intention and interaction or simply perceived by the faithful to manifest the holy, natural locations, human edifices, and consecrated sites can all serve as sacred contexts for the religious believer. This study surveys the cultural landscape of Little Havana, the heart of the Cuban quarter of Miami, Florida. It explores yard shrines, one of the more distinctive urban landscape contributions associated with the Cuban presence in Miami. Although many shrines are built by Catholics, others are erected by followers of the syncretic Afro-Cuban religion Santeria. James Curtis's examination of these spaces, originally published in the 1980s, remains an illuminating entry into a complicated location of cross-cultural religious energy and a powerful demonstration of sacred space within vernacular contexts.

In the summer of 1978 a brief article entitled "Neighbors Irate over Family's Shrine" appeared in the *Miami Herald*.[1] The story told of a group of residents in the predominantly non-Latin city of South Miami who feared that a newly erected seven-foot shrine in the front yard of a Cuban neighbor would lower property values. City officials called in to investigate found that the shrine was located too close to the front property line and thus was in violation of municipal building and zoning laws. Confused and saddened by the turmoil created, the Cuban family stated that the shrine had been built (at a cost of $1,500) in gratitude to Santa Barbara "for answering all of our prayers."

More than an isolated human-interest story, the incident is perhaps symbolic of the bicultural social adjustments, and urban landscape transformations, that have taken place and are continuing to occur in the greater Miami area as a result of Cuban in-migration. In the short span of only twenty years, beginning in 1959, the Cuban population of Dade County has ballooned from about 20,000 to 430,000.[2] Counting the 94,000 non-Cuban Latins residing in the county—mostly Puerto Ricans, Mexicans, and Central and South Americans—Latins constitute approximately 35 percent of the county's population, as compared to only 5 percent in 1960.[3] Moreover, Latins have settled in distinct residential concentrations, thereby greatly accentuating the "Latinization" of selected locales.[4] The city of Miami, for example, is almost 56 percent Latin (207,000 out of 370,000); Hialeah, with a population of 133,000, is over 65 percent Latin, mostly Cuban. The impact of such sudden and fundamental change in the pattern of ethnicity has profoundly altered both material and nonmaterial elements of culture in the region. Nowhere are these transformations better manifested than in Little Havana, a four-square-mile enclave of Cuban culture located a scant mile southwest of downtown Miami.

Little Havana

Often referred to as a city (or "nation") within a city, Little Havana is the nucleus, the core, of Cuban life in Miami. Once a thriving middle-class Anglo neighborhood, dating from the immediate post–World War I era, by the mid-1950s it had deteriorated and was declining in population as urban growth and increased mobility opened up newer housing areas for the middle class in the outlying suburbs.[5] Newly arriving Cuban refugees preferred this area because of its available and affordable housing units and the potential of its vacant shops for business endeavors.[6] It was also served by public transportation and near the central business district, where social services and employment opportunities were most abundant. The neighborhood was reborn as "Little Havana" almost literally overnight. Although its function as the principal receptor area has declined in recent years as the Cuban population has grown in numbers and affluence, spreading out to other settlement areas, Little Havana remains in spirit, if not in actual fact, the traditional Cuban quarter.[7]

In most important respects, Little Havana is a self-contained community that has evolved, by design, to suit the needs and tastes of its residents, and in so doing has embellished the landscape with a pronounced Cuban flavor. Along West Flagler and Southwest Eighth streets (the latter known locally as "Calle Ocho"), the two principal commercial strips that cut through the district, a full complement of goods and services catering to the Cuban population is offered. If so desired, a Cuban who lives in Little Havana and speaks only Spanish could shop, dine out, be medically cared for, attend churches, schools, and theaters—eventually die and be buried without having uttered a word of English.

The commercial landscape of Little Havana reflects in both vivid and subtle ways this impress of Cuban culture. From the older stucco buildings of Spanish and art deco styles, and from the small shopping plazas that have been recently built, neon store signs flash *Joyeria, Ferreteria, Muebleria, Farmacia, Mercado, Zapaeria*, and so on. One frequently encounters small groups of three and four gathered at the countless vest-pocket, open-air coffee counters to sip syrupy, dark, bittersweet *cafe cubano* and consume fresh *pasteles* (pastries).

The newsstands and bookstores in the district display a plethora of Spanish-language books, magazines, and newspapers, including *El Miami Herald*, which has a circulation in excess of fifty thousand. The acrid smell of cured tobacco wafts from the thirty or so small cigar factories located in the area where old men (*tabaqueros*) patiently roll cigars *a mano* (by hand).[8] At Antonio Maceo Mini Park, on Calle Ocho, men play games of dominoes on permanently fixed tables and benches designed specifically for that purpose. Fresh fruits and vegetables are sold in the open-air markets and stands that dot the district. The sweet smell of simmering garlic hangs heavy over the hundred-plus restaurants featuring Cuban and Spanish cuisine, ranging from elegant supper clubs with valet parking to four-stool cafés.

The life and vitality of these places, however, stand in stark contrast to the somberness surrounding the Cuban Memorial Plaza, where flowers and wreaths are faithfully placed at the base of the Bay of Pigs monument in memory of loved ones who fell during that ill-fated invasion. To be sure, the landscape of Little Havana conveys a strong feeling of prerevolutionary Cuba, but the sense of a people in exile remains pervasive. The existence of nearly one hundred officially recognized "municipalities in exile," which function as social and quasi-political organizations composed of former residents of particular municipalities in Cuba, attests to the vitality of this continued sense of Cuban belonging.[9] Many of these groups have converted houses and other buildings in Little Havana into meeting halls where lectures, concerts, and dances are periodically held and where informational and historical newsletters are published.

As befits its population, a people caught inextricably between two cultures, Little Havana is not an isolated community devoid of contact with the surrounding society and environment. Rather, in culture and landscape, it is a mixture of both Cuban and American influences. Cuban and American flags, for example, proudly bedeck the streets of Little Havana during the national holidays of both countries. Cuban grocery shoppers may patronize the neighborhood Winn Dixie or Pantry Pride supermarkets, and then walk to the back parking lot of these stores to barter with itinerant Cuban peddlers selling fresh fish, poultry, fruit, and vegetables. Teenagers sip on *batidos* (exotic fruit milkshakes) from Cuban ice cream shops and eat *grandes macs* from the local McDonald's. In language, as well, especially among the younger Cubans, one now hears a curious mixture of Spanish and English ("Spanglish," as it is known).[10] Signs on some store windows, for example, announce "*Gran* Sale." Young people may be heard shouting to one another, "*Tenga un* nice day."

Although the housing area of Little Havana has been significantly upgraded and changed as a consequence of the Cuban tenure, the residential landscape is not nearly as "Latinized" as the commercial strips in the district. In fact, a quick drive through the area would probably leave the impression that it is largely indistinguishable from neighboring Anglo residential areas. Yet, upon closer inspection, differences unfold. Fences, for example, now enclose many front yards, and wrought iron and tile have been added to some houses for decorative purposes. Even these characteristically Hispanic features, however, remain relatively minor in comparison to what one might expect to find in most Latin communities. If anything, one is impressed more by how little these embellishments reflect the fundamental replacement of culture groups that has occurred in the area. This observation, however, is somewhat misleading, for it fails to include the single most conspicuous landscape element that clearly distinguishes Little Havana from non-Cuban residential areas.

YARD SHRINES

If the Cuban family in the story recounted at the beginning of this essay had lived in Little Havana, it would not have aroused the resentment, or even stirred the curiosity, of neighbors over the construction of its yard shrine. City officials would not have been brought in to search for some minor infraction of local building or zoning laws to force its removal. More commonplace than exceptional, there are literally hundreds of yard shrines gracing the cultural landscape of Little Havana.[11]

The shrines may be found anywhere in the yard area—front, back, or along the sides—although the front yard, especially near the sidewalk, appears to be a favored location. Regardless of placement, however, the front of the shrine always faces the street. Since these are personal shrines, built to suit the religious needs and preferences of individuals, no two are exactly alike; diversity is the standard. In size, the shrines range from about two to ten feet in height, and two to six feet in width. Most are rectangular in shape, although octagonal and circular structures are not uncommon. The most frequently used building materials are brick, cement, stone, and glass; wood is rarely, if ever, used except for trimming. Exterior walls, though, are often stuccoed or tiled. A single cross may adorn the top of a shrine, and use of latticework and other forms of ornamentation are occasionally found, but in general the degree of exterior embellishment is more austere than ornate.

Regardless of size, materials used, or shape, the interiors of the shrines remain visible through either sealed glass side panels or a single glass door enclosing the front of the sanctuary. Pedestaled inside, usually on an elevated platform or altar, stands a single statue. At the base of the statue, and occasionally on a small stairwell leading to the base, one often finds an utterly baffling array of items, including, for example, fresh-cut or artificial flowers, candles, crucifixes, jars of leaves, bowls of water, beads, stones, miniature figures of men or animals, and other assorted paraphernalia.

The statues themselves are of Catholic saints, the Madonna, or

Jesus, each identifiable (at least to the knowing eye) by sex, colors, adornment, and particular symbols, such as a cup, a cane, or a cross. By far, the three saints who are enshrined most commonly in Little Havana are, in order, Santa Barbara, Our Lady of Charity (patron saint of Cuba), and St. Lazarus. Other saints, particularly St. Francis of Assisi, St. Christopher, and St. Peter, are also found, but with much less frequency. Likewise, shrines built in honor of the Madonna and Jesus are not nearly as numerous as those erected to the main three saints.

Santa Barbara is most often portrayed as a young woman dressed in a white tunic with a red mantle bordered with gold trimming. She wears a golden crown and holds a golden goblet in her right hand and a golden sword in her left. Our Lady of Charity is similarly represented as a young woman dressed in a white tunic. Her cloak, however, is either blue or white. She holds a child in her left arm. At her feet, seated or kneeling in a boat, are two or three small male figures looking reverently upward. St. Lazarus is usually depicted as a bent and crippled man of middle age, with open wounds and sores, supported by crutches. Two or three small dog figures often stand at his feet. This particular portrayal of Lazarus is not the image officially recognized or sanctioned by the church; it has evolved from Cuban tradition.

Sacred elements in the landscape often convey much less of the religious context from which they spring than observation alone would suggest. The religious beliefs that inspire the construction of yard shrines in Little Havana are illustrative of this contention. Considering, for example, that a vast majority of Cubans are Roman Catholics, and that most of the shrines are built in apparent homage to saints, one might logically suspect that these shrines are erected by followers of the Catholic faith. This assumption, however, is neither entirely correct nor incorrect. In truth, many of the shrines are built by Catholics, but perhaps an equal number, if not more, are erected by followers of a fascinating, syncretic Afro-Cuban cult religion called Santeria.

SANTERIA: AN AFRO-CUBAN RELIGION

The history of the West Indies is rich in examples of the spontaneous melding of European and African culture traits and complexes.

This process of transculturation—in which different cultural elements are jumbled, mixed, and fused—played an important role in the shaping of present cultural patterns in the region, particularly in the nonmaterial aspects of culture such as language, music, and religion. Besides Santeria in Cuba, other notable examples of religious syncretism in the New World, in which elements of Catholicism were combined with ancient African tribal beliefs and practices, include Vodun (i.e., voodoo) in Haiti and Xango in Trinidad.[12]

Santeria, like other syncretic Afro-Christian folk religions, combines an elaborate ensemble of ritual, magical, medical, and theological beliefs to form a total magico-religious worldview. The Santeria religion evolved among descendents of the Yoruba slaves who had been brought to Cuba from Nigeria beginning in the sixteenth century but particularly in the first half of the nineteenth century.[13] These descendents—known in Cuba as the Lucumi—learned from oral history the tribal religion of their ancestral home. It was a complex polytheistic religion involving a pantheon of gods and goddesses called *orishas*.[14] It was also colorful in its mythology. In many respects it was extraordinarily reminiscent of ancient Greek mythology.[15] The African religion was rather quickly altered, however, as the Cuban Lucumis fell increasingly under the sway of the Spanish culture.[16] Exposure to the Catholic religion, particularly its veneration of numerous saints, greatly influenced the nature of the emergent folk religion.[17] In time, the Yoruba deities came to be identified with the images of Catholic saints.[18] The orishas then became *santos* (saints), and their worship became known as Santeria—literally, the worship of saints. Thus, to the *santero* (the practitioner of Santeria), a shrine may be built to house a statue in the image of a Catholic saint, but the saint is actually representative of a Yoruba god. It is exceedingly difficult to determine accurately, based solely on appearance, whether a yard shrine in Little Havana actually belongs to a Catholic or to a follower of Santeria. In general, however, yard shrines built by practitioners of Santeria are more likely to contain nontraditional religious items such as bowls of water, stones, and jars of leaves.

The followers of Santeria believe in a supreme god called Olodumare, Olofi, or Olorun. He is thought to be a distant, lofty figure. Contact with this supreme deity is attainable only through the orishas, who serve as intermediaries.[19] Thus, worship of god-saints serves as the focus for formal and informal devotional practices; there are no subcults or special rites exclusively in honor of Olodumare.

The saints—who are known both by their Catholic names and their Yoruba appellations—are associated with specific colors and particular symbols or "weapons," such as thunder, fire, or swords. They are considered to have the same supernatural powers ascribed to the African deities.[20] Each is believed to possess specific attributes, which in total govern all aspects of human life and natural phenomena. A santero might seek to invoke the power, for example, of Babalu-Aye (associated with St. Lazarus), god of illness and disease, to cure a particular ailment, or of Orunmila (associated with St. Francis of Assisi), god of wisdom and divination, to bestow knowledge. Others, purportedly, can assure success in a job, ward off an evil spirit, bring back a former lover, and so on.

The numerous deities, however, are not at all venerated equally; some are more favored than others, often leading to the formation of a special subcult devoted to a particular god-saint. In Cuba, as in Miami now, Chango (associated with St. Barbara), god of fire, thunder, and lightning, is the most popular of all the orishas.[21] Chango represents a curious form of syncretism involving a change of sex from the male Yoruba god to the female Catholic saint. Oshun (associated with Our Lady of Charity, patron saint of Cuba), god of love, marriage, and gold, and Babalu-Aye are also extremely popular in Miami. Seven of the most revered and powerful orishas are often worshipped collectively. This group is known among santeros as the "Seven African Powers." The orishas who make up this septet, their associated Catholic images, their colors and weapons, and the human aspects they control are shown in table 1.

The ritual and devotional activities of santeros are confined, in most cases, to private residences. The more important functions, such as initiation into the cult, a funeral, or a consultation in which some form of divination is sought, is presided over by a high "priest" of the religion, called a babaloa.[22] Lesser orders of priesthood attend to the more mundane rites and rituals. The rituals themselves are primitive, bizarre affairs, often involving the consumption of beverages concocted from exotic herbs and roots, the use of incense, oils, and foreign perfumes, drumming, dancing, trance inducement, and animal sacrifices.[23] Many of the liturgical practices, including the

Table 1. The seven African powers				
Orisha	Catholic image	Colors	Human aspect controlled	Weapons or symbols
Changó	Santa Barbara	red/white	passion, enemies	thunder, sword, cup
Elegguá	Holy guardian angel	red/black	messages	iron nails, small iron rooster
Obatalá	Our Lady of Mercy	white	peace, purity	all white substances
Oggún	St. Peter	green/black	war, employment	iron, knives, steel
Orúnmila	St. Francis of Assisi	green/yellow	divination	Table of Ifa (a divination board)
Oshún	Our Lady of Charity	yellow/red/green	love, marriage, gold	mirror, seashells, pumpkins
Yemayá	Our Lady of Regla	blue/white	maternity, womanhood	canoe, seashells, fans

Source: Migene Gonzalez-Wippler, *Santeria: African Magic in Latin America* (New York: Julian, 1973).

phraseology used in prayers and incantations as well as various paraphernalia needed for ritualistic purposes, are also borrowed from Catholicism. A Santeria priest might even suggest to a follower that he or she attend a Catholic Mass, in many cases simply to obtain holy water or even a piece of the consecrated host for use in a subsequent ritual.[24]

THE EXPANSION OF SANTERIA

As surprising as it may seem, Santeria today is neither a predominantly rural nor a lower socioeconomic class phenomenon. Indeed, authorities on the religion confirm that Santeria has permeated all racial groups and socioeconomic classes in Cuba and now in the Cuban community in exile.[25] Santeria is known to be thriving in the larger cities where Cuban refugees have settled, including New York, Los Angeles, Chicago, and particularly Miami. A precise determination of the numbers of adherents to Santeria in Miami is virtually impossible to ascertain, since they do not build public churches or publish membership records. It is believed, however, that their numbers run into the thousands. One rough indication is provided by anthropologist William Bascom, who estimated in 1969 that there were at least eighty-three babaloas, or high priests, practicing in Miami.[26] This may be compared to Havana, the stronghold of Santeria, with tens of thousands of followers, where Bascom estimated the number of babaloas at about two hundred just prior to the Cuban Revolution.[27] Perhaps a better indicator is the existence in Miami of over twelve botanicas, which are retail supply outlets catering to the Santeria trade.

By all scholarly accounts, Santeria is becoming increasingly popular among certain segments of the Cuban exile community. The reason most commonly cited for this kindling of interest is the fear of some Cuban refugees of losing their cultural identity through acculturation to the American way of life.[28] Such a conversion would perhaps represent an attempt to maintain linkage to a more stable past in the face of rapidly changing values and lifestyles. Disenchantment with the Catholic faith is another factor also frequently mentioned as contributing to the apparent expansion of Santeria in the United States. In this respect, the Catholic Church's questioning of the historical validity of certain saints who were popular in Cuba (such as St. Lazarus and St. Christopher), the elimination of many rituals practiced in Cuba, and simply the size and institutionalized nature of the Catholic religion have reportedly prompted some Cuban Americans to seek out alternative religious affiliation, including Santeria.[29] Furthermore, the adaptive nature of the Santeria religion itself has apparently contributed to its expansion. Mercedes Sandoval, for example, concludes that: "Its intrinsic flexibility, eclecticism and heterogeneity have been advantages in helping ensure functional, dogmatic and ritual changes which enable it to meet the different needs of its many followers."[30] Evidently, one of the more important and attractive aspects of Santeria for the Cuban community in Miami is its function as a mental health care system.[31]

In the process of change and modification as practiced in the United States, however, many African chants and dances, the use of certain herbs and roots, and other medicinal and ritualistic elements have been abandoned. One of the more interesting adaptations, for example, involves a change in the Oil of the Seven African Powers, used in the worship of those deities. The "oil" is now available in botanicas in Miami as an aerosol spray. Directions on the side of the container read: "Repeat as necessary. Make your petition. Make the sign of the cross. Air freshener, deodorizer."

Perhaps the apparent expansion of interest in Santeria among certain members of the Cuban exile community is only a transitional phenomenon that will subside, or die out completely, as the process of acculturation speeds ahead; this occurred, for example, in Italian American cult religions.[32] At the present time, however, as one follower of Santeria said, "When we hear thunder in Miami, we know that *Chango* is in exile."[33] Regardless of the future of this particular religious cult, the yard shrines and other contributions to the cultural landscape associated with the Cuban sector reflect the growing social diversity of this rapidly changing cosmopolitan city.

NOTES

1. Sam Jacobs, "Neighbors Irate over Family's Shrine," *Miami Herald*, July 2, 1978, A23.

2. Strategy Research Corporation, *Latin Market Survey* (Miami, 1977), 78; Metropolitan Dade County Office of the County Manager, *Profile of the Latin Population in the Metropolitan Dade County Area* (Miami, 1976).

3. Strategy Research Corporation, *Latin Market Survey*, 78.

4. Metropolitan Dade County Planning Department, *Ethnic Breakdown by Census Tract* (Miami, 1975).

5. Metropolitan Dade County Office of the City Manager, *Impact of the Community Development Program on Private Involvement in the Commercial Rehabilitation of the "Little Havana" Neighborhood* (Miami, 1978), 2.

6. Kimball D. Woodbury, "The Spatial Diffusion of the Cuban Community in Dade County, Florida" (master's thesis, University of Florida, 1978), 33.

7. F. Pierce Eichelberger, "The Cubans in Miami: Residential Movements and Ethnic Group Differentiation" (master's thesis, University of Cincinnati, 1974), 83.

8. William D. Montalbano, "Vanishing Hands," *Miami Herald*, February 4, 1979, Tropic section, 19–21.

9. Ileana Oroza, "The Traditionalist," *Miami Herald*, July 4, 1978, A16.

10. John Dorschner, "Growing Up Spanglish in Miami," *Miami Herald*, September 11, 1977, Tropic section, 6–13.

11. Matthew Creelman, "Count Your Built-in Blessings," *Miami Herald*, July 21, 1979, D3.

12. George E. Simpson, *Religious Cults of the Caribbean: Trinidad, Ja-*

maica, and Haiti (Rio Piedras and Puerto Rico: Institute of Caribbean Studies, 1970), 11.

13. Migene Gonzalez-Wippler, *Santeria: African Magic in Latin America* (New York: Julian, 1973), 1.

14. D. E. Baldwin, *The Yoruba of Southwest Nigeria* (Boston: G. K. Hall, 1976).

15. J. O. Lucas, *The Religions of the Yorubas* (Lagos: C.M.S. Bookshop, 1942).

16. William Bascom, "The Yoruba in Cuba," *Nigeria* 37 (1951): 14–20.

17. William Bascom, "The Focus of Cuban Santeria," *Southwestern Journal of Anthropology* 6, (Spring 1950): 64–68.

18. Gonzalez-Wippler, *Santeria*, 3; Melville J. Herskovits, "African Gods and Catholic Saints in New World Negro Belief," *American Anthropologist* 39 (October–December 1937): 635–43.

19. Isabel Mercedes Castellanos, "The Use of Language in Afro-Cuban Religion" (Ph.D. diss., Georgetown University, 1976), 31–33.

20. Gonzalez-Wippler, *Santeria*, 16.

21. Mercedes C. Sandoval, "Santeria as a Mental Health Care System: An Historical Overview," *Social Science and Medicine* 13B (April 1979): 139; William R. Bascom, *Shango in the New World* (Austin: University of Texas Press, 1972), 13–15.

22. Castellanos, "The Use of Language in Afro-Cuban Religion," 35.

23. Mercedes C. Sandoval, *La religion afro-cubana* (Madrid: Playor, S.A., 1975); Lydia Cabrera, *El monte* (Miami: Ediciones C.R., 1971); Ellen Hampton, "Drums Beating and Animals Shrieking Frighten Southwest Dade Residents," *Miami Herald*, November 25, 1979, B19.

24. Gonzalez-Wippler, *Santeria*, 4.

25. Sandoval, *La religion afro-cubana*, 270–72; Castellanos, "The Use of Language in Afro-Cuban Religion," 163–64.

26. Bascom, *Shango in the New World*, 20.

27. Ibid.

28. Castellanos, "The Use of Language in Afro-Cuban Religion," 164.

29. Sandoval, *La religion afro-cubana*, 272.

30. Sandoval, "Santeria as a Mental Health Care System," 137.

31. Ibid., 137–51; Clarissa S. Scott, "Health and Healing Practices among Five Ethnic Groups in Miami, Florida," *Public Health Reports* 89 (NovemberDecember 1974), 526–27.

32. Rudolph J. Vecoli, "Cult and Occult in Italian-American Culture: The Persistence of a Religious Heritage," in *Immigrants and Religion in Urban Culture*, ed. Randall M. Miller and Thomas D. Marzik (Philadelphia: Temple University Press, 1977), 25–47.

33. Sandoval, *La religion afro-cubana*, 274.

The Archaeology of African American Slave Religion in the Antebellum South

Charles E. Orser Jr.

The religious experience of African American slaves has been the site of multifaceted research. Analysis of the texts of spirituals and reminiscences, attention to African and Muslim as well as Christian religious practices, and acknowledgment of religiously inspired rebellions—all of these have been topics for scholarly investigation. Joining these textual and historical investigations and underscoring the interdisciplinary approach to southern religion, archaeologists with interests in material culture have recently turned their attention to slave religion in the New World. As Charles Orser demonstrates, their contribution is significant.

The archaeology of African slavery in the New World has expanded exponentially within the past twenty years.[1] During this time, several historical archaeologists have diligently set about reconstructing slave life and history at numerous rural and urban archaeological sites. The questions explored by these scholars have been varied, but generally they have been focused on slave diet, the location and size of slave cabins, and the nature of slave material culture. Only a few archaeologists have been bold enough in their analyses to consider ideological issues, such as the role of racism in shaping slave-master relations.[2]

Thus, most historical archaeologists interested in New World slavery have begun their studies of African slaves by taking to heart

Hawkes's dictum that the material aspects of past life are easier to reconstruct than the social and religious institutions.[3] The motivations for conducting slave archaeology at the material level are undoubtedly complex, but one of the primary reasons for such an approach relates to the politics of the present. Until the late 1960s, archaeologists could not imagine that anything of interest or value could be learned by studying relatively recent New World slavery. After all, slavery in the United States ended only in 1865; in Brazil, slavery was officially tolerated until 1889. In society at large, the general attitude seemed to be that if anything at all could be learned about slavery, it could be derived from reading written records. Historians, of course, knew that this was not true, that much remained unknown about slave life, but it took the civil rights movement in America to convince a new generation of archaeologists that the study of the history and culture of African Americans was a valid kind of archaeology.[4] Charles Fairbanks, a pioneer in the field, wrote in the turbulent years of the early 1970s that the archaeology of slavery could "broaden and enrich the knowledge of our American heritage at a time when that tradition is in the midst of rapid and often baffling change."[5] Today, the archaeology of African slavery in the New World is the fastest-growing kind of archaeology being practiced in the Americas. My focus here is only on slavery in the antebellum American South from 1800 to 1861, even though archaeology is also being conducted on earlier sites and on sites associated with free African Americans.[6] Most archaeologists who have an interest in slavery have documented several aspects of slave life, extending from daily foodways to larger social relations. This essay highlights some of this research as it relates to one aspect of slave life, that which Hawkes views as the most difficult to comprehend archaeologically: religion. Before I can develop this theme, however, I must further establish the archaeological relevance of this research.

HISTORICAL ARCHAEOLOGY AND SLAVE IDENTITY

The archaeological understanding of New World slavery as a social institution begins with the concept of "ethnicity." The issue of ethnic identification in archaeology is nothing new. Childe stated several decades ago that "the correlation of cultural with racial [i.e., ethnic] groups is generally hazardous and speculative" and "beset with pitfalls."[7] His observation may be easily understandable in prehistory, where the lines of descent between ancient peoples and peoples known historically may be clouded with the passage of time, the impact of cultural change, and the complexities introduced by diverse population movements. Oddly enough, however, his comment is equally applicable to history, where it may initially be supposed that the agreement between the archaeological past and the ethnographic, or historical, present is a close or near-perfect match. In many cases, a historical archaeologist may be excavating a site for which an abundant and rich documentary record exists. We may thus suppose, and perhaps justly, that a strong correlation exists between the archaeological remains and the historical actors being written about. The need for historical archaeologists to be able to identify ethnic groups in the New World is especially pressing, given the importance of ethnicity in shaping modern life.[8] Historical archaeologists in the United States must be particularly mindful of ethnicity because "ethnicity is a central theme—perhaps *the* central theme—of American history."[9] Given the shared colonial histories of most places in the New World—the United States, Cuba, Jamaica, and Brazil, to name a few—we may easily imagine that the archaeological understanding of ethnicity has prime importance in historical archaeology in general. As a way in which to study ethnicity and the contacts between ethnic groups, New World historical archaeologists have turned to the study of slavery. In addition, slavery has relevance outside the narrow confines of scholarship. To understand this social institution appeals not only to professional anthropologists and historians but also to thousands of nonscholars in society at large.

Embedded within the archaeology of slavery is the once much-debated question of whether the Africans enslaved and brought to the New World had their cultures destroyed by the Middle Passage, the horrendous trip across the Atlantic Ocean. Some scholars, such as Frazier, argue that the process of capture and enslavement—added to the horrors of transoceanic travel—was so traumatic that the people could not be expected to arrive in the New World unchanged.[10] Frazier imagines that these enslaved and traumatized Africans had their cultures ripped from them by their experiences. In this sense, the social landscape of the New World was truly a new one. The slaves' trauma carried over into religion because the horrors of slavery caused their traditional religions to collapse. Any expression of an African belief in the New World was simply a vague memory rather than part of a living cultural tradition.

Many scholars have found Frazier's position difficult to accept: notable among them is Herskovits, who takes as one of his main propositions that Frazier's viewpoint represents a misleading "myth of the Negro Past."[11] This myth, rather than quietly resting among the dust of academic debate, is alive and active in society, helping to perpetuate the idea that African Americans are inferior to European Americans. According to the myth's logic, only an inferior people could "lose" their culture. For Herskovits the proof of the vitality of African culture in the New World can be found in certain "Africanisms," cultural traits from Africa kept alive outside the continent. Herskovits finds several Africanisms in African American methods of planting crops; in postures of sitting, walking, speaking, and dancing; in hairstyles; and in concepts of time and punctuality. Further, he proposes that Africans in the New World were particularly adept at retaining their religious beliefs because, unlike agricultural practices and manners of dress, these ideas could be hidden from view.[12]

Most scholars today have charted an intermediate course somewhere between the positions held by Frazier and by Herskovits. The current most prevalent view contains two central propositions: that Africans did not abandon or lose their cultures during enslavement and the Middle Passage, and that the cultures they forged in the New World were not exact duplications of those in Africa. Through interactions with diverse Africans, Europeans, and Native Americans, enslaved Africans created a syncretic culture in the New World. Members of former African cultures gently transformed some aspects of their cultures, radically altered others, and dropped still others. Accordingly, "one must maintain a skeptical attitude toward claims that many contemporary social or cultural forms represent direct continuities from the African homelands."[13] We must assume that Africans in the New World retained some elements of their traditional cultures in their new homes, but that many of these elements were changed to the point that they may have become unrecognizable.

We may easily and readily accept this syncretic dictum in art, moral perspectives, foodways, and even dress, but what about religion? What did enslaved Africans do about their religions, and how did they express themselves religiously in ways that would leave archaeological evidence?

SLAVE RELIGIONS IN HISTORY

It would be naive to imagine that during the Middle Passage all slaves forgot the gods and spirits they worshipped, feared, and appeased, and that because of their enslavement they lost faith in the rituals and belief systems that had sustained them for generations. Most modern scholars agree that slaves were conservative in their belief systems, and that ideas of cosmology, eschatology, curing, and sorcery inexorably link African Americans to Africa. Raboteau, a leading authority on slave religion, writes, "One of the most durable and adaptable constituents of the slave's culture, linking African past with American present, was his religion."[14] DuBois, the great African American social scientist, notes, "The Negro church of today is the social centre of Negro life in the United States, and the most characteristic expression of African character."[15] Religion thus formed a significant part of the slaves' syncretic culture and was, in fact, one element of life that could mentally tie African men and women in the New World to their kinfolk and way of life still in Africa. Even though the slaves' religious beliefs were altered through contact with others, religious expressions nevertheless retained an African flavor.[16]

Even a cursory examination of the available secondary historical sources on slave religion indicates the complexity of this subject. Nonetheless, at the time of their capture and enslavement, most Africans followed one of two religious traditions: either they were members of large, essentially non-African religions, either Islam or Christianity, or they practiced one of the many "traditional" religions that existed throughout the African continent. Both religious traditions obviously had an impact on African American slave life in the New World. Religion also played a strong role in the lives of free African Americans in the antebellum American South.[17]

Slave owners were divided in their views about slave religion. Some masters were unconcerned as to whether their slaves even had religion. These masters cared little about "the amusements and religion of the Negro so long as they did not affect his working ability."[18] Other slave masters promoted Christianity among their slaves. The comments of ex-slaves from Alabama suggest the range of ways in which slaves could be formally acquainted with Christianity while on the plantation. Molly Ammonds said that her master built his slaves a church with "a floor and seats, and the top was covered with pine boughs" in which the master's father would preach, but Everett Ingram said, "De colored folks used de white church and set in the back."[19]

Many slaves undoubtedly learned about Christianity and Islam while they still lived in Africa. Capuchin missionaries were sent from France, Italy, and Portugal in the seventeenth century to convert as many African men and women as possible, and many slaves had met Christians at the European forts along the coast.[20] Many slaves probably learned about Islam in the same way, and some slave owners were sensitive to the needs of their Muslim slaves. For example, some masters in the American South substituted beef for the pork that usually comprised the slaves' meat ration.[21]

The religions that the slave masters thought they recognized in their plantation quarters, or slave communities, were not always the same religions that planters knew. For instance, many slaves who were identified as being devoted to Islam were also widely known for their largely African-inspired magical powers.[22] African American Christianity was also a multifaceted and syncretic religion in the quarters. In his compelling historical ethnography of the slave communities that stretched along the coast of South Carolina, Joyner proposes that the slaves' Christianity was channeled along two directions. In the first, the slaves incorporated spirit possession and ecstatic trances into their Christian church services; in the second, the slaves continued to believe in witches and evil spirits as "a sort of parallel consciousness" to Christianity.[23]

Some slaves rejected all but their traditional religions, continuing to believe in sorcery, conjuring, and their traditional cosmology. This religion, actually a unified version of several religions, existed as an underground, alternative belief system. The slaves used this religion not only as a form of divine worship but also as a form of resistance.[24] In fact, "nearly all quarter communities organized their own clandestine congregation without the sanction or participation of plantation authorities."[25] The continued tradition of African religion on plantations deeply concerned plantation owners. Many slave owners rigorously attempted to convert their slaves to Christianity, either to Protestantism or, in places like south Louisiana and Spanish-controlled Florida, to Roman Catholicism, simply as a defense mechanism. Of course, the issue of whether to provide religious instruction to their human chattel—which conceivably could lead to open rebellion through the religious principle of inherent human dignity—was a matter of great consternation to slave owners, and the issue was hotly debated across the slave-holding world.[26]

ASSUMPTIONS AND PROBLEMS IN THE ARCHAEOLOGICAL INTERPRETATION OF SLAVE RELIGION

The above comments, albeit brief, indicate that slave religion is an exceedingly complex and multifaceted subject. Although manifestations of African religions appeared in the New World in varying degrees, it seems logical to assume that each would have archaeological correlates. We may further assume that the material expressions of slave religion included both places of worship and associated religious paraphernalia. The contextual union of these elements is easy to imagine. For recognized, plantation-sponsored church observances, we may easily associate places of worship with hymnals, candlesticks, crosses, books, and other readily identifiable pieces of religious material culture. For clandestine slave religious practices, we can understandably envision the difficulty in associating religious places with religious objects. The problem with such identification is well voiced by a Mrs. Channel, who lived on a plantation where it was expressly forbidden for slaves to conduct religious ceremonies: "The slaves would steal away into the woods at night and hold services. They would form a circle on their knees around the speaker who would also be on his knees."[27] One clear object of such religious service, beyond worship, is secrecy. In these clandestine religious observances, we can expect little in the way of easy association between place and object. The locales selected by slaves seeking to conduct traditional rituals were hidden and unpretentious, and the artifacts used for their religious observances were undoubtedly everyday things pressed into service.

The secrecy necessary for the practice of traditional African religion implies that archaeologists will not easily locate places of traditional slave worship. Until such sites can be found, we must concentrate on the possible religious artifacts found in association with slave sites. These objects can serve as tangible, visible reminders that slaves brought aspects of their African religions with them to the New World and that they learned how to adapt them to the new social and political landscapes within which they found themselves.

Many of the powerful religious objects slaves made in the New World might best be described as having to do with magic. By "magic" I mean an interactive religious belief system wherein spells can be cast and warded off, where the future can be foretold, and where the sick can be healed. New World historical archaeologists who search for evidence of slave religion look for the sort of material culture easily associated with religious magic because only in the rarest of contexts can traditional religious items be clearly associated with slaves.

The rarest of contexts, of course, are mortuary settings. One obvious value of such contexts is the underlying assumption of most mortuary studies that material objects buried with the dead were also associated with the deceased while alive. Slaves may have been willing to bury practitioners of traditional religions with African-inspired objects simply because the objects would be forever out of sight, buried for all time in a grave. Slaves could not possibly have imagined that future archaeologists would be fascinated by their daily lives, histories, and struggles. We may expect that some objects interred with the dead had specific religious functions. Burial contexts in Barbados and in the southern United States provide such information, but from different ends of the religious spectrum.

At Newton Plantation, a seventeenth-century sugar estate on the island of Barbados, Handler and Lange found the remains of an old man of African descent, which they named "Burial 72."[28] This individual had been buried with several commonplace objects, such as copper bracelets, white metal rings, and a metal knife. Most interesting, perhaps, were an elaborate necklace and a baked-clay smoking pipe. The necklace contained seven cowrie shells, twenty-one drilled dog canines, fourteen glass beads of various sizes and colors, drilled vertebrae from a large fish, and one large carnelian bead.[29] The clay pipe was a short-stemmed variety of the sort in which a reed or wooden tube was fitted into the bowl to serve as a stem. The bowl was decorated with a series of lines and dots. Handler and Lange judge this pipe to be "of African origin,"[30] possibly from Ghana,[31] because it bears no relationship to any known European pipe of the same period. This pipe, and the necklace—with its cowrie shells and carnelian bead probably from Africa—led them to postulate that the individual they called Burial 72 was probably an "Obeah practitioner or folk doctor." According to seventeenth-century accounts cited by Handler and Lange, the so-called "Obeah negroes" were well known in the slave communities for their African-derived arts of healing and divination.[32] These practitioners were respected and feared, and other slaves often carried charms to protect themselves from the Obeah's power. Handler and Lange interpret the objects found with Burial 72 to be the "toolkit" associated with these powerful people. The pipe and the necklace provide a direct, strong link to the religions of Africa.

A Christianized African burial was discovered a few years later at the first official cemetery in New Orleans, Louisiana. The Catholic fathers of this French colonial settlement on the banks of the lower Mississippi River sanctified this burial ground sometime before 1722. They later deconsecrated it, in 1788, and the French inhabitants of the city removed their ancestors' remains for reburial elsewhere. In 1801, when the city leaders subdivided the former cemetery into lots to be sold for residential development, the only remains not removed were those of the city's poorest classes. At the very bottom of the social hierarchy, of course, were enslaved Africans. Archaeologists excavated thirty-two of these interments as part of a rescue project.[33] Only one of the still-solid cypress caskets contained any religious objects. These objects were a rosary with sixty-three black wooden beads and two silver medals (one emblazoned with St. Christopher, the other with the Madonna and Child) and a glass and white metal medallion with the image of the Virgin Mary etched in gold on the glass face. These items were found with Burial 11.

Burial 11 represents the remains of a forty- to forty-nine-year-old black male who had purposefully notched first mandibular incisors. Tooth mutilation is well known in Africa, and it is tempting to suppose that this individual had spent a portion of his life there.[34] The presence of the rosary, however, implies that he had accepted Christianity at some point in his life. We will never know if his conversion occurred in Africa or in his New World home.

The difference between the material items associated with Burial 11 in New Orleans and with Burial 72 in Barbados may reflect only their temporal disparity. Someone searching for acculturation among slaves may perceive the presence of African objects in the seventeenth-century Caribbean burial and the Roman Catholic objects in the late-eighteenth-century burial in New Orleans as a prime example of the acculturative pressures experienced by African Americans in the New World.[35] Looked at another way, however, the differences between the two burials may be perceived as representing the broad diversity of the African peoples brought to the New World, and how various individuals, at disparate times, accepted and followed different religious traditions. When historical archaeologists think about slave religion, however, their interest invariably focuses on the kind of artifacts found with Burial 72 in Barbados, objects that may reflect something of the slaves' African origins.

The search for African-inspired objects forms the core of the archaeology of slave religion. For the sake of convenience, two sets of religious objects can be readily identified in the archaeological literature: objects that seem to reflect African religious traditions and belief systems, and objects with no clear African influence but that appear to have been used in the pursuit of traditional religious observance. Neither class of items is well known in archaeology, but examples have been found.

OBJECTS OF AFRICAN ORIGIN

Objects with obvious African affiliation are highly sought after by New World historical archaeologists because such objects provide concrete evidence that African peoples retained elements of their cultures in the New World. Regrettably, however, these objects—Herskovits's "Africanisms"—are frightfully few in number in the archaeological record. Nonetheless, two kinds of objects appear to point most clearly to the African religious roots of New World slaves. These objects are earthenware pottery vessels and small, brass ornamental fists.

Upon first encountering pieces of the low-fired, unglazed, coarse pottery at slave sites, archaeologists in the American South assumed that they represented part of a Native American pottery tradition.[36] After all, they bore a remarkable resemblance to the aboriginal pottery ubiquitous in southeastern prehistory and early history. The perception generally held was that, in order to reach the plantations, this so-called Colono-Indian pottery must have been traded by Native Americans to plantation inhabitants. These natives traded the pottery either directly to slaves, who used it in their cabins, or to their masters, who gave it to the slaves for their personal use in the quarters.[37] A careful reading of the ethnographic literature, however, convinced Ferguson that this pottery, which he terms simply "Colono Ware," was actually made by the slaves themselves.[38] Archaeologists working along the eastern coast of the United States and in the Caribbean have documented that Colono Ware appears in many contexts and occurs in both European vessel forms (bowls with standing rings, plates, and small cups and pitchers with handles) and non-European forms (shallow bowls and wide-mouthed pots).[39]

In the course of his detailed and innovative study of several Colono Ware vessels found in South Carolina and Virginia, Ferguson learned that many of the otherwise mundane shallow bowls in this tradition were incised on the bottom with an X, an X enclosed in a circle, or an X with arms extending outward like a reverse swastika.[40] These marks could easily be imagined to represent identification symbols placed on the pots by their makers. Potters throughout eighteenth-century Europe used similar marks on their ceramic wares, and an X is an easy mark to make in wet clay.[41]

The idea that the Xs on the bases of Colono Ware vessels may represent makers' marks is plausible, but Ferguson offers a much more intriguing interpretation. The marks are often found on the interior base of the vessels rather than on the outside, as is true of most makers' marks, and sometimes they resemble the encircled cross of the Bakongo sign of the cosmos; Ferguson thus interprets these crosses as symbols of an African cosmology.[42] The Bakongo—a populous people living in today's Zaire—used earthen pots to contain powerful substances associated with healing and the control of the supernatural.[43] Among the Bakongo, the association of pots with healing extends all the way to Ne Kongo, the renowned founder of their culture. Based on this ethnographic evidence, Ferguson boldly concludes that "South Carolina's marked bowls were made and used by American descendants of the mythical Ne Kongo who cooked medicines in earthenware pots."[44] In addition, these pots, because of their obvious difference from European glazed wards, also served as a form of "unconscious resistance to slavery and the plantation system."[45] These clay pots were a way for slaves to proclaim their traditional cultures in a nonvocalized and relatively nonthreatening manner. The etching of powerful religious symbols on the insides of pots was a further way for slaves to retain a piece of Africa in the New World.

The mundane character of the earthenware pots made it possible for historical archaeologists to overlook the scratched X marks for years. When noticed, these lines were often interpreted to be the cut marks made by knives.[46] The common appearance of the pots, and the nagging uncertainty over exactly who produced them— Native Americans, slaves, or Creoles—clouds the issue of how they were used for religious observances and obscures whether they had a religious function at all. Clearly, much further research is needed on Colono Ware before a definitive statement of its many meanings can be presented.

Objects that cannot be so easily denied as religious in nature are the small, brass, fist-shaped amulets found at the Hermitage, the early nineteenth-century Tennessee plantation home of the U.S. president Andrew Jackson. To date, archaeologists have found three fist amulets in the slave cabin deposits of the Hermitage. Because the temporal context of these objects is in the antebellum period, before the American Civil War, their association with slaves is certain. The fists are small in size and are made of a stamped copper alloy; two of them clench rings, and the third incorporates a hook.

These fist objects are similar in form to the *figas* that are commonly used, even today, throughout Latin America as good luck charms. Figas have occasionally been found at archaeological sites. South found a classic example at Santa Elena, a Spanish outpost located on Parris Island, South Carolina, occupied from 1566 to 1587.[47] The clenched fist of the figa is thought to represent the hand of God grasping the souls of the saved, and as a charm, it is thought to be a powerful protection against the evil eye. Figas are also supposed to repel bullets. A historical connection between the Hermitage and Spanish America can easily be established. Jackson is known to have purchased slaves from the Spanish in the early nineteenth century, and the fists may simply be souvenirs from the Spanish territory.[48]

The fists from the Hermitage are not exactly like figas, however. A true figa has the thumb extending upward between the first and the second finger in a symbolic representation of a cross. The example from Santa Elena is true to this form, but the fists from the Hermitage lack the finger and thumb arrangement and are simply in the form of clenched fists.[49] As a result of this variant form, the alternative possibility remains equally strong: that the fist amulets at the Hermitage may have been used as charms to ward off witches.[50] Writing of his experiences in Brazil in the mid-nineteenth century, Ewbanks notes that symbols of the cross, including figas, were particularly powerful objects, and that "neither witches nor wizards can bear the sight of them."[51] This view has also been expressed in the United States. One former slave in Florida said that an "old witch doctor" charged him $5 to "make me a hand," or a "jack," because "dat be a charm what will keep de witches away."[52] Since *hand* was a widely used term that could refer to any charm regardless of form, the correlation between the warding off of witches and the hand charms at the Hermitage is difficult to make with complete confidence.[53] Still, the connection is plausible.

Both the marked earthenware pottery vessels and the brass fist amulets seem to reflect something about slave belief systems. The meaning of either class of artifacts, however, is ambiguous. The pottery marks may be just makers' marks, and the fists may be simple souvenirs with no deeper significance. Nonetheless, an interpretation that makes reference to slave religion and belief systems is not only appealing, it also adds a substantial new dimension to our understanding of African American slave life.

MUNDANE OBJECTS USED IN TRADITIONAL WAYS

Proposing a religious affiliation for objects like the Hermitage fist charms may be somewhat risky, but both they and the marked pottery vessels do stand out in the archaeological assemblages as unusual objects. Religious interpretations for the functions of these objects—supported by reference to ethnographic and historical information—are entirely plausible. Other artifacts, those that appear even more commonplace in form and supposed function, are decidedly more difficult to associate firmly with the belief systems of enslaved Africans. This troubling archaeological problem is neatly summarized by Adams in his analysis of slave sites at Kings Bay, Georgia:

> Most conjure items were organic, and would not be found or at least distinguished easily. One such item would be a single black cat bone . . . but while cat bones were found, there is no reason to assume these were magical items. A human tooth (lower left canine), however, was recovered in the Kings Bay Plantation Kitchen and it may be the result of magic, because the tooth was extracted after the death of the individual, a child three to four years old. Another tooth from an adult was found in the excavation of the bighouse.[54]

Adams apparently makes the decision about which artifacts were related to magic based on the only available evidence, the archaeological context. This evidence is not without problems, however, because the tooth found at the mansion also could easily have served a magical function as much as any other tooth found during excavation. Thus, at this point, archaeologists of slavery are left to make suppositions often based on plausible, but yet somewhat shaky, grounds.

Even though serious interpretative problems confront archaeologists at every turn, the association of everyday artifacts with religion and magic continue to be made. Numerous examples can quickly be cited. At the Horton Grove slave quarters in North Carolina, for instance, archaeologists found carefully peeled forked sticks between the walls of a late antebellum slave cabin. These sticks—possibly hidden and intentionally incorporated into the cabin's fabric—may have been used as protection from witches in a manner consistent with what some former slaves report.[55] Conversely, these sticks may have had nothing whatsoever to do with witchcraft; perhaps a child stripped the sticks and played with them, eventually losing them during cabin construction. The blue beads often found within slave cabin deposits provide another ready example. When Ascher and Fairbanks reported finding a single hexagonal, faceted, blue bead at an antebellum slave cabin site in Georgia, they proposed a number of interpretations to explain its presence: that it was an "ambassador bead," used as a kind of passport; that it may have played some role in cementing sociopolitical alliances in Africa; or that a Native

American may have traded it to a Georgian slave.[56] Recently, Adams, observing the presence of blue beads at several plantations throughout the American South, proposed that these may signify an Islamic belief in using blue beads "to ward off the evil eye."[57] Adams is careful to note, however, that blue glass beads, like the black, yellow, and red beads he found at the Kings Bay slave cabins, were common items traded to Native Americans. Like Colono Ware pottery, perhaps the beads found their way to slaves through the commercial efforts of European American or even Native American traders. Drilled coins provide still another example. Drilled coins at first seem to represent simple curios used in necklaces until one realizes that former slaves in Georgia have suggested that pierced coins were used as charms to avoid evil. A former slave living in Oklahoma summarized this usage succinctly when he said that slaves "wore a silver dime on a raw cotton thread around their necks to keep from being voodooed."[58] Pierced coins have been found at several plantation sites, including President Thomas Jefferson's Monticello, and other specimens are likely to appear at other sites.[59] The pertinent question, however, is: are these coins to be regarded as religious items, decorative jewelry, or some combination of both? The archaeologist's viewpoint and choice of evidence, at this point in time, seem to decide which interpretation is accepted.

Another excellent example to demonstrate the interpretive problems faced by archaeologists is provided by the common iron pot. Visitors to slave cabins during the antebellum period saw iron pots in every hearth. Rossa Cooley, a Vassar-educated teacher who went to work on St. Helena Island, South Carolina, noted, for instance, that a Miss Towne had reported in 1862: "The household utensils consisted of one pot, in which they [the slaves] cooked their hominy or peas with salt pork."[60] Former slaves made frequent reference to the iron pots they used in their cabins. James Singleton of Mississippi said, "There was a big old iron pot hangin' over de hearth, an' us had 'possum, greens, taters, and de lak cooked in it"; Benny Dillard of Georgia remembered that the slaves he knew boiled their food in the "big old pots what swung on cranes over the coals."[61]

The function of iron pots in slave cabins seems so straightforward that further comment is unwarranted; iron pots were used for cooking. One of the truisms of southern cooking today is that the single-dish meal derives from the slave practice of cooking everything in the same large pot. This easy interpretation is shattered, however, by other slaves' comments that iron pots could have a distinctively religious function. According to ex-slave Charles Grandy of Virginia, an iron pot was commonly used to "catch de sound" of slave religious services: "Sometimes [you] would stick yo' haid down in de pot if you got to shout awful loud"; Marriah Hines, also from Virginia, said, "Couse some of the masters didn't like the way we slaves carried on [at prayer meetings] we would turn pots down, and tubs to keep the sound from going out."[62] Mrs. Channel, cited earlier, made the comment that the leader of a clandestine slave worship ceremony on her plantation "would bend forward and speak into or over a vessel of water to drown out the sound."[63]

The slaves' use of pots to "catch sound" probably had little to do with acoustics. Rather, the use of iron pots in religious observances was an African tradition related to the worship of deities.[64] The iron pot fragments found at sites like Millwood Plantation and at Kings Bay Plantation may relate to more than subsistence.[65] According to Robert Hall: "The iron pot may stand not only for an African baseline but also for the chronological and cultural range of the religious history of Black Americans. By the end of the Civil War black Southerners were scattered along a continuum from the iron pot of African religionists to the silver chalice of the Catholics and Episcopalians."[66]

The same case for religious or magical association might be made for the "mundane" objects found with Handler and Lange's Burial 72 in Barbados. The bracelets and rings may be regarded as more than decorative jewelry; they may represent powerful amulets used for protection. One of the clearest and most remarkable uses of metal rings as protection against evil and as good luck charms was found in the 1930s along the coast of Georgia, in the same region where Adams found metal rings in the archaeological deposits of slave cabins. When the interviewers of the Georgia Writers' Project spoke with George Boddison, they found: "His wrists and arms were encircled by copper wire strung with good luck charms; his fingers were covered with several large plain rings. A copper wire was bound around his head and attached to this wire were two broken bits of mirror which, lying flat against his temples with the reflecting side out, flashed and glittered when he moved his head."[67] The interviewers discovered that he even had a brass ring in his mouth in the place of a lower tooth. Thus, it may be assumed that any ring found at a slave site may have been related in some fashion to a traditional belief system. On the other hand, it may be supposed—with equal conviction, perhaps—that slaves wore some rings and bracelets simply for personal adornment. Some rings may have had dual functions.

One of the interpretive problems caused by such artifacts is that either they appear individually, without clear associations with other religious or ritual objects, or else they are found with artifacts that may have a ritual significance that is not currently understood. Such is the case at Garrison Plantation in Maryland. At this site, Klingelhofer reports the association of incised spoons with small, polygonal objects made of wood, earthenware, and glass.[68] It may well be true that these items represent a slave religious "toolkit," but clear religious associations between them cannot be neatly drawn.[69] Their true function for now must remain a mystery. As Klingelhofer writes, "Until more is known about Negro pagan religions, or games that slaves brought with them or devised in American bondage, the identity of these objects cannot be determined."[70]

One case where strong associations between apparent ritual objects do exist derives from the Jordan Plantation, an antebellum and postbellum site in East Texas. While excavating a cabin thought to have been inhabited by an African American "healer/magician," Brown and Cooper discovered a toolkit composed of five cast-iron kettle bases, numerous pieces of used chalk, bird skulls, an animal's paw, medicine bottles, a tube composed of several bullet casings, nails and spikes, several spoons and knives, and two chert scrapers. Drawing on ethnographical and historical information, Brown and Cooper suggest that all of these objects could have been used together for the conducting of African-style rituals.[71] Kongolese ritual leaders in Cuba draw cruciform patterns on the bottoms of kettles with chalk (similar to the marks on Ferguson's pots, in fact); bird symbolism—associated both with healing and divination—is prevalent throughout Africa; sealed, hollow tubes can be used in certain healing rituals; and spikes and nails are driven into anthropomorphic wooden figures in order to fix spells cast on victims. Brown and Cooper did not find any such figurines, and their interpretations of the religious nature of the objects are otherwise unsupported. Still, their willingness to envision the artifacts as an interacting collection of ritual objects, rather than as individual artifacts with only the most obvious uses, is significant. In order to perceive the possible religious applications of the artifacts at Jordan Plantation we must learn to see them collectively.

In keeping with the idea that much of this religious toolkit would have been hidden from the master's view, Brown and Cooper argue that much African American ritual symbolism may have lacked an expression that could be identified by outsiders. This lack of expression would "keep the behavior operating within the adapting community of African-Americans."[72] Their idea supports Ferguson's notion that the Colono Ware pots—and the Xs scratched on them, for that matter—have a dual function: one religious, one political. Such items allowed slaves to practice aspects of their traditional religions at the same time as they allowed them to embrace an empowerment that existed beyond the reach of the slave system. The slaves' bodies might be held in chains within the system, but their minds were free to maintain their own religious beliefs and their own concepts of personal freedom.

CONCLUSION

This brief essay shows that the archaeology of slave religion is only in its infancy. In the search for answers to questions about slave diet, social relations, and material elements of resistance, some historical archaeologists have found time to examine the religious lives of the African men and women who toiled on the plantations and within the cities of the plantation world. In this essay I have only touched upon some of the discoveries and interpretations historical archaeologists have made over the past few years. The archaeology of New World slavery is such a rapidly growing field that over the next few years it is likely that we will know appreciably more about slave life and religion than we do now.

One of the biases that exists in the present data derives from archaeologists' preoccupation with large plantations. The reasons for this emphasis on the very large estates of the wealthy lower South and Caribbean are varied, but typically they relate to funding and local interest. It has generally been easier to obtain scarce funding for plantation archaeology when a historically important person is associated with the property. For this reason, active archaeological

programs have been conducted at plantations associated with Andrew Jackson, George Washington, Thomas Jefferson, and other
notable members of the elite planter class.[73] In the United States,
the largest estates are typically along the Atlantic coast. Much of
this focus has been driven not by the research design of archaeologists but by the needs of land developers, who have sought to build
huge resorts and retirement communities on prime pieces of coastal
real estate. This prized real estate was also valued in the past by the
wealthiest planters, so the sites that have been studied, usually under the requirements of preservation legislation, have been the large
coastal estates. Federal bureaucrats have easily been able to judge
these large estates, with their famous owners, to be "significant" and
so worthy of federally funded study.

Historically, however, most plantations were not large. The typical plantation in the American South was small in acreage, housed
fewer than ten slaves, and was tilled by the master working alongside the slaves.[74] These kinds of plantations formed the backbone of
the American slave system. Nonetheless, only beginning in the early
1990s have archaeologists turned their attention to these small, unimpressive estates.[75]

In terms of religious beliefs, the distinction between large and
small plantations may not be insignificant. A former slave in Mississippi said, "We didn't hear nothing 'bout hants [haunts] or charms.
It was on the big places where all such as that went on."[76] This comment implies that the size of the plantation may have played a role in
whether and how slaves were able to express their religious beliefs.
We may assume, perhaps, that slaves on larger estates had more an-
onymity and could have more easily maintained elements of a traditional religion than slaves on small plantation farms.

Unfortunately, the intriguing idea that plantation size and religious tradition are linked cannot be addressed at this time. Archaeologists studying slave religion are still too few in number, and
our collective knowledge is too fragmentary to permit a definitive
statement on this matter. There is every reason to believe, however,
that the study of slave religion, along with slave life, will continue
to grow in importance, and that eventually we will be able to write
a more complete account of the religious beliefs and practices of
the African men and women who were held in bondage in the New
World.

NOTES

I would like to thank Larry McKee, staff archaeologist at the Hermitage, for providing information about the fist charms found there. Brian Fagan offered his encouragement during the preparation of this essay, and Chris Scarre kindly assisted as well. I greatly appreciate their support and guidance. I also am very grateful for the encouragement and assistance readily given by Janice L. Orser. Of course, the interpretations and any errors that may result from them are mine.

1. C. H. Fairbanks, "The Plantation Archaeology of the Southeastern Coast," *Historical Archaeology* 18, no. 1 (1984): 1–18; C. E. Orser Jr., "The Past Ten Years of Plantation Archaeology in the Southeastern United States," *Southeastern Archaeology* 3 (1984): 1–12; C. E. Orser Jr., "Archaeological Approaches to New World Plantation Slavery," in *Archaeological Method and Theory*, vol. 2, ed. M. B. Schiffer (Tucson: University of Arizona Press, 1990), 111–54; C. E. Orser Jr., "Bibliography of Slave and Plantation Archaeology (as of December 31, 1991)," *Slavery and Abolition* 13 (1992): 316–37; T. A. Singleton, "The Archaeology of Slave Life," in *Before Freedom Came: African-American Life in the Antebellum South*, ed. E. D. C. Campbell Jr. and K. S. Rice (Richmond: Museum of the Confederacy, 1991), 155–75.

2. See, for example, D. W. Babson, "The Archaeology of Racism and Ethnicity on Southern Plantations," in "Historical Archaeology on Southern Plantations and Farms," ed. C. E. Orser Jr., *Historical Archaeology* 24, no. 4 (1990): 20–28; T. W. Epperson, "Race and the Disciplines of the Plantation," in "Historical Archaeology on Southern Plantations and Farms," ed. C. E. Orser Jr., *Historical Archaeology* 24, no. 4 (1990): 29–36.

3. C. Hawkes, "Archaeological Theory and Methods: Some Suggestions from the Old World," *American Anthropologist* 56 (1954): 155–64.

4. L. G. Ferguson, *Uncommon Ground: Archaeology and Early African America, 1650–1800* (Washington, D.C.: Smithsonian Institution Press, 1992), xxxvi–xxxviii.

5. C. H. Fairbanks, "The Kingsley Slave Cabins in Duval County, Florida," *Conference on Historic Site Archaeology Papers* 7 (1974): 62.

6. See R. L. Schuyler, ed., *Archaeological Perspectives on Ethnicity in America: Afro-American and Asian American Culture History* (Farmingdale, N.Y.: Baywood, 1980).

7. V. G. Childe, *The Aryans: A Study of Indo-European Origins* (New York: Alfred A. Knopf, 1926), 200.

8. C. E. Orser Jr., "The Archaeological Search for Ethnicity in the Historic United States," *Archaeologia Polona* 29 (1991): 109–21.

9. W. Peterson, M. Novak, and P. Gleason, *Concepts of Ethnicity* (Cambridge, Mass.: Harvard University Press, 1982), v.

10. E. F. Frazier, *The Negro Church in America* (New York: Schocken, 1964).

11. M. J. Herskovits, *The Myth of the Negro Past* (Boston: Beacon, 1958).

12. Ibid., 3, 143–206, 137–38.

13. S. W. Mintz and R. Price, *An Anthropological Approach to the Afro-American Past: A Caribbean Perspective* (Philadelphia: Institute for the Study of Human Issues, 1976), 27.

14. A. J. Raboteau, *Slave Religion: The "Invisible Institution" in the Antebellum South* (New York: Oxford University Press, 1978), 4.

15. W. E. B. DuBois, *The Souls of Black Folk: Essays and Sketches* (Greenwich, Conn.: Fawcett, 1961), 142.

16. Raboteau, *Slave Religion*.

17. See M. P. Johnson and J. L. Roark, *Black Masters: A Free Family of Color in the Old South* (New York: W. W. Norton, 1984), 227–29.

18. N. N. Puckett, *Folk Beliefs of the Southern Negro* (Chapel Hill, N.C.: University of North Carolina Press, 1926), 10.

19. G. D. Rawick, *The American Slave: A Composite Autobiography*, Supplement Series 1, vol. 1, *Alabama Narratives* (Westport, Conn.: Greenwood, 1977), 11, 204.

20. J. Duffy, *Portugal in Africa* (Cambridge, Mass.: Harvard University Press, 1962), 44; Raboteau, *Slave Religion*.

21. C. Joyner, *Down by the Riverside: A South Carolina Slave Community* (Urbana: University of Illinois Press, 1984), 171.

22. Raboteau, *Slave Religion*, 5–6.

23. Joyner, *Down by the Riverside*, 142.

24. S. Stuckey, *Slave Culture: Nationalist Theory and the Foundations of Black America* (New York: Random House, 1987), 52–53.

25. T. L. Webber, *Deep Like the Rivers: Education in the Slave Quarter Community, 1831–1865* (New York: W. W. Norton, 1978), 191.

26. Ibid., 43–58.

27. J. B. Cade, "Out of the Mouths of Ex-Slaves," *Journal of Negro History* 20 (1935): 331.

28. J. S. Handler and F. W. Lange, *Plantation Slavery in Barbados: An Archaeological and Historical Investigation* (Cambridge, Mass.: Harvard University Press, 1978).

29. Ibid., 125–32; J. S. Handler, F. W. Lange, and C. E. Orser Jr., "Carnelian Beads in Necklaces from a Slave Cemetery in Barbados, West Indies," *Ornament* 4, no. 2 (1979): 15–18.

30. Handler and Lange, *Plantation Slavery in Barbados*, 132.

31. J. S. Handler, "An African Pipe from a Slave Cemetery in Barbados, West Indies," in *The Archaeology of the Clay Tobacco Pipe, VIII America*, ed. P. Davey (Oxford: BAR, 1983), 251.

32. Handler and Lange, *Plantation Slavery in Barbados*, 32.

33. C. E. Orser Jr., D. W. Owsley, and J. R. Shenkel, "Gaining Access to New Orleans' First Cemetery," *Journal of Field Archaeology* 13 (1986): 342–45; D. W. Owsley, C. E. Orser Jr., R. Montgomery, and C. C. Holland, *An Archaeological and Physical Anthropological Study of the First Cemetery in New Orleans, Louisiana* (Baton Rouge: Louisiana Division of Archaeology, 1985).

34. J. S. Handler, R. S. Corruccini, and R. J. Mutaw, "Tooth Mutilation in the Caribbean: Evidence from a Slave Burial Population in Barbados," *Journal of Human Evolution* 11 (1982): 297–313; T. D. Stewart and J. R. Groome, "The African Custom of Tooth Mutilation in America," *American Journal of Physical Anthropology* 28 (1968): 31–42.

35. For example, T. R. Wheaton and P. H. Garrow, "Acculturation and the Archaeological Record in the Carolina Lowcountry," in *The Archaeology of Slavery and Plantation Life*, ed. T. A. Singleton (New York: Academic, 1985), 239–59.

36. I. Noël Hume, "An Indian Ware of the Colonial Period," *Quarterly Bulletin of the Archaeological Society of Virginia* 17 (1962): 1.

37. S. G. Baker, "Colono-Indian Pottery from Cambridge, South Carolina, with Comments on the Historic Catawba Pottery Trade," *Notebook* [of the South Carolina Institute of Archaeology and Anthropology] 4, no. 1 (1972): 3–30.

38. L. G. Ferguson, "Looking for the 'Afro' in Colono-Indian Pottery," *Conference on Historic Site Archaeology Papers* 12 (1978): 68–86.

39. B. Heath, "Afro-Caribbean Pottery from St. Eustatius, Netherlands Antilles" (paper presented at the Annual Meeting of the Society for Historical Archaeology, Baltimore, 1989); W. B. Lees and K. M. Kimery-Lees, "The Function of Colono-Indian Ceramics: Insights from Limerick Plantation, South Carolina," *Historical Archaeology* 13 (1979): 1–13; R. D. Mathewson, "Jamaican Ceramics: An Introduction to the 18th Century Folk Pottery in West African Tradition," *Jamaica Journal* 6 (1972): 54–56; R. Vernon, "17th-Century Apalachee Colono-Ware as a Reflection of Demography, Economics, and Acculturation," *Historical Archaeology* 22, no. 1 (1988): 76.

40. Ferguson, *Uncommon Ground*, 110–16.

41. R. M. Kovel and T. H. Kovel, *Dictionary of Marks: Pottery and Porcelain* (New York: Crown, 1953), 213.

42. Ferguson, *Uncommon Ground*; for the Bakongo sign of the cosmos, see R. F. Thompson, *Flash in the Spirit: African and Afro-American Art and Philosophy* (New York: Random House, 1983), 109.

43. Thompson, *Flash in the Spirit.*

44. Ferguson, *Uncommon Ground,* 115.

45. L. G. Ferguson, "Struggling with Pots in Colonial South Carolina," in *The Archaeology of Inequality,* ed. R. H. McGuire and R. Paynter (Oxford: Basil Blackwell, 1991), 37.

46. See Ferguson, *Uncommon Ground,* 29, fig. 25, for an example.

47. S. South, *Archaeology at Santa Elena: Doorway to the Past* (Columbia: South Carolina Institute of Archaeology and Anthropology, 1991).

48. L. McKee, *Summary Report on the 1991 Field Quarter Excavation* (Nashville: Hermitage, 1992), 20.

49. South, *Archaeology at Santa Elena,* 72.

50. S. Smith, ed., *An Archaeological and Historical Assessment of the First Hermitage* (Nashville: Hermitage, 1976), 210.

51. T. Ewbanks, *Life in Brazil* (New York: Harper and Brothers, 1856), 245.

52. J. F. Smith, *Slavery and Plantation Growth in Antebellum Florida, 1821–1861* (Gainesville: University of Florida Press, 1973), 199.

53. McKee, *Summary Report,* 21.

54. W. H. Adams, ed., *Historical Archaeology of Plantations at Kings Bay, Camden County, Georgia* (Gainesville: University of Florida, Department of Anthropology, 1987), 204.

55. Singleton, "The Archaeology of Slave Life," 157.

56. R. Ascher and C. H. Fairbanks, "Excavation of a Slave Cabin: Georgia, U.S.A.," *Historical Archaeology* 5 (1971): 8.

57. Adams, *Historical Archaeology of Plantations at Kings Bay,* 204.

58. G. D. Rawick, *The American Slave: A Composite Autobiography,* Supplement Series 1, vol. 12, *Oklahoma Narratives* (Westport, Conn.: Greenwood, 1977), 200.

59. D. Patten, "Mankala and Minkisi: Possible Evidence of African American Folk Beliefs and Practices," *African American Archaeology* 6 (1992): 6.

60. R. B. Cooley, *Homes of the Freed* (New York: New Republic, 1926), 121.

61. G. D. Rawick, *The American Slave: A Composite Autobiography,* Supplement Series 1, vol. 10, *Mississippi Narratives,* part 5 (Westport, Conn.: Greenwood, 1977), 1957; R. Killion and C. Waller, eds., *Slavery Time When I Was Chillun Down on Marster's Plantation: Interviews with Georgia Slaves* (Savannah: Beehive, 1973), 56.

62. C. L. Perdue Jr., T. E. Barden, and R. K. Phillips, eds., *Weevils in the Wheat: Interviews with Virginia Ex-Slaves* (Charlottesville: University Press of Virginia, 1976), 119, 141.

63. Cade, "Out of the Mouths of Ex-Slaves," 331.

64. G. D. Rawick, *From Sundown to Sunup: The Making of the Black Community* (Westport, Conn.: Greenwood, 1972), 39–45.

65. For Millwood Plantation, see C. E. Orser Jr., A. M. Nekola, and J. L. Roark, *Exploring the Rustic Life: Multidisciplinary Research at Millwood Plantation, a Large Piedmont Plantation in Abbeville County, South Carolina, and Elbert County, Georgia* (Atlanta: National Park Service, 1987), 453; for Kings Bay Plantation, see Adams, *Historical Archaeology of Plantations at Kings Bay*, 348.

66. R. L. Hall, "Religious Symbolism of the Iron Pot: The Possibility of a Congo-Anglo Origin," *Western Journal of Black Studies* 13 (1989): 128.

67. Georgia Writers' Project, *Drums and Shadows: Survival Studies among the Georgia Coastal Negroes* (Athens: University of Georgia Press, 1940), 20–21.

68. E. Klingelhofer, "Aspects of Early Afro-American Material Culture: Artifacts from the Slave Quarters at Garrison Plantation, Maryland," *Historical Archaeology* 21, no. 2 (1987): 112–19.

69. Patten, "Mankala and Minkisi."

70. Klingelhofer, "Aspects of Early Afro-American Material Culture," 116.

71. K. L. Brown and D. C. Cooper, "Structural Continuity in an African-American Slave and Tenant Community," in "Historical Archaeology on Southern Plantations and Farms," ed. C. E. Orser Jr., *Historical Archaeology* 24, no. 4 (1990): 16–17.

72. Ibid.,17.

73. See Orser, "Archaeological Approaches to New World Plantation Slavery."

74. K. M. Stampp, *The Peculiar Institution: Slavery in the Ante-Bellum South* (New York: Vintage, 1956), 30–31.

75. S. C. Andrews and A. L. Young, "Plantations on the Periphery of the Old South: Modeling a New Approach," in *Plantations on the Periphery: The Archaeology of Small Slave Holding Sites*, ed. C. G. Faulkner (Knoxville: University of Tennessee Press, 1992).

76. G. D. Rawick, *The American Slave: A Composite Autobiography*, Supplement Series 1, vol. 6, *Mississippi Narratives*, part 1 (Westport, Conn.: Greenwood, 1977), 219.

PRIME MINISTER

WILLIAM MARTIN

Megachurches are as conveniently associated with contemporary southern religion in the minds of some as their rural single-room predecessors were for others. With roots in the move from downtown to the suburbs, the development of "health and wealth" theology, praise music worship, and technologically savvy presentations, these religious institutions are salient features on the southern religious landscape. If a megachurch is a Protestant church with two thousand members, then Joel Osteen's Lakewood Church in Houston, Texas, with its thirty thousand members, qualifies as a gigachurch. In his portrait of Osteen, William Martin plumbs the ministry of this "pastorpreneur" and his appeal in America's popular culture. Martin predicts that the youthful, charismatic, and well-organized Osteen, seen by some as a successor to Billy Graham, will continue to be an important influence on the southern and national religious scene.

For most preachers, Monday is a day of rest. For Joel Osteen, the forty-two-year-old pastor of Houston's mammoth Lakewood Church and the face of the world's most popular religious television program, Mondays have become devoted to meeting his public. On this particular Monday in mid-December 2004, his first book, *Your Best Life Now: 7 Steps to Living at Your Full Potential*, had just hit the top spot on the *New York Times*'s "Advice, How-To and Miscellaneous" best-seller list. To show its appreciation, the book's publisher, Warner Faith, had provided Joel with a private jet and liveried town cars to ease the burden of a book-signing trip that included events in Arkansas and Tennessee on the same day.

At the first stop, a Wal-Mart Supercenter in Little Rock, a few hundred adoring admirers were already lined up as Joel and his wife, Victoria, made their way to the store's book section. Some fans applauded them ecstatically or squealed with delight; others handed them flowers or reached out to touch them, tears of joy streaming down their faces. One woman said to her husband, a tinge of disappointment in her voice, "I thought he was taller. He's no bigger than you are." In fact, Joel is not a particularly imposing figure. A trim five nine, he looks in good shape and stays that way by running, lifting weights, and playing basketball at the YMCA. On television or at any sizable gathering, he wears a conservative dark suit and an attractive but not flashy tie, with thick black hair moussed and curling down his neck past his collar line his only nod to youthful fashion. He is not classically handsome, but his face is instantly appealing, because of both the lively energy in his intense blue eyes and a smile that never seems forced and is seldom missing; he is often referred to as the Smiling Preacher.

As Joel sat down, Lakewood executive director Duncan Dodds announced that the pastor would not have time to listen to testimonies or to personalize his inscriptions. But these restrictions detracted little from the excitement. A large woman laughed and jumped up and down while taking pictures of friends having their books signed. Another woman clutched her autographed book to her breast and said through rapturous tears, "I'm signed. I'm blessed. It's all good!" Many were content simply to let Joel know that they were his greatest admirers, but some used their precious seconds to attempt a more personal connection: "I been keeping up with you since you first started." "You saved my husband's life." "Shake my baby's hand. He needs the anointing." "This is Bailey Ann. She claps when she watches you." One man handed his cell phone to Joel and asked him to say "Hi, Jamie" to his wife. ("She started a new job today and couldn't come.") Joel happily obliged. A young minister who identified himself as Chopper handed the pastor a DVD of his sermons, noting that he often used Joel's. (Among preachers, plagiarism has long been considered more homage than offense.)

A few aisles down, past an area where a young woman from Warner Faith stayed busy opening box after box of copies of Joel's book, Victoria held court with a smaller but no less enthusiastic crowd. A tall blond woman blessed with a beauty queen's features and smile, she wears clothes well. On this day, the vaguely dominatrix look of her high-heeled black boots, black mock turtleneck sweater, and long black leather coat with silver buttons down the front was erased by the warm friendliness she showered on her adorers: "Hi, sweetheart. How are you, darling?" "It's so good to meet you. You look so pretty." "You watch every week? Oh, that's wonderful!" "Bless your heart." "We love you, too."

After two hours, during which Joel signed nearly twelve hundred books, the Osteens hustled back to the airport and headed to Nashville, where a reception was awaiting them at Warner Faith's suburban Brentwood headquarters. The staff there was duly solicitous, giving Joel a plaque for having reached number one on the best-seller list. Though the young house, a Time-Warner subsidiary, publishes the work of several popular religious authors, Joel is clearly its prize of the moment. I was told that a woman who had represented Doubleday in the bidding for Joel's book had commented to her successful competitor, "You have just guaranteed the success of Warner Faith."

It's an audacious claim, especially when you consider that just six years earlier Joel Osteen was largely unknown—probably even to most members of Lakewood Church, whose beloved founder and guiding spirit was his father, John Osteen. And even among those who did know Joel, it is difficult to find anyone who imagined that the mantle would fall to him when his father died in 1999. At the time, Joel was a college dropout who ran the church's television ministry and hadn't preached a single sermon. Yet, within a few years, he's positioned himself as one of the country's premier *pastorpreneurs*, a term often used to describe the leaders of America's rapidly expanding megachurches. Preaching a consistently upbeat, can-do message that some detractors refer to as "Christianity Lite"—references to biblical passages are few, and he rarely takes a stand on controversial political issues—he's attracted one of the largest and most diverse flocks this side of the Vatican. Under his stewardship, Lakewood has grown from an impressive six thousand congregants to more than thirty thousand. His personal-appearance events are packing arenas in major cities around the country, including Madison Square Garden in New York, where an extra night had to be scheduled to keep up with demand, and the American Airlines Center in Dallas, where scalped tickets fetched as much as $100. His television show, *Joel Osteen*, is now broadcast in more than 150 countries. And in mid-July 2005, Lakewood Church moved into the former home of the Houston Rockets, the sixteen-thousand-seat Compaq Center, where he and his staff expect their congregation to swell before long to fifty thousand. In less than a decade, Joel Osteen has outgrown nearly everything he inherited.

The outstripping of expectations was evident that evening, when, following the reception at Warner Faith, Joel headed for yet another book signing, this time at a Barnes and Noble. The store manager, looking at a line that was already outside the door when the Osteens arrived, said, "We knew it would be big but not this big this fast." Joel and Victoria slowly wound their way through the store, their procession made more impressive by the dazzling lights of a camera crew covering the event for a local TV station. Twelve hours into his whirlwind tour, Joel still maintained his infectious grin as he addressed his fans with his familiar greeting: "We just love you guys." The crowd was a bit more upscale than the mostly working-class people at Wal-Mart, but the palpable excitement and the proffered comments were much the same: "Love your show. It kept me going." "I watch you three times a day." "You are so uplifting. I love to see you smiling." "The Lord's with you, boy."

Joel signed another 750 books, bringing the total for the day to nearly 2,000, all without the slightest sign of fatigue or boredom. The day before, he had preached to thirty thousand people packed into four separate ninety-minute high-octane services and had now gone full tilt on one stage or another since daybreak. Minutes after he got into the air, bound for Houston, Joel pulled his tray out before him, laid his head directly on it, without a pillow, and slept soundly until the airplane made the approach for landing.

The story of how Joel Osteen became the leader of the fastest-growing ministry in America begins with his father. The son of a cotton farmer in the East Texas town of Paris, John Osteen wasn't converted until he was eighteen, not long after he had had the feeling that God was tapping him on the shoulder as he left a Fort Worth nightclub (perhaps for being underage). Shortly afterward, he accepted Christ and began preaching in his hometown. After earning degrees from John Brown University and Northern Baptist Seminary, he was ordained as a Southern Baptist minister. He lived for a brief time in San Diego but soon came back to Texas, where, in

1954, he met and married Dolores "Dodie" Pilgrim, a fitting name for a woman about to set sail into uncharted waters. John served as pastor of Central Baptist Church in Baytown and Hibbard Memorial Baptist in Houston.

Not long after arriving at Hibbard Memorial in 1958, John experienced and began to recommend to others what Pentecostal and charismatic Christians call the "baptism of the Holy Spirit," which typically involves speaking in tongues and openness to other "gifts of the Spirit," such as the ability to heal, perform exorcisms, and experience visions. Rather than face a showdown with his Baptist brethren, who preferred to keep a tighter rein on the Holy Spirit, John withdrew from their fellowship and, in 1959, founded Lakewood Church in an abandoned feed store in a predominantly black neighborhood on Houston's northeast side. It was an unimpressive little place, not obviously different from the many churches one sees in such neighborhoods or along highways in Texas and throughout the South, where a small group of believers and a zealous preacher have erected an outpost of faith in the hope of winning their slice of the world for Christ. From the start, however, Lakewood had a great spirit. Nondenominational and inclusive, it welcomed all colors and conditions to what Pastor John referred to as an "oasis of love in a troubled world."

Though hardly a captivating orator, John was a competent preacher with a lively revivalist style. He spoke on conventional topics—the atonement, the Resurrection, the Holy Spirit—but the theme with which he became most closely identified may be found in this passage from one of his sermons: "It's God's will for you to live in prosperity instead of poverty. It's God's will for you to pay your bills and not be in debt. It's God's will for you to live in health and not in sickness all the days of your life."

John was one of many Pentecostal pastors proclaiming this controversial worldview, which went under such names as Word of Faith, Name It and Claim It, Positive Confession, or simply Health and Wealth. The essence of the teaching is that when Christians have sufficient faith, they can ask for healing, for prosperity, or for almost any other legitimate good, and God is honor bound to provide it. That message was a winner at Lakewood. Almost immediately, the church began to expand rapidly, first to a simple but more substantial building hardly larger than the feed store, then to a flat, featureless structure that by 1979 had increased to accommodate more than five thousand worshippers, all sitting on folding chairs. In that time, Lakewood had also become a popular venue for some of the top preachers, teachers, and musicians in Pentecostal and charismatic circles, especially those who shared Pastor John's Word of Faith convictions.

By the early eighties, the Osteen family was flourishing as well. John and Dodie had six grown children (the oldest, Justin, was John's by an earlier marriage that had ended in what is referred to by the family as "an unwanted divorce"). They all lived comfortably in what is now Kingwood. Dodie and daughter Lisa were active in the church's ministry; younger daughters April and Tamara were faithful Christians; son Paul was in medical school; and the youngest son, Joel, was a freshman at Oral Roberts University in Oklahoma. By all accounts, Joel was already an upbeat, optimistic encourager; still, he surprised his family in 1982 when he returned home and told them that he wanted to drop out of ORU and help his dad launch a television ministry. John soon agreed, with the understanding that they would never use the program to ask for money.

His son quickly demonstrated a notable talent for TV production and overall marketing. Lakewood's Sunday service, which Joel directed and produced, was soon being aired locally over Houston's CBS affiliate, KHOU-11, and nationally on the Family Channel. It was hard to drive on a Houston freeway without seeing John Osteen's smiling visage shining down from strategically placed billboards. Not everyone knew exactly where Lakewood was, but few Houstonians were unaware that it existed. This point was brought home to me one evening around that time when, riding around with two of my granddaughters, then about six and four years old, a radio commercial began with "We believe in new beginnings," and the girls immediately chimed in with "and we believe in *yoooooouuuuu!!!*" (The *Houston Press* would later assert that the jingle ranked as one of the most successful marketing campaigns in the city's history.)[1] Joel's efforts helped Lakewood take another giant step: building a seventy-eight-hundred-seat facility in 1987, one that resembled a civic auditorium more than a sanctuary. This was followed by a large family life building in 1991 and a combination education-office building in 1993, making it easy to mistake Lakewood for a well-kept community college with a great deal of parking.

It seemed nothing could stop Lakewood's growth as long as its pastor stayed healthy, and John had frequently predicted that he would be preaching into his nineties. But while in his mid-seventies, John developed some serious medical problems, including a heart condition that necessitated a pacemaker and high blood pressure that weakened his kidneys to such a degree that he required dialysis. One week, in mid-January 1999, he felt so depleted that he called Joel to ask him to preach for him on Sunday morning.

There was no clear reason to think his son would be an able preacher: personal charisma does not pass automatically from generation to generation. Yet it was no surprise that John had confidence in Joel. When John went on preaching missions to foreign countries, particularly to India, where Lakewood had sent millions of dollars to support missionaries and establish Bible schools, orphanages, and medical clinics, Joel and Victoria, who had married in 1987, went along to handle the filming of the revivals and to provide companionship and care. As they might have put it, Joel and John knew each other's hearts. But, unlike his mother and several of his siblings, Joel had never delivered a single sermon; in fact, he had steadfastly refused to do so on numerous occasions. And even when his father called that night and said, "Joel, you're my first choice," the son once again refused. Then Joel hung up the phone and sat down to eat dinner, confident that Lisa or his mother or some other staff member could easily fill the pulpit for a week or two. A few minutes later, however, Joel changed his mind—something came over him, he says—and called back to tell his dad that he would do it.

The days before that Sunday were not easy. He was convinced that he had made a serious error and was setting himself up for colossal public failure. Knowing he'd be preaching for the first time, in front of some six thousand people, he longed to retreat to his familiar and comfortable position behind the camera. To boost his confidence, he even wore a pair of his father's shoes when he stepped onto the broad stage. He spoke rapidly but winningly, drawing laughs from a sympathetic audience with self-deprecating comments and amusing stories about his family. No one, apparently, enjoyed the sermon more than John, who was hospitalized but listened to the service over a telephone. Lisa recalled that when she visited her father after the service, he asked her how she thought Joel had done, and she said, "I thought he was great. You know, Daddy, I think one day he may be standing in front of that camera instead of behind it." Later that same week, on January 23, John Osteen died of a heart attack at age seventy-seven. Before the end of the year, Joel officially became Lakewood's new leader.

In front of packed crowds, Pastor Joel is a superb communicator. He pokes fun at himself, makes no effort to moderate a strong Texas twang, and appears to be talking almost extemporaneously. He seems completely unaffected and can be funny without straining to be a comic. His presence and charisma go a long way toward explaining the astounding popularity of the *Joel Osteen* television program, which in most markets is half an hour long and consists almost entirely of his preaching. But crucial to the success of Lakewood is bringing in its Houston constituents, who provide more than 80 percent of the ministry's $50 million in annual contributions. As with all megachurches—usually defined as Protestant churches with more than two thousand members; at thirty thousand, Lakewood is sometimes called a *gigachurch*—new members are attracted with a vibrant worship experience packed with generous helpings of music and prayer. On a mild Sunday morning in early February 2005, I witnessed a good example of Lakewood's version of a familiar format.

Nearly half an hour before the official beginning of the 8:30 service, worship leader Cindy Cruse-Ratcliff led a sixty-four-voice choir through several numbers that provided background music as the thousands of congregants found their way to seats with the aid of an extensive corps of ushers, part of the thousand or so volunteers needed each weekend. When the time came, Joel and Victoria stepped onto the stage, and Joel gave his standard greeting: "We welcome you to Lakewood. You guys are looking good. You look like more than conquerors this morning. . . . Let's take a few minutes to celebrate the good things God has done in our lives." Victoria, her honey-blond hair cascading over a dramatic black-and-white dress, then offered an enthusiastic endorsement of her husband's words and promised, "If you are coming in here and you have a heart for God, he will never fail you."

With this call to worship completed, Cruse-Ratcliff, the choir, and a ten-piece band launched into a slick, rollicking, often throbbing country-rock-gospel outpouring that had the congregation on its feet for more than half an hour, most with arms upraised, some dancing in a manner not learned entirely in church. In one of the aisles, an older black gentleman, nattily dressed in a gray suit, expressed his pleasure at being in the house of the Lord with a restrained but charming quickstep soft-shoe shuffle. Cruse-Ratcliff, meanwhile, wearing high-heeled boots, a white blouse, and a long black jacket that made her short black skirt seem more modest, prowled the stage almost fiercely, now bouncing, now stomping, now leaning forward in an attitude and expression of pained ecstasy. All of this was magnified on five giant screens and dozens of smaller monitors spaced throughout the auditorium and underscored by a saxophone whose smoky sensuality sounded better suited for Saturday night than Sunday morning.

Cruse-Ratcliff and her colleague, African American singer-songwriter Israel Houghton, compose most of the music used at Lakewood. Typical of the thousands of churches that have converted to "praise music," hymnals have given way to projection screens, and harmony and substantive content have surrendered to unison repetition of simple themes with simple words: "Lord, we declare, who can compare, who would even dare, / 'Cause there is no one like you." Or, in a less complex assessment of divine transcendence, "Who is like the Lord? Nobody! / Who is like the Lord? No, no, no, no, no, nobody!" And, in what seems to be Lakewood's all-purpose signature stanza,

> I am a friend of God,
> I am a friend of God,
> I am a friend of God,
> He calls me friend.

It is not deep, and there's no definitive confirmation that the Almighty actually prefers the praise genre to august anthems, but it is clearly a great deal of fun.

Next, Joel led a prayer for healing, prosperity, new beginnings, and a full measure of joy and peace. He then invited people with any special needs to come to the front of the stage to be prayed for, one-on-one, by a large team of "prayer partners" that includes Joel and Lisa and Dodie, herself a cancer survivor who specializes in praying for people with that disease. This is clearly a moving experience for many, including the partners; after he prayed for a family with two small children, Joel began to weep and returned to his seat for a few moments to gain his composure. (Such incidents, if caught on film, are edited out of the telecast.) After that, Victoria invited parents to bring their children to the front for a special prayer and then announced that it was time to take the offering. She reminded the flock of the need to give a tenth of their income to the church and offered assurance that God would bless them abundantly for doing so, but the whole process, with hundreds of gray plastic buckets whizzing along the rows, took less than two minutes, putting a damper on suspicions that the Osteens are in it for the money. (Remaining true to Joel's father's wishes, this portion of the service is never included in the television broadcast.) Dodie then delivered a brief sermon on how Jesus could rescue us from any trouble if we just had faith to call on him, after which it was time for her son's sermon.

At nearly every service, Joel first greets both the television audience ("It's always a joy to come into your homes. We love each and every one of you, and we know that God has good things in store for you") and the live audience ("You guys are looking good") and then begins by reading a joke: "A man came into the church office . . ." "A Christian lady on an airplane was reading her Bible . . ." That morning he began with one about a man trying to discipline a profane parrot. When the laughter subsided, he said, "All right. Hold up your Bibles and say it like you mean it. Ready?" Thousands of Bibles ascended like blackbirds as Joel led the assemblage in its standard affirmation: "This is my Bible. I am what it says I am. I have what it says I have. I can do what it says I can do. Today I'll be taught the word of God. I boldly confess: My mind is alert; my heart is receptive; I will never be the same. I am about to receive the incorruptible, indestructible, ever-living seed of the word of God. I will never be the same—never, never, never. I will never be the same. In Jesus's name. Amen."

Joel's sermon was "The Dangers of Procrastination," and he opened by identifying procrastination as "one of the greatest enemies we will ever face." He then listed the kinds of things even well-meaning people put off: cleaning the kitchen, taking out the garbage, paying the bills, cutting back on spending ("Listen carefully, Victoria"), losing weight and getting in shape, giving up smoking, practicing good preventive medicine ("Ladies, you know how important it is to have that regular checkup"). He admitted that he suffered the same temptations, which come to us from "the Enemy" (formerly known as Satan), but always felt much better when he did what he knew he should do, which was most of the time now. As in many of his sermons, he urged people to pay attention to their conscience, with gestures that indicated that it was located just below the rib cage.

Joel illustrated his points with simple stories of people he had known or read about, and occasionally he cited a scripture whose words seemed to fit, whether or not the author had that application in mind. As if he had an endorsement deal with Nike, he repeatedly recommended that instead of putting off those things that were nagging at our conscience, we should "just do it!" Despite that note of insistence, his conversational tone invited knowing smiles rather than guilty tears, and his entire manner conveyed encouragement rather than accusation. He wound up by assuring us that if we would stop putting things off and do our part right now, learn to bloom where we are planted, quit looking at what is wrong in our lives and look at what is right, quit letting others steal our joy, quit complaining about what we don't have and start thanking God for what we do have, and stop putting off our happiness and start enjoying life, God would pick up any remaining slack and help us discover the champion in ourselves and, repeating two key Lakewood slogans, allow us to be more than conquerors: victors and not victims. "He will pour out his blessings and favor so you can experience the abundant life that he has in store for you. Amen. How many of you receive it today? I know you do. Amen."

The service ended with Joel inviting people to accept the gift of God's salvation and get on the road to victory. Dozens of people streamed down the aisles, accompanied by sustained applause from those who were not already heading for the exits in an effort to avoid the traffic jam.

An hour later I watched the 10:45 service from the television control room. It was virtually identical, right down to the teasing reference to Victoria's penchant for shopping and her surprised reaction—caught both times on the monitors for the congregation to see but not included in the telecast that aired two weeks later.

Not everyone was initially enthusiastic about Joel becoming the pastor at Lakewood. To some observers, the choice appeared to be rooted in a determination to keep control of the church within the Osteen family. How could a shy young man with hardly any experience as a preacher be up to the task of shepherding one of the largest flocks in America? Among those said to be disappointed was Gary Simons, who is married to April Osteen and was already prominent in the church as a youth pastor and praise-and-worship leader. Simons subsequently left to establish the High Point Church in Arlington, which is modeled along Lakewood lines. Another plausible choice was Jim Graff, who is married to the third Osteen daughter, Tamara, and who was the pastor of a church in Victoria. Joel, however, believes he was more ready than people gave him credit for. "I grew up [in my father's] church," he said, "and I worked with him for seventeen years. That was an education. I kid about being the least likely to take the church, but in one sense, this is all I have ever known. I know how a church works. I just hadn't spoken."

Any residual skepticism about Joel was shattered when attendance at the Sunday morning service began immediately increasing. In fact, Lakewood soon ran out of room, so Joel enlarged the field of his dreams, convinced that "if we hold another service, they will come." When they added a second service in January 2000, attendance doubled. Nine months later, a Saturday night service drew five thousand more. Not long afterward, a 1:00 service on Sunday filled the building once again, and a Spanish-language Sunday afternoon service, led by Latin Grammy Award–winning recording artist and preacher Marcos Witt, drew an additional three thousand worshipers, bringing the average weekly total to thirty thousand.

Joel's youth and energy certainly played a part in his sudden popularity, but another key to his success was his early recognition that he needed competent help. Within a month of becoming pastor he hired Duncan Dodds, who had overseen media for Houston's giant Second Baptist Church before establishing a successful marketing and advertising business, to come to Lakewood to help implement his ambitious vision for the church's television outreach. As executive director, Dodds coordinates media buying and handles the contracts with TV networks and individual stations. Media relations is handled by Don Iloff, Victoria's brother, who performs his duties on a volunteer basis, though he is connected to the church in his capacity as president and general manager of Lakewood-controlled KTBU-TV55. Joining Joel and Dodds on the executive team is Lisa's husband, Kevin Comes, who is in charge of administration, including accounting and other business, and who headed up the transformation of the Compaq Center into a place of worship.

Joel acts as CEO, with responsibility for all major decisions and the overall vision for the church. His main role, however, is to preach. He spends all day Wednesday and Thursday preparing that week's sermon, then two half days practicing and polishing until he has it down cold. "It takes a lot more work," he acknowledged, "than just getting up there with an outline and preaching to people who know your heart, but this is a responsibility, so I'm very careful. It takes the majority of my time. It's basically what I do."

How, I wondered, can Joel spend three days preparing a sermon, another day delivering it four times and, in the months following the publication of his book and the anticipation of the move to new quarters, another full day giving interviews and still have time to fulfill the duties of a pastor of a thirty-thousand-member church? The answer is that he leaves those duties to others. He performs no weddings or funerals, makes no hospital visits, does no pastoral counseling, and turns down outside speaking engagements. Shortly after his father's death, his older brother Paul left a thriving surgical practice in Little Rock and came back home to help Joel, mother Dodie, and sister Lisa run Lakewood's day-to-day operations. Paul and a staff of professionals and volunteers that numbers almost two hundred handle weddings and funerals ("exponentially bigger than you can imagine," said Paul), counseling services, dozens of specialized outreach ministries, discipleship training for new members, a dozen or so "fellowship ministries" (for singles, senior adults, and families who homeschool their children), and hundreds of small groups that meet biweekly all over the sixty-mile area from which Lakewood draws its members. He also oversees an extensive Sunday school program, which is expected to involve ten thousand youngsters now that they've moved into the Compaq Center. Paul and Lisa also share the preaching duties at Wednesday night services.

Although the Osteens seemed slightly amused when I characterized Lakewood as a family-owned business, they did not protest. "Yes, the family is in charge," Lisa agreed. "The board is all family members. Joel decides what he feels like the Lord wants him to do, but we work with attorneys. We call other ministries. We get as much counsel as we can. We have a great accountability to the Lord and to the people and we feel that. We hold ourselves to a high standard." None of them saw this arrangement as a cause for concern. "The beauty of our organization," Paul observed, "is that we don't have to pass things by a thousand boards or a bunch of people with different opinions. If we want to add an extra service next week, we can do it. There's a real beauty about the way we work together. We know our parts. It sounds a lot like the body of Christ."

Inevitably, some wonder about the wisdom of having a small family group exercise almost total control, with little outside accountability, over more than $60 million in annual revenue, a figure almost certain to grow in future years. When I spoke with Joel about the financial scandals that have bedeviled some independent ministries, he revealed that the church did not currently make its budget available to the congregation but that the executive team had been discussing the need to do so. I noted that Billy Graham and other ministries associated with the Evangelical Council for Financial Accountability (ECFA) had been able to deflect much criticism—and, in the process, erect a barrier against temptation—by providing an audited financial statement to supporters. As a family ministry, Lakewood cannot belong to the ECFA, nor is it required to submit 990 forms to the IRS listing income and major expenses, including the salaries of its five highest-paid officials. Joel recognized, however, that nothing was stopping the church from doing this on a voluntary basis. Later that week, I learned that on the day following our conversation, he had spoken to Iloff about the need to provide a more complete picture of the church's finances, "like Billy Graham does." A few days later, I received audited financial statements for the two previous fiscal years.

"We don't set our own salaries," Lisa pointed out. "An outside group approves compensation." (In addition to contributing a substantial portion of his earnings from the book to the church, Joel has stopped taking his $200,000 salary.) And Dodie stressed that she had always told the children, "Daddy's name was always squeaky clean, and we intend to keep it that way." She seemed to feel this had been sufficient, observing, "They are so respectful of their father and of me. You don't hear much criticism about Lakewood Church or about the Osteen family."

Indeed, rather than make an attempt to conceal the family-run nature of Lakewood, the Osteens obviously regard their image as a faithful unit as one of their greatest strengths. From Lakewood's beginning, Dodie has played a prominent role in the worship services. The tiny (size 2 petite), neatly dressed Osteen matriarch still speaks at every service, frequently noting her pleasure in her brood, and it seems that no service passes without some mention of "Daddy." Even when they are not on the program, Lisa and Paul are also present, and the giant screens remind everyone that they will be speaking at the Wednesday night service. Pictures and promos for the church feature Joel and Victoria in affectionate poses, and they have recently brought their two children into a more prominent role. At the Dallas event at the American Airlines Center, six-year-old Alexandra sang "Come Just as You Are" during the invitation. And at a 2005 Easter service, at Minute Maid Park, eleven-year-old Jonathan led the Bible affirmation, then drew warm laughter from the crowd of nearly forty thousand by repeating his father's familiar line, "You sound great, as usual." Just as Joel's sermons often imply that following his own advice has helped him achieve a near-ideal life, so the extensive involvement of his immediate and extended family offers church members another model for their lives.

To watch Joel and the Lakewood team at work and to visit with them offstage is to become aware of dual narratives for explaining the ministry's meteoric success. At one level is a clear sense that the entire venture has been ordained by God and continues to operate under the direct micromanagement of the Holy Spirit. In trying to account for his popularity, Joel mentioned several possible factors—the head start he got by inheriting an already successful ministry, his youth, his consistently positive message—but finally confessed, "I don't know what it is. Maybe it's just God's favor and blessing."

Lisa told me about the first Lakewood service after their father's funeral. "I always sat behind my dad to assist him. So when Joel was sitting there and getting ready to preach—he was so nervous—I was sitting behind him, and I leaned up to say something to him, and in that split second the Lord spoke to me down in my spirit, and he said, 'Lisa, I am transitioning you to work with your brother, and just as you served your dad, I want you to serve your brother as pastor of this church.' I knew that was the Lord who had said that to me, and I was just so happy after that."

Dodie, whose oft-repeated story of surviving metastatic liver cancer serves as a premier warrant for belief in miraculous healing, also finds it easy to accept her son's success as part of a divine plan. "Not long after John died, Joel said, 'Mama, I need to talk to you. I think God is calling me to be pastor of this church.' I said, 'What?!' I thought he was the last one. He didn't want to get up there and pastor, but he felt like it was God's will."

A second set of explanations for Lakewood's success, not perceived as conflicting with the first in any way, is heavy reliance on technology and a great deal of marketing savvy. Although the weekly television show can be seen in almost every home in America, Joel and his associates work constantly to raise the odds that it actually *will* be seen. In addition to repeated showings on religious channels TBN and Daystar, the program currently airs on national network affiliate stations in thirty-five major cities, including the top thirty markets, and on five secular cable channels (ABC Family, USA, Discovery, PAX, and BET). Iloff noted that some people disapprove of having the program appear on USA and BET—"Don't you see the stuff they put on those networks?"—but said, "That's where we need to be: reaching the unreached, telling the untold." Dodds added, "We love Christian television. We are on TBN and Daystar. But we are committed to reaching those who don't believe yet. You have got to go with what they are watching. They are not typically tuning into Christian stations. We try to place our program within the habits and patterns of those people. I am convinced that if they will give Joel five minutes, they will be hooked."

To increase the chances that this will happen, Joel and his media team analyze the Nielsen ratings at the end of each quarter to see how their show is doing and how it might improve. Are they on the strongest station in a market at a time with the highest number of viewers watching television? Is a better time slot available? What is the cost per rating point? "We want to know all the same things you would if you were placing your slicer-dicer on the air," Iloff said. In slightly less commercial terms, Dodds agreed: "We want to make sure we are spending God's money wisely."

The programs themselves are slickly produced, as good or better than any daytime talk show. And even though most people watching never see the joyful-music-and-tear-filled-prayer segments of the service, they still get a feel for the church as cameramen roaming the aisles capture the earnest look, the delighted laugh, the agreeing nod, and above all, the remarkable diversity of the crowd. On an average Sunday, the congregation appears to be about evenly divided among whites, blacks, and Hispanics, with a growing number of Asians, who seem to have a better than average chance of being shown on television. In addition, all the major services are now webcast live. Lakewood has an extensive Web site that provides a wealth of background information about the church, including transcripts of classic John Osteen sermons and some of Joel's first sermons. The site also offers tapes, CDs, videos, and books for sale—bookstore sales account for more than $3 million of the church's annual income—and makes it possible for donors to contribute online.

As an astute observer of both popular culture and other television ministries, Joel realized that people who watched his program would likely have a strong interest in seeing him and other regulars on the program in person. This gave rise to the phenomenally successful tour events called "An Evening with Joel Osteen." At these programs, which Dodds likes to compare to concerts, complete with searchlights scanning the crowd and floor-to-ceiling light columns that move through bright yellow, fuchsia, and purple hues during warm-up segments and musical numbers, the audience not only gets to experience all the ingredients of a typical Lakewood service, including a full choir, but also hears much more explicit references to such pillars of Christian belief as the atoning death and Resurrection of Jesus, topics scarcely mentioned on the half-hour program.

Regular viewers have no difficulty finding out when the tour will visit their city. When Joel occasionally quotes a Bible verse during a sermon, a banner at the bottom of the television screen identifies it and displays the crucial part of the text. Much more frequently, that space advertises future tour stops or reminds people that *Your Best Life Now* and its companion text, *Your Best Life Now Journal*, are now on sale.

With all the growth that occurred as a result of its marketing efforts, the only plausible way for Lakewood to expand even further was to find more space. When Joel learned in 2001 that the Houston City Council was going to be leasing out the Compaq Center, he and his associates put together a proposal and hired Dave Walden, who had served former mayor Bob Lanier as a top aide, to lobby the council on their behalf. Their only competitor was Crescent Real Estate Equities, which owned nearby Greenway Plaza and wanted to tear the building down to make way for additions to that complex. A lively struggle ensued. Crescent argued that the space should be put to more varied use and that giving a religious organization exclusive access to a city-owned facility violated the separation of church and state. The Lakewood forces pointed out that the city had rented the Compaq Center and other facilities to religious organizations over the years and promised to spend tens of millions of dollars on improvements. They also bombarded council members with a phenomenal number of calls, letters, and e-mails asking for their support. Ultimately, Lakewood prevailed, agreeing to pay $12.1 million for thirty years, with a $22.6 million option for a second thirty years. Even though the new facility will hold more than twice as many people as the old one, the current plan is to drop only the 1:00 Sunday service, with the option to resume it if the remaining three English-language services grow too crowded.

In the meantime, Lakewood's staff is considering other ways of growing beyond Houston by establishing satellite churches that would have a local pastoral and teaching staff, with the worship and preaching service beamed in directly from Houston. "I can't speak for the pastor," said Dodds, "but I can see us having Lakewood Philadelphia, Lakewood Atlanta, Lakewood Detroit, and having Joel preach the message every week. I think we could have churches of four thousand to six thousand [in other cities]. I see the potential there from the marketing side. I see the opportunity to expand this ministry and almost franchise it in that way. I think we will get there."

As different as they and their eras may have been, the great popular preachers with an enduring legacy in American religious history—Charles Finney in the 1830s, D. L. Moody in the 1870s, Billy Sunday in the World War I era, Billy Graham in our lifetime—have shared three characteristics: a good organization, a distinctive and appealing personality, and an easily grasped message aimed at a mass audience. Joel's organization has clearly met the competence test, and even his detractors concede that he is an enormously charismatic young man with no apparent dark side or hidden agenda. Still, detractors aplenty exist, and the criticisms they raise pertain directly to Joel's message, which is variously characterized as a barely baptized version of the secular doctrine of Positive Thinking or a damnable heresy that legitimizes materialism and endangers the souls of those who embrace it.

Some of the most vitriolic criticism comes from biblical literalists, who use their Web sites to attack him as "a devil in disguise . . . a flashy smiley joking human being" who is "a stench unto God for twisting God's Holy Word" and for preaching "the doctrines of devils and demons."[2] Specifically, they charge him with being a Word of Faith preacher. Faith healers often espouse this teaching because it provides a convenient explanation for failures; the supplicant lacks the faith to "name it and claim it." (In the process, it also gives healers an inflated rate of apparent success, as people claim cures they have not yet experienced, lest doubt thwart God's willingness to heal them.) Word of Faith advocates also urge people to claim material blessings, including new cars, new houses, and financial windfalls. Some, including a few who have preached at Lakewood, go even further. One night in late 1981 I heard television preacher Kenneth Copeland, host of the *Believer's Voice of Victory* program, tell a Lakewood audience about a farmer whose cotton was withering and dropping to the ground like little brown marbles. When the farmer took his preacher into the field to read some scriptures promising rewards to the righteous, Copeland claimed that they began to hear sounds like popcorn popping, and as they looked about them, they saw the field filling with large, fluffy bolls.

One can understand why some critics place Joel in the Word of Faith camp when he says such things as "You can change your world by simply changing your words" and "When you make declarations of faith, you are charging the atmosphere, and your own words can help to bring it to pass." Joel does not disown such statements nor categorically reject the teachings in question, but he softens them considerably. "I never knew it was such a bad thing to be a Word of Faith preacher," he said, "but I never preach that whatever you say, you can get—'I want five Cadillacs.' 'I'm going to be the president of this company.' I never believed that kind of stuff." When I mentioned what Copeland had said about the magical cotton bolls, he said, "I like Brother Copeland, but I don't believe that. That's just not me. I encourage people to say what God says about you, to say, 'I am strong in the power of the Lord. I can do all things through Christ who strengthens me.'"

Other critics accuse the Osteens of preaching a gospel of prosperity and materialism, a charge with even more evidence to support it. Like his father, Joel often speaks of God's desire that his children do well financially, and prayers at church services frequently invoke God for jobs and promotions and good homes and nice cars. Joel and Victoria live in a large home in tony Tanglewood, as do Lisa and Kevin Comes; Dodie's townhouse is a stone's throw from the senior president Bush's; and Paul lives on a small ranch near Tomball. None of the family members seem inclined to fear that affluence poses much of a danger. During the tour event in Dallas, Lisa made the somewhat surprising statement that "if you look through the Bible from Genesis to Revelation, every person who served him faithfully, God blessed financially." When I asked her about that later, mentioning Jeremiah, who spent time at the bottom of a well and died in captivity, and Stephen, who was martyred, and Paul, who made tents to support his missionary activities, she backed up a bit, noting that she had been thinking mainly about Abraham, Isaac, and Jacob: "The Bible says they had a lot of things. God is just a blessing God. That's my point."

Well aware of the criticism, Joel said,

People will probably laugh, but I don't feel like I am a prosperity preacher. I do believe, though, that God wants us to prosper. I don't see how I could get up there and preach that we need $100 million for the Compaq Center and have a poverty mentality. I just don't think Christians should feel that they have to stay at the lower rung of the ladder. I also point out that prosperity is not just money. It's a healthy relationship with your wife, with your kids; it's a healthy body. We need to get away from the dollar sign on prosperity. In my next book, I'm going to be clearer about that. I believe God wants us to be blessed, but it's only so that we can be a blessing. I think God blessed me by writing this book and giving me a lot of money, but it's not so I can go buy thirteen cars or a bunch of other stuff. After the book started selling a couple hundred thousand copies, I called a friend on staff and asked, "Do I get paid [more] for that?" They gave me some [advance] money. I thought I'd already been paid for it. I didn't know. He said, "Yeah, you get a royalty." I said, "Have you figured that out?!" I had never in a million years thought about doing it for the money, but I thought, "You know what? That's great. I never dreamed that I could be one of the biggest givers in our church, and now I can. I can underwrite a whole wing of this thing." I don't see us changing our lifestyle. It's so I can help more people's lives. We are stewards of God's money.

Joel and his associates are less comfortable with the characterization of his message as Christianity Lite, an appealing but less filling version of the real thing. Dodds contends that such criticisms "come from a lack of experience and full knowledge of what we are doing. I always tell people who say that, 'Just come to church.' There is no way you can sit in our services during a time of worship and not know we are lifting up the name of Jesus. I have heard the criticisms. I just don't think they are valid."

Once again, however, the critics can make an argument. Joel readily acknowledges that he is not an exegetical preacher who begins with a passage of scripture and expounds upon its meaning for his congregation. Even in the early days, when Joel preached such sermons as "The Truth of the Resurrection" and "The Great Commission," it was hardly in a standard fashion; at the 1999 Easter service, after a rather conventional sermon, he told a series of amusing stories about his family, even admitting that they had little to do with the drama of Resurrection. And eventually, those gave way to sermons with Tony Robbins–style titles such as "Developing Your Potential," "Persistence and Determination," "Your Life Follows Your Thoughts," and "Enlarge Your Vision."

"Daddy would often just teach the Bible," Joel said.

I take a little different approach. I may give a whole sermon and give the scripture at the end—"This is what Jesus meant when he said this, that, and the other." I know doctrine is good. We need doctrine, but I think the average person is not looking for doctrine. They are looking to ask, "How do I let go of the past?" "How do I have a better marriage?" "What is wrong with me?" If you want to reach the culture, you need to speak in their terms. When Jesus was here on this earth, he did such practical stuff. He taught using simple examples like the parable of the prodigal son; everybody can relate to that. I tell a lot of stories in my sermons. Most of what I preach is about the simple things.

Jesus indeed told stories, but he also issued some scathing condemnation of sinners, particularly the arrogant, the self-righteous, the corrupt, and those who trust in riches. Joel's sermons are notably free of condemnation. "The Bible says it is the goodness of God that leads us to repentance," he said. "When I talk about sin, I may call it 'making bad choices.' People get so used to being beat over the head. I don't come from that side. I come from the encouraging side. It seems like it resonates with people that God is for them. I feel like I'm doing what God calls me to do. I don't have any agenda to say I'm not going to preach about sin. I write my sermons and pray, and this is what comes out of me."

What about issues of basic social justice, of structures that impede or block personal growth and prosperity, no matter how strongly one believes or how hard one prays? "I don't know that I have a good answer on that," he said. "I feel like the church should be a force. I know that I am all for anything we can do to lift people. On a thirty-minute program, you can't solve the world's problems." As for that knottiest of theological issues, the problem of suffering: "I have a file in my mind called an 'I don't understand it' file. There are some things we are not going to understand, and we must say, like Job, 'Though he slay me, yet will I trust in him.' I think God will give us peace to go through anything. How do you tell somebody why their kid got killed in a car wreck? You just say, 'I can't understand it. I can't explain it to you.' You can't dwell on that. You just know that God is in control. It's a tough issue."

Perhaps in an effort to maintain his uplifting message, Joel has avoided speaking out on today's red state–blue state issues, such as abortion and homosexuality. "I feel there are other issues I am called to more than those," he explained. "I don't know the answers, even on abortion. Somebody asked me what I think of stem cell research. I had to say I don't know. I've heard people talk about it both ways. I don't think a homosexual lifestyle is God's best way, but I'm not going to tell [homosexuals] they can't come to our church. I'm going to be wide open for them." In the same spirit, he has resisted recruitment into the ranks of the religious Right. Iloff, who worked for a time in the White House during the senior Bush administration, admitted that he was tempted at one time to try to get Joel to be more political. "I guess God dealt with me on that, because

I realized, as Joel did from the very beginning, that [politics] could be very polarizing. It could shut the door on his ability to plant the seed of God's message in people's hearts." Politicians are often eager to court his constituency, yet as a general rule, an officeholder who attends Joel's service will be recognized but not asked to speak. And candidates in a current race will rarely be recognized at all.

What does come out of Joel, no matter what topic he is discussing, is unfailingly upbeat and encouraging. Repeatedly, at book signings, at the Dallas appearance, and at the church itself, his followers told me that this was part of the appeal: "You can actually take what he teaches you into real life. It's real useful." "He gives you such a positive outlook on life. When you listen to him, he gives you renewed hope." "He addresses the needs in my life." "He doesn't make you feel dirty, you know? It's just so uplifting." Nonetheless, Joel and his family are sensitive to the charge of theological thinness, so they take comfort in the classic defense used by unconventional but successful evangelists for centuries: it gets results. Virtually every key person I interviewed noted, "We had eighteen thousand people walk the aisles [at Lakewood] last year" to mark a new or renewed relationship with Jesus and that thousands of others from across the country and around the world write or call each week to tell of "giving their lives to the Lord."

After Joel's invitation to new visitors at the end of the Sunday service I attended in February 2005, I followed dozens of people to a "salvation room" behind the stage. There Joel congratulated them, urged them to get into a good Bible church if they didn't intend to keep coming to Lakewood—"This is not the only good church"—and gave each of them a small folder entitled "Your Next Step to a New Beginning," which set forth a bare outline of Christian beliefs, encouraged them to be baptized, and invited them to attend an eight-week New Beginnings class taught on Sunday evenings by Paul. They also received *30 Thoughts for Victorious Living*, a daily devotional guide written by Joel. It wasn't possible to probe the thoughts of these folks, but expressions on the faces of most indicated that they felt something significant had just happened.

The Osteens define salvation as both a transformation in one's earthly life and the promise of eternal life in heaven. They believe in hell, but they don't talk about it much. As Lisa put it: "My dad always said, 'Preach the Bible like it's good news. Don't tell people they're going to hell. Tell them they don't have to go.'" Joel often makes the same point: "God is not mad at you; he is not trying to send you down into darkness. God is on your side. He has already forgiven your sins. All you've got to do is accept the free gift of God's salvation."

Quite appealing, to be sure, but what about Jesus's observation that "the gate is narrow and the way is hard that leads to life, and those who find it are few"? Doesn't the gospel according to Joel sound more like the wide gate and the easy way that leads to destruction? Paul knew the scripture. "I think we've made it clear," he said, "that you have to change your life. Joel is giving a lot of people the opportunity to find the narrow way." Paul contends that, despite the lack of standard theological content, his brother is nonetheless an effective evangelist. "We see the results all the time. I see a guy who is addicted to cocaine, addicted to pornography, on his fourth marriage—it doesn't happen instantly, but in a couple of years, he's married, he's stable, he's got a job, he's got a heart for God. Let me tell you, that's pretty big."

Joel says little about the narrow way in his televised sermons or his book, which elaborates on the themes from those sermons. In the past he has conceded that most of his ministry is not evangelistic and has admitted that the principles he extols will work in anybody's life, whether or not that person is a Christian, but he feels confident that by teaching people how to live as God wants them to live, he is training them for Christian discipleship. And in addition to those he brings into the church, Joel feels his television audience gets the necessary message when he offers a fifteen-second "salvation call" at the end of each telecast, asking viewers to repeat a brief prayer— "Lord Jesus, I repent of my sins. I ask you to come into my heart. I make you my Lord and Savior"—and assuring them that if they say those words, they will be born again. "It's not long and it's not complicated," he acknowledged. "It would be great to have three minutes to really explain it, but I do think I put it out there."

Reluctance to shut the gate or shrink the dimensions of the path does not sit well with everyone in Joel's audience. When he appeared on *Larry King Live* in late June 2005, King asked him about the fate of Jews and Muslims, who "don't accept Christ at all." Joel replied, "I'm very careful about saying who would and wouldn't go to heaven. I don't know. . . . I just think that only God will judge a person's heart. I spent a lot of time in India with my father. I don't know all about their religion. But I know they love God. . . . I've seen their sincerity. So I don't know." That humane, large-spirited response—quite similar to comments Billy Graham has made on occasion—apparently brought a flood of critical calls, letters, and e-mails to the Lakewood office, prompting Joel to issue an abject apology on his Web site, asserting that he believes "Jesus Christ is the *only way* to heaven" and that he regretted that he had not "clearly [communicated] the convictions that I hold so precious." In light of his consistent spirit of "Judge not, that ye be not judged," Joel's repudiation of his apparent instinct in the face of opposition reminded me of another scripture: "The spirit is willing but the flesh is weak."

In a video shown at the tour events, a man says he believes Joel will replace Billy Graham. Clearly, that does not strike Joel's siblings as fanciful. "Joel's impact is huge," Paul pointed out. "He has a humility about him, a power and presence, an ability to use television, and hundreds of pastors are saying, 'This is changing our lives.' It would not surprise me for Joel to be a dominant force in Christianity for quite a few years." Lisa's assessment was even more positive: "The reason they [compare Joel to Graham] is because the anointing is on him to bring in thousands, and that's what we saw with Billy Graham, and still see today. That is only the hand of God on a person. You don't choose that. God chooses. I sort of agree with them."

Billy Graham, of course, is not an office in the Christian Church that must be filled. Because of the enormous growth and diversification within evangelical Christianity over the past half century, much of it a result of Graham's vision and thoughtful leadership, it is unlikely that any single figure will ever dominate it again to the extent that Graham has. Yet Joel Osteen is on a remarkable arc, and it's more than fair to speculate that he is nowhere near his peak. That ambitious outlook seems to be embedded in the Osteen genes. Dodie once told me that her husband announced years ago, "Someday, we'll be meeting in the Compaq Center." Lisa remembered that he had the Astrodome in his sights. For his part, as Joel has said, "I am convinced that in twenty years we'll look up and realize that the Compaq Center isn't big enough to hold all the people.

Hopefully, someone will want to build another stadium by then and Reliant Stadium will be available."

NOTES

Unless otherwise noted, all quotations are from interviews by the author with Joel Osteen, members of his family and church staff, and attendees at church services, book signings, and special events, or were overheard by the author at such events. All interviews and observations were conducted between December 13, 2004, the date of the book trips to Little Rock and Nashville, and mid-April 2005. Quotations from the late John Osteen are from documents viewed during the writing of this essay on the Lakewood Church Web site.

1. *Houston Press*, September 26, 2002.

2. The quotes were from "Chrysti," February 10, 2005, found on http://www.challies.com (accessed June 15, 2005).

Contextualizing the Apocalyptic Visions of McKendree Robbins Long

William D. Moore and Walter H. Conser Jr.

The expression of religious belief and experience through visual representation can take many forms and has been evaluated in divergent ways. In this essay, William Moore and Walter Conser review the construct of "outsider art" and explore its relevance as a category for understanding the artistic career of McKendree Robbins Long. In contextualizing Long's art, they suggest that theological and political disputes at the national level help to situate his career, while conflicts over the meaning of his southern identity subvert his legacy.

The Reverend McKendree Robbins Long (1888–1976), a native of Statesville, North Carolina, who spent much of his adult life as an itinerant preacher, produced a large and compelling oeuvre of religious paintings during the 1940s, 1950s, and 1960s.[1] These works of art have received significant national attention, largely because collectors and curators have classed them with "outsider art." Created in the American South and addressing religious themes, Long's paintings have been compared to those by celebrated figures such as Howard Finster (1915–2001) and Minnie Evans (1892–1987). Finster and Evans, however, were artists without formal academic training who generated art that promoted idiosyncratic theology. In contrast, Long had years of formal education as a painter and situated his canvases squarely within theological and artistic traditions. By placing Rev. Long's images within their historical and artistic context, this essay will argue that the artist was not an eccentric and colorful provincial outsider but instead provides a touchstone for comprehending how cultural critics have treated southern evangelical Protestantism.

Long died largely unappreciated as an artist; his paintings failed to marshal national attention or critical acclaim during his life. A single retrospective held at the Arts and Science Museum in his hometown of Statesville comprised the pinnacle of Rev. Long's artistic recognition before his death.[2] Tommie Long, the artist's son, suggested that his father's canvases be burned after his passing, indicating that even those closest to him lacked appreciation for the artist's vision.[3]

GROWING APPRECIATION OF LONG'S OEUVRE

In the last two decades, however, collectors, curators, and scholars have recognized and celebrated Long's work. Organized by curator David Steel for the North Carolina Museum of Art in Raleigh, a seminal exhibition entitled Signs and Wonders: Outsider Art inside North Carolina included two of his paintings, *Apocalyptic Scene with Philosophers and Historical Figures* (fig. 1), painted around 1963, and *God on His Throne Holding the Book of Seals*, from 1965 (fig. 2).[4] The exhibition's catalog featured these two images, the latter placed prominently opposite the museum director's foreword, thus serving as the frontispiece to the entire volume. A biography of the artist and a self-portrait that Long executed in an academic style early in his career appeared in this publication.[5] Although Long's likeness was painted in a masterful figural style, the photograph shows it in a dilapidated condition with significant paint loss. Lines of chipped pigment indicate that the work previously had been rolled, folded, and stored, lending the image an eerie air of decayed southern grandeur. These lines of missing paint also served to distance the artist from the public, since only portions of the subject's countenance remained to be deciphered.

Subsequently, Long's works were included in Inside Visions, an exhibition mounted in 1992 by the Asheville Museum of Art in Asheville, North Carolina, and in The End Is Near! Visions of Apocalypse, Millennium, and Utopia, organized in 1998 by the American Visionary Art Museum in Baltimore, Maryland.[6] The catalog for

Fig. 1. McKendree Robbins Long, *Apocalyptic Scene with Philosophers and Historical Figures*, c. 1963. Oil on board, 47⅞ x 72¼ inches. Courtesy of the North Carolina Museum of Art, Raleigh. Purchased with funds from the William R. and Frances M. Roberson Endowment for North Carolina Art.

Fig. 2. McKendree Robbins Long, *God on His Throne Holding the Book of Seals*, 1965. Oil on canvas, 52 x 40 inches. Courtesy of Bob Gibson.

the latter exhibition, edited by Roger Manley and published by Los Angeles's Dilettante Press, reproduced eight of Long's most lurid apocalyptic paintings in addition to featuring the compelling damaged self-portrait.[7] In 2001 Tom Patterson, a prolific author in the field of outsider art who resides in Winston-Salem, North Carolina, included Long's *Vision from the Book of Revelation* in his collection *Contemporary Folk Art: Treasures from the Smithsonian American Art Museum*, published by the Smithsonian American Art Museum in association with New York's Watson-Guptill Publications.[8] During these years of Long's rediscovery, institutions, including the Smithsonian American Art Museum, the North Carolina Museum of Art, the Ogden Museum of Southern Art in New Orleans, the Asheville Museum of Art, and the New York State Historical Association in Cooperstown, New York, acquired his works.[9]

Long's posthumous meteoric rise from obscurity culminated in a major retrospective exhibition organized in 2002 by David Steel and Brad Thomas for the North Carolina Museum of Art in conjunction with the Van Every/Smith Galleries at Davidson College of Davidson, North Carolina. Touring for eighteen months at five venues across the state, this exhibition was accompanied by a lavishly produced full-color catalog with contributions by William Ferris and Charles Reagan Wilson, two of the most eminent scholars of the American South.[10] To mark the occasion of the exhibition, *Southern Cultures*, sponsored by the Center for the Study of the American South at the University of North Carolina at Chapel Hill, featured essays by Lee Smith and Hall Crowther, prominent writers and commentators on southern life.[11] *American Art Review* published an illustrated article by curator David Steel, while the *New York Times* took note from far Gotham with an account of the exhibition written by their acclaimed correspondent Stephen Kinzer.[12]

A market for Long's paintings was generated as a result of the attention paid to his work by curators, scholars, editors, and the general public. The Caspari Gallery in New Orleans showed Long's works in 1989.[13] In 2004 the Luise Ross Gallery in New York City mounted the first single-artist exhibition of Long's work outside of the American South.[14] The *New York Times* published a review of the show by critic Ken Johnson, who characterized the artist's biblical paintings as "zany."[15] In the important periodical *Art in America*, Long's work was reviewed contiguous to a notice addressing the celebrated American modernist Mark Rothko, whose art was being shown at the PaceWildenstein Gallery, one of the world's most prestigious art venues.[16] Nearly thirty years after his death, Long finally secured a place for his apocalyptic images that situated him in artistic circles he never had approached in life. In his review of the exhibition at the Luise Ross Gallery, Michael Amy characterized Long's palette as "garish," called his brushstrokes "unctuous," and accused him of distorting space within his compositions. Amy, however, was not entirely damning; his summative evaluation of Long's work proclaimed, "His best pictures are those that effectively convey his fervor."[17]

During the run of Rev. Long's show in New York, the Luise Ross Gallery further promoted his talent by contributing two of his paintings to the 2004 Outsider Art Fair. This event, which included a preview that benefited the American Folk Art Museum, was held January 23–25, 2004, in the Puck Building in New York City's SoHo district, a fashionable neighborhood renowned for being au courant. At this event, Long's paintings were shown alongside works by Henry Darger, a Chicago recluse; William Hawkins, an African American truck driver; and Ben Augustus, a deaf artist with Down syndrome who created black-and-white drawings of nude women based upon photographs in *Playboy* magazine.[18] Following the publicity generated by the Luise Ross Gallery, in June of 2005 an unsigned oil painting on card by the artist, with flaking, warping, abrasions, and a hole, sold for $1,700 at Brunk Auctions in Asheville, North Carolina.[19] By the middle of the first decade of the twenty-first century, owners of works by Long were more likely to consign them to auction than to the fire, as his son had suggested.

OUTSIDER ART

Popular appreciation for Rev. Long's work has risen in proportion to an expansion in the number of museum curators, collectors, and dealers interested in art created by artists who have been described as self-taught or who are perceived to be outside the mainstream of society. Interest in this form of material culture has roots in the romantic and class-based concept of "folk art" codified in the United States in the first half of the twentieth century by Holger Cahill, an arts administrator; Edith Halpert, an art dealer and gallery owner;

Charles Sheeler, a painter and photographer; Edward Duff Balken, a curator and collector; Abby Aldrich Rockefeller, a collector and philanthropist; and many others. These individuals promoted vernacular objects, which they perceived to be created by preindustrial artisans, as a form of national art worthy of study.[20] In celebrating the material culture of the nation's past, twentieth-century Americans expressed a modern sense of alienation and anomie.[21] They projected upon the creators of works of "folk art" a sense of authenticity that they believed was lacking in their own cosmopolitan, sophisticated, industrial lives.[22] The defining characteristic of folk art was that the creators of the works were culturally distant, removed in time and economic status from those individuals who appreciated and collected it. The gulf between the artist and the audience allowed advocates to see the items' creators as being untainted by the problems of modern society, such as commercialization, secularism, and rampant individualism. The anthropologist Charles Briggs has suggested that the use of adjectives like *primitive* or *naive* to describe works of art "provided a protective semantic shield between producers and consumers of folk art."[23]

In the final decades of the twentieth century, writers, curators, and collectors of American folk art began emphasizing the aesthetic value of contemporary artifacts as "folk art." Herbert Wade Hemphill, the first curator of New York's Museum of Early American Folk Art (now the American Folk Art Museum), was central to expanding public interest in, and appreciation for, what came to be called "contemporary folk art."[24] In 1970 Hemphill curated a seminal exhibition at the Museum of Early American Folk Art entitled Twentieth-Century American Folk Art and Artists and later published a book of the same name coauthored with Julia Weissman. Hemphill and Weissman's book featured a spectacular range of art, including paintings by Grandma Moses, who lived in upstate New York; carvings of saints by the Lopez family of Cordova, New Mexico; and concrete grottoes built in Dickeyville, Wisconsin, by Father Mathias Wernerus, a Catholic priest. Hemphill and Weissman explained that their book presented work created by what they distinguished as "everyday people out of ordinary life." They explained, "If there is one characteristic that marks folk artists it is that for them the restraints of academic theory are unimportant, and if encountered at all, meaningless."[25] Robert Bishop, a subsequent director of the Museum of Early American Folk Art, followed Hemphill's precedent in 1979 by including contemporary painters with artists from previous centuries in his *Folk Painters of America*.[26]

In the late 1980s and 1990s, art curators and dealers frequently employed the phrase "outsider art" to describe items that Hemphill and Weissman might have included in their definition of "contemporary folk art."[27] In 1972 the art critic Roger Cardinal coined the term *outsider art* as an English equivalent of the French term *art brut*, popularized by the French artist and collector Jean Dubuffet. Dubuffet, starting in the 1940s, found aesthetic value in works created by individuals in mental institutions, as well as by recluses, convicts, and other marginalized groups.[28] Dubuffet, like Hemphill, elevated visual works that were unconstrained, tempered, or contaminated by what he understood as the flawed principles of Western art. Art brut, or outsider art, therefore, was shaped by the modernist rejection of academic artistic canons and the parallel assertion that art could be valued on its own merits as an individual's authentic expression.

While mavens of the early twentieth century had defined folk art by the temporal or economic distance between the creator and the consumer, dealers and promoters late in the century commodified a cultural gulf. In venues like the annual Outsider Art Fair, established in New York City in 1993, collectors purchased artworks specifically because their creators deviated from norms. In 1992 Roger Manley explained, "By now, it [outsider art] has come to mean an untrained, self-taught artist working for purely personal reasons, often but not always in a somewhat isolated area (either in the wilds of nature or in the faceless confines of an urban tenement), usually beginning creative work later in life after some kind of trauma."[29] In short, an outsider artist was anyone who created art but who did not live in the suburbs, have a formal education, or have training in painting or graphic design. Manley did not specify whether drinking white wine, eating Brie, driving imported automobiles, or attending gallery openings disqualified such individuals as outsider artists.

Cultural historian Eugene Metcalf, in his perceptive article "From Domination to Desire: Insiders and Outsider Art" from 1994, has argued that the construct of "outsider art" is a variety of the touristic preoccupation of modern society in which alienated consumers seek to interact with others whom they perceive to be more authentic or natural and thus less overcivilized, repressed, or inauthentic. For Metcalf, the meaning of outsider art is created not by the artists on the edges of society, but by the insiders who symbolically invert the values of their capitalist, industrial society by glorifying the creativity of those they perceive to be at its margins. In this view, the boundary distancing the commentator from the artist is the defining characteristic of the genre. Significantly, the drawing of this boundary creates unequal power relationships in which individuals in the center of society define what characteristics marginalize others.[30]

Given the dynamics of Metcalf's understanding of outsider art, the art establishment, which has perceived itself to be cosmopolitan and urbane, unsurprisingly has viewed the American South as fertile ground for discovering new untrained artists. The widespread American conception of the South as a benighted rural region of ignorance, poverty, isolation, and fervent religious zeal meshed seamlessly with the qualities that dealers, curators, and collectors sought in outsider art.[31] In the 1980s museums mounted exhibitions celebrating southern outsider folk artists in Columbia, South Carolina; Raleigh, North Carolina; Winston-Salem, North Carolina; Atlanta, Georgia; and Kenner, Louisiana; among other locations.[32] Roger Manley, a multitalented cultural entrepreneur with a graduate degree in folklore from the University of North Carolina, was actively involved in many of these installations, which often featured the works of Minnie Evans, Howard Finster, and James Harold Jennings, an artist who created sculptural objects from lumber scraps and house paint in converted school buses outside Winston-Salem before committing suicide in 1999.[33]

Southern artists' embrace of religious imagery further served to distance these individuals from the cognoscenti who collected and canonized their creations. Secularized white-collar sophisticates could view religious belief, particularly evangelical Protestantism, as exotic, as alien, even as quaint. The supposed omnipresence of charismatic Christianity in the South served to define the region as a land apart from mainstream, secular, pluralistic, modern America. In seeing the South as drenched in Protestantism, however, many writers have failed to recognize denominational distinctions and competing faiths within the region.[34] Curators and connoisseurs have presented southern religion as monolithic, but close scrutiny reveals a bewildering complexity of theological distinctions and diverse worship practices, which can inform the production of artists.

Even within communities of religious believers, American culture has assigned a marginalized status to makers of religious images. As the historian Colleen McDannell has shown, American denominations have long privileged the word over the image. Both the biblical story of the Golden Calf and sixteenth-century Protestant reformers urged believers to shun visual representations of religious ideals. Makers and users of religious imagery historically have been shunted to the margins of American belief systems. In twentieth-century America, high-status religious groups embraced the idea of an abstract God that could not and should not be represented visually and materially.[35] Scholars have recognized in the South an extreme version of this Protestant emphasis upon the word, whether spoken or written.[36] For devotees of the Bible, divine revelation is verbal. In this understanding, those who used images and objects to express their spirituality thus fell into a secondary class of "outsiders."

Exhibitions of southern folk art have continued a historically grounded practice of defining the American South as a region apart, as culturally distinct from the rest of the nation. As pursued by cultural institutions, this regional differentiation has served at least two agendas. For individuals outside the region, defining the states of the old Confederacy as divergent gave urban cosmopolitans a population to which they could feel economically, educationally, and culturally superior. In contrast, for southerners, regional distinction was a matter of pride. In their eyes, all of the same distinguishing characteristics elevated the region; the South was a place of tradition, of honor, of family, of creativity, and of moral rectitude.[37]

McKendree Robbins Long's paintings were introduced to the art world and to the marketplace in this intellectual climate. Long hailed from a region, the American South, that had a reputation as a fertile environment for fostering artists untainted by education, training, or wealth. His works visually addressed theological concerns that were of great importance to evangelical Christians but of little concern to urban, educated secularists. With these attributes Long's compositions entered the art market under the classification of "outsider art," thus retroactively defining the artist as an "outsider."

Closer scrutiny of Rev. Long and his paintings indicate that he is a poor candidate for the marginal status that the art world has assigned to him. A well-traveled, educated individual trained in art both in the United States and in Europe, McKendree Robbins Long's expressed religious beliefs were not idiosyncratic; rather, they were well within the mainstreams of southern Protestant theology. Moreover, Long's paintings derive from established visual traditions in Western culture and indicate a sophisticated and encompassing familiarity with both fine art and popular visual culture. The sources for his paintings range from the works of the fifteenth-century German artist Albrecht Dürer to mass-market reproductions of paintings by the popular American religious painter Warner Sallman, and are comparable to religious compositions by the English painter John Martin and the American illustrator Harry Anderson.

LONG'S BIOGRAPHY

Born in Statesville, North Carolina, on July 20, 1888, McKendree Robbins Long was the son of Benjamin Franklin Long and Mary Alice Long, both the well-educated offspring of affluent families.[38] As the son of a prominent family in a genteel southern town, Long was educated at the Webb School at Bell Buckle, Tennessee, and the Horner Military Academy in Oxford, North Carolina, before enrolling in 1906 in Davidson College, a Presbyterian school located twenty miles south of Statesville.[39] Having demonstrated an early aptitude for drawing, in 1907 Long began to study art under Duncan Smith at the University of Virginia.[40] Long's accomplishments with Smith won him a scholarship to New York's Art Students' League. William Merritt Chase and F. Luis Mora were among the prominent instructors teaching at this famous school during Long's enrollment.

Long studied at the Art Students' League, specializing in portraiture, for two years before winning, in February 1911, a $1,200 scholarship for American students to study the fine arts abroad.[41] While sojourning in London, the artist gained acceptance into a school led by Philip de László, a prominent Hungarian portraitist.[42] During his time in Europe, Long visited Paris, Amsterdam, and Madrid and studied art by the Old Masters, including Rembrandt and Velázquez.[43]

Upon returning to the United States, Long reestablished residence in Statesville and undertook a career as a portraitist of prominent North Carolinians. According to an article published in the *Statesville Landmark* in 1914, Long's likeness of Cyrus B. Watson, a distinguished attorney and Democratic politician, was hung in the state Supreme Court building in Raleigh. This same article predicted, "Mr. Long's future as an artist is one that North Carolina will be duly proud of, as he continues to work at home and in the great art centers."[44]

Long married Mary Belle Hill, a resident of Statesville, on June 24, 1914. They had a child in 1915, and another in 1918. With war raging in Europe, in the summer of 1918 Long enlisted in the U.S. Army as a noncombatant. While stationed in France, the artist served as an ambulance driver.

Following the war, the artist returned to North Carolina, where his work was featured in single-artist exhibits sponsored by local women's clubs in Raleigh, Greensboro, and Charlotte.[45] Mrs. W. T. Bost wrote about Long's Raleigh show for the *Greensboro News*, noting, "One of the portraits, in which the women found great pleasure, was that of the artist's sister, Mrs. Ed. M. Land, of Goldsboro, a prominent club woman of the state."[46] Although his sister's role in acquiring these opportunities for public exposure may be assumed, Long's status as a North Carolinian contributed to the success of the endeavors. Newspaper notices of the events consistently commented positively upon the artist's residency and nativity. Ruth Huntington Moore, of the Peace Institute, for example, asserted, "Mr. Long is a North Carolinian, and it seems to me that the people of his state should be very proud of him and should rally around him and 'hold up his hands.'"[47]

While these exhibitions were composed primarily of landscapes and the portraits upon which Long had built his reputation, they also included paintings that foreshadowed the religious works for which he would later become renowned. The exhibition in Raleigh contained an oil sketch entitled *Study for the Temptation*.[48] More notably, the Greensboro show contained a painting inspired by the book of Revelation entitled *Angel with Book*. A reporter for the *Greensboro Daily News* characterized this work as "remarkable."[49]

During the early 1920s, while North Carolina's women's clubs were showcasing his paintings, Long was embarking on a second career. While studying in London, Long had regularly attended the Metropolitan Tabernacle, a Baptist church most famous for being the home pulpit of the Victorian evangelist C. H. Spurgeon. This English congregation rekindled the faith in which the artist had been raised in North Carolina. In 1912 Long was baptized in London to reconfirm his relationship with God. He felt drawn to the ministry. Ten years later, back on the western shore of the Atlantic, the painter fulfilled his calling and was ordained as a minister at the First Presbyterian Church in Statesville, North Carolina, in 1922.

For the next four decades, Rev. Long served as an itinerant minister, traveling throughout North Carolina and preaching in states as distant as Oklahoma. Although he did not paint during these years, he referred to European religious paintings in his sermons, acquiring the informal title "Picture Painter of the Gospel." Just as Aimee Semple McPherson, Long's near contemporary, used the new technology of radio to spread the gospel, Long recorded sermons for Troutman's Radio Service in Statesville.[50] In the 1920s, as American fundamentalism blossomed after the First World War, Long's theology became increasingly conservative, based on a literal interpretation of the Bible.[51] By 1935 he discovered that his new understanding of faith was at odds with Presbyterianism and was ordained as a Baptist.

Following the Second World War, Long curtailed his preaching and resumed painting. He established a studio in his backyard and created images based on the Bible, overwhelmingly illustrating passages from the New Testament. In the early 1960s the minister told a reporter that he was undertaking the task of creating illustrations of the book of Revelation in which John foresees the end-times.[52] Long, like many other Christians, was convinced that John's prophecies were being enacted around him. In many of Long's paintings, which he considered visual sermons, the artist incorporated figures from current events and history into biblical scenes, thus blurring genre distinctions as he had in his verbal preaching.

Throughout the last years of his life, Long exhibited his biblical paintings at regional institutions. An exhibition of Christian art mounted at Statesville's St. John's Lutheran Church in 1969, which included forty-eight paintings drawn from as far away as New York City, featured Long's *Wrongside Fishing under Man—Resultless.*[53] Three years later, in 1972, Long's portrait of Jesus, entitled *He Still*

Loves and Saves, was judged to be the most popular painting at an art show in Fort Mill, South Carolina.[54]

In 1972 Frank Sherrill of Statesville organized a retrospective of Rev. Long's paintings at the city's Arts and Science Museum that showcased approximately one hundred works from both before and after the itinerant lacuna in his artistic career.[55] Mildred Huskins, who reported on the exhibit for the *Statesville Record,* preferred Long's earlier work. She wrote: "These are portraits, still lifes, and landscapes in rich color showing intense feeling and great talent. They are mellow with age and prized possessions of many individuals who have loaned them for exhibit." In contrast, his later paintings she characterized as "brilliant in color and great imagination."[56]

Long died of pneumonia on May 8, 1976, at the age of eighty-seven. Robert Hill Long, the painter's grandson, eulogized him with a poem entitled "Grandfather Long the Last Time," which mourned the emotional and psychic distance between the aged preacher, weakened by time, and his pony-tailed grandson. The poet wrote:

Is this the God-haired evangelist whose supper prayer was as
    big as a circus tent?
who painted himself arm in arm with Dante
grinning on a crag in hell
while Russian cosmonauts plunged into a lake of fire?[57]

Long's Theology

To make sense of Long's impulse to visually merge the book of Revelation with historical figures and current events, his paintings must be understood within the historical and cultural context of the 1950s and 1960s. The religious and apocalyptic paintings from the end of his career reflect responses to his cultural and religious milieu. Following the Second World War, as Long returned to his easel, the United States was assuming an expanded international role through the Truman Doctrine and the deployment of American troops to Korea. While the Korean War's geopolitical ramifications were complex, American society often portrayed it as a conflict between the forces of totalitarian, atheistic communism and freedom-loving, God-fearing America. For, by the 1950s, as the sociologist Will Herberg noted, to be a Protestant, Catholic, or Jew were just three, roughly similar, modes of being American. Dwight Eisenhower stated this pluralistic American religious self-identification in 1952: "Our government has no sense unless it is founded in a deeply felt religious faith and I don't care what it is."[58]

Although the Korean War remained within the arena of conventional arms, the potential for escalation into a nuclear conflict was widely recognized in American society, fueled by the cold war with the Soviet Union. By the 1950s, B-52 bombers, under the direction of the Strategic Air Command and armed with nuclear weapons, were kept in the air twenty-four hours a day, ready to strike foreign targets on command. Popular culture commented on the threat inherent in this state of global readiness in movies like *Fail Safe* and *Dr. Strangelove*, which told stories of commands gone awry and the ensuing nuclear holocaust. Children participated in "duck and cover" exercises in their public schools, and homeowners privately built bomb shelters to protect themselves from nuclear explosions and radioactive fallout.

As the Korean War was prolonged into the cold war and defense strategists discussed "Mutually Assured Destruction," America's domestic scene witnessed hearings by the House Committee on Un-American Activities, the confrontation between Alger Hiss and Whittaker Chambers over espionage, and the rise of Senator Joseph McCarthy, Representative Richard Nixon, and the John Birch Society. The passage of the Internal Security Act of 1950 allowed for the deportation of "subversives." Atomic scientists, college professors, and labor leaders found themselves under investigation. In 1955, in this context of national and international anxiety, Congress, in an attempt to staunch subversion, added the phrase "In God We Trust" to government-issued currency. Similarly, the phrase "under God" was added legally to the nation's Pledge of Allegiance.[59]

While Congress dealt with the political situation, the courts handed down decisions that radically changed the American social situation, especially in the South. In 1954 the U.S. Supreme Court ruled in *Brown v. Board of Education* that racial segregation in schools was unconstitutional. Coming in the wake of the official desegregation of the armed forces in 1948, the court's decision propelled other changes in American race relations. In December of 1955, for example, Rosa Parks refused to give up her seat on a bus in Montgomery, Alabama, sparking the Montgomery bus boycott, which ushered civil rights leader Dr. Martin Luther King Jr. onto the national stage.

The period in which Rev. Long began to paint his images of the Apocalypse was a time of anxiety, an era that gave rise to the massive transformations and revitalizations that are popularly associated with the 1960s. Scholars have suggested that it is impossible to understand the movement against the war in Vietnam without recognizing the background of the civil rights movement, just as it is impossible to comprehend the Cuban missile crisis without the context of the conflict of the 1950s between the United States and the Soviet Union over nuclear deployment.[60]

Three interrelated and somewhat overlapping themes inform the evangelist's paintings and assist in their analysis. These concepts are fundamentalist revivalism, apocalyptic millennialism, and expectant restorationism. Central to Long's itinerant ministry was his insistence on the necessity of a conversion experience in order for an individual to become a true Christian. Familiar to southerners as the need to be "saved," or the need to be "born again," this event would preferably take place at a revival meeting such as those presided over by Rev. Long. This approach to religion, with its characteristic emphasis on renunciation of sin, breaking with one's past, and adoption of a new identity, has a long history in southern Protestantism, ranging from George Whitfield in the colonial era through Billy Graham in the twentieth century.

Long expresses this emphasis on conversion in his recorded sermons and in two paintings from the 1960s. In *Masters and Servants of the Hereafter* (fig. 3), Long presented a straightforward depiction of the results of accepting Christ as one's savior or of rejecting him. Since Long believed that the whole point of preaching was to confront the individual with the importance of making such a choice, the implication was clear. Choose Christ and go to heaven to enjoy music, drink, literature, and a foot massage while becoming one with Christ—or reject Christ and go to hell to suffer excruciating pain for all eternity. In *Christ Leads the Faithful into the Heavenly Paradise* (fig. 4), Long again presents those who have chosen to follow Jesus, now symbolically robed in white, being ushered into a blissful existence. David Steel has pointed out that Long painted many of his own family members into this image, but it is also significant that this is one of the few depictions by Long to include

Fig. 3. McKendree Robbins Long, *Masters and Servants of the Hereafter*, 1967. Oil on masonite, 28 x 44 inches. Courtesy of Margaret DuB. Avery.

Fig. 4. McKendree Robbins Long, *Christ Leads the Faithful into the Heavenly Paradise*, c. 1960–65. Oil on canvas, 41 x 54 inches. Courtesy of the Van Every/Smith Galleries, Davidson College, Davidson, North Carolina.

Native American and African American faces as well.[61] Thus, both in sermons and in paintings, Long insists that all people need to seek redemption through an acceptance of Jesus and a dedication to his ways. If one experiences such a conversion, then heavenly paradise will be the reward.

If revivalism is clear in Long, the qualifier of "fundamentalist" may be more problematic. According to George Marsden, fundamentalism was a subdivision of Protestant evangelicalism characterized by its rationalism and its strident opposition to modernism. With such an emphasis on rationalism, fundamentalists distanced themselves from those evangelicals and Pentecostals who prized emotionalism, speaking in tongues, and other such "gifts of the Spirit."[62]

Equally important, however, was the virulent opposition to modernism in any of its forms. For fundamentalists, modernism could be acknowledging progress in science or morality, maintaining optimism about the future, harboring an openness toward the theory of evolution, exercising a willingness to put the scriptures into their historical contexts, accepting the importance of human experience for theology, or working for the Kingdom of God here on earth. Against these innovations the fundamentalists stood foursquare.

Controversy between fundamentalists and modernists ranged widely throughout American Protestantism during Long's lifetime. In the 1890s, for example, the Presbyterian Church witnessed heresy charges brought against three of its seminary professors. In each case conservatives (or fundamentalists) battled liberals (or modernists). Similar struggles took place within the southern Baptist and Methodist denominations. Of course, the most familiar symbol for the conflict between modernists and fundamentalists was the Scopes trial in 1925, in which a high school biology teacher in Tennessee was charged with teaching evolution in his classroom.[63] These clashes provided the context in which the young McKendree Long grew up, was educated theologically, and cast his lot, ultimately switching from the Presbyterians to the Baptists in the 1920s as he sought a more conservative affiliation.

Long's antimodernism is pervasive. In his recorded sermons he vilifies modernist ideals as the "modern foe" and cries out, "Down with modernism." Further, in three of his paintings from the 1940s through the 1960s, he clearly consigns those he considered modern

Fig. 5. McKendree Robbins Long, *Charon Ferrying Figures across the River Styx*, c. 1948. Oil on canvas, 36 x 48 inches. Courtesy of Allen and Barry Huffman.

to the flames of hell. In *Charon Ferrying Figures across the River Styx*, Long portrays Pablo Picasso, Fillippo Marinetti, and Helena Blavatsky on their way to hell (fig. 5).[64] Each of these figures represented modernity and attacks upon tradition: Picasso in art, Marinetti in poetry, and Blavatsky in religion. In Long's view, their activities condemned them to eternal damnation.

Similarly, Long's *Apocalyptic Scene with Philosophers and Historical Figures* contains a veritable who's who of the damned (see fig. 1). Mao Tse-tung, Benito Mussolini, Joseph Stalin, and Adolf Hitler are already consumed in the fiery lake, with Charles Darwin, Karl Marx, Sigmund Freud, Friedrich Nietzsche, and Albert Einstein among the others about to meet a similar fate.[65] Long himself, as described by his grandson, watches over the spectacle, smiling while chatting with Dante about the foolhardiness of unbelievers.

Finally, in *The Fifth Angel Opens the Bottomless Pit*, Long illustrates Fidel Castro and Nikita Khrushchev about to be consumed by

Fig. 6. McKendree Robbins Long, *The Fifth Angel Opens the Bottomless Pit*, c. 1965. Oil on canvas, 41¾ x 52½ inches. Courtesy of Margaret DuB. Avery.

scorpion-tailed beasts (fig. 6). A golfer occupies the lower-right-hand corner of the painting. Long's grandson Ben Long IV has identified this figure as a portrait of Dwight Eisenhower, disguised with a beard and mustache after the painter's daughter disagreed with placing the leader of the free world in hell.[66] Eisenhower had provoked the evangelist's wrath by playing golf on Sundays and thus publicly disregarding the Sabbath as a day of rest. The upper-right corner of this work contains a Soviet cosmonaut falling from the sky. This image may have been Long's response to a comment attributed to an early Soviet cosmonaut who claimed that he had flown through the heavens and had found God nowhere.

Clearly, Long's roster of the damned as cataloged in these compositions is a response to the aforementioned social dislocations of the 1950s and early 1960s. Just as the Bible states that God passed a righteous judgment on sinners in the past and promised that those who opposed his ways in the future would likewise feel his wrath,

McKendree Long was here passing judgment on the personalities, ideologies, and movements that were so prominent in his era and that he held responsible for the troubles of his times. Because he was a trained and talented portraitist, viewers of his works have the opportunity to make informed guesses in a game of historical identification and allusion. In the spirit of 1950s television games, Long's audiences can play "Name That Damned." Interpreters of Long's works should not lose sight of the role that Long claimed for himself—namely, the regent of the Lord who on his own authority condemned Mussolini, Hitler, Stalin, Mao, Khrushchev, Castro, Picasso, Freud, Blavatsky, and Einstein to the everlasting agonies of hell. Nor should scholars underestimate the didactic purposes to which the artist dedicated these works, for in his opposition to "modernism," Long sought to depict in unequivocal terms for all to see his own analysis of the age and to enlist recruits in the battle that he believed was under way. In their attempts to visually interpret biblical prophecy in relation to current events, Long's paintings were functionally similar to the lithographic *Millerite Chart of 1843* created in the antebellum period by followers of William Miller to inform the public of Christ's imminent return.[67]

Apocalyptic millennialism is the second significant theme visible in Long's paintings. Millennialism refers to the biblical prophecy of the Second Coming of Jesus and his thousand-year reign. While the millennial prophecies in the Bible have been widely interpreted, with numerous alternative meanings adduced from various texts, McKendree Long's understanding falls into that school scholars call premillennialism. A basic understanding of this interpretation places Christ's return before his thousand-year reign. (An alternative postmillennialist interpretation claims that the thousand-year reign precedes Jesus's appearance.)[68]

Broadly speaking, in this premillennialist interpretation the Antichrist appears on earth and begins a reign of terror referred to as the tribulation. This era concludes with the battle of Armageddon in which Christ defeats the Antichrist and then establishes his millennial kingdom.

Long's paintings seek to show the meaning of the book of Revelation, with its cosmic conflict of good and evil, righteousness and sin, and the ultimate victory of Christ over Satan. While many of Long's works depict apocalyptic scenes, two images painted in the

Fig. 7. McKendree Robbins Long, *The First Angel Sounds His Trumpet*, c. 1965. Oil on canvas, 46 x 54 inches. Courtesy of the Van Every/Smith Galleries, Davidson College, Davidson, North Carolina.

mid-1960s deserve special attention. *The First Angel Sounds His Trumpet* (fig. 7) is a premillennial insistence upon the imminence of the Lord's return. As a couple lounge in a boat enjoying the day and its natural beauty, the Day of Judgment arrives. As the angel overhead sounds his trumpet, the relaxing people are taken by surprise.[69] In this work, Long hearkens back to his revivalist preaching to insist that being saved should take precedence over all else—family development, national improvement, environmental awareness, or, in this case, the simple enjoyment of the beauty of nature. The "endtimes" are imminent, he asserts. The Day of Judgment is near, and the only relevant question is, as a church message board once put it: "How Are You Spending Eternity? Smoking or Nonsmoking?"

The same apocalyptic dimension can be seen in Long's *The Reaping of the Earth in Judgment* (fig. 8). In this composition, Christ,

Fig. 8. McKendree Robbins Long, *The Reaping of the Earth in Judgment*, c. 1965. Oil on canvas, 48 x 48 inches. Courtesy of Bob Gibson.

armed with a sharp sickle and with nail holes in his feet serving as evidence of the sacrifice he has made for humanity, is in the process of reaping the harvest, judging the living and the dead, and separating the saved from the damned. A pool of blood has collected at Christ's feet. For Long, nothing short of the return of Christ will set the world right. Moral striving, good deeds, well-intentioned activities are not sinful; however, for this premillennialist they ultimately count for nothing. Instead, in Christ's return to earth, the end-times are under way. In this image, Long once again expresses himself both as a preacher of premillennial expectations and as a painter of apocalyptic visions.

Expectant restorationism is the third important theme in Long's biblical paintings. Restorationism, at its simplest, can have a range of meanings, from the reestablishment of certain practices as nominally justified by scriptural precedent through the reunion of the divine and the human, a renewal of the harmony between God and humankind that originally existed in the Garden of Eden before the rupture between the sacred and the human took place. Restorationism is a broad concept and one familiar in American religious history. Many Christian groups, for example, have sought to restore biblical or early Christian practices in their ritual, community life, and ethical practice. Biblical precedents have served as justification for groups as diverse in their beliefs as the celibate Shakers and the advocates of complex marriage within the Oneida community; for denominations as different as Methodists, Pentecostals, and Mormons; and for religiously influenced social movements such as abolitionism, pacifism, and Sabbatarianism.[70]

For McKendree Long, however, restoration was not to take place here on earth, but rather in heaven after death. Long's high hopes for a restoration were not of this world but of the next. In *God on His Throne Holding the Book of Seals* (see fig. 2), a rainbow, the symbol of God's covenant with the world and of his faithfulness, surrounds God the Father, as Christ, to the right of the composition, displays the wounds on his hands to indicate the sacrifice he made on behalf of humankind. Similarly, in *Christ Leads the Faithful into the Heavenly Paradise* (see fig. 4), a rainbow appears in the middle ground as Jesus, replete with wounds on his hands and feet, leads long lines of believers into paradise. The landscape is of Edenic charm, with flowers and trees in full bloom. Long has represented an Arcadian bounty in which human and divine relationships are finally restored through the Savior's pain. Through the inclusion of Native Americans and African Americans in the scene, Long also affirms the imminent restoration of the unity of the human race.

Hope is a familiar motif in southern Christianity, as it is in many religious traditions. Indeed, the book of Revelation, despite its gruesome imagery and violent scenes, was intended as a message of hope, as a proclamation of a "new heaven and a new earth" promised for the future. Thus, for all of the violence and chaos of Long's paintings, the overarching import is one of hope and salvation for those who choose a life of faithfulness to the Lord's commands. By using biblical imagery and drawing upon strains of fundamentalist, evangelical Christian theology, Long was able to convey a message of hope in the face of the American social and political anxieties omnipresent in the cold war environment of the mid-twentieth century. Rather than being idiosyncratic and bizarre personal statements, Long's paintings are replete with mainstream symbols that explicate complex tenets central to American systems of theology for those who have the visual and religious background to read his manifestos.

Art Historical Sources

Long's life experiences prepared him extraordinarily well to translate his theological understandings into visual form. His compositions were not naively born from raw passionate belief, untainted by academic theory. Rather, Long's works are sophisticated theological statements created by an artist well versed in European and American artistic traditions who was also attuned to the popular visual culture of his time and place. Long's European sojourn as a youth had taken him to many of the continent's major art centers and had exposed him to the art of the Great Masters of the Western tradition. His subsequent career as an itinerant preacher familiarized him with American visual culture, which infused his paintings with a religious familiarity not commonly found in laypeople's cultural expressions.

Long did not hide his sophisticated knowledge of European art history. His *The Fourth Horseman*, executed between 1961 and 1965, bears a prominent and elaborate inscription dedicating the work to Albrecht Dürer, whom Long describes as his "old friend of Nürnburg." David Steel has asserted that Dürer's images exerted little influence on the artist's work; however, Long's *The Woman Arrayed in Purple and Scarlet and the Two Beasts* clearly is derived from the master's woodcut *The Whore of Babylon*[71] (figs. 9 and 10). Specifically, Long's woman, who rides a multiheaded beast and holds aloft a goblet in her right hand while sporting a tiara, is similar to Dürer's handling of the same figure. The head of the second beast in Long's painting also is reminiscent of one of Dürer's seven monstrous faces.

Dürer's influence on Long's compositions is evident throughout the southerner's later artistic production. Most notably, Long's *The Vision of the Sixth Angel* includes fire-breathing lions being ridden by

Fig. 9. McKendree Robbins Long, *The Woman Arrayed in Purple and Scarlet and the Two Beasts*, c. 1965. Oil on masonite panel, 40 x 48 inches. Courtesy of Bob Gibson.

armored figures that seem to be based on a detail of Dürer's *The Fifth and Sixth Trumpets* (1498). David Steel suggests that a crowd being driven over a cliff in this work by Long may be derived from Dürer's woodcut *The Martyrdom of the Ten Thousand*.[72] A painting of this scene by Dürer from 1508 is in the Kunsthistorisches Museum, Vienna, and it may also have been known to the evangelist. Long's *The Seventh Angel Pours Out His Vial upon the Earth*, from the second half of the 1960s, may be derived from Dürer's *Opening of the Fifth and Sixth Seals* (1498). Both of these works portray destruction raining down from above and feature figures in the foreground covering their heads and cowering before God's judgment. Both paintings also include a large triangular element. In Long's painting this shape represents a volcano, while in Dürer's print it is an abstraction of God's power.

Long's respect for Dürer may be indicative of a broader aware-

Fig. 10. Albrecht Dürer. *The Whore of Babylon*, 1498. Woodcut. The Metropolitan Museum of Art, Rogers Fund, 1918 (18.65.8). Image © The Metropolitan Museum of Art.

ness of religious works of the northern Renaissance. The chaos and destruction in Long's works reverberate with paintings by Hieronymus Bosch (1450–1516) and Pieter Brueghel (1525/30–69). The suffering figures falling into the lake of fire in the top left corner of Long's *Apocalyptic Scene with Philosophers and Historical Figures* (see fig. 1) are not unlike the bizarre naked sinners in Bosch's *The Last Judgment* of 1502. Long's themes and compositions also are reminiscent of Brueghel. The latter's magnificent *The Triumph of Death* of 1562, held by the Prado in Madrid, shows humans fighting an army of skeletons in a rectangular composition with a distant vanishing point and elevated land masses on both the right and left margins. In comparison, Long's *The Vision of the Sixth Angel* depicts mankind annihilated by a demonic cavalry in a similar composition. Animated skeletons, like those of Brueghel's army of death, appear repeatedly in Long's oeuvre. Long's *The Fifth Angel Opens the Bottomless Pit* (see fig. 6) approximates Brueghel's *The Fall of the Rebel Angels* (1562), held by the Royal Museum of Fine Arts in Brussels, with both compositions bearing strong vertical lines featuring angels, demonic beasts, and grotesque human figures.

Long's paintings from the 1960s that represent heaven as a colonnaded white city utilize a convention of Anglo-American religious paintings that represents sublime otherworldly experiences through awe-inspiring architectural settings. The English painter John Martin (1789–1854) is among the most noteworthy figures in this tradition, epitomized by his *Belshazzar's Feast* of 1820, which was widely printed and distributed as a steel mezzotint.[73] American artists Thomas Cole (1801–1848), Frederic Church (1826–1900), and Erastus Salisbury Field (1805–1900) also produced works in this visionary tradition, which gained a broad popular dissemination in the twentieth century through circus spectaculars like the Ringling Brothers' "Solomon and the Queen of Sheba" and the cinematic efforts of D.W. Griffiths and Cecil B. DeMille.[74]

John Martin's influence on Long may be seen most clearly in *Apocalyptic Scene with Philosophers and Historical Figures* (see fig. 1). As discussed above, this work presents sinners in a cavern suffering in the flames of hell. Long's conception of hell is closely related to John Martin's engravings of the underworld, which he produced starting in 1824 for an edition of Milton's *Paradise Lost* published by Septimus Prowett. In particular, Long's work exhibits many similarities to Martin's 1824 mezzotint *Satan Arousing the Fallen Angels* (fig. 11). Like Long's tour de force, Martin's mezzotint depicts two figures standing to the right of the composition looking down on a sea of fire located in a cavern; souls suffer in seas of flame while demons perch on subsidiary crags.

The Prowett edition of *Paradise Lost* featured several Martin engravings that are variations on the theme of flaming chasms of the damned, including works entitled *Satan on the Burning Lake; Satan, Sin, and Death;* and *Pandemonium.* These reproductions have profoundly affected American conceptions of hell, impacting everything from amusement park thrill rides to fraternal initiation scenery created by firms like Sosman & Landis and the Twin City Scenic Studios.[75] By drawing upon Martin's vision of a fiery netherworld, Long borrowed a framework for his theological argument and utilized an art historical source that would resonate with viewers of his work. The artist's use of Martin's formats places him firmly in an American tradition of borrowing visual imagery that also includes Field, Cole, DeMille, the Ringling Brothers, and early-twentieth-century scenic design firms.

As indicated, Long's apocalyptic scenes are related to historical artworks, but they also were created within the context of the sacred and secular visual culture that was concurrently being created by Long's contemporaries. Within religious material culture, Long's paintings are sympathetically consistent with images by Warner Sallman and Harry Anderson. Long's compositions also resonate with both commercial illustration and paint-by-number kits omnipresent in the United States during the mid-twentieth century.

Warner Sallman (1892–1968) was arguably the most important American religious artist of the twentieth century.[76] Sallman's *Head of Christ*, first marketed by the Warner Press in 1941, is pervasive.[77] In 1984 the publishing firm of Kriebel and Bates estimated that this single image had been reproduced more than an astounding 500 million times.[78] Trained in art at the School of the Art Institute of Chicago from 1909 to 1913 and in Christianity at the Moody Bible Institute from 1914 to 1917, Sallman was almost an exact contemporary of Long. While Long sought to spread the gospel through itinerant preaching, Sallman served as art director of the *Covenant Companion* of the Evangelical Covenant Church based in the Midwest.[79]

Sallman's paintings were designed to serve the same function that

Fig. 11. John Martin, *Satan Arousing the Fallen Angels*, 1824. Mezzotint.
25.9 x 25.3 cm. Special Collections, University of Wisconsin–Milwaukee
Libraries.

Long envisioned for his work: to motivate individuals to commit their souls to Jesus. With the hopes of converting adults, Sallman produced images for the Salvation Army, creating paintings for chapels and magazine illustrations for the publication *The War Cry*.[80] Evangelicals also broadly used reproductions of Sallman's works in the years following World War II to spur adults and children toward conversion experiences. His images of a loving Christ interacting with contemporary figures were marketed to parents and Christian educators as tools for saving youths from the adverse effects of modernity in American life, including juvenile delinquency and sexual promiscuity.[81]

Not surprisingly, many thematic and compositional parallels can be found within Sallman's and Long's oeuvres. These similarities are most notable when comparing Long's *The Good Shepherd* of the early 1960s with Sallman's *The Lord Is My Shepherd* (originally also entitled *The Good Shepherd*) from 1942 (figs. 12 and 13).[82] Both of these works portray Jesus as a shepherd in flowing robes standing by a body of water and surrounded by a flock that includes a single black sheep. Both of the central figures hold a crook in their right hands while cradling a lamb in their left. While Sallman carefully expunged all threatening elements of the biblical references from his scene, Long introduced tension by depicting predatory wolves and a cougar who would feast on the sheep should they stray.[83] In Sallman's painting Christ's identity is assumed but not specified; Long, however, leaves no doubt as to the Savior's identity by crowning him with a halo and delineating wounds on his hands and feet. Both Sallman and Long owe a debt to Bernhard Plockhorst (1825–1907), a German artist whose *The Good Shepherd* from the late nineteenth century was widely distributed at the beginning of the twentieth.[84]

Long's *Christ Blesses the Child* (1952; now in the collection of the Van Every/Smith Galleries at Davidson College) bears a striking resemblance to Sallman's *He Careth for You* of 1954.[85] Both images include a seated Christ figure with flowing hair and a beard dressed in biblical robes surrounded by pale blossoms. Three individuals dressed in twentieth-century American garments interact with the Savior; however, the dynamics of the people meeting their Savior differ between the two compositions. Produced for evangelical purposes, Sallman's image presents three adorable, white, middle-class children who are being reassured that Christ will look after them. Not intended to appeal to a large audience, Long's treatment in-

Fig. 12. McKendree Robbins Long, *The Good Shepherd*, c. 1960–65. Oil on canvas, 39¾ x 50⅛ inches. Courtesy of Catherine Taylor Egerton.

Fig. 13. Warner Sallman, *The Lord Is My Shepherd*, 1942. Oil on canvas, 40 x 30 inches. © 1943 Warner Press, Inc., Anderson, Indiana. All rights reserved. Used with permission.

cludes an unidentified baby portrayed sitting on Jesus's lap while a woman holds the child's foot. In a compelling self-portrait, Long captures himself weeping while on his knees at the Lord's feet.[86] As with *The Good Shepherd*, Long's Christ is differentiated from Sallman's by the halo and crucifixion wounds.

Harry Anderson (1906–1996), Sallman's friend, was born almost two decades after Long but produced comparable Christian images. Anderson's most famous illustration, entitled *What Happened to Your Hands?* (1945), for example, depicts a bearded Christ with flowing hair and white robes sitting in a garden. In this work Anderson presents three cute middle-class children in twentieth-century clothing examining the wounds in Jesus's palms. The art historian David Morgan has indicated that Anderson's painting was the inspiration for Sallman's *He Careth for You.*[87]

Anderson was trained as an artist and illustrator at the Syracuse School of Art in New York State. After graduation in 1931, he moved to New York City to pursue a career in commercial art. He created many illustrations for advertising campaigns, including commissions for Coca-Cola and the Ford Motor Company, and editorial art for popular magazines such as the *Saturday Evening Post*, *Good Housekeeping*, and *Ladies' Home Journal*. In the 1940s Anderson was associated with the studio of Haddon Sundblom, the famous illustrator responsible for Coca-Cola's images of Santa Claus.[88]

Anderson experienced a religious conversion in the 1940s and joined the Seventh-Day Adventist Church. T. K. Martin, the art director at the Adventists' *Review and Herald*, capitalized upon Anderson's newfound faith and recruited him to produce work for the church's extensive publishing efforts.[89] Subsequently, Anderson split his time between producing illustrations for Madison Avenue and generating religious images for the Adventist Church.

Because Christ's imminent return is central to the teachings of the Seventh-Day Adventists, who derive institutionally from the nineteenth-century Millerites, Anderson's pictures frequently addressed prophetic themes.[90] Produced in the same decades in which Long was painting, Anderson's images frequently portray Americans interacting with Christ, angels, and Satan. One of Anderson's scenes of resurrection shows a family, composed of a father, mother, son, and daughter, emerging fully clothed from the grave. Another of Anderson's illustrations portrays people on the rooftops of New

York City's commercial buildings greeting winged angels carrying scrolls. In *The Prince of Peace*, a work from 1961 that resonates thematically, if not stylistically, with Long's paintings, Anderson depicts a towering spectral Jesus knocking on the exterior of New York City's United Nations building (fig. 14). In all of these composi-

Fig. 14. Harry Anderson, *The Prince of Peace*, 1961. © Review & Herald Publishing Association. Used by Permission.

tions, Anderson made clear, as Long did, that the Apocalypse was fast approaching and that biblical prophecy had relevance for twentieth-century Americans.

Warner Sallman and Harry Anderson were not outside of the American artistic tradition; their products, whether created for religious organizations or for multinational corporations, were viewed and appreciated by millions of Americans. Moreover, Christian imagery was not created and manipulated exclusively by socially and politically conservative artists in the middle of the twentieth century. In the 1970s Christian imagery entered the work of Rick Griffin (1944–1991), an artist who drew cartoons for *Surfer* magazine, designed psychedelic posters for Bill Graham's rock concerts at the Fillmore West, and codified the iconography of the Grateful Dead through his innovative concert posters and album covers. In 1973 Griffin's artwork for the Grateful Dead's album *Wake of the Flood* featured a man with a sickle, inspired by the twentieth chapter of Revelation.[91] Later in the decade, Griffin produced illustrations for a modern retelling of the Gospel of John.[92]

THE FEMALE FORM

While Rev. Long's religious themes have served to marginalize him for some commentators, the artist's portrayal of scantily clad women with prominent breasts has offended other critics' sensibilities and contributed to his perceived status as an outsider.[93] Yet, when Long is understood within an accurate and nuanced historical and cultural context, the artist's interest in the female nude places him at the center of American society rather than at its fringe.

The representation of the nude female torso was commonplace in American culture in the middle decades of the twentieth century. Women's breasts were portrayed in a wide variety of media crossing definitional boundaries. Possibly most famously, Marilyn Monroe graced the centerfold of the first *Playboy* in 1953. Hugh Hefner was not alone in publishing the female form; the more respectable *Esquire* magazine published pinup art by Alberto Vargas (1896–1942) and others.

During this period, a fascination with the female form was not limited to men's magazines. This preoccupation appeared in both high art and popular culture. Another near contemporary of Rev.

Long, Thomas Hart Benton (1889–1975), portrayed naked women in his compositions of the 1930s derived from the Bible and from classical sources. His paintings *Susannah and the Elders* and *Persephone* both exploit and comment upon the titillating aspect of nudity, while simultaneously situating the characters from these ancient stories within a twentieth-century American milieu. Illustrators like Rudolph Belarski (1900–1983), Earle Bergey (1901–1952), Robert McGinnis (1926–), and others produced eye-catching covers featuring attractive scantily clad women for paperback book publishers throughout the middle decades of the twentieth century.[94] In the same years, science fiction pulp magazines depicted buxom women threatened by horrendous monsters.[95]

Even the mass-market, do-it-yourself paint-by-number kits marketed in the 1950s capitalized on an American appreciation of female beauty and sexuality.[96] Consumers could purchase sets to create their own version of Plockhorst's *The Good Shepherd*, but hobby shops also offered customers supplies to create images of female nudes relaxing by a waterfall or reclining on a sofa.[97] The museum curator William L. Bird has noted that Palmer Paint, the leading manufacturer of paint-by-number kits in the 1950s, developed new designs for distribution based on sales of other kits and customer correspondence.[98] Thus the manufacture of paint-by-number nudes testifies to the centrality of naked women to American visual culture in this period.

SITUATING LONG'S PAINTINGS

Rev. McKendree Long's apocalyptic visions, then, are the products of an artist trained in one of America's finest art schools who subsequently continued his studies in Europe. While sojourning on the continent, he visited cities renowned for their art collections and studied the Old Masters. Upon his return to North Carolina, his early pictures received positive critical review when they were exhibited for the state's women's clubs.

The body of religious imagery Long produced upon returning to the easel after his career as an evangelist comments upon social and political stresses related to cultural modernization and contemporary international relations. These compositions are imbued with beliefs connected to fundamentalist revivalism, apocalyptic millennialism, and expectant restorationism, all concepts that were common if not ubiquitous in the mid-twentieth-century South. Long, who had spent decades as an itinerant preacher, understood his paintings to be a continuation of his calling to preach the gospel.

In composing such apocalyptic visions, Long drew upon European and American visual traditions that linked religion to art and derived from recognized masters, including Albrecht Dürer and John Martin, while also forming part of an American art historical lineage that includes painters like Thomas Cole and Erastus Salisbury Field, among others. Further, the art historical traditions that informed Long's apocalyptic scenes also have shaped the appearance and identity of circuses, movies, amusement parks, and the material culture of fraternalism.

Long's paintings are comparable to those of his contemporary American professional artists who were simultaneously creating religious visual culture. While employed by religious denominations, these other Christian artists expressed many of the same theological concepts as Long, including apocalyptic millennialism and expectant restorationism, and their works were designed to serve purposes similar to Long's own understanding of painted sermons. The similarities evident in these individuals' artistic productions suggest sources shared among them, made available through broadly distributed reproductions.

Long's paintings exhibit a proclivity for buxom, scantily clad women, just as the female torso was popularly portrayed in American visual culture in the years that Long was creating his apocalyptic art. In the middle decades of the twentieth century, the female form appeared in formats as diverse as popular books and magazines, religious and mythological paintings by internationally recognized artists, and do-it-yourself kits marketed to the suburban middle class.

In recent years, Long's paintings have been included in exhibitions dedicated to outsider artists, marketed at outsider art fairs, and reproduced in museum catalogs documenting the genre. Advocates of outsider art argue that the artists who create it have exhibited an intuitive artistic talent unfettered by convention. McKendree Long and his artistic career have been misrepresented by the art market and by those who seek to classify his oeuvre without contextualizing it historically, theologically, or artistically.

As theorists, including Eugene Metcalf and Charles Briggs, have suggested, outsider art is a cultural construct developed by empowered insiders who define individuals as being Other. For these thinkers, the endeavor of codifying and exhibiting outside art is a form of self-discovery similar to anthropology. By establishing boundaries that distinguish insiders from outsiders, curators, dealers, and collectors better understand their own identity and place in the world.

The marketplace and the art world have defined McKendree Robbins Long as an outsider due, not surprisingly, to attributes of region and of faith, qualities that defined cultural conflict in American society throughout the twentieth century. These cultural rifts made the Scopes trial of the 1920s a media circus and drove Jerry Falwell to found the Moral Majority in 1979.

Both his religious faith and his regional identity have obscured the details of Long's biography, his artistic influences, and his larger historical context. Writers awash in late-twentieth-century secularism, and thus victims of anomie, have mistakenly identified Long as a primitive oddity for whom they feel both repulsion and attraction. Having treated his belief as regional exoticism, they have respected him for his perceived authenticity while simultaneously condemning him as unsophisticated. Conversely, southerners have celebrated and lionized this native son of North Carolina as a means to codify and define a culture that is distinct from the rest of the nation. Ultimately, however, Long must not be considered an "outsider" but should be understood as a figure who exemplifies how American cultural critics have viewed and interpreted southern evangelical Protestants.

NOTES

This essay is derived from lectures the authors presented as public programming at Wilmington, North Carolina's Louise Wells Cameron Art Museum in April 2003. The authors would like to extend their thanks to Cary Wilkins, librarian at the Morris Museum of Art, Augusta, Georgia. Charlotte Emans Moore provided invaluable editorial assistance. Brad Thomas and Jessica Cooley of Davidson College were also gracious and generous in assisting to secure images for this chapter.

1. David Steel, "The Art of Reverend McKendree Robbins Long," *American Art Review* 15 (March–April 2003): 122–27.

2. Mildred Huskins, "Long's Art Exhibit Well Received," *Statesville (N.C.) Record*, March 5, 1972; Brad Thomas, "The Life of Reverend McKendree Robbins Long," in David Steel and Brad Thomas, *Reverend McKend-*

ree Robbins Long: Picture Painter of the Apocalypse (Davidson and Raleigh, N.C.: Davidson College and the North Carolina Museum of Art, 2002), 35.

3. Thomas, "The Life of Reverend McKendree Robbins Long," 36.

4. "Exhibition Checklist," in Roger Manley, *Signs and Wonders: Outsider Art inside North Carolina* (Raleigh: North Carolina Museum of Art, 1989), 132.

5. Manley, *Signs and Wonders*, vii, 78–89.

6. *Inside Visions* (Ashville, N.C.: Ashville Art Museum, 1992); Hank Burchard, "Millennial Art: Apocalypse Wow!" *Washington Post*, June 6, 1997, N59.

7. Roger Manley, *The End Is Near! Visions of Apocalypse, Millennium, and Utopia* (Los Angeles: Dilettante, 1998), 46–53.

8. Tom Patterson, *Contemporary Folk Art: Treasures from the Smithsonian American Art Museum* (New York: Watson-Guptill, 2001), 62–63.

9. Randolph Delehanty, *Art in the American South: Works from the Ogden Collection* (Baton Rouge: Louisiana State University Press, 1996), 239.

10. Steel and Thomas, *Reverend McKendree Robbins Long*.

11. Lee Smith, "Saturday Night and Sunday Morning," and Hal Crowther, "Float Fishing in the Ring of Fire," both in "'All Wrought Up': The Apocalyptic South of McKendree Robbins Long," *Southern Cultures* (Spring 2004): 50–60.

12. Steel, "The Art of Reverend McKendree Robbins Long"; Stephen Kinzer, "Painterly Sermons Mix Severe and Sensual," *New York Times*, July 1, 2002, E1, E3.

13. Jesse W. Nash, "Rev. McKendree Long's Paintings," *New Orleans Art Review*, September–October 1989, 17.

14. Exhibition notice, Luise Ross Gallery, "Salvation and Smothered Passions: Reverend McKendree Robbins Long, 1888–1976," McKendree Robbins Long biography file, library of the Morris Museum of Art, Augusta, Ga.

15. Ken Johnson, "McKendree Robbins Long—'Salvation and Smothered Passions,'" *New York Times*, January 16, 2004, E2:39.

16. Stephen Westfall, "Mark Rothko at PaceWildenstein," *Art in America* 92 (September 2004): 129.

17. Michael Amy, "McKendree Robbins Long at Luise Ross," *Art in America* 92 (September 2004): 129–30.

18. N. F. Karlins, "Outsider Art Fair 2004," *Artnet Magazine*, http://admin.artnet.com/magazine/reviews/karlins/karlins1–28–04.asp (accessed December 2, 2006). For Darger, see Brooke Davis Anderson, "Darger, Henry," in *Encyclopedia of American Folk Art*, ed. Gerald C. Wertkin (New York: Routledge, 2004), 115. For Hawkins, see Lee Kogan, "Hawkins, William," in Wertkin, *Encyclopedia of American Folk Art*, 227–28.

19. Brunk Auctions, "Auction Program with Prices Realized June 11, 2005," 7, http://www.brunkauctions.com/Highlights/2005Auctions/June/June2005prices.pdf (accessed December 3, 2006).

20. Wanda Corn, *The Great American Thing: Modern Art and National Identity, 1915–1935* (Berkeley: University of California Press, 1999), 292–337. For the codification of American folk art, see the essays in Virginia Tuttle Clayton, ed., *Drawing on America's Past: Folk Art, Modernism, and the Index of American Design* (Chapel Hill: University of North Carolina Press, 2002). For Balken, see Charlotte Emans Moore, "Another Generation's Folk Art: Edward Duff Balken and His Collection of American Provincial Paintings and Drawings," in *A Window into Collecting American Folk Art: The Edward Duff Balken Collection at Princeton* (Princeton, N.J.: Princeton University, Art Museum, 1999), 16–23.

21. Eugene W. Metcalf Jr., "The Politics of the Past in American Folk Art History," in *Folk Art and Art Worlds*, ed. John Michael Vlach and Simon J. Bronner (Ann Arbor, Mich.: U.M.I. Research, 1986), 27–50.

22. For the classic statement concerning antimodernism and alienation in American industrial society, see T. J. Jackson Lears, *No Place of Grace: Antimodernism and the Transformation of American Culture, 1880–1920* (New York: Pantheon, 1981).

23. Charles L. Briggs, "The Role of *Mexicano* Artists and the Anglo Elite in the Emergence of a Contemporary Folk Art," in Vlach and Bronner, *Folk Art and Art Worlds*, 195.

24. Lynda Roscoe Hartigan, "Hemphill, Herbert W. Jr.," in Wertkin, *Encyclopedia of American Folk Art*, 229–30. Hemphill's personal collection of artworks was subsequently acquired by the Smithsonian Institution. See Lynda Roscoe Hartigan, *Made with Passion: The Hemphill Folk Art Collection* (Washington, D.C.: Smithsonian Institution Press, 1990). Hemphill was preceded by Sidney Janis. See Sidney Janis, *They Taught Themselves: American Primitive Painters of the Twentieth Century* (New York: Dial, 1942).

25. Herbert W. Hemphill Jr. and Julia Weissman, *Twentieth-Century American Folk Art and Artists* (New York: E. P. Dutton, 1974), 9.

26. Robert Bishop, *Folk Painters of America* (New York: E. P. Dutton, 1979).

27. For a discussion of the divergence of "outsider art" from "folk art," see Gerard C. Wertkin, "Authentic Voices, Stammered Words," in Karekin Goekjian and Robert Peacock, *Light of the Spirit: Portraits of Southern Outsider Artists* (Jackson: University Press of Mississippi, 1998), 11–17.

28. Manley, "Seed and Shadow," in *Signs and Wonders*, 6–8. See also Roger Cardinal, "Outsider Art," in Wertkin, *Encyclopedia of American Folk Art*, 351–54.

29. Roger Manley, "Beyond the Outside," in *Inside Visions*.

30. Eugene W. Metcalf Jr., "From Domination to Desire: Insiders and Outsider Art," in *The Artist Outsider: Creativity and the Boundaries of Culture*, ed. Michael D. Hall and Eugene W. Metcalf Jr., with Roger Cardinal (Washington, D.C.: Smithsonian Institution Press, 1994), 221–27.

31. Fred Hobson, "Benighted South," in *Encyclopedia of Southern Culture*, ed. Charles Reagan Wilson and William Ferris (Chapel Hill: University of North Carolina Press, 1989), 1100–1101.

32. David Steel, introduction and acknowledgments to Manley, *Signs and Wonders*, x. See also Tom Stanley, *Worth Keeping: Found Artists of the Carolinas, the Catalogue for an Exhibition* (Columbia, S.C.: Columbia Museums of Art and Science, 1981).

33. Manley, *Signs and Wonders*, 66; John Hood, "Jennings, James Harold," in Wertkin, *Encyclopedia of American Folk Art*, 253–54; Tom Patterson, "Roadside Art: Beating a Path to the Homemade World of James Harold Jennings," *Art Papers*, November–December 1987, 26–31; Goekjian and Peacock, *Light of the Spirit*, 59–63.

34. Charles Reagan Wilson, *Judgment and Grace in Dixie: Southern Faiths from Faulkner to Elvis* (Athens: University of Georgia Press, 1995), 80.

35. Colleen McDannell, *Material Christianity: Religion and Popular Culture in America* (New Haven, Conn.: Yale University Press, 1995), 8–11.

36. Wilson, *Judgment and Grace in Dixie*, 78.

37. The literature on the construction of the southern identity is vast. One point of entry to this discourse is John Shelton Reed, *My Tears Spoiled My Aim and Other Reflections on Southern Culture* (Columbia: University of Missouri Press, 1993). Particularly useful is the chapter entitled "The South's Mid-life Crisis."

38. The best current biography of Long is Thomas, "The Life of Reverend McKendree Robbins Long." Information not cited elsewhere is drawn from this source.

39. "Mr. Mac Long's Art Studies," *Statesville (N.C.) Landmark*, May 27, 1913, 1.

40. "Long Paintings to Be Exhibited," *Statesville (N.C.) Record*, March 3, 1972, 1.

41. *Statesville (N.C.) Sentinel*, February 1911, McKendree Robbins Long biography file.

42. "Mr. Mac. R. Long's Success," *Statesville (N.C.) Landmark*, n.d., McKendree Robbins Long biography file. For de László, see Suzanne Bailey and Sandra De Laszlo, *A Brush with Grandeur: Philip Alexius de László (1869–1937)* (London: Paul Holberton, 2004).

43. "Mr. Mac Long's Art Studies."

44. "Statesville Artist Winning Fame," *Statesville (N.C.) Landmark*, March 8, 1914.

45. "M'K. R. Long's Work Shown at Exhibition," *Greensboro (N.C.) Daily News*, May 8, 1922; Art Department of the Woman's Club, *Exhibition of Paintings and a Literary Evening* (Raleigh, N.C.: Woman's Club, 1921), McKendree Robbins Long biography file; Thomas, "The Life of Reverend McKendree Robbins Long," 27.

46. Mrs. W. T. Bost, "A Fine Arts Evening Is Held at Raleigh," *Greensboro (N.C.) News*, February 24, 1921.

47. Ruth Huntington Moore, "Mr. Long's Pictures," *Raleigh (N.C.) News and Observer,* February 28, 1921. See also Charles E. Raynal, "McKendree Robbins Long—An Appreciation," *Greensboro (N.C.) News*, February 21, 1921.

48. Art Department of the Woman's Club, *Exhibition of Paintings*, no. 33.

49. "M'K. R. Long's Work Shown at Exhibition."

50. Thomas, "The Life of Reverend McKendree Robbins Long," 28. For McPherson and radio, see Tona J. Hangen, *Redeeming the Dial: Radio, Religion, and Popular Culture in America* (Chapel Hill: University of North Carolina Press, 2002), 57–79.

51. For a brief overview of fundamentalism in the 1920s, see Lynn Dumenil, *The Modern Temper: American Culture and Society in the 1920s* (New York: Hill and Wang, 1995), 175–91.

52. Conrad Paysour, "Minister Artist: He Begins a Mighty Big Task," *Charlotte (N.C.) News*, July 25, 1961.

53. Harold Warren, "Annual Festival Features Christian Art," *Charlotte (N.C.) Observer,* March 30, 1969.

54. Thomas, "The Life of Reverend McKendree Robbins Long," 35.

55. "Long Paintings to be Exhibited."

56. Huskins, "Long's Art Exhibit Well Received."

57. Robert Hill Long, "Grandfather Long the Last Time," in Robert Hill Long, *The Power to Die* (Cleveland: Cleveland State Poetry Center, 1987), 103.

58. See Will Herberg, *Protestant, Catholic, Jew* (Garden City, N.Y.: Anchor, 1955; rev. ed., 1960). Dwight Eisenhower is quoted in the *New York Times*, December 23, 1952, 16.

59. For a provocative analysis of the impact of the cold war on American society, see Edward Pessen, *Losing Our Souls! The American Experience in the Cold War* (Chicago: Ivan R. Dee, 1993).

60. See Maurice Isserman, *America Divided: The Civil War of the 1960s* (New York: Oxford University Press, 2000).

61. David Steel, "Catalogue of Works," in Steel and Thomas, *Reverend McKendree Robbins Long*, 96.

62. See George M. Marsden, *Fundamentalism and American Culture: The Shaping of Twentieth-Century Evangelicalism, 1870–1925* (New York: Oxford University Press, 1980).

63. See Bradley J. Longfield, *The Presbyterian Controversy: Fundamentalists, Modernists, and Moderates* (New York: Oxford University Press, 1991); and Edward J. Larson, *Summer for the Gods: The Scopes Trial and America's Continuing Debate over Science and Religion* (New York: Basic, 1997).

64. Steel, "Catalogue," 92.

65. Ibid., 94.

66. Ibid., 72.

67. David Morgan, *Protestants and Pictures: Religion, Visual Culture, and the Age of American Mass Production* (New York: Oxford University Press, 1999), 123–59.

68. On the complicated topic of millennialism, see Timothy P. Weber, *Living in the Shadow of the Second Coming: American Premillennialism, 1875–1925* (New York: Oxford University Press, 1979); Paul Boyer, *When Time Shall Be No More: Prophecy Belief in American Culture* (Cambridge, Mass.: Harvard University Press, 1992); James H. Moorhead, *World without End: Mainstream American Protestant Visions of the Last Things, 1880–1925* (Bloomington: Indiana University Press, 1999).

69. Steel, "Catalogue," 70.

70. See Richard T. Hughes, ed., *The American Quest for the Primitive Church* (Urbana: University of Illinois Press, 1988); and Richard T. Hughes, ed., *The Primitive Church in the Modern World* (Urbana: University of Illinois Press, 1995).

71. Steel, "Catalogue," 68.

72. Ibid., 76.

73. Michael J. Campbell, *John Martin: Visionary Printmaker* (London: Campbell Fine Art and York City Art Gallery, 1992). For an appreciation of Martin's importance to Victorian culture, see Christine Alexander, "'The Burning Clime': Charlotte Brontë and John Martin," *Nineteenth-Century Literature* 50 (December 1995): 285–321.

74. Richard C. Mühlberger, "Field, Erastus Salisbury," in Wertkin, *Encyclopedia of American Folk Art*, 164–65. See, in particular, Fields's work entitled *Burial of the First Born of Egypt*, reproduced in C. Kurt Dewhurst, Betty MacDowell, and Marsha McDowell, *Religious Folk Art in America* (New York: E. P. Dutton, 1983), 110. For Solomonic circus spectaculars, see William D. Moore, *Masonic Temples: Freemasonry, Ritual Architecture, and Masculine Archetypes* (Knoxville: University of Tennessee Press, 2006), 37–39.

75. Moore, *Masonic Temples*, 84. For fraternal scenery, see C. Lance Brockman, ed., *Theatre of the Fraternity: Staging the Ritual Space of the Scottish Rite of Freemasonry, 1896–1929* (Jackson: University Press of Mississippi, 1996). See also C. Lance Brockman, ed., *The Twin City Scenic Collection: Popular Entertainment, 1895–1980* (Minneapolis: University of Minnesota, University Art Museum, 1987), 96.

76. Jack R. Ludlum, *Master Painter: Warner E. Sallman*. (Macon, Ga: Mercer University Press, 1999).

77. McDannell, *Material Christianity*, 28–31.

78. David Morgan, "Warner Sallman and the Visual Culture of American Protestantism," in *Icons of American Protestantism: The Art of Warner Sallman*, ed. David Morgan (New Haven, Conn.: Yale University Press, 1996), 26.

79. Erika Doss, "Making a 'Virile, Manly Christ': The Cultural Origins and Meanings of Warner Sallman's Religious Imagery,"in Morgan, *Icons of American Protestantism*, 78–82.

80. Ludlum, *Master Painter*, 74–80.

81. Betty A. DeBerg, "The Ministry of Christian Art: Evangelicals and the Art of Warner Sallman, 1942–1960," in Morgan, *Icons of American Protestantism*, 122–47.

82. Ludlum, *Master Painter*, 89–90; Steel, "Catalogue," 54.

83. Morgan, "Warner Sallman and the Visual Culture of American Protestantism," 46.

84. Morgan, *Protestants and Pictures*, 329–37.

85. Ludlum, *Master Painter*, 154.

86. Thomas, "The Life of Reverend McKendree Robbins Long," 33.

87. Morgan, "Warner Sallman and the Visual Culture of American Protestantism," 212n23.

88. Raymond H. Woolsey and Ruth Anderson, *Harry Anderson: The Man Behind the Paintings* (Washington, D.C.: Review and Herald, 1976). See also Kent Steine, "Harry Anderson: The Art of Loose Realism," *American Art Archives*, http://www.americanartarchives.com/anderson,harry.htm (accessed December 29, 2006).

89. For an account of the Adventists' evangelical publishing at the time, see Alonzo L. Baker, *Belief and Work of Seventh-Day Adventists* (Takoma Park, Wash.: Review and Herald, 1942), 39–43.

90. For histories of Adventism, see R. W. Schwarz, *Light Bearers to the Remnant* (Boise: Pacific, 1979); and Gary Land, ed., *Adventism in America: A History* (Grand Rapids, Mich.: William B. Eerdmans, 1986).

91. Gordon McClelland, *Rick Griffin* (New York: Perigree, 1980), 78.

92. *The Gospel of John*, paraphrased by Chuck Smith, illustrated by Rick Griffin (Costa Mesa, Calif.: Maranatha! Music, 1980).

93. See, for example, Kinzer, "Painterly Sermons Mix Severe and Sensual."

94. Piet Schreuders, *The Book of Paperbacks* (London: Virgin, 1981); Thomas L. Bonn, *Undercover: An Illustrated History of American Mass Market Paperbacks* (New York: Penguin, 1982).

95. Many of these covers are reproduced in Frank M. Robinson, *Sci-*

ence Fiction of the 20th Century: An Illustrated History (New York: Barnes and Noble, 1999).

96. For the paint-by-number phenomenon, see William L. Bird Jr., *Paint by Number* (Washington, D.C.: Smithsonian Institution, National Museum of American History, and Princeton Architectural Press, 2001).

97. Brennen Jensen, "Rec Room Rembrandts: Smithsonian Institution Revisits the Artistry and Kitsch of Paint-by-Number," *Baltimore City Paper,* April 18, 2001; Sasha Archibald and David Serlin, "By the Numbers: An Interview with William L. Bird, Jr.," *Cabinet* 15 (Fall 2004), http://www.cabinetmagazine.org/issues/15/paintbynumbers.php (accessed December 29, 2006).

98. Bird, *Paint by Number,* 40–43.

Flannery O'Connor and the Southern Code of Manners

Matthew Day

Arguing that the characteristic American novel, particularly in its southern mode, is based not on class struggles as in Europe but rather on the peculiar institution of race, Matthew Day examines the way in which the work of Flannery O'Connor provides a vocabulary of manners and social distinctions differentiating whites and blacks. Utilizing an enriched literary realism, O'Connor unpacks notions of grace as a kind of moral sensibility embodied in the lives of her literary figures and also as a theological reflection upon fallen humanity's opportunities. Day concludes that O'Connor laments the substitution of the mere forms of grace for its substance. Beyond that, in the complexity of race, O'Connor finds the mystery, the shadows, and the ambiguity that make for great literature.

Lionel Trilling worried that the United States would never produce a classic novel because we lacked the basis for writing one—a European-styled struggle between the ancien régime and the nouveau riche. Since the novel is a historical by-product of the clash between the emerging middle class and the entrenched aristocracy, he reasoned, it is essentially a cultural archive for the vocabulary of manners distinguishing these two classes. Thus, any country lacking economic theater on this grand scale will also lack the catalog of social distinctions that serious literature demands. "American fiction," he wrote in *The Liberal Imagination*, "has nothing to show like the huge, swarming, substantial population of the European novel, the substantiality of which is precisely a product of class existence."[1] Trilling thought that only this vaguely Tocquevillean thesis could explain, among other things, our lingering inability to produce a homegrown Balzac. In this light the United States, rather than living up to Walt Whitman's tender hope, is instead the sort of general literary disappointment about which most families only whisper.

Of course, Trilling was bracingly wrong about America lacking a bona fide class struggle. We might say in hindsight that he mistook a perceived national lack of interest for such matters as evidence of its absence. But what happens if we politely disregard this oversight and choose instead to modify Trilling's underlying Platonism? What if we suggest that alongside the classic European novel there is something like a classic American novel? The idea is nothing new. When Melville sat down to write "Hawthorne and His Mosses" in 1850, he thought we were well on our way to writing it. Then again, Melville tended to be a better propagandist for the nascent American literary tradition than a robust critic. In the twentieth century John Dos Passos quietly suspected that he might have already bagged this mythological creature—but from this distance, he now looks like a brilliant pamphleteer and a second-tier novelist. Yet, ignoring these untimely visions of cultural success, might it still be the case that somewhere along the way the United States shed what Melville once memorably called its "literary flunkyism"?[2] If so, sticking to the Trilling line of thought, the question that must be answered is: What is the American equivalent to European class?

In recent years a number of critics and theorists have suggested that American literature has always been, at bottom, a reflection on our peculiar institution of race. For example, Toni Morrison has argued that we should be rereading the American canon for the "dark and abiding presence that moves the hearts and texts of American literature with fear and longing."[3] I take her point to be that for political, moral, and aesthetic reasons we must observe how our (white) men and women of letters have hired a black or Africanist literary persona to do their narrative dirty work for them. While this suggestion may seem modest at first blush, Morrison is proposing nothing less than a systematic reexamination of how the American canon works as a whole. The hermeneutical ambitions of this project are seen most clearly when we find her arguing that the idea of America itself is a consequence of this Africanist presence. Her thesis is that as the blossoming literary tradition explored the anxieties of political freedom through a language of color, a young and quintessentially (white) American cultural identity was born. "Africanism is the vehicle," Morrison writes, "by which the American self knows itself as not enslaved, but free; not repulsive, but desirable; not helpless, but licensed and powerful; not history-less, but historical; not damned, but innocent; not a blind accident of evolution, but a progressive fulfillment of destiny."[4] From this vantage point, before there could ever be "Walt Whitman, an American," there first had to be a black, nameless, and silent persona to define what it means to not be an American. For this reason, the dominant cultural traditions of the United States rest on the foundations of a literary Africanist presence.

The intelligence and rigor of Morrison's interpretive enterprise is compelling, and her case must be taken seriously. However, one need not accept the grand historical premise that the idea of America depends on an Africanist presence to appreciate how her mindfulness of race reveals a possible answer to our question—particularly when sharpened into a regionally specific claim and read in a certain light. It seems promising to think along with Morrison and argue that for southern literature at least, the American equivalent to European class has indeed been race. So, rather than hearing only the echoes of a provincial class struggle in southern fiction, we should also expect to find a vocabulary of manners and social distinctions differentiating whites from blacks. The challenge is finding a southern author who, to lean on Trilling once more, believes "that scaling the moral and aesthetic heights in literature one has to use the ladder of social observation."[5] I believe this is where a nuanced appreciation of Flannery O'Connor and her relationship to the American canon comes into play.

Despite the traditional proclivity for discussing "the grotesque" in her work, I argue that O'Connor is best read as doing for the American short story what Henry James did for the American novel. That is to say, both writers struggled to take inherited forms of literary realism and, for lack of a better word, enrich them. In the case of James, this enriched realism can be attributed to two narrative talents. First, James tried capturing "the air of reality" through what he called the "solidity of specification," the meticulous description of well-drawn characters set against precisely noted backgrounds.

Or, as he put it in *The Art of Fiction*, the merit upon which all literary merits rest is an author's ability "to render the look of things, the look that conveys their meaning, to catch the colour, the relief, the expression, the surface, the substance of the human spectacle."[6] It is this commitment to "catching the colour" of life itself, for example, which accounts for the obsessive social observations in a novel like *The Bostonians*. Second, James pushed beyond mere description by cultivating an unparalleled power "to guess the unseen from the seen, to trace the implication of things, to judge the whole piece by the pattern." This is a tall order, and reliably intelligent readers like Gore Vidal think he may have pulled it off only in *The Golden Bowl*.[7] Nevertheless, for James the duty of the literary artist could be paraphrased as the commandment: "Become one of the people on whom nothing is lost!" My proposal is that we begin thinking of Flannery O'Connor as this kind of accomplished literary figure, a writer who accepted James's artistic challenge of becoming the sort of person on whom nothing is lost.

As she noted in *Some Aspects of the Grotesque in Southern Fiction*, "every writer, when he speaks of his own approach to fiction, hopes to show that in some crucial and deep sense, he is a realist."[8] Yet, she found herself surrounded by a mid-twentieth-century American literary culture that insisted on a pinched notion of realism that forced ambitious authors to either praise the sober virtues of middle-class families or expose the kinky things those families were doing in their bedrooms. She writes: "We have become so flooded with sorry fiction based on unearned liberties, or on the notion that fiction must represent the typical, that in the public mind the deeper kinds of realism are less and less understandable."[9] O'Connor's artistic search for this *deeper kind* of literary realism is in many ways a Jamesian enterprise because it begins with a scrupulous eye for social manners. Manners are so important for great literature, she once observed in a Jamesian mood, "that any kind will do. Bad manners are better than no manners at all."[10] However, where James became a great writer by quitting the United States and chronicling the lives of displaced, moneyed Americans amid the disintegrating culture of Old Europe, O'Connor came into her own only after she returned to Georgia and began to archive the no less baroque complexities of southern culture. More to the point, O'Connor's fiction has endured the slings and arrows of literary fortunes largely because her writing is knotted with the grainy details of the southern catalog of manners that regulates white-black relations. To my mind few writers have understood so clearly, or represented with such unalloyed artistic force, how southern culture inherits not only the vile history of slavery but also the vast collection of folk traditions that both sides of the color line developed over time. As she commented in 1963:

> It requires considerable grace for two races to live together, particularly when the population is divided about fifty-fifty between them and when they have our particular history. It can't be done without a code of manners based on mutual charity. . . . Formality preserves that individual privacy which everybody needs and, in these times, is always in danger of losing. It's particularly necessary to have in order to protect the rights of both races. When you have a common code of manners based on charity, then when the charity fails—as it is going to do continuously—you've got those manners there to preserve each race from small intrusions upon the other. The uneducated Southern Negro is not the clown he's made out to be. He's a man of very elaborate manners and great formality which he uses superbly for his own protection and to insure his own privacy. . . . The South has survived in the past because its manners, however lopsided or inadequate they may have been, provided enough social discipline to hold us together and give us an identity.[11]

This sensitivity to the southern "code of manners" appears throughout O'Connor's work, but few examples demonstrate her keen eye better than this single sentence describing how two black farmhands speak to their white boss's son: "When they said anything to him, it was as if they were speaking to an invisible body located to the right or left of where he actually was."[12] With an economy of expression that the genre of the short story demands, O'Connor reveals a world where black men receive death sentences simply for looking white men in the eyes. She has, to invoke James's formula, discerned the awful legacy of slavery and the gothic complexity of southern culture in the pattern of this isolated exchange. There is, however, something else about O'Connor's archive of social distinctions that is distinctive: the issue of grace.

For the white women who populate this fictional landscape, the southern code of manners reserves a kind of prearticulate, vernacular model of feminine virtue that might be called "gracious living." This folk ideal of gracious living is closer to what Wittgenstein called a "form of life" than a laundry list of normatively required behaviors. Gracious living is a particular kind of moral sensibility, an ethos that is expressed by the "habits of choice" that O'Connor's characters manifest in every domain of their lives.[13] Manners are, in other words, the embodiment of the southern woman's moral life. In this way, O'Connor shares the canonical literary interest in the personal microcosm of "table manners, toilet habits, conventions of dress . . . and all the other 'decencies' of behavior'" that we find not only in James but also in novelists like Austen, Dickens, and George Eliot.[14] Throughout her writing, I find that O'Connor is pitch-perfect when it comes to fleshing out the details of this enigmatic social virtue. It is, for example, what brings the matriarch of *Everything That Rises Must Converge* to show up at her YMCA "reducing classes" dressed in hat and gloves, and what leads Mrs. Hopewell in *Good Country People* to insist "that people who looked on the bright side of things would be beautiful even if they were not," and the ultimate reason why Mrs. Turpin in *Revelation* puts on her "good patent leather pumps" to take her husband to the doctor.[15] In this portrait of the South a good woman—a *graceful* woman—is one who has cultivated an unflappable sense of propriety and decency. Taken together, as Olympia Dukakis put it in *Steel Magnolias*, these habits of choice demonstrate that "you were brought up right."

In my proposed reading of O'Connor, however, this scrupulous anthropological attention to the particular is more than just a sound art. James liked to say that a novel's *moral significance* depends on the amount of "felt life" it captures, and I think the same thing can be said about O'Connor if we replace *moral significance* with *theological significance*. More pointedly, O'Connor considered the social observation of manners to be one and the same with her Christian literary project because the *artistic* and the *theological* were treated as identical. To see how these two projects dovetailed in her own mind, consider the following passage from *The Teaching of Literature*:

> It is the business of fiction to embody mystery through manners, and mystery is a great embarrassment to the modern mind. About

the turn of the century, Henry James wrote that the young woman of the future, though she would be taken out for airings in a flying-machine, would know nothing of mystery or manners. James had no business to limit the prediction to one sex; otherwise, no one can very well disagree with him. The mystery he was talking about is the mystery of our position on earth, and the manners are those conventions which, in the hands of the artist, reveal that central mystery.[16]

In other words, unlike transparently philosophical writers like Camus and Sartre, who explicitly attend to The Big Idea, with authors like James and O'Connor it is through their attention to narrative detail that the really big questions get asked. Or, as Martha Nussbaum, another Jamesian disciple, is fond of saying: everything about a piece of literature, "the selection of genre, formal structures, sentences, vocabulary . . . all of this expresses a sense of life and of value, a sense of what matters and what does not, of what learning and communicating are, of life's relations and connections."[17] From this perspective, good literature is a morally and, according to O'Connor, theologically salient activity.

This lesson is driven home when we remember that *grace* was a theologically loaded term for O'Connor—it meant God's love for, and forgiveness of, humanity. She insisted throughout her career that the fundamental challenge for any Catholic writer was to discern the presence of grace as it appears in the world; and that as a result, every good story must have "a moment of grace" in which fallen humanity is given an opportunity to be restored. The reason for this is that in her estimation the central mystery of life and literature is the enduring Christian riddle that human existence, "for all its horror, has been found by God to be worth dying for."[18] The hard business of literature was to confront the mysteries of the Christian Incarnation, Crucifixion, and Resurrection through a style that never separated theological concerns from dramatic sensibilities. In all of O'Connor's work, John Updike once observed, there is "the pinpoint tunnel to Jesus at the end of all perspectives."[19]

These wide-ranging commitments make for a lot of balls to keep in the air at once. Nevertheless, in O'Connor's best work she manages to pull off this juggling act, striking the right balance between aesthetic details and theological concerns. In my estimation there is no better example of O'Connor on top of her game than *Revelation*. Painted in broad strokes, the story explores how Mrs. Turpin, a woman who embodies what I've been calling the southern virtue of gracious living, is slowly unhinged after being told to "go back to hell where you come from, you old wart hog."[20] Rather than attempting to rehearse bits and pieces of the story, I have selected a passage where the main themes of the story come together:

> Sometimes at night when she couldn't go to sleep, Mrs. Turpin would occupy herself with the question of who she would have chosen to be if she couldn't have been herself. If Jesus had said to her before he made her, "There's only two places available for you. You can either be a nigger or white-trash," what would she have said? "Please, Jesus, please," she would have said, "just let me wait until there's another place available," and he would have said, "No, you have to go right now and I have only those two places so make up your mind." She would have wiggled and squirmed and begged and pleaded but it would have been no use and finally she would have said, "All right, make me a nigger then—but that don't mean a trashy one." And he would have made her a neat clean respectable Negro woman, herself but black. . . . [Other times] Mrs. Turpin occupied herself at night naming the classes of people. On the bottom of the heap were most colored people, not the kind she would have been if she had been one, but most of them; then next to them—not above, just away from—were the white trash; then above them were the home-owners, and above them the home-and-land owners, to which she and Claud belonged. Above she and Claud were people with a lot of money and much bigger houses and much more land. But here the complexity of it would begin to bear in on her, for some of the people with money were common and ought to be below she and Claud and some of the people with good blood had lost their money and had to rent and then there were colored people who owned their homes and land as well. There was even a colored dentist in town who had two red Lincolns and a swimming pool and a farm with registered white-face cattle on it.[21]

This is classic O'Connor, where indirect theological reflection is effortlessly woven into a densely stratified puzzle of southern culture. To my mind one of the softest literary touches that O'Connor ever displayed appears with the unnamed black dentist, a figure who marks what Nabokov once called the "subliminal co-ordinates" on which a story is plotted.[22] Although he remains the mere suggestion of a character, and in that sense remains what Morrison calls a "dark and abiding presence" in the story, the two red Lincolns and registered whiteface cattle are essential for the Jamesian literary endeavor of capturing a "world so beautifully and so disastrously solid."[23] Another remarkable quality is how quietly she has drawn our attention to the way distinctions based on race and distinctions based on class feed off each other in the South. So instead of a single code of manners separating white from black, there is a vast library of folk traditions used for distinguishing one kind of white from another, as well as one kind of black from another. O'Connor makes this diversity of discriminating criteria explicit when she has Mrs. Turpin state matter-of-factly: "There's a heap of things worse than a nigger. . . . It's all kinds of them just like it's all kinds of us."[24] While the complexity of southern cultural distinctions quickly overwhelms Mrs. Turpin's social imagination, O'Connor has thus far examined only the white side of the equation. A bit later in the story, she gives us a glimpse of the "elaborate manners" the black side of the color line has assembled for its own protection when one of Mrs. Turpin's hired farmhands patronizingly tells her: "She sho shouldn't said nothin ugly to you. . . . You so sweet. You the sweetest lady I know."[25]

Perhaps even more subtle than all of this, however, is the way O'Connor exposes the foul underbelly of the white woman's ideal of gracious living. In O'Connor's fictional world, the form of grace has displaced the substance of grace. That is to say, the sense of grace as attention to the markers of style and decorum has left no room for her substantive, theological understanding of grace as love, charity, and forgiveness. Or, as O'Connor herself once explained: "Often the nature of grace can be made plain only by describing its absence."[26] When considered in this light, the Jamesian aesthetic strategy of thickly describing the cultural meaning of grace is also seen as an attempt to simultaneously draw our attention to the absence of the substantive theological meaning. In fact, through her doggedly Christian narrative voice, O'Connor suggests again and again that the southern ideal of a graceful woman is morally suspect, a tradition that ultimately depends on repugnant distinctions based on race and class. Thus, we find the matriarch of *Everything That Rises Must Converge* looking at the changing landscape of race relations in twentieth-century America and concluding: "They were better off when they were [slaves]. . . . It's ridiculous. It's simply not realistic. They should rise, yes, but on their own side of the fence."[27] This trenchant literary eye leads to O'Connor's complex and ambivalent judgment of the South's enduring cultural institutions. Her writing reveals a political vision that is almost Augustinian in tone, in this case crediting the inherited code of manners for establishing enough discipline to forge a coherent cultural identity while criticizing that ethos because there is very little grace in this form of graceful living.

Yet, unlike some of O'Connor's most dedicated readers, I do not find this theological preoccupation with the graceless forms of modern life to be her lasting contribution to the American canon. In *The Comedy of Redemption*, for example, Ralph Wood submits that O'Connor is an important literary voice because she was more interested in undermining the secular assumption that human dilemmas have human solutions than in addressing any particular injustice. He argues that when it comes to the injustice of southern racism, O'Connor's snapshots of the South are significant because: "They are not moralistic accounts of blacks breaking free from the fetters of racist injustice, nor of whites being condemned for their inability to accept the brave new world of racial equality. They are stories about the grace that makes clowns of us all, liberals no less than reactionaries, the old no less than the young, the genteel no less than the uncouth."[28] In part, I agree with Wood's assessment: O'Connor continues to demand our attention precisely because she refused the easy comforts of moral didacticism. However, I would add that this quality of her writing has more to do with her Jamesian inheritance than her "Catholic" or "theological" heritage. More to the point, I believe that O'Connor is a canonical literary voice— someone worthy of rereading—because she managed to out-James the master himself when it came to capturing the "substance of the human spectacle" in America. From the beginning of our country's literary tradition, American writers have echoed Nathaniel Hawthorne's complaint that one cannot create enduring art in "a country where there is no shadow, no mystery, no picturesque and gloomy wrong, nor anything but a commonplace prosperity, in broad and simple daylight."[29] This image of a crude and simple society, a culture whose most prominent feature is that "the items of high civilization, as it exists in other countries, are absent from the texture of American life," was Trilling's fear and James's conviction.[30] However, where these writers saw nothing but excessive thinness and blankness, O'Connor managed to find in the American South the necessary accumulation of history and custom, manners and types, that great literature requires. Looking back on her work, it does not look like the product of an artist making do with a thinly composed and historically impoverished culture. It is instead a testament to an expansive literary imagination that grasped the significance of a society burdened with the kind of moral complexity that Toni Morrison has asked us to discover in the canon of American literature—the complexity of race.

NOTES

1. Lionel Trilling, *The Liberal Imagination* (New York: Charles Scribner's Sons, 1976), 262.

2. Herman Melville, "Hawthorne and His Mosses," in *Norton Edition of Moby Dick* (New York: Norton, 1967), 546.

3. Toni Morrison, *Playing in the Dark* (New York: Vintage, 1992), 33.

4. Ibid., 52.

5. Trilling, *The Liberal Imagination*, 212.

6. Henry James, *Literary Criticism*, vol. 1 (New York: Library of America, 1984), 53.

7. Gore Vidal, "The Golden Bowl of Henry James," in *United States: Essays 1952–1992* (New York: Random House, 1993): 177–86.

8. Flannery O'Connor, *Mystery and Manners* (New York: Farrar, Straus and Giroux, 1962), 37.

9. Ibid., 37–39.

10. Ibid., 29.

11. Flannery O'Connor, "Flannery O'Connor: An Interview," in *Conversations with Flannery O'Connor*, ed. Rosemary Magee (Jackson: University Press of Mississippi, 1987), 103–4.

12. Flannery O'Connor, *The Complete Stories* (New York: Farrar, Straus and Giroux, 1971), 368.

13. Wayne Booth, *The Company We Keep* (Berkeley: University of California Press, 1988), 8.

14. Gertrude Himmelfarb, *The Demoralization of Society* (New York: Vintage, 1994), 22.

15. O'Connor, *Complete Stories*, 406, 275, 491.

16. O'Connor, *Mystery and Manners*, 124.

17. Martha Nussbaum, *Love's Knowledge* (New York: Oxford University Press, 1990), 5.

18. O'Connor, *Mystery and Manners*, 146.

19. John Updike, *Hugging the Shore* (Hopewell, N.J.: Ecco, 1994), 291.

20. O'Connor, *Complete Stories*, 500.

21. Ibid., 491.

22. Vladimir Nabokov, "On a Book Entitled *Lolita*," in *Lolita* (New York: Vintage, 1955), 316.

23. Lionel Trilling, *Beyond Culture* (New York: Viking, 1965), 195.

24. O'Connor, *Complete Stories*, 495.

25. Ibid., 504.

26. O'Connor, *Mystery and Manners*, 204.

27. O'Connor, *Complete Stories*, 408.

28. Ralph Wood, *The Comedy of Redemption* (Notre Dame, Ind.: University of Notre Dame Press, 1988), 113.

29. Nathaniel Hawthorne, Preface to *The Marble Faun; or, The Romance of Monte Beni*, in *The Centenary Edition of the Works of Nathaniel Hawthorne*, 10 vols., ed. William Charvat et al. (Columbus: Ohio State University Press, 1962–1980), 4:3.

30. James, *Literary Criticism*, 351.

ENCOUNTERS IN SOUTHERN RELIGION AND CULTURE

MEETINGS AT THE BUDDHIST TEMPLE

Signposts to a Changing South

BARBARA LAU

Religious diversity is an increasingly familiar aspect of religious life in the South. Since 1985 Greensboro, North Carolina, has been home to a Theravada Buddhist community composed of refugees from Cambodia and Laos. More recently, American converts have joined these cradle Buddhists, and a temple complex with resident monks has grown up on the ten-acre site. In her ethnographic examination of this religious community, Barbara Lau explores how these Tar Heel Buddhists—now both Southeast Asian and southern—have had to make adjustments to traditional religious practices in their new religious context. Unpacking the variety of levels influenced by this fascinating example of cultural and religious blending, Lau places this Buddhist community in the evolving religious landscape of the South.

WOOD FOR SALE. It is a small sign made of plywood, painted white with red letters. Nailed to a short stake, it is stuck in the ground next to the driveway. Across the pavement a larger sign, mounted on much taller posts, reads: GREENSBORO BUDDHIST CENTER. WAT GREENSBORO. Made of carefully joined pine boards, its raised letters are painted gold. Above it, the stars and stripes of an American flag fly next to an orange Buddhist wheel of life on a background of yellow. Straddling the driveway, these simple identifying markers signify an intriguing, perhaps unexpected, set of invitations to pass-

Fig. 1. Coming around the curve on Liberty Road, visitors can easily find the Buddhist temple. Photo by Cedric N. Chatterley, © 2001.

ersby. Their juxtaposition also reveals an emerging synchronicity between a deeply vernacular culture and a Buddhist worldview on the southern landscape. Many years ago, as I passed between these two signs for the first time, I probably didn't take much notice. But the significant ways they would shape my time and understanding of a new community and its search for points of cultural intersection would soon become evident.

Phramaha Somsak Sambimb, a Buddhist monk, had arrived a few years before my first visit to serve the Southeast Asian refugees who made their way to the South from poverty-stricken and war-torn Cambodia and Laos. He found himself on the residential fringes of Greensboro, North Carolina, among a community of Buddhists struggling with a new language and a new economy in a predominantly Christian environment. In 1992, a research interest in ethnicity and dance brought me to the Greensboro Buddhist Center and my first meeting with the monk. I learned that Theravada Buddhism is the predominant religion in Cambodia, Laos, Thailand, Burma, and Sri Lanka. Buddhist practice, Sambimb explained, is a belief system of values, ethics, and morals that guide day-to-day living. Following the teachings of the Buddha, these believers embrace characteristics such as compassion, forgiveness, generosity, gratitude, and respect for elders. The Buddhist philosophy, symbolized by the wheel of life, promotes ideas about reincarnation and karma—actions and thoughts in one's lifetime impact lifetimes to come on the journey to enlightenment, a state of spiritual purity. In the American context, Buddhist beliefs provide key survival strategies for many Cambodians and Laotians as they recover from the trauma of war and face the challenges of resettlement. Learning more about this history, I began to understand some of the ways that Buddhism was going to operate in the lives of these new southerners. My ethnographic research began with an exploration of the process that initially brought these refugees to North Carolina.

By design, Lutheran Family Services, the resettlement organization, placed the newly arrived Cambodian and Lao families in small clusters, in apartments or rental houses a few minutes' walk from one another, instead of creating a village environment by consolidating everyone in a single apartment complex or housing development. While this strategy may have minimized potential backlash from the larger community to the arriving foreigners, it simultaneously created a need for a place for the new arrivals to gather, socialize, and, most important, to worship.

Establishing a temple was a high priority for these new North Carolina communities, but a temple is only a building without monks. Monks are integral to the practice of Theravada Buddhism. In this socioreligious system, the people of the community are responsible for providing for all of the monks' earthly needs. In exchange, the monks provide for the spiritual needs of the community. As scholar Robert Lester explains, "The monk exists to support the lay society as much as the layman exists to support the monk. The layman and monk define each other's existence, exist for each other, and are catalysts to each other's way of life. By his purity and wisdom the monk moves the layman to acts of charity, respect, and reliance which in turn 'activate' the monk to compassionate service to society. That which characterizes the Theravada way of life is neither the way of the monk nor the way of the laity but the interaction, the reciprocation between the two."[1] So, to continue being Buddhists, the community needed both a sacred place and religious leadership.

The Southeast Asians in Greensboro were painfully aware of this and made great efforts to locate monks for their new temple.

Finding religious leadership, however, proved difficult for several reasons. First, there was a shortage of Khmer- and Lao-speaking Buddhist monks. Many had been forced to leave the monkhood or were executed during the 1970s. The monks who survived were in great demand. The Southeast Asian communities in Greensboro were small and not particularly wealthy. In Greensboro, a monk, in addition to encountering all of the same challenges and adjustments faced by other refugees, might have to live alone at the temple, whereas customarily, many monks reside in each temple. These circumstances made the job even more difficult and perhaps less appealing to monks who might also have the option to serve in a larger, more established community that had the resources to support several monks.

Established by the Khmer Aid Group of the Triad, the Buddhist Center first purchased property in 1986 with a generous downpayment grant from the Z. Smith Reynolds Foundation. The Buddhist community was facing a monthly mortgage payment, utility bills, and the property taxes on a house and the land surrounding it. A monk would provide a focal point for fund-raising efforts. And without a monk, the community could not hold the calendrical Buddhist ceremonies.

The community limped along for several years, recruiting monks from Thailand or from other U.S. cities, who would come and stay in Greensboro for several months but then leave the monkhood or move to another temple. These failures disheartened many. Temple leader Kep Kong remembers that time: "No monk, nobody pay money, no ceremony in here. So I go to get one monk, his name is Duong Chang, to help me. That time we had a Lao monk, cannot speak Cambodia. Thai monk cannot speak Cambodia, and Sri Lanka monk, cannot speak Cambodia, come to stay in the temple. Until we have Maha Somsak come."[2]

Phramaha Somsak Sambimb responded to a request to come to Greensboro from Washington, D.C., to help conduct a Buddhist ceremony. Sambimb grew up bilingual, speaking both Thai and Khmer—the predominant language of Cambodia—and later he learned to speak Lao. He received the title Phramaha after passing a series of tests about Buddhism and Buddhist scripture. He could have become a professor at Buddhist University in Thailand, but he had always been interested in working directly with people, and he saw a need for his services in Greensboro. A weekend visit turned into a life's commitment. Later evaluating the situation that had faced him in Greensboro when he arrived in 1989, Sambimb shared his philosophy:

> I not blame the people, I not blame anybody. I not blame the Buddhist monk because Buddhist monk depend on the people, the people depend on the Buddhist monk. We have to come together, the temple and the house, or the people. We have to come together, help each other, support each other, like try to cultivate more harmony. That the big problem for temple, you know, because temple have no budget, nothing, you know, except the donation from the people, and the leader is mean, the monk. Each temple have to be strong enough, and, you know, more patient, more tolerant, you know, for how to unite the people together? That hard, you know.[3]

With exceptional skill and courage, Sambimb succeeded in bringing the people together. Since 1989, he has marshaled enough resources to double the size of the temple grounds with the purchase of an adjacent house and lot. Together, he and his supporters have created a home for the Southeast Asian community. He is very serious when he considers the temple a "home" for the community. Sambimb believes that this is a very traditional and important role for the temple in the lives of Southeast Asians: "I can tell you that the temple in our meaning looks like the second home for the people. So the temple should have everything, to provide the way for the people, in the peace way. We try to provide whatever is possible here to let the people understand, here, it look like their country."[4]

An indicator of the community's success, Wat Greensboro marked its twentieth anniversary in 2005. Its membership—"cradle" Buddhists from Cambodia, Laos, and Thailand—were fishermen and farmers who now support their families through factory work and small businesses. Much has changed in their lives, but these growing families have also had an impact on the greater Greensboro community. In addition to shopping at the local Food Lion or Harris Teeter, Greensboro residents, refugees and longtime Americans alike, now check the shelves of Asian markets, tucked into strip malls and stocked with dried fish, vegetables, spices, jasmine rice, and cooking utensils—the immigrants to procure materials required for their kitchens, and the Americans to prepare their new favorite Asian recipes. Southeast Asians are also joined by Americans in their purchases of the distinctly aromatic incense, beeswax candles, and golden statues central to a Buddhist religious practice.

On most days, Southeast Asian teenagers arrive at school dressed in popular American street-style clothes, speaking English laced with the slang they hear on television—a stark juxtaposition to the Khmer or Lao language spoken at home. Many of these students' parents have become longtime employees in the furniture and textile industries that hug Interstate 85, one of the Piedmont region's primary transportation corridors. Occasionally, their early-rising neighbors witness Cambodian wedding processions: drummers, family members carrying trays heaped with gifts, and a groom walking under an umbrella supported by his attendants, wending their way along streets lined with brick ranchers and late-model cars. Some of those neighbors receive invitations to the wedding receptions, at which the brides and grooms are attired in white, American-style wedding dresses and crisp tuxedos.

Like familial traditions, Buddhist ceremonies are also subject to the influence of the "American" context. The calendar of ceremonies has had to change to accommodate American work schedules, and so most holidays are now celebrated on Sundays. In addition, certain ceremonies require several monks and so are planned for successive weekends at temples in different cities throughout the state so that each celebration has the appropriate number of monks. Changing these dates has also resulted in changing communications strategies. Instead of people going to the monks or the astrologers to learn the date of a ceremony, an annual calendar listing Buddhist ceremonies is now created on the temple's computer for distribution to Southeast Asian and American community members. Many temples now employ Web sites as communications tools as well.

These changes have put pressure on the monks to reexamine and in some cases change their roles. For example, the monks have had to learn to drive cars, a practice generally unacceptable in their homelands, in order to pick students up from school or to transport elders to medical appointments. The monks cannot walk from

Fig. 2. In the shadow of a pagoda built to provide an appropriate space for funerals, Phramaha Somsak Sambimb uses a small tractor to move brush. Photo by Cedric N. Chatterley, © 2002.

house to house each morning collecting alms as they do in Southeast Asia, so they must rely upon the laypeople to bring food to the temple. Most important, Phramaha Sambimb has seen his attention shift from a primarily inward focus on the temple and religious contemplation to duties that require him to spend more time directed outward to the larger community. "The monk have to help the community, help all people who need help. I give them everything, whatever, guidance, whatever they need, even take them somewhere see doctor, see unemployment, see apply for a job, do something like contact with lawyer, go to hospital. That one way to keep them, empower them, you know."[5]

At the temple, Sambimb has also played an important role in creating educational opportunities that reflect the needs of growing Southeast Asian American families. Cultural education classes in dance, music, language, and Buddhism have been offered after school, on weekends, and during summer vacations for boys and girls. Families no longer work together in the fields or on the waterways, and children cannot simply walk home as their parents did.

Great efforts have been made to locate teachers and support the transmission of traditional Khmer and Lao cultural knowledge to the next generation.

One important rite of passage for young men in Theravada Buddhist cultures involves spending some time serving as a novice monk. Growing into manhood, these young monks learn about religious philosophy, personal responsibility, and community traditions. In Southeast Asia, this experience also provides young men with educational opportunities they might otherwise not have received. In the United States, many Cambodian families feel this experience is an essential stepping-stone to adulthood. "We want him to become a novice [monk] because we want him to know about our Khmer traditions, to know this is Buddhism," explains Chhorn Chiep, the father of a high school–aged boy. "It's to understand life. From ancient times, Khmer boys have to be novices."[6]

For several weeks, months, or even years, young Khmer boys become monks to honor their parents and to learn how to be good men. They are initiated in an elaborate ceremony in which they don

Fig. 3. Chamroeun Kong and Johny Sitha Ksa cut firewood and learn to meditate as part of their training as novice monks at the Buddhist temple. Photo by Cedric N. Chatterley, © 2002.

the monk's orange robe and take on a religious life. They learn to meditate and control their emotions. They learn to chant in Pali, the ancient language associated with the written Sanskrit used in Buddhist holy scriptures. They discipline their bodies through hard work and modest meals served only in the morning hours, and they learn humility by living in debt to the generosity of others.

For some families, this kind of cultural education has saved young men who had drifted into violence, drug use, or gang involvement. Savoeun San's brother Savon is one example. Several years ago, Savon Thach moved to Greensboro from Long Beach, California, the largest Cambodian community in the United States. He had become embroiled in street fighting, gambling, and illegal behavior. "My older brother, Saphon Sok, he lectured the thug out of our brother Savon. He made him realize he's Khmer, and going to the gangster life is not the life that you want to live. After Savon quit school, he came over to the temple and started to be a monk."[7] Finding a very traditional solution to a modern problem, some families have even sent their sons to Cambodia to live in village temples, helping them find an internal fortitude in the disciplined life demanded by the monastic rules of Theravada Buddhism. This choice suggests that embracing Buddhism more deeply can help these young men be more successful in a non-Buddhist environment. They no longer need the robes to remind them of the core values this simple cotton cloth represents.

The saffron-robed monks may be one of the most iconic ways Buddhism is seen on the southern landscape. However, after two decades, they no longer draw the curious eyes of neighbors when they check the mailbox, a welcome change from earlier days, when vandals targeted the property with verbal taunts and destructive actions or hailed Phramaha Sambimb on the street as "Mr. Big Handkerchief."

The changing attitudes of the neighbors are linked in important ways to physical changes made to the temple grounds by hard-working monks and laypeople, modifications to make it "look like their country." Exerting his astute leadership, Phramaha Sambimb knew that working to create a truly "Buddhist" space, an effort that could be viewed by some as a challenge to the Judeo-Christian hegemony of a Bible Belt state, could instead offer multiple invitations and opportunities for social, economic, and spiritual engagement.

From the road, the two houses that front the temple grounds resemble the other homes on the street; their southern-style facades act as a buffer to the passing traffic and neighborhood curiosity. Temple leadership wisely chose a path of harmony with the neighborhood by making few changes to the outward faces of the houses. Decisions about paint colors and landscaping were often influenced by a desire not to offend the existing residential aesthetic. Ceremonial needs have, however, significantly reshaped the two houses and ten acres of land that now make up the Greensboro Buddhist Center. In the early 1990s, the number of people attending temple ceremonies outgrew the small concrete patio behind the house on the initial property. With money raised from the community and tremendous sweat equity, the patio roof was extended and a larger concrete floor was poured, creating a covered space, or *sala,* that could accommodate several hundred people. Ceiling fans made the space more comfortable and an outdoor food preparation area relieved overcrowding in the small indoor kitchen. After the adjacent property was purchased, half of the open field between the two houses became an overflow parking lot, while the other half was groomed as a ceremonial ground to accommodate the growing number of Buddhist celebrants. This expansion was welcomed by many neighbors, who had been inconvenienced by the ad hoc parking strategies and traffic jams on Buddhist holidays in the past.

Phramaha Sambimb has also added a number of visual Buddhist elements to the Greensboro temple, often in a simple, symbolic fashion that identifies the space as Buddhist but does not offend or confront neighbors and outsiders. For example, he affixed an eight-spoke Buddhist wheel of life to the front exterior face of the temple. This symbol also appears in orange on the small yellow flags stretched on strings between buildings and trees across the property on ceremonial days. In 1995 Sambimb learned how to weld metal pipe, and together with An Heng, a skilled builder, constructed metal gateways and wooden Buddhist wheels to create symbolic entryways into the sala. The acute angle of the gate frames is reminiscent of the soaring rooflines of Southeast Asian temples, offering a subtle but powerful reminder that crossing these thresholds signifies entrance to a sacred Buddhist space. These small but key additions to a typical southern "homeplace" are analogous to the impact that the growing Southeast Asian community is having on the larger social

Fig. 4. This simple temple gate welcomes worshippers to the *sala*, or gathering place, at the Greensboro Buddhist Center. Photo by Cedric N. Chatterley, © 2000.

landscape. They also mark the temple as a place open to all Buddhists, be they Khmer, Lao, Thai, Vietnamese, or American.

The altars at the Greensboro Buddhist Center reflect new approaches and new attitudes in the community of practitioners as well. On the stepped platforms that support the altar, Buddha statues imported from Thailand are surrounded by Cambodian *mak bang* (flower sculptures made of folded paper) and Lao umbrella trees. This is quite unusual, even in the United States, where most temples are identified with a single nationality or ethnic group. Finding ways to bridge these divides concerns Southeast Asians now living in diaspora communities across the globe. A shared Buddhist heritage and the annual calendar of ceremonies offer many Southeast Asians the opportunity to build upon their commonalities and quiet the history of ethnic and national boundaries and forces that divide them. Many Americans do not differentiate between those of Lao, Thai, Cambodian, and Vietnamese heritage (or indeed, on occasion, Chinese, Japanese, Korean, Hmong, Filipino, Hawaiian, Tongan, or Montagnard), lumping them together as pan-Asian. Given the small size of these communities, developing alliances across these boundaries could have important political benefits in the future.

In Southeast Asia, temples are encircled by thick stone and concrete walls. With a similar intent, chain-link and wooden privacy fencing was chosen to surround the Greensboro temple, defining the sacred space using materials common to the local landscape. Each of these additions and improvements was made possible by the hard work, ingenuity, skill, and self-reliance of the monks and community members—work-ethic values often shared, and increasingly recognized, by their southern neighbors.

Many of these changes were gradual—the transformation of the grounds into a Buddhist temple was a process I witnessed over the course of many visits and many years. I didn't always understand what I was participating in; the seemingly simple activity of cutting and selling firewood was one whose deeper implications it took me a long time to really understand. In the mid-1990s I was able to spend several months making daily visits to the temple. I knew that spending time with Phramaha Sambimb meant doing whatever he was doing and assisting him in whatever way I could. I drove him all over the state, sometimes with other monks from other temples, to weddings and funerals, to home ceremonies, to the hardware store. And we worked wood. At that time he was expanding the temple's garden plots and building henhouses. He began to pull downed trees out of the wooded sections at the rear of the grounds, cutting them into stove-sized lengths and splitting them for firewood. He learned how to use chainsaws, taught me how to sharpen them, and, after borrowing a mechanical splitter from the family next door, purchased one for the temple's use. In addition to creating resources valuable to the larger community, he was stoking the woodstoves that warmed the temple houses. Through this process, he found ways to communicate with his new neighbors around a common interest and repaid their friendliness with stacks of neatly cut wood. Before they knew it, they were building relationships and in some cases doing business. To repay a local tree-service company for taking down a few big trees he could not handle, the monk allowed them to drop off trees and branches from other job sites. More downed trees meant more wood. It began to stack up. Two other monks whom Phramaha Sambimb had known in Thailand came to live in Greensboro, one of whom possessed extensive skills as a carpenter.

Together, we built lean-to–style sheds to keep the growing wood-piles out of the rain. The piles were everywhere and they kept multiplying. Young people from the Cambodian community were often enlisted to assist us with the splitting and stacking. Heating with wood saved money, often in short supply during those years. The monk explains, "You know I saw a lot of wood. I not want to throw away, I want to share to warm the neighbor, like share the warm for the people and sell some for my gas, for my electricity, I have to do that way. We don't have enough money for support the temple, so what way can we do, I think useful, yeah."[8] After a while, the monks had much more wood than they could use or give away—and I had much stronger muscles.

The sign advertising wood for sale was installed at the temple's front gate. It was an invitation open to anyone passing by to stop in, stock up on firewood, and in the process meet the Buddhists. Many people accepted the invitation, but Sambimb's aim was to do more than sell firewood. He wanted a chance to talk to people, to help them understand who he was and what he was doing in North Carolina. To keep his customers coming back and the conversation flowing, his strategy was "you know, they buy one, I give them two free, I give more than friendly."[9] He understood that building social relationships might be challenging, especially with the working-class neighbors who bought wood by the truckload. Commerce was often accompanied by conversations, sometimes tough ones about religious beliefs—but selling wood, engaging in business, building mutual dependence, being generous and self-reliant: these were strategies with currency, strategies that enabled the monk to engage with the heart of the population, not just the middle-class social workers, resettlement volunteers, and school officials who took the initiative to visit the temple.

This is not to say that all of the interactions in the temple's driveway at that time were positive. Along with adding a traditional element to the temple grounds, the fence was necessary to protect the community inside from visitors with less than honorable intentions. Pranks and serious threats have lived alongside the more respectful and friendly interactions between the larger community and the temple. Sambimb attributes much of this to ignorance, a lack of exposure to Buddhism, and to fears about people from different cultures. I was involved in one difficult conversation while the monk and I were shopping one day at the local hardware store. A woman, who I later learned lived very near the temple, approached me and blurted out, "You his wife?" I tried to explain to her that Buddhist monks were forbidden to marry, but she had another agenda. She followed with, "I just can't understand why he doesn't accept Jesus Christ as his Lord and Savior." No amount of explaining would appease her, and I learned that this discussion was an ongoing one, that she came by to "talk" to the monks on a regular basis.

But two decades of quiet persistence have reaped rewards. As Phramaha Sambimb reveals, "And now they know me, they know who I am and they know what I am doing here and they understand what I am doing here, so they treat me very well, whatever I need them to do and I want to do something for the temple, they very good cooperation with me. I think everything better, better, better every year. Even the neighbor in this area."[10]

To cement his connections and to express his good intentions toward the neighbors, Phramaha Sambimb has made good use of the food, herbs, and fruit grown in the temple gardens and orchards. Sharing food with the neighbors is a deeply southern tradition, one that engenders reciprocity and embraces a vernacular culture built on generosity, humility, tolerance, and self-reliance. He has found a way to "give back" to the larger community, to counteract ideas about immigrants as "takers" who should be feared and sent back to their homelands. Metaphorically, he is using food and wood to nourish understanding, to help grow relationships, and to clear new roads of communication. And he did all of this without asking for help or handouts, subsidies or charity.

Sambimb has also managed to pass this sentiment on to the next generation, whose members are not merely looking at what being in America can do for them. "So we come to America," twenty-year-old Ran Kong explained, "and we have nothing. We carry nothing with us from Cambodia. All that we have is ourselves and our culture." Like many others of her generation seeking to distinguish themselves and their communities within the American cultural mosaic, Ran asked, "What can we give back to America? What can we show Americans about us? Like, try to teach that we're more than just refugees, or that we're more than just immigrants. You know, that we have more than just the Khmer Rouge to make us important in this world."[11]

One of these givebacks is Buddhism. Many Americans have crossed the temple gate to learn more, finding its ancient philosophy relevant to their lives. For more than twenty years, Americans have interacted with these immigrants—at work, in school, and in their neighborhoods—but it has only been more recently that Americans have in greater numbers sought spiritual connection. The Buddhism in North Carolina Project, created by students in 2001 at the University of North Carolina at Chapel Hill, began mapping the changing religious landscape of the state. To date they have documented more than thirty temples and seventy-five Buddhist communities with histories that date to the late 1970s. Their work reveals that "Buddhism has come to the land of barbeque, Baptists, and basketball."[12]

At first, I saw other Americans only during the annual New Year festival at the Greensboro Buddhist Center. They were often friends and coworkers, teachers and neighbors who had been invited to share in the food and fun of the day. But their numbers have grown, and they are beginning to arrive with a different kind of curiosity. On a Buddhist altar, the candles represent the "dharma," or teachings of the Buddha, the light that shines in the darkness of life's suffering. As the monk sees it, "That why I say now the sun is rise in the West, you know, they rise with it, because most Western people, they study Buddhism and not only study, some of them they just become a monk, they practice meditation, they do something more by Buddhist way. They happy to do that because that is the real peace, you know."[13]

More and more Americans are arriving in search of that "peace" and instruction in meditation and Buddhist philosophy. For a while the temple was offering meditation classes every Sunday evening and the classes were growing, but proficiency in English has proved to be a bit of a barrier. The monk who led these classes was an American who had studied and been ordained in Thailand. He was later called to live at a Lao temple in High Point, North Carolina, but in his place two other Americans chose to become monks and live at the Greensboro temple. Unfortunately, they are not yet knowledgeable enough to lead these classes, and Phramaha Sambimb does not feel prepared to maintain the weekly instruction schedule. He does, however, encourage anyone who is interested to learn how to practice meditation, and to embrace Buddhist ethics, the Four

Fig. 5. Folklorist Barbara Lau confers with Phramaha Somsak Sambimb at the Greensboro Buddhist Center. Photo by Cedric N. Chatterley, © 2006.

Noble Truths and the five precepts—abstinence from killing, lying, stealing, sexual misconduct, and drinking fermented beverages. In response to a recent question about how Buddhism may have affected Greensboro, he replied, "We can say that we add a little bit, not more. But anybody who comes to study Buddhism, they change their mind, they change everything. The one who used to drink, they stop drinking, used to do bad thing, do bad, say bad, now they stop. I think that change, yeah. It useful, you know, they change, that Buddhism."[14]

Buddhism has come to the American South in the minds and hearts of immigrant practitioners and through converts who have found its spiritual philosophy in books, lectures, retreats, and pilgrimages. True believers like Phramaha Somsak Sambimb have carved out a place for Buddhism to live in harmony within an evolving southern religious landscape. Using the land itself, he has transformed the social web of his Greensboro, North Carolina, neighborhood with wood and vegetables. His successes may seem small, but they are deeply significant. Recently, a young African American woman arrived at the temple gate. She had grown up in the neighborhood adjacent to the temple's back fence. As a teenager, she and her friends regularly pushed through that fence, to play and party among the temple's trees and to taunt the ducks living on the pond. Despite Phramaha Sambimb's efforts to reason with these teens, their families, and their pastors, the vandalism continued. As he would have when she was a teenager if she had presented herself, he welcomed the young woman at the temple that day. He offered her food and his time. She had come to apologize, to acknowledge her wrongdoing and to ask for forgiveness, which, of course, she received. This small act speaks loudly. It confirms the common ground between faiths, realizing the potential that nurturing relationships and understanding across difference can inspire true enactments of the values those faith traditions share. Taking responsibility for past transgressions and receiving forgiveness and redemption allow us to hold each other in the light of dignity and respect.

NOTES

1. Robert C. Lester, *Theravada Buddhism in Southeast Asia* (Ann Arbor: University of Michigan Press, 1973), 130–31.

2. Kep Kong, interview with the author, Greensboro, N.C., April 24, 2000.

3. Phramaha Somsak Sambimb, interview with the author, Greensboro, N.C., April 15, 1997.

4. Ibid.

5. Phramaha Somsak Sambimb, interview with the author, Greensboro, N.C., October 25, 2006.

6. Chhorn Chiep, interview with the author, Greensboro, N.C., December 21, 2002.

7. Savoeun San, interview with the author, Greensboro, N.C., June 1, 2003.

8. Sambimb, interview, October 25, 2006.

9. Ibid.

10. Ibid.

11. Ran Kong, interview with the author, Greensboro, N.C., November 25, 2000.

12. See the project Web site: http://www.unc.edu/ncbuddhism/index.html.

13. Sambimb, interview, October 25, 2006.

14. Ibid.

FEEDING THE JEWISH SOUL IN THE DELTA DIASPORA

MARCIE COHEN FERRIS

Adaptations in folkways and foodways are often realities in trans-planted cultures. Identity arising from more than one world re-sults in complicated negotiations, nowhere more evident than in the food prepared for family and friends. "Eating is inseparable from religion," writes Marcie Cohen Ferris, and in Judaism, she continues, the act of eating is both communication and commu-nion. Her essay demonstrates the applicability of food as an index to place, kinship, occupation, race, and Jewish-Gentile relations.

Mention "The Delta" and vivid images come to mind of a dramatic, flat landscape etched by rows of cotton and bounded by the Missis-sippi River. One imagines catfish, juke joints, barbecue, and pickup trucks in a world inhabited by white planters, poor white share-croppers, and black blues musicians. Although the Mississippi and Arkansas Delta is largely populated by black and white working-class laborers and upper-class white landowners, the region is also shaped by a small group of Jewish southerners, now numbering no more than three hundred, whose families first arrived in the Delta in the late nineteenth century as peddlers and fledgling merchants.[1] Between the Mississippi River levee and Highway 61, amidst the shotgun houses, cotton fields, and Baptist churches of the Delta, are a handful of synagogues, Jewish cemeteries, Jewish-owned clothing stores, and businesses that were central to the economies of small Delta towns prior to the coming of discount stores like Wal-Mart. Less visible but nonetheless present are the adapted folklore and foodways of a transplanted culture, for feeding the Jewish soul, both spiritually and physically, has challenged Delta Jews from their first arrival in the region through today.

In the town of Blytheville in the Arkansas Delta, my family's Jewish identity separated us from our white and black Gentile neighbors. Contrary to popular belief, this division was more respectful than mean-spirited. Biblical identification of Jews as the "chosen people" carries weight in the South; because of our distant lineage to Moses, Jewish families had a special status in the Delta. Although there were violent incidents of antisemitism such as the 1960s temple bombings in Jackson and Meridian, Mississippi, most antisemitic expressions were far more benign actions such as exclusion from debutante parties, garden clubs, country clubs, and occasional comments about Jewish tightfistedness. My family attended synagogue—known to non-Jewish locals as "the Jewish church"—and offered up prayers to a deity, which helped to secure our acceptance in town. More than Judaism, it was the fact that we had not *always* lived in the community that separated us from the Gentiles. Because generations of history did not intimately link "our people" with "their people," our place in the local hierarchy of white society was never clear.[2]

My Jewish ancestors arrived in the Delta in the early 1920s. We lived within the Delta world of cotton planting, fall ginning, church socials, and football and the Jewish world of weekly Sabbath services, visiting rabbis, and preparation for the Passover seder in the spring and the High Holy Days of Rosh Hashanah and Yom Kippur in the fall. We ate *between* these two worlds in a complicated culinary negotiation of regional, ethnic, and religious identity. Within Jewish homes in the Delta, African American cooks and domestic workers set bountiful tables and prepared the cuisine for which the region is famous. Their meals featured elegant dinners of standing rib roast, as well as down-home southern Gentile meals of barbecue and fried catfish. Less familiar dishes served at Jewish tables in the Delta included matzah balls, kugels (dairy casserole), tortes, and tzimmes (baked sweetened vegetables and fruits), foods that tied Jewish worlds to central and eastern Europe.

Food writer Craig Claiborne was "initiated into the joys" of Jewish foods in the home of Sadie Wolf, who lived across the street from the Claiborne family in Indianola, Mississippi. Claiborne recalls visiting the Wolfs' home one Passover when daughter Anita had eaten her fill of traditional holiday foods. "If somebody feeds me one more matzah ball I'm going to kill them," protested Wolf. As Claiborne recalls in his memoir, it was the "talent and palate" of African American cooks who blended "soul food"—a mix of African and American Indian flavors—with creole cuisine that made the southern kitchen unique.[3] Although separated by a gulf of race and class, African Americans and Jews in the Mississippi and Arkansas Delta were brought together by a culinary exchange that has existed since the late nineteenth century.

Throughout the nation food strongly defines ethnic and regional identity. But in the South, and especially in the Delta, a region scarred by war, slavery, and the aftermath of Reconstruction and segregation, food is especially important. Historian David Blight suggests that the South was conquered during the Civil War, and afterwards the slow process of rebuilding and "re-imagining" the South began. Blight contends that while the South is no richer in history and memory than any other region, more of its collective energy is devoted to defining the past through literature, storytelling, and monument-making.[4] We should add food traditions to this list, because southerners also use food to define the history of their region. For generations, southerners, including southern Jews, have struggled to understand their experience through memory-making, and much of that struggle takes place at the dinner table. In this tradition Delta Jews connect to family and regional history at every meal, Oneg Shabbat, and Sisterhood luncheon.

Food historian Joan Nathan argues that because of their "wandering history" Jews always adapted their lifestyles and foodways to local cultures. Apart from matzah (the Passover unleavened bread), *haroset* (the Passover apple and nut spread), and *cholent* (a traditional slow-cooked Sabbath stew), she argues that there are no specifically Jewish foods; rather, foods are associated with Jewish countries of origin. Since more than two-thirds of American Jews trace their roots to eastern Europe, Polish and Russian foods such as rye bread, borscht, and herring in sour cream became known as Jewish foods in America.[5] Eastern European Jews were not the only Jews to learn to "make do or do without" while adjusting their tastes to regional food traditions and local ingredients. Earlier waves of Sephardic and Ashkenazic Jews left many culinary traditions in the Old World, but not all. After arriving in the South, Jewish immigrants revived their memories of stewed fish dishes flavored with lemon, olive oil, and almonds, bean soups, roasted goose, duck, chicken, kugels, challahs, kuchens (coffee cake), and tortes. Jewish women gave these recipes to African American cooks, who integrated these dishes into the culinary tradition of the South.

From the handful of Conservative and Orthodox Jews in the Delta, who closely adhere to the Jewish dietary rules, or *kashrut*, to the most liberal Reform Jews, who do not recognize these culinary restrictions, eating is inseparable from religion. Anthropologists, folklorists, and food historians agree that food is invested with symbolic meaning and that any food-related activity—from a simple meal at home to the most elaborate public celebration—is an act of communication.[6] In Judaism, food is both communication and communion. This concept is central to understanding the power of food in ethnic and regional communities like the Delta.

For observant Jews, eating is an act of divine law dictated from the Bible and expanded in the Talmud, the ancient rabbinic commentaries related to the Torah, the first five books of the Bible. As Blu Greenberg, an orthodox *rebbetzin* (wife of a rabbi) and an authority on the precepts of traditional Jewish life, explains, "Kashrut is not simply a set of rules about permitted and forbidden foods; kashrut is a way of life."[7] This way of life determines which foods are prohibited, how certain foods should be prepared, and how animals should be slaughtered. For example, Jews are allowed to eat meat only from animals that chew their cud and have cloven hooves, fish that have both fins and scales, and no combinations of dairy and meat dishes. Even this rudimentary explanation of kashrut hints at the predicament of Jews in the Delta, who are surrounded by a cuisine that celebrates *treyfe* (nonkosher) foods like pork, catfish, shrimp, crawfish, and wild game such as rabbit, squirrel, and deer. (Catfish is not kosher because it has no scales and is a nocturnal scavenger.)

Less observant Jews in the Delta ignore kashrut and eat Jewish foods like bagel and lox on Sunday morning as their only expression of Jewishness, a practice referred to as "kitchen Judaism."[8] For Delta Jews who position themselves between these two poles of observance, daily choices about food either connect them to or distance them from their Jewish identity. Thus, one encounters Jews who enjoy a pork barbecue sandwich at restaurants but avoid serving or eating pork at home. Some Jewish families keep separate dishes at home for serving nonkosher foods like shrimp and pork barbecue so that the "regular" dishes are not tainted by these forbidden foods—a "southernism" of kashrut that requires separate sets of dishes for meat and dairy items.

Sylvia Klumok Goodman and her sister Ann Klumok Bennett grew up in the Delta town of Moorhead, Mississippi, where their African American cook, Evalina Smith, prepared Jewish foods under the tutelage of their mother, Fannie Klumok. Smith created her own names for these foreign-sounding dishes. Gefilte fish was "filthy fish," *chremslach* (fried Passover fritter) became "himself," and haroset was "roses." "She might not have pronounced all these dishes correctly," said Sylvia, "but she could cook them as well as any Jewish *yenta* from the old country, actually better."[9]

The world of Delta families like the Klumoks, who lived "Jewishly" in a world dominated by the Mississippi River, cotton, churches, and the blues, reveals a unique expression of American Judaism. Although they were far removed from Jewish butcher shops, bakeries, grocery stores, and even synagogues, Delta Jews frequently drove to Greenville, Greenwood, Clarksdale, Vicksburg, and Blytheville to socialize and worship. Regular trips were made to Memphis to buy kosher meat and "kosher-style" and Jewish foods like bagels, rye bread, pastrami, and corned beef.[10]

Jewish foodways in small towns throughout the Delta illustrate how "country Jewish" life was distinctive from that of "city Jews" in Memphis, where it was possible to socialize almost exclusively with other Jews. Strong Jewish social ties in the Delta created a sense of Jewish community through monthly dinner clubs, Sisterhood and B'nai B'rith activities, deli lunches, seders, Jewish golf tournaments, dances, and youth activities that reinforced Jewish identity. Foodways of Delta Jews reveal a regional Jewish culture shaped by a deep sense of place, isolation, kinship ties, agricultural occupations, the influence of white and black Protestant cultures, and a long history of racial and class divisions.

"Cotton Has Been Good to the Jewish People"

Morris Grundfest was born in Russia in 1869. He came to New York in the late 1890s, married Mollie Bernstein, and after the birth of their two children, the couple came to the Mississippi Delta. They were drawn by family already settled in the South and their belief that the South was an "open place" that presented opportunity with its many farms and plantations. Like so many southern Jewish immigrants, Morris Grundfest began as a pack peddler, walking between farms and plantations to sell goods to white and black families. Eventually, the Grundfests opened M. Grundfest's, a dry goods store in the nearby town of Cary. Later, stepping outside the retail sphere, Morris Grundfest purchased two hundred and twenty acres of Delta farmland and established himself as both a shopkeeper and a cotton planter.[11]

Betty Grundfest Lamensdorf, the great-granddaughter of Mollie and Morris, and her husband, Ben, farm the original acreage known as "the Grundfest place." "People are surprised you're Jewish and a farmer," said Ben Lamensdorf, who has raised cotton in the Delta for over forty years, "but we were farming a long time ago in Israel. We just went from sheep herders to raising cotton. Cotton has been good to the Jewish people who came to the Mississippi Delta."[12]

Morris's son Ike raised cotton in the Delta, ran his father's store after his death in 1925, and married June Flanagan, an Episcopalian. Their store was open six days each week, except for Rosh Hashanah and Yom Kippur, when Ike Grundfest closed it for half a day. Betty and her sister, Ann Grundfest Gerache, worked in the store after school and on Saturdays, the busiest shopping day of the week. "The labor would come in on Saturday to receive their pay, and then they'd buy their week's groceries. They usually ran about fifteen dollars," said Betty. "That would hold you for a whole week. And then, when everyone had gotten their groceries and visited and everything, we'd take the people and their groceries back to their houses."[13]

Despite the racial and class divisions that separated them, African Americans in the Delta found that Jews like the Grundfests were fair employers and shopkeepers. African Americans could try on clothes and shoes in Jewish-owned stores, and they were often employed as sales clerks. The Grundfests also provided transportation and housing for the black laborers who worked for them, an arrangement shaped by long-held Delta rules of race and class. "We knew that there was something different about them [Jewish southerners]," said writer Cliff Taulbert, an African American who grew up in nearby Glen Allan. "You didn't really expect them to do the same types of things that you'd expect a white person to do. And I guess, in our minds, we divided the two—there were white people in Glen Allan and there were Jewish people in Glen Allan. They may have felt they were white, but we never did."[14]

Some white gentile southerners may have questioned the racial status of their Jewish neighbors as well. Historian Leonard Rogoff argues that although southern Jews were accepted as white, their "precise racial place was not fixed," especially after Reconstruction, with the arrival of thousands of eastern European Jews whose "swarthy" complexions concerned white southerners.[15] The newly arrived Jews quickly realized that skin color in the South determined where they fell in the socioeconomic order. Jews in the Delta were accepted as white, and many joined local White Citizens' Councils during the 1950s and 1960s. Journalist Jack Nelson argues that the few resident Jews who became members of the councils did so either out of fear of antisemitism or because they too were "hard-rock segregationists."[16]

With their own racial identity questioned in a region plagued by nativism and growing antisemitism, Jews bridged the chasm between white and black cultures in their roles as merchants, cotton brokers, and music agents. A less visible but equally compelling source of identity was associated with food—at the Jewish dinner table, in the synagogue kitchen, and in Jewish-owned grocery stores and dry goods stores throughout the Delta. Here Jews encountered white and black Gentile neighbors, customers, domestic workers, cooks, and caterers, and southern and Jewish foods mixed. At times, the food choices emphasized Jews' "southerness," and at other times, the selections emphasized their "otherness."

With income from farming and their store, the Grundfests could afford to hire African Americans as cooks and domestic workers. Having full-time household help in the Delta—even with the meager salaries African American women were paid weekly—was often only possible for families where the wife worked in the family store and could not do the housework herself. In their Delta home, June Flanagan Grundfest supervised the work of African American employees, including Alice Watson, the family's cook, and Edna Davis, the housekeeper and the children's nurse.

Ann Grundfest Gerache described the family's daily meals as "southern country food." The Grundfest home was next door to the family store, and any ingredients Alice Watson needed were either found in the store or grown in the family's garden. "Mother didn't like to cook," said Ann. "She loved to garden. She did not like being inside cooking, because you worked half a day for every meal, and then it was gone in thirty minutes." Not allowed the luxury of "likes and dislikes," and limited to few options for work, African American cooks like Watson prepared three meals a day for white families like the Grundfests every day except Sunday. Watson worked a "double day," caring for the Grundfests during the day and beginning another round of labor with her own family when she returned home at night.[17]

In addition to her vegetable and flower gardens, June Grundfest raised squabs and chickens and tended a strawberry patch, plum and pear trees, and a fig tree from which she made delicious jams and jellies. The foods that Ann and Betty associate with their mother are a southern and Jewish mix of homemade jams and pickles, salted pecans, and blintzes, topped with June's homemade strawberry jelly, which their father, Ike, ate each Sunday evening. "If she put salted pecans on the table," said Ann, "it meant a celebration."[18] The pecans were grown locally on the place and were buttered, salted, toasted in the oven, and then put away for "company" and special occasions.

As Hortense Powdermaker observed in her sociological studies of Indianola in the 1930s, black domestic workers like Alice Watson were "the chief liaison agent between the races."[19] The Grundfest girls were not allowed to help with the cooking, work considered inappropriate for well-to-do southern white women and girls, but after school they would slip into Watson's kitchen at the Grundfest home, where they sat on the kitchen counter and visited with Watson while she cooked. On occasion, Watson slipped the girls a forbidden cigarette. Ann and Betty recalled the cooking of "Ma Mary," who lived nearby and weighed cotton that the laborers picked in their cotton sacks during the fall harvest. "Ann and I used to walk down there and eat," said Betty. "She'd go out into her garden and pick the butter beans, peas, and okra. We'd sit at this little table and she'd bring the bread in a skillet from the wood-heated oven. That was the best food. It just stuck in my memory how good it tasted."[20] Powdermaker collected a similar story from one of her female informants in the 1930s who said that the "happiest memory of her childhood" was when the family's black cook took her home, "across the tracks," to play with her children and eat turnip greens.[21] The narrative confirmed Powdermaker's belief that whites long cared for by black workers sentimentalized those relationships in their memories of nurturance and caring, often centered at the table.

The ample meals at the Grundfest table included several meats, bowls of fresh vegetables, rice and gravy, hot biscuits and cornbread, preserves, and two or three desserts. Ann found oppressive the amount of food and the ritual associated with their meals. "I'm not going to put all this food on my table," she brashly told her mother when she married. "We're going to have one meat, two vegetables, and I don't know if I'm going to have dessert."[22] In the Delta in the 1950s, Ann's declaration was considered a radical act.

Holidays were divided between June's Episcopal family in Blanton, Mississippi, where they celebrated Thanksgiving and Christmas, and Ike's Jewish family in Greenville and Clarksdale, where they visited on Sunday afternoons and at Passover and High Holy Days to attend religious services. The Grundfests belonged to temples in both Greenville and Vicksburg, which were fifty miles and thirty-seven miles respectively from Cary. At Christmas, June's aunt, Elizabeth Darden, oversaw an elegant dinner prepared by three African American cooks who were expected to work on the holiday. The feast included a turkey and all the trimmings, a coconut cake and ambrosia for dessert. Ike's sisters, Kate Grundfest Sebulsky and Hattie Grundfest Brownstein, worked in "ladies' ready-to-wear." During market trips to Memphis and St. Louis they bought kosher salamis, pastramis, and rye bread, treats that were served with homemade chopped liver when the family visited on Sundays.[23]

Beyond June's Sunday evening blintzes and the aunts' deli foods, Jewish foods were rarely eaten by the Grundfest family until they began to participate in the local community Passover seder, which was organized by Jewish families in the Rolling Fork area in the 1950s. Gefilte fish was bought in Jackson, and other dishes for the seder were prepared by Jewish women in Rolling Fork, Cary, and Anguilla. June always contributed a 1950s-style congealed salad. The dessert was individual "sham tarts," a Delta version of the German-Jewish *shaum* torte, a meringue served with fresh strawberries and whipped cream. Ann Gerache continues to serve the same dessert at family seders, where it has become known as "Mamaw's

Slip and Slide Cake" because of its tendency to melt and slip on warm spring seder evenings.[24]

LIVING JEWISHLY IN A GENTILE WORLD OF CATFISH AND PORK BARBECUE

Food traditions in the Grundfest family tell us much about the defining issue faced by Jews in the Delta since the late nineteenth century: the tension between the pull of assimilation as Jews began to make the Delta their home and the religious imperative to follow Jewish laws and foodways that by definition serve to set Jews apart from their Gentile neighbors. This tension touched all Jews in the Delta, regardless of their expression of Judaism and level of observance.

In the 1950s writer David Cohn, a native of Greenville, where his eastern European immigrant parents had opened a dry goods store, wrote that the Jews of the Delta had conformed so completely to the way of life of their Gentile neighbors that "they had not even clung to the many items of cookery gathered by their forebears during their peregrinations through Russia, Rumania, Hungary, Poland, Germany, and the Baltic States." Cohn underestimated the tenacity of food and the strength of food memories even in situations of great duress. In the Mississippi Delta Jews preserved food memories passed down by Jewish grandmothers and African American cooks alike. Despite intermarriage, a deep attachment to the South, and the strong influence of the white and black Protestant world in which they lived, Delta Jews preserved Jewish foodways in "the most southern place on earth."[25]

As with Ike Grundfest and June Flanagan, there was a high rate of intermarriage among Jewish families in the Delta because of the limited number of potential Jewish mates for young adults who chose to remain in the region. When Ike and June married in the 1930s, they had a tacit understanding that they would respect both their Jewish and Episcopal religious upbringings and would not influence their children's decisions about religion. "We observed everything," their daughter Ann explained.[26] For Ike, this amounted to little or no participation in formal Jewish life, but he was conscious of his Jewish identity. Being with his Jewish sisters on Sunday afternoons and enjoying the deli foods they served him and his family was Ike's weekly expression of Jewishness.

When Ann Grundfest married her first husband, Robert Em-
mich, a Vicksburg Jew, in the early 1950s, they agreed that a decision had to be made about their children's religion. "You can't have
Christmas *and* Hanukkah," Robert told Ann. "You have to decide
how you want to raise your children, and you must do one or the
other."[27] They chose Judaism for their children, and with this choice
came Jewish food. Ann learned to prepare Jewish foods rarely seen
in her childhood home as she turned to Jewish cookbooks, in-laws,
Sisterhood friends, and the rabbi for advice and their recipes.

Families like the Emmichs encouraged their high school–age
children to attend regional Jewish summer camps, like the Henry
S. Jacobs Camp in Utica, Mississippi, and supported the creation of
Jewish youth organizations like the Mississippi Federation of Temple Youth, which later became the Southern Federation of Temple
Youth or SOFTY. Jacobs Camp and similar programs across the nation were evidence of a revitalization of Jewish education beginning
in the 1970s. An attempt to counter rising rates of intermarriage and
assimilation, Jewish summer camps, adult education weekends, and
retreats emphasized spirituality, ritual, and a sense of community in
nontraditional settings outside the synagogue.[28] Jewish parents in
the Delta pushed their college-age children to enroll at a college or
university with a significant Jewish population like the University of
Alabama or the University of Texas.[29] When Ann Grundfest joined
a Jewish sorority at the University of Alabama, her "preference" for
Judaism was set. "I remember one Shabbos dinner, the hostess, a
mother of one of my sorority sisters, had a whole baked fish with a
creole sauce over it," she recalled. "It was the first time I'd ever seen
anything like that."[30] Ann was used to fried chicken or roast beef at
special dinners. If fish was eaten, it was either shrimp prepared in
a creole fashion, such as jambalaya or étouffée, or fried fish such as
catfish or crappie (a local white fish) served often at outdoor fish
fries. From the colonial era to the present, Jewish families of central
European and Sephardic descent frequently served baked or stewed
fish dishes with a sauce for Sabbath meals.[31]

Whether or not one found Jewish life at college, what mattered most
in the Delta was having a religion and a place to pray. Denomination was less important than demonstrating one's attachment to a
religious community and a belief in God. "The South is not known

as the Bible Belt for nothing," explained David Orlansky, a native of Greenville. "People probably take religion more seriously here than many other areas. It's important for people to belong to something, not necessarily to any particular church or religious affiliation, but just to be affiliated with something."[32] Gene Dattel, raised in the Mississippi Delta communities of Sunflower and Ruleville, observed that "100 percent of Jews belonged to congregations in the Delta."[33] Their smaller numbers required a visible demonstration of religious commitment.

This concern was raised when in May of 1889 a small group of Jewish men in Port Gibson, thirty miles south of Vicksburg, sought financial support from congregations around the country to help them build a synagogue. "Our Christian fellow citizens often ask why the Israelites have no church," they explained. "They think we Jews care for nothing but business. For our children's sake, and in order to command the proper respect, we must have a Temple."[34] In 1892 Temple Gemiluth Chassed was dedicated in Port Gibson. Its Moorish architectural style is unique in the state. Jews throughout the Delta organized congregations during this same period. Vicksburg's Anshe Chesed Congregation was founded in 1841, Greenville's Congregation B'nai Israel, now Hebrew Union Congregation, was founded in 1880, Greenwood's Ahavath Rayim in 1893, and Clarkdale's Temple Beth Israel was founded in 1896.

An article published in 1870 in *The Israelite* by Rabbi Max Lilienthal, who officiated at the dedication of Vicksburg's Anshe Chesed Synagogue, described the gala affair attended by both Jewish and Gentile citizens from the city, as well as guests from Natchez, New Orleans, Baton Rouge, Mobile, Montgomery, and Jackson. Lilienthal, a German-ordained rabbi, was a distinguished leader of Reform Judaism in both New York and Cincinnati and traveled to officiate at many American congregations throughout the nineteenth century. Notable figures such as the governor of Mississippi, the mayor of Vicksburg, and most of Vicksburg's clergy also attended. "With true genuine southern hospitality and Jewish sociability no effort was spared to make me feel quite at home," wrote Lilienthal. "I have attended at many a consecration of larger temples in larger cities and congregations, but I have found nowhere more sincere enthusiasm, more deep felt interest in our holy cause, than among our good brethren of Vicksburg."[35]

Yeager's Brass Band from New Orleans, plus a midnight banquet aboard the steamboat, the *Frank Pargond*, convinced Lilienthal that a congregation in the Delta was unique. They understood that the two unspoken rules in the Delta were to demonstrate your respect for "the Lord" and to show everyone a good time, which meant foot-stomping music, free-flowing alcohol, and abundant food. Although the ball lasted until three o'clock in the morning, the new synagogue was filled at nine o'clock by all "the Israelites living or staying in Vicksburg."[36] Vicksburg's Jewish merchants honored the occasion by closing their businesses from Friday noon until the following Monday morning, an unprecedented act in an agricultural community where retailers did most of their business on Saturdays.

The prosperity that made possible the new synagogues, as well as the lavish parties attending their openings, had its basis in the cotton economy, which affected everyone in the Delta, including Jewish merchants, their families, and rabbis. In 1874 Rabbi Aaron Norden of Natchez received a letter from temple officers informing him that his promised annual salary of $2,500 would have to be reduced to $2,000 due to a poor cotton season. The letter declared that the proposed salary of $2,500 was made "when the prospects for a good crop were very flattering and indications for a good business season was then thought more than likely to follow such a crop." Rabbi Norden replied to the Temple officers: "I have assurances from several of the members, and from appearances in general, [that] commercial affairs in this community are much more flourishing this year than they were last year."[37] The rabbi informed his congregants that he knew as much about the financial circumstances of the cotton economy in Natchez as they did.

In Jackson and Canton, Mississippi, the Wiener family paid close attention to the cotton market. Every year at the Passover seder, the family appointed one member to record seder "statistics" on the inside covers of the family *haggadahs* (the small book of prayers and songs used at the Passover seder). The names of seder guests, those who were away at college, illnesses, and recent births and deaths were recorded, along with a description of the seder highlights and praise for tasty dishes, such as "Sally's matzo balls, Thelma's Haroses, and Tinka's ice cream and meringues." A summary of local as well as national and international events, including the market price of cotton and soybeans, was also a part of each haggadah entry. At the April 12, 1912, seder, a participant recorded, "July cotton closed today: 11.06; low for season, 8.66. Last year of Boll Weevil and Vardaman."[38] (James K. Vardaman, elected governor of Mississippi in 1904, ran a campaign steeped in racism.) From the late 1890s to the present, each entry also included the weather, flood conditions on the Mississippi River, whether the azaleas had bloomed early or late, and the market price of cotton and soybeans.[39] "If there was too much rain or it was too cold, it could be devastating for cotton," said Kathryn Loeb Wiener, who came from a family of cotton factors in Montgomery, Alabama. "Cotton was currency, cotton was still king."[40]

Practicing Judaism in an overwhelmingly gentile world like the Delta was challenging, and for most Jews in the region, it meant adjusting religious practices to live in a farming society that conformed to both a southern and Protestant time table. For Jewish merchants like those in Vicksburg in the 1870s, this meant keeping their stores open on Saturdays—the Sabbath and holiest day of the Jewish calendar. In the 1940s and 1950s, Jewish retailers were overwhelmed with business from both white and black families that began early on Saturday morning and continued late into the evening. "This street on Saturday night when I was growing up," said Joe Erber of Greenwood's downtown, "'till one thirty, two o'clock in the morning would be packed with people. The Mississippi Delta was an agricultural-based economy, . . . and the farmers all paid off on Saturdays."[41] Jewish merchants did what they had to do to make a living, and those who kept their stores open on the Sabbath hoped that God might understand the business cycles of the Delta.

Many stores were owned by Jewish families who were either close friends or relatives, and children of these merchants spent Saturday visiting from store to store and assisting with sales and other chores. "You ran from aunt to uncle, because our father had a brother who had a store a few doors down," said Shirley Fleischer Solomon, describing the scene in Shaw, Mississippi, where her parents had a small dry goods store.[42] This scene of family togetherness was repeated throughout the Delta on Sabbath mornings and was a common experience shared by Delta Jews.

Although most opened their stores on Saturdays, Jews in Greenwood observed the Sabbath by going to Friday evening services at Orthodox Congregation Ahavath Rayim. "We've tried to honor our forefathers, our ancestors," explained Joe Erber, whose grandfather was a charter member of the congregation. "We've never been perfect. We've done the best we can with what we've got."[43] Erber, a postal worker and part-time police officer, continues to serve as a lay leader at the synagogue. Harold and Lucille Hart of Eudora, Arkansas, located across the river from Greenville, also tried to do their best "Jewishly." With little access to Jewish institutional life, the Harts' religion focused on the basic tenets of Judaism. "You don't have to know a whole lot about tradition in order to get to heaven," said Mr. Hart. "Just live right."[44] In Clarksdale, Temple Beth Israel changed the time of their Friday night services to six o'clock to allow the congregation to attend services as well as the local football games. In the Delta, football was a religion.

Such examples of Jewish "self-sufficiency" allowed the isolated Jews of the Delta to maintain their religious beliefs without adhering to the letter of the law. Jews faced special challenges in the Delta regarding their burial practices. Local Protestant funeral directors knew little about Jewish ritual, and usually one or two Sisterhood and Brotherhood members constituted the *hevra kaddisha*, or burial society, that stepped in on such occasions. Abe Barkovitz drove seventy miles from Hayti, Missouri, to attend Temple Israel in Blytheville each week and depended on a visiting student rabbi to instruct him in preparing a Jewish body for burial. "The Rabbi did a prayer, 'Excuse us, O Lord, for we know not what we do,'" said Barkovitz. "And then we would proceed with the directions that he had brought with him."[45]

Congregants frequently led services because hiring a permanent rabbi or even securing the services of a visiting student rabbi from Hebrew Union College in Cincinnati was too expensive for small Jewish communities. Assuming this responsibility forced congregants to assume leadership roles and become personally active in Judaism in ways they would never have done had there been a rabbi to lead the congregation. "I think some of us come more since we don't have a rabbi," said Marion Metzger about attendance at Vicksburg's Congregation Anshe Chesed. "I didn't mean that because we didn't like the rabbi, because whoever happens to be saying the service, we all try to support them."[46] In Vicksburg a rabbi is hired only for the High Holy Days season and stays in a local bed-and-breakfast for that twelve-day period. During other times of the year, three or four congregants take turns reading the services. In a modernization of the worship service, an organist and her daughter from the Baptist church provide the music. (American Reform congregations have had organs since 1841 at Congregation Beth Elohim in Charleston.) Thelma Havard and Sophie Smith, African American housekeepers who work for Anshe Chesed, unlock the temple, put out the books, the wine, the candles, and prepare the sanctuary for the Sabbath.

Isolated Jews in small Delta communities made lengthy road trips to the nearest synagogue for services and religious school, to purchase Jewish foods, and to visit Jewish family and friends. Traveling thirty to seventy miles each week was a common fact of life for Delta Jews. "We grew up, and my parents grew up, traveling somewhere to go to Sunday school or temple," said Leanne Lipnick Silverblatt of Indianola. "You know you have to do it, and you just do it."[47] Food and visiting eased the burden of such trips, which could mean enjoying bagels and lox, strudel, and pound cake with family or, just as likely, stopping at the Dixie Pig, a favorite barbecue restaurant in Blytheville, or a café like the Resthaven in Clarksdale, owned by the Chamouns, a Lebanese family known regionally for their kibbe, stuffed grape leaves, and baklava. "We do not ride on the High Holiday, so our family, as well as a number of other families from small Delta towns, would spend the High Holy Days in Greenwood with our relatives," says Ann Klumok Bennett, who grew up in Moorhead. With Jewish food supplies brought in from Memphis and Birmingham, "meals were very festive with many family members and close friends participating."[48]

Obtaining Jewish food supplies in the Delta was one of the biggest challenges of being far from a center of Jewish population. Jewish women in the Delta never traveled without an ice cooler in the trunk of their cars to keep their foods fresh. No traveler went to Jackson, Memphis, St. Louis, Birmingham, New Orleans, and especially to New York without promising to return with bagels, lox, corned beef, and dark loaves of pumpernickel. Women charged relatives and friends traveling outside the region with this task, and returning empty-handed required a good explanation. Cecile Gudelsky remembered her grandfather bringing Jewish foods with him on the train when he returned from St. Louis to Paragould, Arkansas. He sat with friends on the way to St. Louis, but on the return trip he sat alone because the smell of salami and pastrami was too much for his companions.[49]

Delicatessens and kosher butcher shops like the Old Tyme Delicatessen in Jackson and Rosen's, Segal's, and Halpern's in Memphis were known in the Delta by word of mouth as well as through advertisements in Jewish newspapers like the *Hebrew Watchman* and the *Jewish Spectator*. Advertisements guaranteeing "prompt attention given out-of-town orders" encouraged Delta Jews to mail-order foods that would be delivered by bus and train.[50] Gilbert Halpern, the son of Thelma and Louis Halpern, who opened their Memphis delicatessen in 1946, remembered their busy mail-order business at Passover time. After the restaurant closed at the end of the day, the building turned into a packing business at night. Gilbert personally delivered food supplies to families in the Delta and Arkansas, and he remembered the warm reunions when those same families visited his deli in Memphis.[51]

Preparing for Passover posed challenging logistics for Jewish homemakers in the Delta. In Shaw, Bess Seligman did the trips to Memphis. "I was the 'delivery boy,'" said Seligman. "I went to Memphis and took everybody's order and brought back the meat and the perishable foods. The matzah, the flour, the potato starch, and all that, we would ship by bus or by train, because we couldn't put it all in a car."[52] In Moorhead, Fannie Klumok ordered her kosher meats and other Passover foods from Rosen's Delicatessen in Memphis. The primary Passover order arrived several days before Passover. "Each day as she assessed our needs," said Sylvia Klumok Goodman, mother "called Rosen's and they would send us the current day's request by Greyhound bus." Fannie Klumok hired two African American men and three additional African American women to help with the Passover cleaning and preparations. "Nonkosher and non-Passover foods were either given to the black workers or stored at a gentile's house until after Passover," said Sylvia.[53] Passover was the one week a year when the Klumok family observed the dietary laws of kashrut.

Because she worked at the family's store in Indianola and could not be home to oversee the kosher-keeping skills of her domestic workers, Fannie Klumok outlawed any dairy products in the home for that week. Relying on African American cooks to prepare daily southern fare was acceptable to her, but their involvement in Jewish tradition and dietary laws was another matter. Race and class shaped the Klumoks' daily decisions, including preparations for a southern

Jewish Passover. "We had kosher meats and no dairy on Passover as my mother was afraid that our cook and maid wouldn't be able to keep the dishes separate. I never knew that you could eat matzah with butter until I went to college and learned that dairy wasn't prohibited during Passover."[54] Fifty Jews and Gentile friends attended the Klumok seder, for which Fannie annually prepared three hundred pieces of gefilte fish made from a mixture of locally available carp and buffalo fish.

In Chatham, Mississippi, Rabbi Fred Davidow described his Lithuanian great-grandmother Sarah Stein and her oldest child, Fannie Stein Schwartz, his maternal grandmother, as an "island of kashrut" in the Delta. Stein and Schwartz kept kosher themselves but did not prepare kosher food for their families. Davidow explained that the problem of obtaining meat for Stein was "solved not by importing kosher meat, but by importing *shohets* (Jewish butchers)." Her husband, V. A. Stein, made sure his wife could keep kosher by paying for a shohet's passage from Europe to Mississippi. When it became difficult to keep shohets in Chatham, V. A. Stein went to Cincinnati to confer with an Orthodox rabbi about his dilemma. The rabbi gave him permission to slaughter poultry only for his wife, and he returned home with a *halif* (a kosher butcher's knife) and the rabbi's instructions on kosher slaughtering.[55]

Sarah Stein and her daughter Fannie created their own interpretation of kashrut. Allowing no pork or shellfish in the home, observing kashrut during the week of Passover, and ignoring treyf eaten outside the home enabled the Stein women to make peace with their religion while accepting the fact that they lived in a Gentile world of catfish and pork barbecue.

In Ruleville, Flo Silverblatt Selber's mother, Eva, tried to keep kosher by salting the family's meat to remove any traces of blood and keeping a kosher home during the week of Passover.[56] Eva Silverblatt taught her African American cook Georgia Lee to make strudel, blintzes, kreplach (noodle dumplings filled with meat or vegetables), stuffed cabbage, *mandelbread* (sweet bread), and matzah kugel. Lee and Silverblatt also prepared turnip greens, black-eyed peas (flavored with kosher salami), and fried chicken for the family's Sunday noon dinner. Eva Silverblatt drew the line on certain non-kosher southern dishes like ham and bacon, and other foods associated with poor whites and blacks, such as biscuits with white gravy flavored with bacon fat. These foods were forbidden according to Eva's personal rules of kashrut.

Fannie Klumok maintained a similar system of kashrut at her home in Moorhead. Evalina Smith, her African American cook, prepared two batches of vegetables at every meal, one without pork for Fannie and one with pork for her husband, Sol, and their four children. Kosher pots and pans and glass plates were set aside for visiting Orthodox salesmen and the rabbi. When Fannie's father visited, the pork mysteriously disappeared from everybody's food.[57]

Evalina Smith prepared the Sunday noon meal at the Klumok home, at which there might be ten to twenty-five guests, including salesmen and visiting relatives. Her menu illustrates the family's complete acceptance and celebration of Delta cuisine. Smith made homemade rolls to go with the shrimp cocktail, followed by a green salad, fried and broiled chicken, roast beef, tomato sandwiches, butter beans, fried corn or corn on the cob (sometimes both), crowder peas, lady peas, mashed potatoes, sweet potatoes with marshmallows, and asparagus or cauliflower with béchamel sauce and melted cheddar cheese. She also served two desserts, such as rice pudding, homemade ice cream, strawberry shortcake, and fresh watermelon when it was in season.[58]

Sol Klumok picked up Smith at 6:00 A.M. and drove her home each night at about 8:30. She received fourteen dollars a week in salary. Sylvia Klumok explained the system of "deputy motherhood" that occurred each day at the Klumok home. Evalina Smith "ordered us around and was the boss of the house while my mother was working at our store in Indianola," said Sylvia. "She always had black gospel music or blues playing in the kitchen. Sometimes she'd grab my hand, and we'd dance together."[59]

Pearl and William "Bill" Borowsky of Manila, Arkansas, who had immigrated from Russia and Poland, were among a small number of families in the Delta who kept an absolutely kosher home with no allowances for family preferences or for the difficulties of obtaining kosher supplies. The Borowskys' daily food "would have to be described as Jewish," said their daughter Fruma Borowsky Kane. "There was very little southern influence."[60] In the 1920s Bill Borowsky came to visit an uncle who owned the Tiger-Levine Store, a local dry goods business in Manila. Bill met Pearl while traveling through Oklahoma City as a young salesman. They married, returned to Manila, and eventually bought the business, which they operated for the rest of their lives.[61]

As observant Jews, the Borowskys followed Orthodox practices as much as possible given the restrictions of life in Manila, where even a *minyan* (the ten men necessary for worship according to Jewish law) was impossible. The family's kosher meat and other food supplies were delivered from Memphis, St. Louis, and Chicago. Founding members of Temple Israel in Blytheville in the late 1940s, the Borowskys were active participants in the Sisterhood and Brotherhood. Huddy Cohen of Blytheville recalled a "close call" with Pearl that illustrated her commitment to Jewish law. After driving together to the funeral of an old friend in Helena, Cohen realized that they might not make it back to Manila before the Sabbath began at sunset. "Won't God forgive you if we're just a few minutes late?" asked Cohen. "After all, we were doing a mitzvah." "No, I have to be home," replied Borowsky. "That's the law."[62] They arrived just in time for Pearl to light her Sabbath candles.

"Mother cooked from her head and her heart," said Fruma Kane.[63] She was known for elegant kosher holiday meals that she prepared at home, since the family did not travel on the Sabbath and on other holidays. Pearl prepared all her family's meals, including traditional European delicacies such as sweet and sour tongue, candied fruit peel (which required seven days of preparation), and lighter-than-air sponge cakes and angel food cakes. She allowed her African American housekeeper to assist only with washing and chopping vegetables so that kashrut was never breached. Although both shared experiences of marginalization, African American and Jewish women were not equal players. Judaism did nothing to erase the long-standing racial division between white and black women, and at times, particularly during the Jewish holidays and concerning matters of kashrut, Judaism reinforced the division.

In less observant southern Jewish homes, Jewish women cooked the family's meals instead of hiring African American cooks due to cost, personal preference, or sometimes regional experience. In my home in Blytheville, a division of labor in the kitchen existed that was based on state of origin. My mother, Huddy Horowitz Cohen, a native of Connecticut, prepared Jewish holiday dishes and the family's daily meals, which rarely featured anything southern because of her Connecticut upbringing. "I thought it was my job to do the cooking," says Cohen. "I was at home, and could handle it, but I did need help with the cleaning."[64] Cohen left one aspect of cooking—southern food—to "an expert," and that expert was Richie Lee King, an African American housekeeper born in Arkansas who worked for my family from 1955 to the early 1980s. King did the household cleaning, and on special occasions she prepared southern specialties like fried chicken, cornbread, vegetable stew, and sweet potato pie and also helped serve at the family's annual Rosh Hashanah and Yom Kippur dinners.

Alfred and Rebecca Fendler, natives of Krakow, Poland, came to Manila in 1910 and opened a cleaning and pressing business. "They could not keep kosher in a town like Manila, but they did their best," said Oscar Fendler, their son, who practiced law in Blytheville for over sixty years. "We never had any pork in our home during all of the time Dad and Mother lived." Rebecca Fendler slaughtered her own chickens, salted beef that she bought from the local butcher, and prepared European-inspired dishes such as *gedempte* (well-stewed) meat, goulash, tongue, roast goose, liver, blintzes, knish, latkes (potato or matzah meal pancakes), and borscht. Unlike Pearl Borowsky, Rebecca Fendler included southern foods in the family's diet, foods such as locally caught perch and crappie, fried chicken, homemade fruit preserves, but no catfish. "That food was not considered proper," said Oscar Fendler.[65] Catfish was treyf and before it was farm-raised was considered a "trash" fish eaten primarily by African Americans.

As Rebecca Fendler's decision about catfish reveals, the foods Jews chose to eat positioned them in Delta society, and these choices were not limited to the broader categories of "southern" and "Jewish." There were subcategories. Delta Jews could eat southern food, but it was important to eat only those foods associated with their own race and class, including foods prepared by African American cooks, who understood what was appropriate fare in a white home. Fried chicken was appropriate, chitterlings ("chitlins") were not.

A similar hierarchy existed for the Jewish foods a Delta Jewish woman would serve to her family and her gentile guests. Foods associated with higher class, German-Jewish tastes—roast chicken, tortes, sponge cakes, and kuchens—were acceptable to serve for family and Gentile company. Heavier foods of eastern European cuisine—kugels, kiskha, tzimmes, and cholents—were more questionable. Some Delta Jews avoided foods associated with Jews from the shtetl, the small villages of eastern Europe. Although outwardly accepted by the white society around them, Delta Jews were mindful of their "otherness" and vigilantly strove to maintain status in the community, even at the dinner table.

Because of their small numbers and the lengthy drives between home and synagogue, Jews in the Delta often gathered together at holiday time for community seders, Rosh Hashanah dinners, Yom Kippur break-the-fasts, and Hanukkah latke parties. Depending on the number of participants, these events might be held in private homes, at the synagogue, in a Jewish social club like Vicksburg's B.B. (B'nai B'rith) Literary Association, the Olympia Club in Greenville, or at a local restaurant. Jennifer Stollman observes that the annual Sisterhood-sponsored "deli lunch," still held in Greenville, not only raises money for the synagogue and brings members together but helps to "demystify" the Jewish community to the hundreds of Gentiles who come to purchase corned beef sandwiches.[66]

The minutes of Jewish women's groups in the Delta reveal the importance of these food events and social activities for small congregations. Throughout the 1950s the Annie Weinberg chapter of B'nai B'rith women in Blytheville sponsored a constant round of congregational potluck suppers, community seders, Oneg Shabbats, Hanukkah suppers, dinners for the rabbi, and meals associated with Sisterhood and Brotherhood meetings. Jewish women participated in the chapter's activities from Blytheville, a center for buying and selling cotton, as well as the nearby Arkansas communities of Osceola, Manila, Luxora, and Joiner, and Hayti and Caruthersville in Missouri. The organizational minutes' frequent mention of the "kitchen fund" and needed kitchen supplies like refrigerators and steam tables, donations of serving dishes, and redecoration of the recreation hall suggests that significant money and time were dedicated to these activities.[67]

The B'nai B'rith Literary Association, or "B.B. Club," as it was known in Vicksburg, was organized in the 1880s by the Jewish community. Architect William Stanton designed its elegant building standing at the corner of Clay and Walnut Streets, which was completed in 1887. The club included a banquet hall for five hundred guests, which was frequently filled to capacity for balls, banquets, lectures, and wedding receptions. In the 1890s the club's eighty

members reflected the size and affluence of Vicksburg's Jewish community at that time. "The club and club house is known all over this
part of the Mississippi valley as the center of the most lavish, yet
refined, hospitality, while its cuisine under the direction of its accomplished caterers, past and present, is no less celebrated," wrote
the authors of *Picturesque Vicksburg* in 1891.[68] Local Jewish grocers
and butchers like D. J. Shlenker, Sol Fried, and A. A. Ehrman supplied the club's caterers with food and drink for all occasions. Due
to the decline in congregational membership, the building was sold
in 1967 to the Vicksburg Police Department. Recently, this historic
property was purchased by Laurence Leyens, the mayor of Vicksburg and a descendant of an early Vicksburg Jewish family. Leyens
has restored the B.B. Club to its 1890s grandeur, and it is once again
a popular location for community social functions.

Living in small communities where there were few other Jews—
in some cases only a single family—Delta Jews developed networks
to sustain their social and spiritual worlds. From formal dances at
the B.B. Club in Vicksburg in the 1950s where Jewish youth were
entertained by the music of the Red Tops, a popular African American band, to monthly dinner clubs and Sunday afternoon family visits, the dispersed Delta Jewish community gathered for friendship
and courtship. The active calendar of Jewish social life reflected the
lifestyle of the Gentile community in the Delta where both blacks
and whites are known for their hospitality, high standards of en-
tertaining, and love of a good time. Delta people have a sense of
space and distance that distinguishes them from people in the city,
and they willingly travel an hour or more on lonely Delta roads to
attend a good party. Harry Ball describes the social life of Washington County in the Delta from the 1880s to the early decades of the
twentieth century in his diary. Ball recalls a "full-dress ball" at the
Jewish social club in Greenville, which was attended by two hundred people, "the largest public ball we have ever had."[69] Decades
later during the civil rights movement of the 1960s, such hospitality
was not extended to Jewish "freedom riders" from the Midwest and
Northeast who threatened the Jewish community's tenuous position
in the racially charged, violent state of Mississippi.

Folklorist Carolyn Lipson-Walker argues that the experience of
Jews in the South was defined by mobility, and larger towns like
Greenville, Vicksburg, Clarksdale, and Blytheville served as "mag-

nets" for Jews who lived in the smaller towns. Lipson-Walker suggests that unlike Jewish ghettos and neighborhoods in the Northeast, in the South there is a "temporary recurring community" that Jews re-create each time they gather for a social function, a meal, or holiday worship.[70] Today Delta Jews view their parents' generation in the 1940s and 1950s and their ancestors as models of Delta Jewish sociability. "People from Clarksdale, Greenwood, Greenville, Vicksburg, they would get together once or twice a month for dances and so forth," said Earl Solomon Jr. "And they still talk about all the parties they used to have."[71] Leanne Lipnick Silverblatt of Indianola remembers the Young People's Jewish League, or the YPJL as it was called by her parents, which sponsored a monthly supper club. "They met every month or so to eat—Jewish couples from all over the Delta belonged," said Silverblatt.[72]

The biggest Jewish social event in the Delta now takes place each year in October. Begun fifteen years ago as a fund-raiser for the Henry S. Jacobs Camp in Utica, the Delta Jewish Open Golf Tournament draws over one hundred participants from communities throughout the Delta and from other parts of Mississippi. "The fact that they're so scattered, there's a real bond among them," said Macy Hart, former director of Jacobs Camp. "Here's a chance for them to come together, have some fun, do something for a good cause that they created to begin with."[73] After the sun has set and the Sabbath is officially concluded, the festivities begin with a Saturday evening social hour at Greenville's Hebrew Union Temple and hors d'oeuvres prepared by the congregation. Fred Miller, whose family were longtime members of a small synagogue in Rolling Fork that has now closed, operates the grill for the dinner. The tournament begins Sunday morning with a blessing, "*lahdlik ner shel* golf balls," said by congregant Barry Piltz. (The Hebrew phrase means "to light the candle," or in this version "to light [or drive] the golf balls.") After the blessing, Piltz blows the tournament's opening shofar (ram's horn).[74] More food and partying follow a full day of golfing and visiting.

As Jewish population has diminished in the Delta, social functions have become even more important in sustaining Jewish life in the region. Delta Jews were hit particularly hard by the decline in the overall population of the Delta. This decline is associated with the arrival of the boll weevil in the early 1900s, the mechanization of cotton picking in the 1940s, the "great migration" of black laborers out of the Delta to industrial cities like Chicago, and the movement after World War II of veterans and young adults from their rural communities to cities like Memphis and Chicago. These changes, accompanied by the decline of downtown business districts and the growth of regional discount stores like Wal-Mart, pushed third and fourth generation Jews out of their small mercantile businesses in the Delta and into professions located in cities.

In the 1930s there were over two dozen Jewish-owned businesses in Blytheville.[75] Today there are no Jewish-owned businesses downtown. Temple Israel held its last service in the fall of 2004. Congregants donated the sanctuary's stained-glass windows and a Torah to Congregation Beth Sholom in Memphis, a vital synagogue of 325 families, where several Blytheville residents now worship.

Jews who remain in Delta communities—older adults and sons and daughters who work with family businesses and farms—are bound together by kinship and the challenge of maintaining Judaism in their region. While their Judaism is different from that of Jews outside the South, for Delta Jews it is the "real thing" despite their different ritual practices, accents, and food traditions. Judaism in the South is not defined by "faith, theological principles, or affiliation only," says Carolyn Lipson-Walker, who argues that in the South "the criterion for who and what is Jewish is more visceral than rational." Lipson-Walker believes that southern Judaism is a mix of "loyalties, historical memories, beliefs, and cultural expressions," and chief among those cultural expressions is food.[76] Although Delta Jews share the same religious heritage as urban Jews in the Northeast, they are bound to their gentile Delta neighbors by fried chicken, cornbread, and field peas.

Eli Evans, the unofficial dean of the Jewish South, grew up in Durham, North Carolina, where his father, E. J. "Mutt" Evans, was the first Jewish mayor in the 1950s. Eli Evans became the first Jewish student-body president at the University of North Carolina at Chapel Hill in 1958. In his personal biography of growing up Jewish in the South, *The Provincials,* Evans writes about the complicated negotiation of regional and religious identity:

> I am not certain what it means to be both a Jew and a Southerner—
> to have inherited the Jewish longing for a homeland while being

raised with the Southerner's sense of home. The conflict is deep in me—the Jew's involvement in history, his deep roots in the drama of man's struggle to understand deity and creation. But I respond to the Southerner's commitment to place, his loyalty to the land, to his own tortured history, to the strange bond beyond color that Southern blacks and whites discover when they come to know one another.[77]

Evans's words eloquently capture the spirit of Jewish life in the Delta. Delta Jews value their own expression of religion and ethnicity, yet their world is defined by the region's rules of race, class, intermarriage, strong family ties, social activities, deep sense of place, intimate ties to Gentile white and black neighbors, and the agricultural economy. They are also defined by a sense of Jewish self-sufficiency and by the inventiveness required to obtain Jewish foods, supplies, and educational and cultural resources for their Jewish community. The rich cultural world of the Delta that is expressed in the region's music and food is an equally important part of the region's Jewish life. Delta Jews are southerners, and this allegiance to region profoundly influences their Judaism. "I love the South. I can't imagine living anywhere besides the South," said Fred Miller of Anguilla. "We believe in our Jewish heritage for sure, but I think that there's no one who was born in this area who doesn't feel a real kinship with the South—and with the history of the South. Right or wrong, we are and were part of it."[78]

NOTES

I would like to thank Dr. Stuart Rockoff, director, history department, Goldring/Woldenberg Institute of Southern Jewish Life, Jackson, Mississippi, for his review of earlier versions of this article. I am indebted to Mike DeWitt for his interviews of Jewish southerners in the Delta.

1. Stuart Rockoff, interview with the author, Jackson, Miss., September 3, 2003.

2. See David Goldfield's theory of social "place" in "A Sense of Place: Jews, Blacks, and White Gentiles in the American South," *Southern Cultures* 3, no. 1 (1997): 58.

3. Craig Claiborne, *A Feast Made for Laughter* (Garden City, N.Y.: Doubleday, 1982), 47, 31.

4. David W. Blight, "Southerners Don't Lie; They Just Remember Big," in *Where These Memories Grow: History, Memory, and Southern Identity*, ed. W. Fitzhugh Brundage (Chapel Hill: University of North Carolina Press, 2000), 348–49; W. Fitzhugh Brundage, "No Deed but Memory," in Brundage, *Where These Memories Grow*, 2, 7.

5. Joan Nathan, *Jewish Cooking in America* (New York: Alfred A. Knopf, 1994), 3, 4.

6. See Frederik Barth, *Ethnic Groups and Boundaries: The Social Organization of Culture Difference* (1969; repr., Prospect Heights, Ill.: Waveland, 1998), 15; Mary Douglas, *Implicit Meanings: Selected Essays in Anthropology* (1975; repr., London and Boston: Routledge, 1999), 231–51; Claude Levi-Strauss, "The Culinary Triangle," in *Food and Culture: A Reader*, ed. Carole Counihan and Penny Van Esterik (New York: Routledge, 1997), 28; Sidney W. Mintz, *Tasting Food, Tasting Freedom: Excursions into Eating, Culture, and the Past* (Boston: Beacon, 1996), 7. See also Susan Kalcik, "Ethnic Foodways in America: Symbol and the Performance of Identity," in *Ethnic and Regional Foodways in the United States: The Performance of Group Identity*, ed. Linda Keller Brown and Kay Mussell (Knoxville: University of Tennessee Press, 1984), 37–65.

7. Blu Greenberg, *How to Run a Traditional Jewish Household* (New York: Simon and Schuster, 1983), 95.

8. Jenna Weissman Joselit, *The Wonders of America: Reinventing Jewish Culture, 1880–1950* (New York: Hill and Wang, 1994), 171, 293–94; see also Barbara Kirshenblatt-Gimblett, "Kitchen Judaism," in *Getting Comfortable in New York: The American Jewish Home, 1880–1950*, ed. Susan Braunstein and Jenna Weissman Joselit (New York: Jewish Museum, 1990), 77, for a discussion of the term *kitchen Judaism*.

9. Sylvia Klumok Goodman, e-mail to the author, June 4, 2001.

10. "Kosher-style," explains historian Jenna Joselit, was an American invention that allowed Jews to ignore the rigor of the Jewish dietary laws by choosing which rules of kashrut they wished to observe and which they chose to ignore. Joselit, *The Wonders of America*, 173–74.

11. Betty G. Lamensdorf, interview with the author, Cary, Miss., June 28, 2001; Betty G. Lamensdorf, telephone conversation with the author, October 21, 2003.

12. Ben Lamensdorf, in *Delta Jews*, directed by Mike DeWitt (Mike DeWitt Productions, 1999).

13. Lamensdorf, interview.

14. Cliff Taulbert, in DeWitt, *Delta Jews*.

15. Leonard Rogoff, "Is the Jew White? The Racial Place of the Southern Jew," *American Jewish History* 85, no. 3 (1997): 195; see also Jen-

nifer Stollman, "Building Up a House of Israel in a 'Land of Christ': Jewish Women in the Antebellum and Civil War South" (Ph.D. diss., Michigan State University, 2001), 275.

16. Jack Nelson, *Terror in the Night: The Klan's Campaign Against the Jews* (New York: Simon and Schuster, 1993), 41.

17. Ann G. Gerache, interview with the author, Vicksburg, Miss., June 27, 2001; see Jacqueline Jones, *Labor of Love, Labor of Sorrow: Black Women, Work, and the Family, from Slavery to the Present* (New York: Vintage, 1985), 127–30, 325, for a discussion of the daily lives of African American female domestic workers and what she describes as the "double day."

18. Gerache, interview.

19. Hortense Powdermaker, *After Freedom: A Cultural Study in the Deep South* (1939; repr., New York: Atheneum, 1968), 118.

20. Lamensdorf., interview.,

21. Powdermaker, *After Freedom*, 31–32.

22. Gerache, interview.

23. Ibid.

24. Ann G. Gerache, in Southern Jewish Foodways Survey, survey conducted by author, October 3, 1998, Southern Historical Collection, Wilson Library, University of North Carolina, Chapel Hill.

25. James C. Cobb, *The Mississippi Delta and the World: The Memoirs of David L. Cohn* (Baton Rouge: Louisiana State University Press, 1995), xii, 171.

26. Gerache, interview.

27. Ibid.

28. Jonathan D. Sarna, *American Judaism: A History* (New Haven, Conn.: Yale University Press, 2004), 323.

29. Gertrude Philippsborn, *The History of the Jewish Community of Vicksburg, from 1820 to 1968* (Vicksburg, Miss.: published by the author, 1969), 56.

30. Gerache, interview.

31. Claudia Roden, *The Book of Jewish Food* (New York: Alfred A. Knopf, 1997), 28, 326.

32. David Orlansky, in DeWitt, *Delta Jews*.

33. Gene Dattel, "Growing Up Jewish and Black in Mississippi" (lecture, Southern Jewish Historical Society Annual Conference, Memphis, November 1, 2003).

34. Kenneth Hoffman, "The Jews of Port Gibson, Mississippi," in *100th Anniversary Celebration Program*, Gemiluth Chassed Synagogue, October 20, 1991, Museum of the Southern Jewish Experience, Jackson, Miss.

35. Max Lilienthal, "Consecration of the New Temple in Vicksburg, Miss.," *Israelite* (Vicksburg, Miss.), June 3, 1870, 9–10—Anshe Chesed file, American Jewish Archives, Cincinnati.

36. Ibid.

37. Letter from Samuel Ullman and Temple B'nai Israel committee to Rabbi A. Norden and his reply, July 1874, Temple B'nai Israel Archives, Natchez, Miss.

38. Passover haggadah, April 17, 1992, April 1, 1912, collection of Kathryn L. Wiener, Jackson, Miss.

39. Kathryn L. Wiener and Julian Wiener, interview with the author, Jackson, Miss., 1992, Collections of Institute for Southern Jewish Life, Museum of the Southern Jewish Experience, Jackson, Miss.

40. Kathryn L. Wiener, interview with the author, Jackson, Miss., June 26, 2001.

41. Joe Erber, in DeWitt, *Delta Jews.*

42. Shirley Fleischer Solomon, Shaw, Miss., interview with the author, 1993, Collections of Institute for Southern Jewish Life.

43. Erber, in DeWitt, *Delta Jews.*

44. Harold Hart, interview with the author, Eudora, Ark., October 1991, Collections of Institute for Southern Jewish Life.

45. Abe Barkovitz, interview with the author, Hayti, Mo., April 1991, Collections of Institute for Southern Jewish Life.

46. Marion Metzger, in DeWitt, *Delta Jews.*

47. Leanne Silverblatt, in DeWitt, *Delta Jews.*

48. Ann Klumok Bennett, in Southern Jewish Foodways Survey, July 2001.

49. Cecile Gudelsky, e-mail to the author, July 17, 2001.

50. Segal's Kosher Delicatessen advertisement, *Hebrew Watchman* (Memphis), March 30, 1928; Halpern's Kosher Snack Shop advertisement, *Hebrew Watchman*, December 12, 1946; Rosen's Kosher Delicatessen advertisement, 291 N. Main St., Memphis, *Hebrew Watchman*, August 10, 1939; advertisements for Dalsheimer's Brothers and Albert Seessel and Son, *Jewish Spectator* (Memphis), 1908, 23rd anniversary edition of the *Jewish Spectator* (Memphis); all in Temple Israel Archives, Memphis.

51. Gilbert Halpern, interview with the author, Memphis, December 20, 2001.

52. Bess Seligman, interview with the author, Shaw, Miss., April 1991, Collections of Institute for Southern Jewish Life.

53. Sylvia Klumok Goodman, e-mails to the author, May 25, 2001, August 25, 2003.

54. Ibid.

55. Rabbi Fred Victor Davidow, "Greenville, Mississippi," in *Jews in Small Towns: Legends and Legacies*, ed. Howard V. Epstein (Santa Rosa, Calif.: VisionBooks International, 1997), 244, 245.

56. Florence Silverblatt Selber, in Southern Jewish Foodways Survey, October 1998–June 2001.

57. Sylvia Klumok Goodman, e-mail to the author, August 25, 2003.

58. Sylvia Klumok Goodman, e-mail to the author, June 4, 2001.

59. Ibid.

60. Fruma Borowsky Kane, in Southern Jewish Foodways Survey, September 26, 1998.

61. Carolyn Grey LeMaster, *A Corner of the Tapestry: A History of the Jewish Experience in Arkansas, 1820s–1990s* (Fayetteville: University of Arkansas Press, 1994), 98.

62. Huddy Horowitz Cohen, interview with the author, Memphis, December 22, 2001.

63. Kane, in Southern Jewish Foodways Survey.

64. Huddy Horowitz Cohen, telephone conversation with the author, October 13, 2003.

65. Oscar Fendler, interview with the author, Blytheville, Ark., April 1991, Collections of Institute for Southern Jewish Life; Oscar Fendler, in Southern Jewish Foodways Survey, September 22, 1998.

66. Jennifer Stollman, "We're Still Here: Delta Jewish Women in the Twentieth Century" (lecture, Southern Jewish Historical Society Annual Conference, Memphis, November 1, 2003).

67. Temple Israel Sisterhood minutes, Blytheville, Ark., October 12, 1955, March 11, 1956, August 26, 1956, September 23, 1956, November 11, 1956, March 10, 1957, box 418, American Jewish Archives, Cincinnati; "Temple Israel Fiftieth Anniversary Pamphlet and History," May 11, 1997, collection of author; LeMaster, *A Corner of the Tapestry,* 255.

68. H. P. Chapman and J. F. Battle, *Picturesque Vicksburg* (Vicksburg, Miss.: Vicksburg Printing and Publishing, 1891), 105–7, manuscript collection 10, American Jewish Archives, Cincinnati.

69. James C. Cobb, *The Most Southern Place on Earth: The Mississippi Delta and the Roots of Regional Identity* (New York: Oxford University Press, 1992), 138.

70. Carolyn Lipson-Walker, "Shalom Y'all: The Folklore and Culture of Southern Jews" (Ph.D. diss., Indiana University, 1986), 99, 98.

71. Earl Solomon Jr., in DeWitt, *Delta Jews.*

72. Leanne Lipnick Silverblatt, in Southern Jewish Foodways Survey, November 1998.

73. Macy B. Hart, in DeWitt, *Delta Jews.*

74. "Delta Jewish Open Scheduled for October 7," *Deep South Jewish Voice,* August 2001, 3.

75. LeMaster, *A Corner of the Tapestry,* 255.

76. Lipson-Walker, "Shalom Y'all," 43–44.

77. Eli N. Evans, *The Provincials: A Personal History of Jews in the South* (1973; repr., New York: Free Press, 1997), 22.

78. Fred Miller, in DeWitt, *Delta Jews.*

"THERE IS MAGIC IN PRINT"

*The Holiness-Pentecostal Press and
the Origins of Southern Pentecostalism*

RANDALL J. STEPHENS

*While the Holiness-Pentecostal movement is widely recognized
in the South, questions about its origins and spread in the region have not been fully answered. Analyzing the Holiness and
Pentecostal press as an instrument for dissemination of information and for community building, Randall Stephens argues that
southern Pentecostals in their early organizational years dissented
from prevailing racial and gender conventions. Beyond that, this
network of newspapers and periodicals enabled southern Pentecostals to imagine their religious community as a counterculture to
national and even some regional developments at the same time as
they understood themselves as a restoration of early Christianity.*

I believe the dear Southland will receive [a] great blessing this
time. She is ripe for it. I pray that she may not miss it.
                                                    —Frank Bartleman

I am so glad of all God is doing in the South-land and am pleased
to put my name on record for all [Pentecostalism] stands for.
I received the Baptism of the Holy Ghost at Azusa St., Los
Angeles, Cal., on July 2, 1906. My heart has been overflowing
with His sweet peace and love ever since.
                                                    —Mary Radabaugh

Testimonials similar to these flooded Holiness and Pentecostal periodicals throughout the United States from 1906 to 1910, making the

religious press instrumental in the revival's formation and perpetuation.[1] As correspondents penned their sentiments, Pentecostalism entered the South through the enthusiastic reports of an unconventional revival occurring in Los Angeles. William Seymour, an African American holiness preacher originally from Louisiana, began his revival with integrated meetings in a rundown former African Methodist Episcopal (AME) church on Azusa Street. Soon after the revival began in April 1906, the gatherings received the attention of *Los Angeles Times* reporters, who lampooned the attendants for their religious excesses. The spiritual acrobatics performed at the Azusa mission—including jumping, dancing, falling prostrate on the floor, shouting, speaking in tongues, and prophesying—made its participants easy targets of ridicule. One *L.A. Times* reporter denigrated the meeting as a "Weird Babel of Tongues." The writer mercilessly parodied Seymour: "An old colored exhort, blind in one eye, is the major-domo of the company. With his stony optic fixed on some luckless unbeliever, the old man yells his defiance and challenges an answer."[2] The press, whether positive or negative, helped spread Pentecostalism far beyond the confines of L.A. Subsequently, Frank Bartleman, a major leader at Azusa, claimed that the *L.A. Times* gave "us much free advertising" and made thousands aware of the revival who otherwise would never have come in contact with it.[3]

The press, secular and sacred, became essential in promulgating the movement in the States and abroad. Yet scholars have written so little on the origins of Pentecostalism in the South that the role of the press in these early years has received scant attention.[4] At least two factors make this religious movement significant in larger cultural terms and worthy of critical study. First, by sheer numbers of adherents Pentecostalism is arguably the most important mass religious movement of the twentieth century.[5] Second, southern Pentecostals, at least in the first few years of the movement, frequently transgressed racial and gender hierarchies in a region dominated by Jim Crow and intense patriarchalism.

Historians of southern religion have clearly demonstrated the massive impact of evangelicalism on the region.[6] But Pentecostalism in particular has seldom been investigated. Consequently, many questions about the origins of this movement remain unanswered. Currently we do not know why Pentecostalism proved so successful in the South, often overshadowing other sects and mainline denominations.[7] It is also still somewhat unclear how the doctrine and practice of the southern Holiness movement served as catalysts for the new sect. Moreover, it would be helpful to determine the degree to which southern Pentecostals were in fact dissenters from prevailing racial and gender conventions. The Holiness and Pentecostal press sheds considerable light on these matters and offers some clues as to how Pentecostals imagined their religious community and transmitted and sustained their countercultural vision.

Grant Wacker, the preeminent historian of American Pentecostalism, argues that periodicals "constituted by far the most important technique for sustaining national and world consciousness" among Pentecostals.[8] Much as was the case with earlier revivals in America, the press defined and invented the movement, unifying its discourse and orienting it along communal lines.[9] Without question, other forms of communication, including the preached word, pamphlets, broadsides, and books, were also critical to the spread of southern Pentecostalism, but in the earliest period the press was more crucial. The immediacy of newspapers and the ways in which they allowed individuals throughout the United States to correspond with one another made them an unusually potent medium. Roughly three quarters of a century before the Pentecostal revival Alexis de Tocqueville piercingly observed, "Only a newspaper can put the same thought at the same time before a thousand readers."[10] And Holiness as well as Pentecostal adherents distinguished themselves as avid readers of religious books and papers. W. B. Godbey, one of the most influential southern Holiness authors and evangelists, perfectly summed up his coreligionists' sentiments. "Let us remember that there is magic in print," he wrote in his autobiography, "rendering it far more influential than words spoken." Spoken words, thought Godbey, faded away soon after they were uttered, but the printed word could last indefinitely and influence far more individuals as a result.[11] Though many scholars describe Pentecostal religious culture as fundamentally oral based and antimodern, from the beginning believers relied heavily on print culture and shrewdly manipulated modern technologies.[12]

A paper published from the Azusa Street mission, the *Apostolic Faith*, and a barrage of other Holiness periodicals served as springboards for southern Pentecostalism.[13] They were the primary agents through which the emerging Pentecostal community first imagined itself.[14] Within their pages, radical Holiness people wrote and read about the restoration of New Testament gifts occurring in Los Angeles.[15] These papers described the interracial worship taking place at Azusa and highlighted the prominent roles of women in the revival. They also covered the gift of speaking in tongues, not a feature of the Holiness movement, and convinced many Holiness adherents that the more zealous Pentecostals were the rightful bearers of gospel truth. As editors tantalizingly described the strange new "gifts of the Spirit" manifested at Azusa, they also provided space for elaborate testimonies. Men and women, some barely literate, from Tennessee, South Carolina, Georgia, Florida, Alabama, and Mississippi wrote to the papers to express their hunger for experiences equal to those occurring in the West.[16] Accordingly, the reportage on the Azusa revival persuaded southern Holiness leaders like the white evangelist Gaston Barnabas Cashwell and the African American minister Charles Harrison Mason to make pilgrimages to Los Angeles in search of their "Pentecost" and the baptism with the Holy Ghost. The revival that began in California spread rapidly into the South, prompting A. J. Tomlinson, the first general overseer of the Church of God (Cleveland), to apply the well-worn incendiary metaphor to this region: "The Fire is spreading for miles and miles in every direction."[17]

The newspaper accounts that followed the Azusa revival were the culmination of a movement steeped in a long tradition of theological perfectionism and religious radicalism. And although Pentecostalism was a relatively new religious sect in the early twentieth century, its roots were firmly planted in the Holiness revival of the late nineteenth century. As early as 1867, a new agency led by northern Methodists, the National Camp Meeting Association for the Promotion of Holiness, began disseminating Holiness doctrine in revivals throughout the North. These Holiness advocates disapproved of the alleged impiety of mainline denominations. They also despised the growing wealth, smugness, and elaborateness of their churches. Lower- and middle-class communities throughout America expressed in religious terms the same discontent that motivated the Populist movement.[18] Dissatisfied with the churches of their youth, they formed new religious communities committed to the theological doctrine of perfectionism.[19] These former Methodists, Presbyterians, and Baptists were convinced that the Holy Spirit had descended. They traced its origins to the early church as revealed in the book of Acts. Hence, the Holiness revival produced zeal for "Spirit Baptism" (a divine empowerment of believers) and for other gifts of the New Testament church, such as healing and prophecy.[20]

Already by the late nineteenth century the National Camp Meeting Association had introduced many southerners to perfectionism. In September 1872 this organization held its first meeting below the Mason-Dixon Line. John Inskip, president of the organization, and other northern evangelists who officiated had reason to be cautious in the postwar South. However, the *Knoxville Daily Chronicle* assured its readers that Holiness promoters knew "no North, no South, no East, no West," but were motivated by one goal, the propagation of holiness. Some Tennesseans remained unconvinced, imagining these northerners to be paid agents of the government with more sinister designs.[21] This suspicious faction proved the minority. Most of the roughly six thousand congregants in attendance at Knoxville and other later revivals eagerly received the doctrine of entire sanctification, a second work of grace following salvation, in which, they thought, the believer was made free from sin. At subsequent camp meetings throughout the region, such colorful southern evangelists as "Uncle" Bud Robinson, L. L. Pickett, Beverly Carradine, Mary Lee Cagle, H. C. Morrison, John Lakin Brasher, and W. B. Godbey drew thousands of new recruits into the Holiness ranks.

Editors and correspondents in newly established Holiness papers wrote of their commitment to perfectionism. Accordingly, the Virginia-born evangelist G. D. Watson expressed the perfectionist sentiment in his periodical *Living Words* (Pittsburgh), arguing that anyone "born of God doth not commit sin."[22] Other initiates believed that when they were entirely sanctified God removed their "carnal mind," cleansing them of "all sin."[23] Readers soon mastered the terminology and practice of this doctrine.

These papers exercised power over converts' lives in numerous other ways as well. Widely circulated Holiness periodicals such as the *Christian Alliance and Missionary Weekly* (New York), the *Firebrand* (Shenandoah, Iowa), the *Gospel Trumpet* (Anderson, Indiana), the *Way of Faith* (Columbia, South Carolina), *Zion's Outlook* (Nashville), the *Holiness Advocate* (Lumberton, North Carolina), the *Way of Life* (Cartersville, Georgia), and *Live Coals of Fire* (Royston, Georgia) told black and white adherents which books to read, which evangelists to follow, who and what to pray for, and which doctrines to accept or reject.[24] Papers regularly featured full-page advertisements for Holiness literature available at reasonable prices. Editors sold the works of authors from the Wesleyan canon—John Wesley, John Fletcher, Madam Guyon, and Adam Clark—as well as texts by the newer lights who had reshaped Wesleyanism—Phoebe Palmer, Daniel Steele, W. B. Godbey, S. A. Keen, and G. D. Watson.[25]

The Holiness press also created a strong sense of fellowship, even where no physical community existed. Spread out across the South, many Holiness people could not attend in person the various revivals reported throughout the region. But within the pages of their newspapers, they entered an imagined community that united them. In an 1899 issue of *Live Coals of Fire*, one initiate from Hartwell, Georgia, wrote that after reading testimonies and reports of the "warfare of God" in this paper, he felt as if he were in the midst of a "red-hot testimony meeting." Furthermore, he believed that if he did not write to the paper to testify about his own experience, he would somehow lose the fullness of his faith.[26] A Mobile, Alabama, judge named Price experienced something similar. For years he subscribed to northern Holiness papers like the *Christian Standard* and knew the names and read the editorials of a host of Holiness preachers. Yet he had never met any of these in person.[27] Converts all over the South felt the same sense of community and solidarity.

Devotion to the new Holiness periodicals ran high. Many readers announced that they would read only Holiness newspapers, leaving secular and denominational publications to "worldlings." Methodist officials fumed at the exclusiveness of the new craze. One Holiness believer wrote to the journal of the South Carolina conference of the Methodist Episcopal Church, South to announce the cancellation of his subscription. "Dear Brother: Please stop my advocate, as I take The Christian Standard and Way of Life," he bluntly stated. The Methodist editor thought this gentleman's disloyalty incredible and rebuked him and other Holiness enthusiasts who looked for spiritual sustenance outside the confines of official southern Methodism.[28]

As Holiness folk met with opposition among mainline groups, they found other ways to spread their message. Numbers of converts, eager that more might know about entire sanctification, circulated their older newspapers among friends and neighbors. Some believed so wholeheartedly in the mission of Holiness periodicals that they became ardent newspaper agents, selling or giving out copies at revivals, local stores, and on street corners.[29] Miller Willis, an eccentric evangelist based in Georgia, even worked out a program of Holiness print evangelism. He suggested to the readers of the *Christian Witness* (Boston) that they start up circulation libraries in their churches. Once proponents won over their congregations, they should introduce a "good holiness paper" to them and "get it into as many homes as you can." Willis found, too, that reading selections from Holiness books and papers from the pulpit yielded tremendous results.[30] Like Willis, Irving E. Lowery, an African American minister in the Methodist Episcopal Church of South Carolina, aggressively pitched Holiness newspapers. In the pages of the *Christian Witness* he urged black ministers of the South Carolina conference to subscribe to this northern Holiness journal. At the Kingstree, South Carolina, conference meeting in 1887 he gave away 110 free copies of the *Christian Witness* in an attempt to entice new subscribers.[31] Pentecostals expressed an equally zealous devotion to their periodicals.

Two radical Holiness papers in particular, the *Pentecostal Herald* (Louisville, Kentucky) and *God's Revivalist* (Cincinnati), were perhaps most instrumental in the transition from Holiness to Pentecostal. Though one paper was published in a border state and the other in a northern one, both exerted profound influence upon the South. These papers represented the translocal Holiness movement as a whole by eschewing geographic as well as social boundaries.[32] In the 1890s and early 1900s, scores of southerners, soon to be Pentecostals, corresponded with both publications, seeking advice, offering their viewpoints, and reporting on local revivals.[33] The *Pentecostal Herald* received letters from Holiness proponents in all the former Confederate states. Though exact figures are difficult to obtain, it is clear that the *Pentecostal Herald* and *God's Revivalist* maintained large circulations. In 1893 the *Pentecostal Herald* had a circulation of 15,000, which rose to 30,000 in 1920, 38,000 in 1934, and 55,000 in 1942. In just one week in early 1898, the *Herald* gained 1,078 subscribers. Nearly as successful, the *Revivalist* reported 20,000 copies circulated monthly by the summer of 1899.[34]

The editors of these publications vigorously spread the message of Holiness, which they considered essential to a vital Christian life.

The editor of the *Pentecostal Herald*, Henry Clay Morrison, was motivated by a single-minded enthusiasm. Lying in bed one night in 1888, Morrison felt that if he could multiply himself into a "score of men," he could widely disseminate his message. At this point he struck on the idea of publishing a paper. It might do the work of hundreds of preachers, reasoned Morrison. He envisioned the paper inspiring a return to plain folk religion and the "old paths" of Methodism. Morrison had no experience in newspaper publishing, but that seemed inconsequential to him. Small presses cost as little as $125, and paper and supplies were also relatively inexpensive. Taking advantage of increasingly low-cost equipment and materials, others, too, soon established presses dedicated to sanctification and radical religion.[35]

The aptly titled *God's Revivalist*, edited by the impassioned Martin Wells Knapp, claimed to be under the sole proprietorship of God, published in "His" interests. In this paper, Knapp employed Pentecostal language that well foreshadowed the hyperbolic vocabulary of the tongues movement. Using apocalyptic imagery, Knapp published accounts of "Revival Dynamite," "Revival Tornados," "Lightning Bolts from Pentecostal Skies," and "Revival Fire."[36] Southern Holiness folk were electrified by Knapp's paper and others like it. Between 1893 and 1900, twenty-three new Holiness sects emerged in the South. And from the Methodist Church alone, the exodus of members numbered roughly one hundred thousand.[37] On a practical level, radical commitments precluded participation in secular entertainments, such as theatergoing, attending sporting events, or social dancing. The faithful frequently prohibited the consumption of alcohol, tobacco, coffee, Coca-Cola, or anything else that "blunted" one's "moral quality."[38] As editors broadcast their peculiar social beliefs in newspapers scattered throughout the region, southern stalwarts constructed a countercultural environment that would easily be accommodated within the domain of Pentecostalism.

The scrutiny that Holiness groups applied to mainline churches was as demanding as their opposition to popular culture. Within the pages of their periodicals they held their churches accountable for any delinquency in doctrine or morality. Editors and correspondents lamented the growing indifference or outright opposition to perfectionism in mainline churches. Speaking of the late nineteenth century, the ardent Church of God evangelist J. W. Buckalew bemoaned: "Mr. John Wesley said when the Methodist church gave up the doctrine of holiness they would be a backslidden and fallen church. They have surely given it up for the people have quit getting their [sanctification] experience."[39]

At the same time Holiness folk battled doctrinal declension, they resisted the growing embourgeoisement of Methodist, Baptist, and Presbyterian churches. Subsequently, they reacted against mainline churches and the "diversion of enthusiasm from the salvation of souls to the building of institutions," as one historian put it.[40] Because increasingly formal mainline churches could not accommodate the needs of their poorer members, many made the departure into more ecstatic, unconventional Holiness churches. Once settled in the new sects, members felt free to act and dress as they pleased. According to Mickey Crews, the predominately rural Church of God (Cleveland) became a countercultural bulwark against its social betters.[41] Many southern Holiness papers denounced eating pork, the wearing of neckties for men, and fashionable dresses or jewelry for women. They also opposed contemporary attitudes toward recreation, status, and race.

Holiness and later Pentecostal churches were the most integrated religious bodies in the South. Hence, *God's Revivalist* frequently corresponded with and supported African American Holiness evangelists like Amanda Berry Smith. Occasionally, the paper included features hinting at an openness to integrated services. In 1901 a published letter to the *Revivalist* asked the question of whether blacks and whites worshiped together in biblical times. Kentucky-based evangelist W. B. Godbey emphatically answered yes, offering proof-texts to back up his position.[42]

Black and white Holiness folk integrated their newspapers by featuring the work of evangelists of both races within their publications. African American C. P. Jones reported on white Holiness activities in South Carolina, Georgia, and Tennessee in his journal, *Truth* (Jackson, Mississippi). Jones lauded the efforts of leading white southern evangelists such as J. M. Pike, N. J. Holmes, and Charlie Tillman. Simultaneously, white-operated papers like the *Christian Witness* and *Zion's Outlook* featured African American evangelists in their pages and published editorials by leading black ministers.[43] In Georgia, the white Holiness leader W. A. Dodge lent his support to black ministers like W. J. Adams. There is evidence that

Dodge's own paper, the *Way of Life*, maintained a significant black readership. In the pages of the *Pentecostal Herald*, Adams recalled that quite a number of African Americans in Georgia "subscribed [to] this paper, and took it as long as he published it. Dodge, also, sold holiness books and tracts, and a few of the [African American] preachers went to his home for these books and papers so often until we called it the 'Power House.'"[44] Concerned with the spread of Holiness among African Americans, Dodge encouraged Adams to publish his own paper and helped name the new periodical, the *Herald of Full Salvation*.[45] The perfectionist press served as a type of liminal space where blacks and whites could interact and freely share their ideas about Christian perfection.

At the apex of the Jim Crow era, the Fire-Baptized Holiness Church and the Church of God (Cleveland) proved exceptional with regard to interracialism. Few southerners approved of Holiness views on race. In fact, some evangelists, like Richard Baxter Hayes of the Fire-Baptized, bore reproach for challenging racial norms. After asking a few African Americans to lead in singing a song at an 1898 revival in Carlton, Georgia, "a man who weighed over two hundred pounds" confronted Hayes, brandishing a stick and accusing Hayes of "showing Negro equality." In retaliation for Hayes's breaches in racial, social, and religious etiquette, his meeting tents were burned down several times, a Baptist minister punched him in the face, he was shot at, and he regularly faced hostile crowds.[46]

Like Hayes, the preacher B. H. Irwin often drew protests in communities where he held meetings. The radical Irwin introduced to southerners further works of grace beyond sanctification and helped create a contentious climate in the years before Pentecostalism arrived. Conflict and social upheaval followed Irwin wherever he ministered, be it in the West or the South. The *Way of Faith* recounted one such instance, in which "masked murderers" broke up Irwin's meeting by firing revolvers and throwing chairs at congregants. Most likely, these were local toughs who lashed out at the preacher who night after night condemned their many vices. Irwin escaped without injury, which confirmed his saintliness, according to the columnist reporting on the affair.[47] A similar melee occurred at an African American Holiness revival in Lexington, Mississippi. In 1897 C. P. Jones and C. H. Mason, founders of what would become the Church of God in Christ, held open-air meetings after being barred from a local Baptist church. Amid one service a sniper opened fire on the congregation, wounding several attendees. Mason remained optimistic. Elated, he noted that a local newspaper had reported the episode. As a result, news of the movement spread throughout the area.[48]

Others seemed to court confrontation as if to prove their anointing. Soon after A. J. Tomlinson began publishing a small Holiness paper in Culberson, North Carolina, he encountered strong opposition to his views. In August 1901, Tomlinson was approached by a Baptist minister enraged by what he read in Tomlinson's paper, *Samson's Foxes*. The minister believed Tomlinson exaggerated the spiritual and material squalor of poor southern whites in the area. Unable to take such criticisms lightly, and equipped with an enormous ego, Tomlinson surmised that his antagonist was unknowingly fighting against God. This and a series of other confrontations, including vandals firing bullets into Tomlinson's home at night, put the Holiness preacher and his family in grave danger. However, recounting violent incidents like these in his paper, he reasoned, affirmed the Holiness cause.[49]

Holiness and later Pentecostal churches also faced attacks for upsetting life in mill towns. In 1910 a tumultuous Pentecostal tent meeting in Alabama City, Alabama, kept workers up late, infuriating mill bosses and local residents. Leaders of the community stepped in to counter the revivalists' work. Owners of a nearby cotton mill continued to operate into the night in order to keep workers away from the meetings. The *Gadsen Evening Journal* and the *Gadsen Daily News* satirized the revival and reported on the religious frenzy occurring there. The preacher leading the event retaliated, hurling epithets at the Gasden editors. Town officials accused the Pentecostals of disturbing the peace and attempted to place a 9:00 P.M. curfew on the gathering. When this did not work, police arrested the revival's leaders while vigilantes burned meeting tents and chairs.[50]

These struggles, vividly narrated in the local press, meant genuinely different things to Holiness and Pentecostal believers on one hand and secular authorities on the other. For the former it became a cosmic battle between God's people and demonic forces. For the latter it seemed to pit societal order against communal breakdown and chaos. Community leaders were rightly troubled. Holiness and then Pentecostal converts were empowered in such a way that they felt an overwhelming sense of religious and social superiority. Local opposition, always deemed diabolical, only confirmed them in their spiritual pursuits.

Perhaps the most fierce confrontations of all were those that unfolded within the pages of southern denominational papers. Southern Baptists and Methodists could not bear Holiness doctrinal hubris any more than they could tolerate their ecstatic worship practices. Holiness people, mainline church leaders protested, disrupted congregations and communities and stirred up theological controversy wherever they ventured. In the Methodist Episcopal Church, South's official organ, the *Christian Advocate,* one writer blasted the religious bigotry of exclusivist Holiness folk. "This sort of medievaelism," he inveighed, "is a gross anachronism, out of place in the nineteenth century."[51] Other southern Methodists recoiled at what they considered the pious pretensions of the movement. Of course, Holiness adherents did tend to describe the Spirit's leading as an intimate affair. On this account, one southern Methodist official satirized them on the front page of the *Christian Advocate.* It was, he scoffed, as if they had a private wire running into heaven, "along which they receive direct instructions from God concerning all the petty and trivial details of their daily conduct."[52] If nothing else, anti-Holiness commentators could dismiss the faithful for not living up to their supposed ideals. In the *Religious Herald* a Virginia Baptist man described the failings of one adherent who was his neighbor. Though this sanctified sister claimed to be without sin, she did not offer any help when the layman's wife became seriously ill. She did, however, the author wryly commented, send over a newspaper advocating her strange new beliefs.[53]

Holiness stalwarts easily shrugged off such criticisms. Holiness folk and Pentecostals found deep meaning in all forms of physical and emotional suffering. Both published their many persecutions and trials in their newspapers with an air of satisfaction. Their expectancy that God would restore the New Testament church on earth gave them a heightened sense of mission. Moreover, like the apostles, they were persecuted for their radical views.

Just as uprooted Holiness people longed for a return to the old-fashioned religious zeal of their youth, they also yearned for the restoration of the true church. Social critic W. J. Cash observed that Holiness churches held themselves to be "the one true Church among a host of Byzantine pretenders."[54] Accordingly, a pronounced primitivist streak, long the hallmark of America's new and more radical sects, was especially strong within southern perfectionist groups. Holiness leaders proclaimed this restorationist message repeatedly in their publications and facilitated a climate of expectancy among the movement's followers. They called for a return to "Christ and the apostles, to the days of pure primitive Christianity, to the inspired word of truth."[55]

A radical Holiness group in Kansas took restorationism one step further. In January 1901, the *Kansas City Times*, the *Kansas City Journal*, the *St. Louis Post-Dispatch*, the *Topeka Daily Capital*, the *Topeka State Journal*, and the *Chicago Blade* began reporting on an unusual revival led by Holiness evangelist Charles Fox Parham. Using the Pentecost account in Acts, chapter 2, Parham and the students of his Topeka Bible school concluded that speaking in tongues was the necessary confirmation of Holy Spirit baptism.[56] Theological subtleties were lost on the secular press, which announced, "Parham's New Religion," "New Sect in Kansas Speaks with Strange Tongues," "A Queer Faith," and "Strange Gibberish: 'Students' Talk but No One Understands Them."[57]

Parham's own paper, *Apostolic Faith*, never spread the news of the Topeka revival as thoroughly as did the secular press. Despite wide-reaching reports, this first wave of Pentecostalism remained regional, limited primarily to Kansas, Missouri, Texas, and Arkansas. The next phase of the movement, following the revival at Azusa Street, bore Parham's imprint. However, through massive Holiness-Pentecostal press coverage, the west coast revival became much more influential than its midwestern precursor.[58]

When news of the Azusa Street revival reached the South in 1906, heralding a restoration of New Testament Christianity, it took hold of much of the Holiness movement, re-forming it along Pentecostal lines. The *Apostolic Faith*, published from Azusa Street beginning in September 1906, reached thousands of anxious southerners who pored over its pages in anticipation of the baptism of the Holy Ghost. The first issue ran five thousand copies, but by May 1908 the Azusa Street mission was publishing fifty thousand copies every month. This paper reported the activities of the Los Angeles revival and served as a forum for burgeoning Pentecostal sects scattered around the globe.[59] Certain papers, including the *Apostolic Faith*, were so revered that they were thought to have curative, nearly magical powers. Some adherents believed that "when applied like a balm to the site of infirmity," these newspapers would bring relief to converts.[60] The *Apostolic Faith*'s power of persuasion was immense.

Along with the *Apostolic Faith*, the southern radical Holiness press proved crucial to the transmission of Azusa's Pentecostal message. Leaders like Frank Bartleman eagerly promoted the Azusa message in southern Holiness and Pentecostal papers. Bartleman wrote glowing editorials. He provocatively recounted the miracles at Asuza in the *Way of Faith*, the *Apostolic Faith*, *Word and Work* (Framingham, Mass.), and a number of other periodicals.[61] Soon after the revival began in April 1906, the *Holiness Advocate*, published in Clinton, North Carolina, featured it in its pages. The editor, Rev. A. B. Crumpler of the Pentecostal Holiness Church, wrote that he had sent out "scores of letters of inquiry to persons who have been in touch with the work [at Azusa] from the beginning." And he, like others, became "profoundly convinced that God is in the movement."[62] Not only did many radical Holiness papers give approval to the Azusa revival, they also began to question the sufficiency of Holiness doctrine and experience. The challenge prompted many Holiness believers to withdraw from the movement and declare allegiance to Pentecostalism.

Other papers rapidly became instruments of this process. Shortly after the California revival began, reports of it appeared in J. M. Pike's South Carolina–based the *Way of Faith*. This paper reprinted accounts of men and women speaking in tongues and performing miracles at Azusa. The editor convinced many Holiness people that they had somehow been denied the full gospel. A North Carolina Holiness preacher, Gaston Barnabas Cashwell, reasoned similarly and wrote in to the *Apostolic Faith* with his testimonial: "I began to read in the *Way of Faith* the reports of meetings in [the] Azusa Mission, Los Angeles. I had been preaching holiness for nine years, but my soul began to hunger and thirst for the fullness of God. . . . After praying and weeping before God for many days, [Jesus] put it into my heart to go to Los Angeles to seek the baptism with the Holy Ghost."[63]

Cashwell made the long journey west in November 1906. Once at Azusa, however, he recoiled at the interracial fellowship he found there. But soon he overcame his prejudice and asked Seymour and other African American ministers in attendance to pray that he might receive the baptism. Subsequently, Cashwell spoke in tongues and felt empowered to return to the South as an evangelist of Pentecost.[64]

After returning from Azusa, Cashwell went to Dunn, North Carolina, where he rented a tobacco warehouse to hold a revival through December and January.[65] He intended Dunn to be a virtual reenactment of Azusa. It was: with healings, speaking in tongues, interracial fellowship, and mystical religious experiences. The southern Holiness press also reported on the Dunn revival and helped encourage the uninitiated to seek their "Pentecost." Not long afterward, Cashwell mounted a barnstorming tour of the South. He preached his new message in Memphis, Tennessee; High Point, North Carolina; Danville, Virginia; West Union, Clinton, and Lake City, South Carolina; Toccoa and Valdosta, Georgia; and Birmingham, Alabama. But perhaps Cashwell's most effective tool was his new paper, the *Bridegroom's Messenger*, published in Atlanta. In the October 1, 1907, inaugural issue, he forthrightly summarized its singular purpose: "We believe that . . . the South [should] have a paper in which nothing contrary to this great Pentecostal truth is allowed to enter."[66] At first Cashwell printed four thousand monthly issues, but by September 1908 he was publishing eight thousand copies per month. Half of these were sent out for free, the other by subscription. The *Bridegroom's Messenger* became the mouthpiece for Pentecostalism in the Southeast. It published announcements for revivals throughout the region, and it gave considerable space for testimonies. Moreover, the paper ran features that cultivated the nascent movement's theology. Consequently, Cashwell's paper and his tireless evangelism helped guide the Church of God (Cleveland), the Fire-Baptized Holiness Church, and the Pentecostal Holiness Church into the Pentecostal fold.[67]

A few months after Cashwell embraced the Azusa message and began his tour of the South, Charles Harrison Mason, a leader of the Memphis-based African-American Church of God in Christ, also made the pilgrimage to Azusa. Writing to the *Apostolic Faith* in 1907, Mason remarked, "I had a great desire to come to Los Angeles. I had preached the Pentecost to my people and they were hungry for it." The outbreak on the West Coast, Mason believed, was prophecy fulfilled. Once at Azusa, Mason recalled that he "surrendered perfectly to [Christ] and consented to Him." Next, he began singing a song in "unknown tongues" and received what he described as an agonizing vision of Christ's crucifixion. After this experience, he felt confirmed that the Church of God in Christ must adopt the Pentecostal message.[68] Following a disagreement with the non-Pentecostal wing of his denomination, Mason led his camp into the movement. Like his contemporaries, he soon began publishing his own Pentecostal paper, the *Whole Truth*, which served to unify the otherwise loosely organized new church.

After initially reading about Azusa, Mason and Cashwell expressed a longing to receive something more than what they thought the Holiness movement could provide. However, not only did the Holiness movement come under suspicion for being inadequate in their eyes, so, too, did numerous independent sects and denominations, including Southern Methodists, Southern Baptists, and Free-Will Baptists. Editors of the southern radical Holiness press seized on the tensions between established churches and newer sects and printed accounts of religious dissatisfaction in their papers. In this manner, the *Evening Light and Church of God Evangel* (Cleveland, Tennessee) published a letter from a Baptist preacher to his wife. The clergyman described his heightened attraction to the ecstatic Pentecostals. After explaining how devotees spoke in tongues, performed healings, and seemingly cast out devils at a revival, he exclaimed: "Compared with [the Pentecostal revival], any meeting of Baptists is as the silence of death."[69] Similarly, G. G. Miller, a Pentecostal minister, concluded that traditional churches had become ineffective or spiritually dead. In July 1908 he wrote to the *Way of Faith* describing revival services he held in Berrydale, Florida. Shortly after setting up his tent between a Methodist and a Mormon church, he denounced the Methodists and asked the local minister to "show five conversions in ten years," but the preacher could not. Triumphant, Miller reported that after two weeks of meetings, he saw "thirty-six professions [at] the altar; three reclaimed, sixteen converted, eleven sanctified and six Baptized with the Holy Ghost."[70] For these preachers and others like them who corresponded with the emerging Pentecostal press, the sedate forms of conventional evangelicalism could not compete with the liberating emotionalism of the new sect.

State denominational as well as Holiness papers went on the defensive and warned readers to guard themselves against the fanaticism of "tonguers." These public conflicts replicated some of the same tensions that once existed between mainline groups and the Holiness movement. In some ways, though, the stakes were even higher now. A Methodist minister in Florida who once battled local independent Holiness bands soon encountered a new nemesis, Pentecostalism. In the pages of the *Florida Christian Advocate* he cautioned Florida Methodists to beware of the "tongue crowd" or "fanaticism gone to seed." This new zealous sect drew many members away from his church while threatening his pastoral authority.[71] The Holiness movement seemed tame by comparison. Southern Baptists also mounted an attack. An article that appeared in a 1908 issue of the *Baptist Argus* (Louisville, Kentucky) is characteristic of this posture. Following an investigation of tongues speech, this paper published its findings. Non-Pentecostal missionaries from India, China, and Japan were cited in order to disprove the validity of the gift. One missionary described what he heard spoken by Pentecostals as unintelligible, little resembling an actual language.[72] In the competitive sphere of foreign missions allegiance was critical.

The ensuing skirmish that broke out between non-tongues-speaking Holiness people and Pentecostals might be said to resemble what Sigmund Freud called "the narcissism of minor differences."[73] Yet, for all the similarities between the two groups, the conflict took the form of outright warfare. The success of Pentecostalism in the South often depended on the competitive drive against traditional religion. Moreover, according to Grant Wacker, the new Pentecostal message compelled converts to attest that their former religious experiences were not just incomplete but inauthentic.[74] Such challenges were ubiquitous in Pentecostal papers. This, of course, infuriated those who stayed within the Holiness movement. Editors of non-Pentecostal Holiness papers crowded their pages with vitriolic screeds against what they called "tongues people." The tongues movement was "An Open Door for Heresy," "A Confusion of the Devil," full of "BORDER LAND HOLINESS PEOPLE" and backsliders.[75]

Yet southern Pentecostals thought mainline evangelicals and Holiness folk impeded spiritual freedom when they failed to accept Pentecostal doctrine and practice. Bearing so close a resemblance to Pentecostalism, the Holiness movement came under particular suspicion. Whereas Holiness people espoused only two works of grace (salvation and sanctification), most southern Pentecostals adopted a third: Holy Ghost baptism, culminating in tongues speech.[76] They referred to their faith as the Full Gospel, and in the incipient Pentecostal press, new converts to the movement criticized their sanctification experience as incomplete.

Testimonies of the three works of grace, instead of two, crowded the pages of these papers. Personal salvation histories, written and read by inductees, revealed how Pentecostals imagined and constructed their religious community in line with Azusa. Typical of these was E. G. Murrah's, who entitled his testimony "Three Epochs in My Life." Writing from Atlanta to the *Bridegroom's Messenger*, Murrah reminisced about his salvation fifty-five years before, and his sanctification some thirty years later. Not entirely satisfied, Murrah felt something lacking, and upon contact with Pentecostals he sought and received the baptism of the Holy Ghost. Murrah soon spoke in tongues and rhapsodized, "Never in my life of over 55 years on the way to heaven did I feel so . . . full of glory and of God."[77]

The new sect offered to overwhelm human emotions, washing away despair through the hope of euphoric religious experience. Pentecostal experience might also serve as a great leveler. Eager southerners read that at Azusa no distinctions were made to differentiate who could receive the gifts of the Spirit. The gift of foreign tongues, for instance, required no educational or cultural experience. Indeed, as at Azusa, in the South social and cultural distinctions were purposefully confounded. At a revival in Southern Pines, North Carolina, narrated in the June 1907 issue of the *Holiness Advocate*, Anna Kelly described how a "sister McLaughlin" received the gift of language. In confirmation of this experience, she recounted, "a highly educated doctor of Southern Pines told me he could understand what [sister McLaughlin] said except one word, and that she spoke the purest Latin." God, Kelly continued, "is just as able to give languages as He is to confound them."[78]

Racial and gender divisions were also not as clearly demarcated as they were in the society as a whole or in mainline churches. The Holiness movement set the tone for this, offering women and African Americans opportunities unavailable elsewhere.[79] Nowhere was this perhaps more clear than in the Church of God (Anderson), which struggled to maintain interracial communion and some degree of gender equality throughout its history.[80] In the earliest years, female Holiness evangelists like Maria Woodworth-Etter were extremely popular among both southern whites and African Americans. She, like others, frequently preached to racially integrated crowds in the region.[81] Writing in the *Holiness Advocate*, one woman maintained that when a believer received the baptism with the Holy Ghost, she would come to see that scripture did not prohibit women from preaching. For her it was clear that "God don't call all women to preach neither does He call all men to preach. But if He does call and they fail to obey—woe is pronounced upon them."[82] At Azusa this tradition continued. The *Apostolic Faith* published testimonials from both men and women, African Americans and whites. In theory and in practice the Spirit was said not to discriminate by color or sex. As such, potentially anyone could be a spiritual conduit.[83] It is doubtful, however, that Azusa's egalitarian message was received with equal enthusiasm in the Southeast.[84]

The southern Pentecostal press only occasionally broached the subject of race. Even periodicals edited by African Americans, including *Whole Truth* and *Voice in the Wilderness*, showed remarkable inattention to matters of racial justice. Yet when the press did grapple with issues of race, it must have made a strong impact upon its readers.[85] A. A. Boddy, an English participant at Azusa, commented on the astounding interracialism of the revival in his paper *Confidence* (Sunderland, England). Cashwell reprinted Boddy's stunning observations in the *Bridegroom's Messenger*: "One of the remarkable things was that preachers of the Southern States were willing and eager to go over to those negro people at Los Angeles and have fellowship with them, and through their prayers receive the same blessing. The most wonderful thing was that, when those white preachers came back to the Southern States, they were not ashamed to say before their own congregations that they had been worshipping with negroes, and had received some of the same wonderful blessings that had been poured out on them."[86]

Black and white southern Pentecostals attended tent revivals together and wrote in each other's papers. But there were limits to the degree of interaction. When necessary, southern Pentecostals evaded reprisals for race mixing by segregating their tent meetings or by having blacks and whites meet at separate times.[87] The extent of gender and racial equality in the South should not be exaggerated. Social equality was not Pentecostals' primary concern. Moreover, the Pentecostal revival emanating from Azusa offered a type of spiritual liberation that transcended, they thought, more immediate forms of social liberation.[88]

While Holiness and Pentecostal writers occasionally addressed racial and gender inequalities in their papers, they showed extreme inattention, if not hostility, to politics and social issues. One looks in vain for references to labor, voting rights, economic distress, or lynching in their publications. They were obsessed with exposing duplicitous Methodist and Baptist ministers and denouncing pleasures of the flesh, but said nothing about robber barons or the unfair treatment of workers. There are a few exceptions. In the late nineteenth and early twentieth centuries certain Holiness periodicals, like the *Pentecostal Herald* and the *Battle Axe* (Danville, Va.), championed the Prohibitionist cause. Their zeal for Prohibition was equally matched by fervent antitobacco crusading. Such specific moral interests seldom translated into larger political concerns. A poem entitled "For Whom Will You Vote" printed in an 1894 issue of the *Revivalist* well illustrates Holiness and Pentecostal attitudes toward politics. "*I am one of God's electioneering agents,*" the poet declared. "In this contest men, women, and children can vote. Then vote for Jesus! Vote for Jesus!! Vote for Jesus!!!"[89]

When initiates rhapsodized about the revival, they seldom referred to the fact that it brought some form of gender, racial, or political equality. Instead, they recounted its spiritually transformative possibilities. And, reading of the signs and spiritual wonders at Azusa, southern converts to Pentecostalism craved similar experiences. The sect's newspapers advertised what converts needed. Simultaneously they met those needs and provided believers with a new vocabulary of expression.[90] Most of those who sought "their Pentecost" were not disappointed. In his published testimony, Rev. R. F. Wellons recounted the gravity of his salvation and sanctification experiences, yet he commented that when he read of the California revival, he "began to hunger and thirst after more of the real water of life." Similarly, Berta Maxwell of Fayetteville, North Carolina, wrote that after she read of Azusa she "became hungry for a deeper death to self and a fuller something."[91] Because of the extensive press coverage of Azusa, some knew more clearly what they sought and were able to voice their needs accordingly. M. H. Alexander, writing to the *Bridegroom's Messenger* from Pasley, North

Carolina, epitomized this pattern: "In the Fall of 1906 I began to read how the power was falling in California and people were speaking in tongues and the sick were being healed. . . . My heart began to leap within me; I realized that this was what I needed; so I began to see how clear the word of God taught it [and] I began to ask the dear Lord to give me this wonderful blessing."[92] Such testimonies attest to the degree that newspaper accounts formed the lived religious experience of southern Pentecostals.

In the Pentecostal press, those who received Holy Ghost baptism described being bodily possessed by the Spirit of God. In this sense, their ecstasy became all the more dramatic because of its divine origin. As Ann Taves suggests, these individuals fervently believed that they were not the agent or cause of their experience. When they sang in tongues, prophesied, or performed miracles, it was through the direct working of God. With this new revelation in full view, Pentecostals perceived themselves as at the center of God's restored order.[93]

In part, the more radical sects in the South favorably received Pentecostalism because of the movement's sharpened restorationist vision. The Pentecostal press generated this phenomenon, reporting such messages as "Many are being saved, sanctified, filled with the Holy Ghost, and speaking in tongues" and "Pentecost is the same today as it was 1900 years ago."[94] The restorationist trope filled accounts of revivals in Florida, Tennessee, Georgia, the Carolinas, and Alabama. In their published testimonies, converts occupied an anachronistic space, proclaiming freedom from nineteen hundred years of church history and dogma. Writing from Birmingham, Alabama, Rev. M. M. Pinson claimed, "Those who get the baptism of the Spirit in my meeting speak and sing in other tongues . . . as on the day of Pentecost, and at the house of Cornelius. It surely works as of old, for Jesus is the same yesterday, today, and forever."[95]

Certainly, by 1906 radical Holiness people were well attuned to the restorationist message, but newspaper accounts of the younger movement piqued their interest in new ways. Accordingly, for those wanting assurance that their experience was in fact a restoration of the apostolic faith, the Pentecostal press seemed to offer the most literal rendition as well as a faith free from the taint of the past. Pentecostalism, mused B. F. Lawrence, was unencumbered by the burden of history; "it leaps the intervening years crying, '*Back to*

Pentecost.'"[96] Most of all, their conviction that they were reenacting the book of Acts, attested to by the signs and wonders narrated in their papers, gave them confidence in Pentecostalism's credibility and purpose.

Without the network of newspapers that enabled southern Pentecostals to imagine their community in accord with the Azusa revival, it is doubtful that the movement would have been as successful in the South as it was. The reportage of the Azusa revival allowed individuals in the region to reconstruct their religious experience along Pentecostal lines. Once in attendance at revivals, southern converts began to experience firsthand what they had only read and heard about before. In turn, numbers of converts from southern revivals reported their experiences in Pentecostal papers, bringing the message full circle—and back into print. So, whereas radical Holiness sects set in motion the doctrines and religious practices that would feed southern Pentecostalism—theological perfectionism, intense religious experience, counterculturalism, and restorationism—it was the burgeoning Holiness and Pentecostal press that served as the major instrument of transition.

NOTES

The author wishes to thank the following for their insightful comments on earlier versions of this essay: Fitzhugh Brundage, David Hackett, Matt Harper, Ben Houston, Charles E. Jones, Susan Lewis, Donald G. Mathews, David Roebuck, Beth Stephens, Grant Wacker, Brian Ward, David Harrington Watt, Bland Whitley, Daniel Woods, and Bertram Wyatt-Brown.

1. The term *Holiness-Pentecostal* denotes the interlocking networks and similar religious outlooks of the two movements. The doctrines of a second, purifying work of grace (usually called entire sanctification), the baptism of the Holy Spirit, and the premillennial Second Coming of Christ were important to both. Although Pentecostalism and speaking in tongues arose after 1900, Pentecostalism had its origins in the Holiness revival of the 1880s and 1890s. Donald W. Dayton, *Theological Roots of Pentecostalism* (Metuchen, N.J., and London: Scarecrow, 1987), 87–113. To distinguish Holiness from Pentecostal churches in the United States, J. Gordon Melton asserts that the Pentecostals, unlike the Holiness people, seek and receive "the gift of speaking in tongues as a sign of the baptism of the Holy Spirit." *The Encyclopedia of American Religions*, vol. 1 (Tarrytown, N.Y.: Triumph, 1991), 41.

2. *Los Angeles Times*, April 18, 1906, sec. 2, p. 1.

3. Frank Bartleman, *Azusa Street* (South Plainfield, N.J.: Bridge, 1980), 48.

4. Southern historians, in general, have failed to take into account the impact of Pentecostalism in the New South. Donald Mathews points out that before Edward Ayers's *The Promise of the New South: Life after Reconstruction* (New York and Oxford: Oxford University Press, 1992), "the major synthesizers of southern history," including U. B. Phillips, William Dunning, C. Vann Woodward, George Tindall, Wesley Frank Craven, and E. Merton Coulter, had "not been forced to explain the role of religion in southern life." "'We have left undone those things which we ought to have done': Southern Religious History in Retrospect and Prospect," *Church History* 67 (June 1998): 306.

5. Pentecostalism has not attained scholarly attention commensurate with its size. Today, Pentecostalism is the second largest subgroup of global Christianity. It claims approximately 11 million American adherents and a worldwide following of more than 430 million. Grant Wacker, "Searching for Eden with a Satellite Dish: Primitivism, Pragmatism and the Pentecostal Character," in *Religion and American Culture*, ed. David G. Hackett (New York and London: Routledge, 1995), 440. Wacker, a prominent historian of Pentecostalism, defines Pentecostals as believing in a postconversion experience known as baptism in the Holy Spirit. Pentecostals, he says, believe that a person who has been baptized in the Holy Spirit will manifest one or more of the nine spiritual gifts described in 1 Corinthians 12 and 14 (441).

6. David Edwin Harrell suggest that if southern religious experience is not qualitatively distinct, it is, nonetheless, quantitatively different from that of other sections of the United States. The South has been the most solidly evangelical section of the country. According to Harrell, excluding "the Mormon havens in Utah and Nevada, the most homogenous religious states in the nation are in the South. The Bible Belt was a well entrenched stereotype by the early twentieth century, and it was one with clear substance to it." This region, remarks Harrell, "was a reservoir where the old-time message had remained intact amid the challenges of the twentieth century." Introduction to *Varieties of Southern Evangelicalism*, ed. David Edwin Harrell (Macon, Ga.: Mercer University Press, 1981), 2, 3. Samuel Hill asserts that although secularization has grown in the recent South, it "scarcely made a dent in the fabled religiosity of the southern people." Introduction to *Varieties of Southern Religious Experience*, ed. Samuel S. Hill (Baton Rouge and London: Louisiana State University Press, 1988), 3. Ted Ownby argues that the South can be rightfully called an evangelical culture "if we realize that people who rarely attended church and who lived far

outside the evangelicals' moral code nevertheless found ways to express their beliefs in the virtues of the dominant religion." Revivals, Ownby suggests, became the locus where sinners as well as saints expressed their commitment to southern Christian culture. *Subduing Satan: Religion, Recreation, and Manhood in the Rural South, 1865–1920* (Chapel Hill and London: University of North Carolina Press, 1990), 162.

7. We currently know little about how mainline denominations and local communities responded to the supposed threats these groups posed. Vinson Synan, *The Holiness-Pentecostal Tradition: Charismatic Movements in the Twentieth Century* (Grand Rapids, Mich., and Cambridge: Eerdmans, 1997), 66–67.

8. Grant Wacker, *Heaven Below: Early Pentecostals and American Culture* (Cambridge, Mass.: Harvard University Press, 2001), 264. At a 1915 convention of the Pentecostal Holiness Church, leaders of the denomination recognized this all-important aspect. They reported: "There is perhaps no agency among us greater than the printing press. Hence, we are admonished by the Word of the Lord to give attendance to reading." F. L. Bramblett, D. R. Brown, and Hugh Bowling, "Report of Committee on Books and Periodicals," in *Minutes of the Fifth Annual Session of the Georgia and Upper South Carolina Convention of the Pentecostal Holiness Church Held at Canon, Ga., Nov. 17–19, 1915* (n.p., 1915), 8–9. In the late nineteenth century the newspaper industry experienced extremely rapid growth. Between 1870 and 1900 the number of daily newspapers quadrupled, while the number of copies sold daily increased nearly sixfold. Michael Emery, Edwin Emery, and Nancy L. Roberts, *The Press in America: An Interpretive History of the Mass Media* (Boston: Allyn and Bacon, 2000), 157. Technological advancements, including the development of high-speed presses, the invention of the typewriter, and the shift from rag to wood-pulp paper, greatly contributed to this boom. George H. Douglas, *The Golden Age of the Newspaper* (Westport, Conn.: Greenwood, 1999), 83–86; Kevin G. Barnhurst and John Nerone, *The Form of the News: A History* (New York: Guilford, 2001), 105–6. I would like to thank David G. Roebuck for alerting me to the importance of these changes.

9. For an examination of how the press imagined the First Great Awakening, see Frank Lambert, *Inventing the "Great Awakening"* (Princeton, N.J.: Princeton University Press, 1999), 87–124; Harry S. Stout, *The Divine Dramatist: George Whitefield and the Rise of Modern Evangelicalism* (Grand Rapids, Mich.: Eerdmans, 1991), 113–32; and T. H. Breen, "Retrieving Common Sense: Rights, Liberties, and the Religious Public Sphere in Late Eighteenth Century America," in *To Secure the Blessings of Liberty: Rights in American History*, ed. Josephine F. Pacheco (Fairfax, Va.: George Mason University Press, 1993), 55–65. On the role played by the press in

the Third Great Awakening, see Kathryn Long, *The Revival of 1857–58: Interpreting an American Religious Awakening* (New York: Oxford University Press, 1998), 26–45. Long reveals, "Although the Reformed clergy shaped the narrative of the 1857–58 Revival for later historians, newspapers told the story to most Americans in the spring of 1858." Religious and secular papers emulated each other's writing styles and helped organize and unify the language used to describe the event (27).

10. Alexis de Tocqueville, *Democracy in America*, ed. J. P. Mayer (Garden City, N.Y.: Anchor, 1969), 517.

11. W. B. Godbey, *Autobiography of Rev. W. B. Godbey, A. M.* (Cincinnati: God's Revivalist, 1909), 10.

12. On the orality of Holiness and Pentecostal culture, see J. Lawrence Brasher, *The Sanctified South: John Lakin Brasher and the Holiness Movement* (Urbana and Chicago: University of Illinois Press, 1994), xii, 69; Deborah Vansau McCauley, *Appalachian Mountain Religion: A History* (Urbana and Chicago: University of Illinois Press, 1995), 257; Elmer T. Clark, *The Small Sects in America* (Nashville: Abingdon, 1965), 85, 98; Cheryl J. Sanders, *Saints in Exile: The Holiness-Pentecostal Experience in African America Religion and Culture* (New York and Oxford: Oxford University Press, 1996), 49–52, 56; and Robert Mapes Anderson, *Vision of the Disinherited: The Making of American Pentecostalism* (New York and Oxford: Oxford University Press, 1979), 223–27. For an examination of how readily radical evangelicals embraced modern advertising techniques, radio, and drama, see Betty A. DeBerg, *Ungodly Women: Gender and the First Wave of American Fundamentalism* (Minneapolis: Fortress, 1990); Douglas Carl Abrams, *Selling the Old-Time Religion: American Fundamentalists and Mass Culture, 1920–1940* (Athens: University of Georgia Press, 2001); Quintin J. Schultze, ed., *American Evangelicals and the Mass Media: Perspectives on the Relationship between American Evangelicals and the Mass Media* (Grand Rapids, Mich.: Academie, 1990); Lillian Taiz, *Hallelujah Lads and Lasses: Remaking the Salvation Army in America, 1880–1930* (Chapel Hill: University of North Carolina Press, 2001), 4–5, 74–75, 79–90; Wacker, "Searching for Eden with a Satellite Dish," 445–46; and Edith Blumhofer, *Aimee Semple McPherson: Everybody's Sister* (Grand Rapids, Mich.: Eerdmans, 1993), 266–68.

13. Joe Creech argues that Azusa was only one of many *historical* points of origin for Pentecostalism. However, he acknowledges its *symbolic* and theological importance. "Visions of Glory: The Place of the Azusa Street Revival in Pentecostal History," *Church History* 65 (September 1996): 406–8, 420. On the massive impact of the Azusa Street meeting, see Cecil M. Robeck Jr., "Pentecostal Origins from a Global Perspective," in *Altogether in One Place: Theological Papers from the Brighton Conference on World Evangelism*, ed. Harold D. Hunter and Peter D. Hocken (Sheffield, U.K.:

Sheffield Academic, 1993), 166–80. Robert Mapes Anderson estimates that Pentecostals published as many as seventy-four different newspapers in the early years of the movement. *Vision of the Disinherited*, 75.

14. Benedict Anderson describes the unifying character of newspapers, which, as an extreme variant of print capitalism, "made it possible for rapidly growing numbers of people to think about themselves, and to relate themselves to others, in profoundly new ways." Accordingly, the Holiness-Pentecostal newspapers' role in unifying the discourse of Pentecostals proved particularly effective. *Imagined Communities: Reflections on the Origins and Spread of Nationalism* (London and New York: Verso, 1998), 36, 32–35. For other examples of the press creating coherent religious discourse, see Evelyn Brooks Higginbotham, *Righteous Discontent: The Women's Movement in the Black Baptist Church, 1880–1920* (Cambridge, Mass.: Harvard University Press, 1993), 11; and Nathan O. Hatch, *The Democratization of American Christianity* (New Haven, Conn., and London: Yale University Press, 1989), 73, 75, 76, 146.

15. The leading sects that constituted the radical Holiness movement were the Apostolic Faith (Kansas), the Fire-Baptized Holiness Church, the Church of God (Cleveland, Tennessee), the Pentecostal Holiness Church, and the Church of God in Christ.

16. Edward Ayers notes that new musical styles (jazz, the blues, and country music) entered the South at roughly the same time as Holiness-Pentecostalism did: "Those who played and those who preached incorporated new ideas and styles from outside the South into their own distinctly Southern vocabularies." *The Promise of the New South*, 373.

17. A. J. Tomlinson, "Journal of Happenings: The Diary of A. J. Tomlinson, 1901–23," September 25, 1908, Dixon Pentecostal Research Center, Cleveland, Tenn.

18. For a typical postwar Holiness philippic, see George Hughes, *Days of Power in the Forest Temple: A Review of the Wonderful Work of God at Fourteen National Camp-Meetings from 1867 to 1872* (Boston: John Bent, 1873), 10–17. For more on the connection to Populism, see Joseph Whitfield Creech Jr., "Righteous Indignation: Religion and Populism in North Carolina, 1886–1906" (Ph.D. diss., University of Notre Dame, 2000); Norman Kingsford Dann, "Concurrent Social Movements: A Study of the Interrelationships between Populist Politics and Holiness Religion" (Ph.D. diss., Syracuse University, 1974); and Randall J. Stephens, "The Convergence of Populism, Religion, and the Holiness-Pentecostal Movements: A Review of the Historical Literature," *Fides et Historia* 32 (Winter–Spring 2000): 51–64.

19. Wacker indicates that in the last two decades of the nineteenth century evangelicals across the ideological spectrum "exhibited a deep and

enduring fascination with the work of God's Spirit." "The Holy Spirit and the Spirit of the Age in American Protestantism, 1880–1910," *Journal of American History* 72 (June 1985): 54. For a history of the Holiness movement in America, see Melvin Easterday Dieter, *The Holiness Revival of the Nineteenth Century* (Lanham, Md., and London: Scarecrow, 1996). On the southern extension of the revival, see Briane K. Turley, *A Wheel within a Wheel: Southern Methodism and the Georgia Holiness Association* (Macon, Ga.: Mercer University Press, 1999). Examples of these new sects include the Fire-Baptized Holiness Church, the Church of God (Anderson, Indiana), the Pentecostal Church of the Nazarene, and the Apostolic Holiness Union.

20. On healing, see Raymond J. Cunningham, "From Holiness to Healing: The Faith Cure in America, 1872–1892," *Church History* 43 (September 1974): 499–513; and Jonathan Baer, "Redeemed Bodies: The Functions of Divine Healing in Incipient Pentecostalism," *Church History* 70 (December 2001): 735–71. For an analysis of the transformation from Holiness to Pentecostal, see Dayton, *The Theological Roots of Pentecostalism*. On the millennial expectations of Holiness-Pentecostal groups, see Timothy Weber, *Living in the Shadow of the Second Coming: American Premillennialism, 1875–1925* (New York: Oxford University Press, 1983).

21. "National Camp Meeting," *Knoxville Daily Chronicle*, September 24, 1872, 1; September 25, 1872, 1. Seven years later, southern Methodists in Texas were similarly apprehensive about the Holiness movement. Their chief periodical writers lambasted Holiness "cranks" as prideful fanatics and disturbers of denominational peace. They were, as one critic wrote, outside agitators from the North bent on driving congregants "mad" and causing women to become "boisterous and rough." "Sanctification—So Called," *Texas Christian Advocate*, November 1, 1897, 4; November 29, 1879, 2. These fears are not at all surprising. The postbellum battles between the Methodist Episcopal Church and the Methodist Episcopal Church, South revealed intense lingering sectional hostilities. See Hunter Dickson Farish, *The Circuit Rider Dismounts: A Social History of Southern Methodism, 1865–1900* (Richmond, Va.: Dietz, 1938), 25–26, 78, 101, 107, 161; Daniel Stowell, *Rebuilding Zion: The Religious Reconstruction of the South, 1863–1877* (New York: Oxford University Press, 1998), 130–45.

22. *Living Words*, April 1903, 7.

23. *Bridegroom's Messenger*, October 1, 1907, 2.

24. The Church of God paper, the *Gospel Trumpet*, boasted of 60,000 subscriptions in 1908. To this the editor hoped to add another 140,000 by 1909. *Gospel Trumpet*, December 10, 1908, 15. In 1896 J. M. Pike, editor of the *Way of Faith*, wrote that his publication had a circulation of 8,000 to 10,000 in South Carolina alone and reached nearly every state in the

Union. "Advertisements," *Way of Faith*, August 5, 1896, 4. W. A. Dodge's Georgia Holiness paper, the *Way of Life*, ran at 6,000 issues during the peak of its influence. Around 1890, one-year subscriptions for the *Way of Life* cost $1. J. William Garbutt, *William Asbury Dodge: Southern Holiness Pioneer*, ed. Kenneth O. Brown (Hazelton, Pa.: Holiness Archives, 2001), 69. In 1900 the editor of the *Firebrand* reported a circulation of 10,000 issues, some for regular subscriptions and others for sample copies. *Firebrand*, November 1900, 1. Two Holiness papers, the *Way of Faith* and the *Pentecostal Herald*, focused almost exclusively on the movement's peculiar views concerning eschatology, healing, and entire sanctification. By the mid-1890s the vast majority of southern Holiness folk had adopted beliefs in healing and, more important, a pessimistic end-times theology known as premillennialism. Holiness adherents cited a number of reasons for accepting premillennialism. Most felt rejected by mainline churches and came to see the world as fundamentally corrupt, even irredeemable. Southern premillennialists believed Christ would return before the millennium to take his loyal followers into heaven. Hence, they grew increasingly uninterested in social reform. If anything made the southern Holiness movement unique it was the nearly unanimous adoption of these views. Every issue of the *Way of Faith* for 1896 included pieces on either the premillennial coming of Christ, healing, or both. Readers of Southern Methodist periodicals would have rarely, if ever, seen articles on these themes. For an excellent treatment of premillennialism among early Pentecostals, see D. William Faupel, *The Everlasting Gospel: The Significance of Eschatology in the Development of Pentecostal Thought* (Sheffield, U.K.: Sheffield Academic, 1996).

25. The *Way of Life* listed 157 books for purchase in an 1891 issue. These ranged in price from 10¢ for Wesley's ever-popular *Plain Account of Christian Perfection* to $3 for a two-volume set of Frances R. Havergal's poetry. "Our Book List," *Way of Life*, June 24, 1891, 4. An 1885 issue of the *Christian Witness* advertised 211 books and tracts for sale from a wide range of Holiness-affiliated authors and hymn writers. "Books and Tracts on Christian Holiness," *Christian Witness and Advocate of Bible Holiness*, November 5, 1885, 7.

26. *Live Coals of Fire*, October 27, 1899, 4.

27. Eva M. Watson, *George D. Watson, Fearless for the Truth* (Salem, Ohio: Schmul, 2001), 54.

28. "Denominational Loyalty," *Southern Christian Advocate*, August 26, 1886, 4.

29. Emma Christmas, "An Experience," *Way of Faith*, January 8, 1896, 5; November 25, 1895, 4. The *Way of Faith* solicited this help with ads calling on readers to circulate Holiness papers and magazines. For one dime,

agents' names would be added to the Holiness Exchange List, a document "sent to all publishers of holiness literature." These publishers would then mail sample copies to those on the list. *Way of Faith*, March 25, 1896, 7.

30. W. C. Dunlap, *Life of S. Miller Willis: The Fire Baptized Lay Evangelist* (Atlanta: Constitution, 1892), 140.

31. I. E. Lowery, "The Colored Ministers and Bishop Taylor's Steamer," *Christian Witness and Advocate of Bible Holiness*, March 8, 1887, 2.

32. Southern Holiness and Pentecostal folk seldom identified with the shibboleths of sectionalism. In their papers they never championed the Lost Cause, as the mainline press so often did. Historian Roger Glenn Robins finds radical Holiness representative of a growing late nineteenth-century transregional culture. The connections perfectionist advocates made with other believers throughout the country—much like Populists, temperance enthusiasts, and women's rights activists—undercut regional and local affiliations. Moreover, Holiness people came to think of themselves as part of a larger religious family that obliterated many sectional, class, and racial barriers. "Plainfolk Modernist: The Radical Holiness World of A. J. Tomlinson" (Ph.D. diss., Duke University, 1999), 47, 48, 103–5; Robert Wiebe, *The Search for Order, 1877–1920* (New York: Hill and Wang, 1967), 47, 53. Holiness advocates often testified to being cleansed of all sectional prejudice. For examples of this phenomenon, see Dunlap, *Life of S. Miller Willis*, 26; "That They May Be One," *Zion's Outlook*, February 7, 1901, 8; and Timothy Smith, *Called unto Holiness: The Story of the Nazarenes, the Formative Years* (Kansas City, Mo.: Nazarene Publishing House, 1962), 178.

33. For example, A. J. Tomlinson, a founder of the Church of God (Cleveland), avidly read and corresponded with *God's Revivalist*, the *Christian and Missionary Alliance*, and *Way of Faith*. Robins, "Plainfolk Modernist," 264. Joseph H. King, a leading figure in the Fire-Baptized Holiness movement and later in the Pentecostal Holiness Church, recalled being strongly influence by Holiness papers like the *Way of Life*, the *Vanguard* (St. Louis, Mo.), and the *Christian Witness*. *Yet Speaketh: Memoirs of the Late Bishop Joseph H. King* (Franklin Springs, Ga.: Publishing House of the Pentecostal Holiness Church, 1949), 43, 81.

34. Percival A. Wesche, *Henry Clay Morrison: Crusader Saint* (Berne, Ind.: Herald, 1963), 62. I am indebted to William Kostlevy for providing me with this source. *Pentecostal Herald* (Louisville, Ky.), February 9, 1898, 1. The editor of the *Revivalist*, Martin Wells Knapp, changed the name to *God's Revivalist* in 1901. Lloyd Raymond Day, "A History of God's Bible School in Cincinnati, 1900–1949" (master's thesis, University of Cincinnati, 1949), 22.

35. Wesche, *Henry Clay Morrison*, 52. Other Holiness enthusiasts reasoned the same. Before W. A. Dodge began his *Way of Life*, he had no

experience publishing or editing a paper. Likewise, Texas Holiness minister Denis Rogers edited and published his paper, *True Holiness*, though he "knew nothing about the printing business and had scarcely seen [the] inside of a printing office." Rogers made up for his deficiencies by taking courses in typesetting and editing at a printing office in McKinney, Texas. Garbutt, *William Asbury Dodge*, 40; Denis Rogers, *Holiness Pioneering in the Southland* (Hemet, Calif.: n.p., 1944), 28. In January 1904 A. J. Tomlinson purchased a small treadle press for $125. With this easy-to-operate machine, Tomlinson began publishing the *Way* from his home in Culberson, North Carolina. Joel R. Trammell, "Publishing the Gospel," *Church of God History and Heritage* (Winter 1998): 2. Years before M. M. Pinson helped establish the Assemblies of God, he bought a press and type in New Orleans, Louisiana, for approximately $300. He intended to reach thousands with a planned Holiness paper. However, an insolvent business partner wrecked the venture. M. M. Pinson, "Sketch of the Life and Ministry of Mack M. Pinson," September 6, 1949, 6, Flower Pentecostal Heritage Center, Springfield, Mo.

36. Martin Wells Knapp, "The Revised Name," *God's Revivalist* (Cincinnati), January 3, 1901, 1. The apocalyptic titles appeared in the *Revivalist*, January 1894, June 1894, January 1893. *Lightning Bolts from Pentecostal Skies; or, Devices of the Devil Unmasked* was also the title of an influential book Knapp published in 1898. For the most incisive discussion of Knapp's role in the radical Holiness movement, see William Kostlevy, "Nor Silver, nor Gold: The Burning Bush Movement and the Communitarian Holiness Vision" (Ph.D. diss., University of Notre Dame, 1996), 21–48. Similar to Knapp's contention that God was the proprietor of his paper, in 1908 the Pentecostal paper *Latter Rain Evangel* began publication, identifying the "Holy Sprit" as its exclusive editor. Wacker, *Heaven Below*, 139. On Holiness adherents' use of Pentecostal imagery, see Dayton, *The Theological Roots of Pentecostalism*, 174–75.

37. Synan, *The Holiness-Pentecostal Tradition*, 41–43.

38. Turley, *A Wheel within a Wheel*, 149–80, 65.

39. J. W. Buckalew, *Incidents in the Life of J. W. Buckalew* (n.p., n.d.), 55.

40. Charles Edwin Jones, "The Holiness Complaint with Late-Victorian Methodism," in *Rethinking Methodist History: A Bicentennial Historical Consultation*, ed. Russell E. Richey and Kenneth Rowe (Nashville: United Methodist Publishing House, 1985), 62, 63. Jones also alludes to the return to an evangelism of the past in *Perfectionist Persuasion: The Holiness Movement and American Methodism, 1867–1936* (Metuchen, N.J.: Scarecrow, 1974), 79–82. Smith traces these volatile years of "come-out-ism" in *Called unto Holiness*, 27–47. On the Holiness reaction to Methodism and the restorationist thread, see Turley, *A Wheel within a Wheel*,

151–67, 172–80. David Edwin Harrell Jr. discusses such religious revolts occurring in the South from 1885 onward in "The Evolution of Plain-Folk Religion in the South," in Hill, *Varieties of Southern Religious Experience*, 32–42. Similarly, James N. Gregory shows how Holiness and Pentecostal sects flourished among the Okies in the 1930s and 1940s. Hungry for the familiar world of plain-folk, revivalistic Christianity, Okies flocked to the new sects, which catered to their sense of cultural loss. *American Exodus: The Dust Bowl Migration and Okie Culture in California* (New York and Oxford: Oxford University Press, 1989), 191–221.

41. Mickey Crews, *The Church of God: A Social History* (Knoxville: University of Tennessee Press, 1990), 38–41.

42. *Revivalist*, June 1897, 6; W. B. Godbey, "Question Drawer," *God's Revivalist*, January 31, 1901, 12. A caveat: Holiness and Pentecostal groups' equality of fellowship seldom generated institutional equality. Donald G. Mathews, "'Christianizing the South'—Sketching a Synthesis," in *New Directions in American Religious History*, ed. Harry S. Stout and D. G. Hart (New York and Oxford: Oxford University Press, 1997), 103.

43. "Spreading among the White Baptists: The Holiness Work in South Carolina," *Truth*, December 3, 1903, 10; *Zion's Outlook*, October 10, 1901, 12. See articles written by Irving Lowery and L. P. Cushman from 1885 to 1887 in the *Christian Witness and Advocate of Bible Holiness*.

44. "Rev. W. A. Dodge's Work among the Colored People," *Pentecostal Herald*, February 24, 1904, 4.

45. Turley, *A Wheel within a Wheel*, 170. For a discussion of other black periodicals, see David Douglas Daniels, "The Cultural Renewal of Slave Religion: Charles Price Jones and the Emergence of the Holiness Movement in Mississippi" (Ph.D. diss., Union Theological Seminary, 1992), 247–48.

46. W. M. Hayes, *Memoirs of Richard Baxter Hayes* (Greer, S.C.: n.p., 1945), 35, 28, 29, 33, 36, 44–45, 24.

47. "A Murderous Assault on Evangelist B. H. Irwin," *Way of Faith*, August 12, 1896, 1.

48. Crews, *The Church of God*, 17–18, 93–107; Daniels, "The Cultural Renewal of Slave Religion," 251–52.

49. By 1902 *Samson's Foxes* had obtained 620 subscribers. Trammell, "Publishing the Gospel," 1; Tomlinson, "Journal of Happenings," August 18, 1901, December 11, 1901.

50. See selections from the *Gadsen Evening Journal* and the *Gadsen Daily News*, in Dorothy Womack Oden, *The History of the Alabama City Church of God* (Montgomery: Herff Jones, 1988), 9–13. See also I. A. Newby, *Plain Folk in the New South: Social Change and Cultural Persistence, 1880–1915* (Baton Rouge: Louisiana State University Press, 1989), 406.

At other times, Pentecostals provoked hostility for their opposition to local churches and secret societies. Kurt O Berends, "Social Variables and Community Response," in *Pentecostal Currents in Mainstream Protestantism*, ed. Edith L. Blumhofer, Russell P. Splitter, and Grant A. Wacker (Urbana and Chicago: University of Illinois Press, 1999), 68–69. For their uproarious street meetings, Salvation Army adherents were also lambasted by the secular press, which accused them of "encouraging civil and sexual disorder." Taiz, *Hallelujah Lads and Lasses*, 70. However, the Holiness-Pentecostal challenge to mainstream culture was largely apolitical. Consequently, some scholars have been quick to criticize or dismiss the movement. In the 1940s, Liston Pope's study of labor unrest in Gaston County, North Carolina, indicted church leaders for not standing "in opposition to the prevailing economic arrangements or to the drastic methods employed for their preservation." *Millhands and Preachers: A Study of Gastonia* (New Haven, Conn.: Yale University Press, 1942), 330. Robert Mapes Anderson concludes that Pentecostalism represented a dysfunctional and maladjusted reaction to social pressures. Because of Pentecostals' negative appraisal of society and their pessimistic outlook for the future, they were an apolitical, "conservative bulwark of the status quo." As such, they channeled their social protest "into the harmless backwaters of religious ideology." *Vision of the Disinherited*, 239. Similarly, R. Laurence Moore argues that the otherworldliness of Pentecostals cut short social protests by diffusing class hostilities. *Religious Outsiders and the Making of Americans* (Oxford and New York: Oxford University Press, 1986), 140–42. These appraisals misconstrue Pentecostals as mere ciphers, when in fact, as Clifford Geertz suggests, religious groups "do not merely interpret social and psychological processes in cosmic terms—in which case they would be philosophical, not religious—but they shape them." *The Interpretation of Cultures: Selected Essays* (New York: Basic, 1973), 124, 93, 119. For an assessment of the positive role of faith in Pentecostalism, see Grant Wacker, "The Functions of Faith in Primitive Pentecostalism," *Harvard Theological Review* 77, no. 3 (1984): 355, 356, 363.

51. "Our Attitude toward Exclusivists," *Christian Advocate*, August 8, 1889, 8.

52. "The Leading of the Spirit," *Christian Advocate*, July 2, 1896, 1.

53. *Religious Herald*, August 22, 1907, 1.

54. W. J. Cash, *The Mind of the South* (New York: Vintage, 1941), 297.

55. Herbert M. Riggle, quoted in Steven Ware, "Restorationism in the Holiness Movement, Late Nineteenth and Early Twentieth Centuries," *Wesleyan Theological Journal* 34 (Spring 1999): 200. For an analysis of earlier forms of restorationism, see Hatch, *The Democratization of American Christianity*, 71.

56. Through the gift of foreign tongues, Pentecostals hoped to fulfill

the "great commission" and evangelize the world in their generation (Acts 1:8; Matt. 28:20). On the millenarian-missions aspect, see James R. Goff Jr., *Fields White unto Harvest: Charles F. Parham and the Missionary Origins of Pentecostalism* (Fayetteville and London: University of Arkansas Press, 1988), 15, 164; and Synan, *The Holiness-Pentecostal Tradition*, 92. To their disappointment, many first-generation Pentecostals entered the mission field and discovered that they did not have the gift of foreign tongues. Subsequently, the gift was interpreted as unknown or unintelligible tongues (glossolalia). Anderson, *Vision of the Disinherited*, 16–19, 90–92; Goff, *Fields White unto Harvest*, 154. Although the manifestation of spiritual gifts and exercises in America was at least as old as the First Great Awakening, the revival Parham inaugurated was unparalleled. Whereas in earlier revivals signs like speaking in tongues and healing were occasional, often dissipating with a revival's termination, Pentecostals normalized and rationalized these experiences as necessary to a total Christian experience.

57. *Kansas City Times*, January 27, 1901; *St. Louis Post-Dispatch*, January 25, 1901; *Topeka Daily Capital*, January 6, 1901, 2; *Topeka State Journal*, January 7, 1901, 4; Goff, *Fields White unto Harvest*, 79–83; Sarah E. Parham, *The Life of Charles F. Parham: Founder of the Apostolic Faith Movement* (New York and London: Garland, 1985), 59–66.

58. Anderson, *Vision of the Disinherited*, 69. Douglas J. Nelson contends that Azusa featured throngs "from every race nationality and class. . . . Never before in history had any such group surged into the church of a black pastor." "For Such a Time as This: The Story of William J. Seymour and the Azusa Street Revival" (Ph.D. diss., University of Birmingham, 1981), 196, 194, 196–99, 201, 204.

59. Bartleman, *Azusa Street*, 213. Bartleman noted that as many as fifty letters a day came to the Azusa mission from the United States and abroad. Pentecostal leaders well knew how instrumental the press would be in propagating the revival. Several years after Azusa, A. J. Tomlinson continued to believe that newspapers would spread the revival far and wide: "Thousands will believe and say good by [*sic*] to old forms and creeds, and will be stanch [*sic*] followers of Christ. (Acts 9:35)." A. J. Tomlinson, *The Last Great Conflict* (Cleveland, Tenn.: Walter E. Rodgers, 1913), 118.

60. Occasionally, believers "proved so respectful—or fearful—of the supernatural power embedded in their periodicals that persons who had not received Holy Spirit baptism were not allowed to touch them." Wacker, *Heaven Below*, 94.

61. Throughout his ministry, Bartleman authored more than 550 articles, 100 tracts, and 6 books. C. M. Robeck Jr., "Bartleman, Frank," in *Dictionary of Pentecostal and Charismatic Movements*, ed. Stanley M. Burgess and Gary B. McGee (Grand Rapids, Mich.: Zondervan, 1988), 50–51.

62. *Holiness Advocate*, May 15, 1907(?), 4. Ironically, Crumpler later rejected the Pentecostal faction and eventually returned to the Methodist Episcopal Church, South.

63. *Apostolic Faith*, December 6, 1907, 3.

64. Synan, *The Holiness-Pentecostal Tradition*, 113–14; Gary Don McElhany, "The South Aflame: A History of the Assemblies of God in the Gulf Region" (Ph.D. diss., Mississippi State University–Starkville, 1996), 30–31. The phenomenon of racial equality inspired Bartleman to note that "The 'color line' was washed away in the blood" at Azusa. *Azusa Street*, 54.

65. *Apostolic Faith*, January 7, 1907, 1; Vinson Synan, *Old Time Power: A Centennial History of the International Pentecostal Holiness Church* (Franklin Springs, Ga.: LifeSprings Resources, 1998), 98–101.

66. *Bridegroom's Messenger*, October 1, 1907, 1.

67. *Ibid.*, September 15, 1908, 1.

68. C. H. Mason, "Tennessee Evangelist Witnesses," *Apostolic Faith*, February–March 1907, 7.

69. *Evening Light and Church of God Evangel*, July 1, 1910, 2.

70. *Way of Faith*, July 23, 1908, 13.

71. Rev. E. J. Hardee, "Wauchula Letter," *Florida Christian Advocate*, August 20(?), 1907, 3. In Georgia, Wesleyan Methodists faced very similar if not more devastating circumstances. See the myriad of articles condemning the new movement in their denominational publication, the *Wesleyan Methodist*, between 1907 and 1910.

72. *Baptist Argus*, January 23, 1908.

73. Sigmund Freud, *Civilization and Its Discontents*, trans. James Strachey (New York: W. W. Norton, 1962), 61–62. From this vantage the newly converted Pentecostal Reverend H. H. Goff saw "the holiness people as I never saw them before. They are the foolish virgins without the oil." *Fifty Years on the Battlefield for God* (Falcon, N.C.: n.p., n.d.), 51. Gaston Barnabas Cashwell, like many Pentecostals during these early years, could "not see how any honest man or women can claim to have the pentecostal baptism and not have the pentecostal evidence [speaking in tongues]." *Apostolic Evangel* (Royston, Ga.), April 3, 1907, 3. The anti-Pentecostal offensive from the Holiness camp was particularly brutal. Renowned Holiness evangelist W. B. Godbey wrote extensively against tongues and accused Pentecostals of worshiping the devil. *Spiritualism, Devil-Worship, and the Tongues Movement* (Cincinnati: God's Revivalist, n.d.). Some criticisms, like those of Parham, were racially based. Alma White, leader of the Pillar of Fire Holiness Church, made truculent denunciations of Azusa for its interracial character.

74. See Grant Wacker, "Travail of a Broken Family: Evangelical Responses to Pentecostalism in America, 1906–1916," *Journal of Ecclesiastical*

History 47 (July 1996): 526, 505–28. Pentecostals, Charles Edwin Jones points out, believed that speaking in tongues was the initial evidence of Holy Spirit baptism. This thoroughly offended Holiness adherents, who did not possess "the gift," resulting in discord. "Tongues-Speaking and the Wesleyan-Holiness Quest for Assurance of Sanctification," *Wesleyan Theological Journal* 22 (Fall 1987): 117–24. Contemporary outside observers of Pentecostalism knew of this progression from more established churches to unencumbered sects. Hence, newspaper reporter Grover C. Loud observed that the religion born of the Holiness Revival demanded "an even stronger revival for its own perpetuation." *Evangelized America* (Freeport, N.Y., and New York: Books for Libraries, 1971), 280. This "freedom of the Spirit" motif, as Samuel Hill points out, had long permeated southern religious history. If spiritual freedom was imperiled, evangelicals frequently believed the act of leaving mainline churches was justified. Baptists in eighteenth-century Virginia and O'Kellyites, Stoneites, Campbellites, and antimission Baptists in the early nineteenth century all made the exodus, at least in part, in the interests of practicing according to their own beliefs. *One Name but Several Faces: Variety in Popular Christian Denominations in Southern History* (Athens and London: University of Georgia Press, 1996), 80, 81.

75. Winfred R. Cox, "An Open Door for Heresy," *God's Revivalist and Bible Advocate*, May 23, 1907, 10; Oswald Chambers, "Third Work of Grace—A Confusion of the Devil," *God's Revivalist and Bible Advocate*, February 14, 1907, 1; "Border Land Holiness People," *Nazarene Messenger* (Los Angeles), April 15, 1909, 12; Amanda Coulson, "The Tongues People as I Saw Them," *Pentecostal Advocate* (Peniel, Tex.), May 18, 1911, 7.

76. Although some radical Holiness sectarians had spoken of a third work of grace before the advent of Pentecostalism, Parham and Seymour were the first to define and disseminate the notion of tongues speech as evidence of Spirit baptism. Synan, *The Holiness-Pentecostal Tradition*, 89, 105.

77. *Bridegroom's Messenger,* October 1, 1907, 2.

78. Edith Blumhofer, *Restoring the Faith: The Assemblies of God, Pentecostalism, and American Culture,* (Urbana: University of Illinois Press, 1993), 71–72; *Holiness Advocate*, May 15, 1907(?), 8; Wacker, *Heaven Below*, 48.

79. For a discussion of the role of women leaders in the nineteenth-century Holiness movement, see Lucille Sider Dayton and Donald W. Dayton, "'Your Daughters Shall Prophesy': Feminism in the Holiness Movement," *Methodist History* 14 (January 1976): 67–92.

80. Cheryl J. Sanders writes that blacks make up 20 percent of current Church of God (Anderson) membership. Equally astonishing, the first black congregation in the denomination was founded and pastored by a

woman, Jane Williams, in Charleston, South Carolina, in 1886. *Saints in Exile*, 22, 33. See also Anthea D. Butler, *Women in the Church of God in Christ: Making a Sanctified World* (Chapel Hill: University of North Carolina Press, 2007).

81. For more on Woodworth-Etter, see Wayne E. Warner, *The Woman Evangelist: The Life and Times of Charismatic Evangelist Maria B. Woodworth-Etter* (Metuchen, N.J., and London: Scarecrow, 1986).

82. *Holiness Advocate*, March 1, 1906, 5.

83. On gender equality at Azusa, see Nelson, "For Such a Time as This," 197–98, 204. This stands in sharp contrast to the prevailing view of southern Methodists at this time. Representative of southern mainline opinion, one Methodist Episcopal Church, South leader noted, "If Christ had intended that women should preach, it seems likely that he would have chosen some of them to be apostles." *Christian Advocate*, May 30, 1895, 3.

84. Joe Creech argues that the Church of God (Cleveland), even after it became Pentecostal, was antagonistic to "racial mingling, and women had little place in the C. O. G. hierarchy." "Visions of Glory," 415. Additionally, David G. Roebuck posits that the Church of God limited the roles of women ministers because "the original premise upon which they ministered—that Spirit-baptism in these 'last days' equips women for ministry—failed to impute authority to women." David G. Roebuck, "Limiting Liberty: The Church of God and Women Ministers, 1886–1996" (Ph.D. diss., Vanderbilt University, 1997), 4. Wacker, too, observes that "other priorities eclipsed self-conscious gender concerns of any sort—traditional, progressive, or otherwise." *Heaven Below*, 176.

85. Wacker, *Heaven Below*, 234.

86. A. A. Boddy, "The Southern States," *Confidence*, September 1912, 209, reprinted in *Bridegroom's Messenger*, September 1, 1912, 1.

87. Pinson, "Sketch of the Life and Ministry of Mack M. Pinson," 9, 13.

88. For instance, Edith Blumhofer notes that for every story of women being affirmed in leadership there is also one of frustration and suppression. "Women in American Pentecostalism," *Pneuma* 17 (Spring 1995): 19. The Pentecostal press occasionally sent mixed signals, elevating women to leadership status while denigrating them to a subservient role. In the same issue of the *Church of God Evangel*, J. A. Giddens advocated women's right to preach, while E. B. Culpepper cautioned women: "You will have all you can do without running [your] husband's [business] or [the] business of the church." *Church of God Evangel*, May 6, 1916, 4. On this ambiguous legacy Cheryl Townsend Gilkes, drawing on oral tradition, remarks that although the major black Pentecostal bodies denied women ordination, women nonetheless assumed powerful roles as exhorters, church mothers, missionaries, teachers, and deaconesses. "'Together and in Harness': Women's Traditions in the Sanctified Church," *Signs* 10 (Summer 1985): 683.

89. *Revivalist*, May 1894, 4. See also "Don't Get Excited over Politics," *Pentecostal Herald*, September 20, 1899, 9. On this point, Samuel Hill's analysis of southern Baptists and Methodists is particularly appropriate. Even more than other conservative evangelicals, Holiness and Pentecostal adherents considered the conversion and Spirit baptism of individuals to be virtually the sole task of the church. The "Great Commission" took priority. All other interests, be they political, social, or cultural, were either peripheral or antithetical to these primary goals. *Southern Churches in Crisis* (New York: Holt, Rinehart, and Winston, 1967), 73, 77–81.

90. This process bears striking resemblance to that taking place in early twentieth-century advertising culture. Roland Marchand and T. J. Jackson Lears describe how advertisements held the power to realize consumers' dreams, linking them to a larger culture and giving them solace in the modern world. As Marchand indicates, advertisements "contributed to the shaping of a 'community discourse,' an integrative common language shared by an otherwise diverse audience." Marchand, *Advertising the American Dream: Making Way for Modernity, 1920–1940* (Berkeley, Los Angeles, and London: University of California Press, 1985), xx; Lears, *No Place of Grace: Antimodernism and the Transformation of American Culture, 1880–1920* (New York: Pantheon, 1981). See also Lears, "From Salvation to Self-Realization: Advertising and the Therapeutic Roots of the Consumer Culture, 1880–1930," in *The Culture of Consumption: Critical Essays in American History, 1880–1980*, ed. Richard Wightman Fox and T. J. Jackson Lears (New York: Pantheon, 1983), 3–38.

91. *Holiness Advocate*, June 1, 1907, 8, 6.

92. *Bridegroom's Messenger*, April 15, 1908, 3. The Cane Ridge revival in Kentucky, which occurred more than one hundred years before Azusa, owed its success to similar modes of transmission. Historian Paul Conkin observes that ministers who participated in the ecstatic outdoor meetings spread the word through the pulpits of numerous southern congregations. Ministers retold the story of the revival to their audiences. As a result, "an almost immediate irruption of physical exercises roughly similar to those" being described occurred among the preachers' listeners. *Cane Ridge: America's Pentecost* (Madison: University of Wisconsin Press, 1990), 69–70.

93. Ann Taves, *Fits Trances and Visions: Experiencing Religion and Explaining Experience from Wesley to James* (Princeton, N.J.: Princeton University Press, 1999), 9, 332, 333, 334.

94. *Bridegroom's Messenger*, October 1, 1907, 2.

95. Ibid., December 1, 1907, 1.

96. B. F. Lawrence, "The Apostolic Faith Restored," in *Three Early Pentecostal Tracts*, ed. Donald Dayton (New York and London: Garland, 1985), 12.

Scottish Heritage, Southern Style

Celeste Ray

Kirkin' O' the Tartan worship services began in America in 1941 and are but one familiar example of the overlap between southern- and Scottish-heritage-based identity in the contemporary South. In this essay, anthropologist Celeste Ray examines the forging of a Highland Scot grievance experience based on the battle of Culloden and its analogy with the southern tradition of the Lost Cause. Understanding these movements as examples of revitalization, this essay probes the symbolic and functional dimension of these heritage affiliations.

During the past four decades, growing interest in Americans' cultural and ancestral ties to Scotland has produced hundreds of new clan and heritage societies and a steadily increasing number of Scottish Highland games. Scottish American ethnic awareness and organization has had other, briefer, periods of popularity in our nation's history. However, the growth of Scottish cultural groups and gatherings has proved most dramatic in the late-twentieth-century South, where a unique and distinctly regional style flavors events and perceptions of Scottish origins. Today, approximately half of all Scottish American societies base their associations in the South and more than one-third of the over two hundred annual Highland games/Scottish festivals occur in the region.[1]

The popularity of the Scottish-heritage movement in the South is partly due to its double celebration of a "reclaimed" Scottish ethnicity and its particular relationship to southern regional identity. Southern Scottish-heritage societies emphasize kinship and bill clan society activities as family reunions. Scottish Highland games in the South are more likely to have barbecue stands, fiddle competitions, and time designated for religious events. At southern games, singers perform the Scottish tune "Bonnie Dundee" with the Confederate lyrics "Riding a Raid," reenactors combine Confederate jackets and caps with their Scottish kilts, and bagpipe band renditions of "Dixie" leave crowds either cheering, in tears, or both.

American celebrations of Scottish heritage draw on romantic nineteenth-century interpretations of Highland manners and Scottish identity—a mythic Scottish past that in the South blends harmoniously with nostalgic visions of antebellum southern society and the Lost Cause. Celebratory and commemorative reflections on ancestral experience commonly merge historical realities, religious inheritance, and folk memories with selected (and often invented) traditions to interpret the past in a form meaningful for the present. Southerners take to the Scottish-heritage movement so well because its present form draws on parallel mythologies, rather than actual cultural continuities, that underlie the construction of both Scottish and southern identifies. Both derive from perceived historical injuries, strong attachments to place and kin, and links between militarism and religious faith, and both have produced symbolic material cultures.

Scottish-heritage celebration in the South offers alternative interpretations of "southernness." In heritage lore, the southern experience and identity unfold in continuous tradition from Scottish culture and history, rather than from a relationship to slavery or Jim Crow. Members of the southern Scottish American community are of the generations that experienced desegregation and the reinvention of the new South. By attributing southern distinctiveness to Scottish roots, a post–civil rights movement celebration of "southernness" takes on an uncontroversial, multicultural dimension focused on ethnic identity rather than race relations. Mourning the Old South's defeat or displaying the Confederate battle flag acquires less problematic meanings in the Scottish-heritage context. The "new southerner" involved in Scottish heritage is no longer just a white, Anglo southerner, but an ethnically Celtic southerner with other reasons for being different and unassailable justification for celebrating that difference.

HIGHLANDISM AND THE FORGING OF IDENTITY
THROUGH DEFEAT

The Scottish American community celebrates a conception of Scottishness engendered largely by the poet and novelist Sir Walter Scott long after the ancestors of many Scottish Americans had left Scotland. The celebrated heritage is that of one region of Scotland: the Highlands. How the Highlands came to represent the whole of Scotland is quite similar to the way in which plantation owners came to represent southerners generally.

As southern identity focuses on the Lost Cause of Lee and Davis, the Scottish identity of southern Scottish Americans centers on the lost cause of Bonnie Prince Charlie, whose bid to regain the British throne for the Stuart dynasty ended in 1746 on a Scottish moor called Culloden. Chief among the Jacobites who had supported Charles Edward Stuart against the Hanoverians were the Highland Scots. Although the Highlanders were the most ardent Jacobites, Charlie's defeat resulted in second-class status within Britain for all Scots, and Scotland itself became merely "North Britain" for over a century.

As in the American South, cultural attributes of the vanquished, once no longer a threat, became idealized. Post-Culloden legal proscriptions against Highland cultural expression banned tartan as a symbol of Jacobitism and outlawed bagpipes as "instruments of war." Yet, ironically, the fetishism of Highland culture followed these prohibitions. What the Hanoverian government labeled the dress of traitors, and Lowland Scots had previously associated with cattle thieves, became the Scottish national dress. Lowlanders forsook the ancient Highland/Lowland cultural divide to don tartan and an elaborate and accessorized version of the kilt.

Nineteenth-century Scotland cultivated a particular type of romanticism called Highlandism, or Balmoralism after Queen Victoria's Highland castle. Sir Walter Scott's writings ennobling the hitherto "savage" Highlander, and the subsequent Balmoralism, promoted the well-known militaristic image of the Scot not only as a Highlander but as a bagpiping, kilted soldier. Through the romance of Highlandism, all Scots became defeated Jacobites and Highlanders. It is this image that represents the identity that Americans of Lowland Scots, Scots-Irish, and Highland Scots ancestry alike have "reclaimed" in the heritage movement. It is this identity that articulates well with white southern identity in Scottish-heritage celebration. Created by the battle-driven histories of Scotland and the South, both cultural stereotypes exhibit a certain inventiveness in explaining away defeat by emphasizing the virtues and chivalry of the losers and the romance of lost causes. In southern Scottish-heritage celebration, "Scottish" heritage incorporates the main themes of the Old South Myth—themes originally borrowed *from* Scottish Highlandism.

THE INTEGRATION OF PARALLEL LOST CAUSES

In both the southern and Scottish cases, military defeats become symbolic of the loss of distinctive agrarian ways of life. Folk models position the South's defeat as the end of an aristocratic, privileged, and care-free world for people who valued the extended family and maintained a love of the land and a sense of place. Likewise, the Battle of Culloden marks the demise of Highland Gaelic society and a romanticized, though not prosperous, way of life for a people with clan ties to specific hills and glens. These defeats have become not merely significant in regional histories, but *the* dates after which everything changed for the worse.

Southern antebellum houses, fashions, and manners always stand in opposition to the Reconstruction era. During the forty years following Culloden, legal proscriptions against tartan, bagpipes, and communal clan land ownership accompanied the advent of exorbitant rents and large-scale emigration. Highlanders' sufferings during these years occupy a place in Scottish-heritage literature and event oration comparable to that of Reconstruction in the lore of the South.

In both the plantation legend and Highlandism, the failures of the Confederacy and of Prince Charlie appear to cause major social and economic changes that nonetheless were well underway at the time of the events. Yet the myths portray both the Highland clan system and southern society as functioning smoothly until the dramatic demise of their respective causes at Culloden and Appomattox. The harmonious, pristine, and unchanging nature imputed to plantation and Highland ways of life in commemorative rituals, song, and conversation intensifies indignation at their loss. Southerners comforted themselves in defeat by imagining a noble past, a chivalric pre-war arcadia quite different from northern industrial capitalism. The Highland way of life likewise acquired such romantic associations that even its privations polished nicely into stereotypically Highland sensibility, thriftiness, and efficiency.

In Scottish-heritage lore, Culloden is the reason for broken clan ties and the forced exile of Americans' gallant Jacobite ancestors; in southern lore, the Civil War explains "the fall" of illustrious ancestors and their forced removal from the plantation. Hence, within the southern Scottish American community, "heritage" entails a double sense of loss. Discussion of genealogical research explores what might be now had it just not been for event X in one's southern or Scottish past.

Already familiar with Lost Cause rhetoric and dispossession themes, southerners easily incorporate the experiences of "wronged" Scottish ancestors. It is a central premise in today's heritage lore that the majority of colonial Scottish immigrants fled their homeland as political refugees after Culloden in what is called the Scottish diaspora. Scottish American beliefs that post-Culloden hardships resulted in ancestral immigration inculcate a certain sense of loss and injury—both for the transgenerational loss of a cultural heritage and homeland, and through a revived sense of indignity over ancestral sufferings. John Shelton Reed suggests that white southerners traditionally stand in a certain relationship to the South's Lost Cause and share what he calls a "grievance identity" because of that stance.[2] Such an identity finds a corollary in these particular southerners' "other" heritage of a Scottish identity constructed after Culloden and also grounded in defeat.

Taking on a "Scottish" identity, southerners of Highlander, Lowlander, or Scots-Irish backgrounds stand together on one side of another lost cause, "remember" the wrongs done to the Highlanders, and feel the pique, sometimes passionately, that the injury still smarts. Grievances of southern Scottish clans include the saga of legal, economic, and cultural repression of Highlanders, the Hanoverian Duke of Cumberland's butchery, and subsequent eviction and forced emigration; southern stories relate parallel grievances of Sherman's March, Republican-implemented "reconstruction," and carpetbaggers. These are often integrated and subtly compared in campfire storytelling and song at Highland games, in heritage publications, at public rituals, and in general discourse about ancestral experience.

A further lament combining southern and Scottish grievances is the tenet that the Civil War deprived the South of its Scottishness. In North Carolina, home to the largest colonial settlement of Highland Scots, the use of the Gaelic language for religious services does seem to have ceased after the Civil War.[3] Following the war, "Scotch fairs" (agricultural fairs) degenerated to occasions for gambling and heavy drinking until their abolition about 1871. Community members suggest that Scottish consciousness succumbed to the overarching implications of the war and the new identity forged by that experience. According to heritage philosophy, coping with the war's devastation meant sublimating Scottish ethnicity, not to an American identity but to a new southern unity. The significance of Culloden faded since most everyone had lost someone in the War of Northern Aggression.

These rationales pardon ancestors for "forgetting to remember." Since heritage lore claims Scottish ancestors did not desert the ancient clan homelands for adventure or profit, but under persecution, they may not be accused of forsaking a heritage that their descendants now value. Those ancestors involved with the Civil War are no less forgiven—their experience being an inheritance itself. Heritage celebration entails reverencing the ancestors; romanticized grievances maintain their venerability in public memory. That a heritage lost was forcibly lost makes its reclaiming particularly potent.

As with Highlandism in Scotland, the plantation legend has become systemic in a southern sense of identity and in the world's conceptions of American southernness. To let go of grievances at this point, in either the Scottish or southern case, would be to let go of the romance as well. Attempts at revising regional identities, even grievance-based identities, are not often popular, especially when such identities have endeared their possessors to the outside world in legend, in public culture, and through tourism.

THE SOUTHERN TAKE ON THE SIR WALTER METHOD

Highlandism developed between 1780 and 1860 with the major thrust of Britain's empire building. Drawing on antebellum origins, southern postbellum lore developed mostly between 1880 and the first quarter of the 1900s. While contemporary southerners recognize the familiar feel and language of Scottish heritage, they credit this to cultural continuity, and, well, heritage. Southern myths are indeed built on a Scottish model, but not of a continuous tradition.

Southern myths assumed a model with which southerners were already well acquainted—the model created through Highlandism and the writings of Sir Walter Scott. Southerners named pets, plantations, and the occasional child after characters and places in Scott's novels. They generally identified with Scott's chivalrous castle- and glen-dwelling characters, who exhibited the best of courtly manners and hospitality, viewing them as models rather than as ancestors. The motifs of Highlandism yielded many parallels for southerners based on assumed spiritual and intellectual kinship rather than "heritage" as is claimed today.

Making aristocrats of patriarchal chieftains, Scott medievalized and feudalized what had been a nonfeudal, pastoralist society in the Scottish Highlands. Southern mythologizing likewise revised a slave society into a courtly realm of knightly lords and beautiful belles. The images and traditions made famous by Scott's Waverley novels provided a favorable analogy to fairly self-sufficient southern plantations in the Cameloting of the Old South. The chivalric moonlight-and-magnolias depiction of antebellum southern society evoked many of the same values and themes as Highlandism.

The lore of the Scottish-heritage movement in the South has been over two centuries in the making. Romantic constructs developed in Highlandizing the Scottish identity proved popular with southerners, who drew from them in idealizing their own Lost Cause. This process produced many apparent similarities between the Scottish Highlands and the antebellum South that Scottish-heritage celebration, and some scholarship, stretches to suggest cultural continuity between the American South and Celtic lands.[4] Southerners are argued to be more Scottish than northern Scottish Americans because of these "authenticating" cultural ties claimed to extend hundreds, even thousands, of years. Certainly Scottish immigrants did contribute to southern culture, but as in the creation of the Old South model, the impact of Sir Walter Scott and Highlandism in current heritage lore cannot be overemphasized.

Scott's influence was much the same in effect in Scotland and in the American South. In Scotland it offered a Highland regional identity that appealed to the Scottish nation. In the South it flavored a postbellum regionalism that appealed to both northerner and southerner. The romanticization of the Highlands and the South was a relief from the tragic consequences of both civil conflicts. It provided a means for reacceptance, as well as remasculinization, of the defeated as representatives of past, but idyllic, ways of life.

The stereotypical image of a Scot as a bagpiping, kilted soldier finds masculine parallels in the characters of southern myth. The Highland soldier is not unlike the military model of the southern gallant: a gentleman and a colonel. Highlanders and southern men have somehow become both heroic in defeat *and* famed for loyal military service to their former enemies following those defeats. Both the South and the Scottish Highlands have disproportionately contributed to their national militaries since their respective disasters. While the Spanish-American War allowed southerners to re-affirm their American patriotism, Scottish Highlanders often took "the king's schilling" rather than face emigration, and their role in British empire-building aided their conversion through Highland-ism from traitors to loyal "King's men." "Having been enshrined in their lost cause," writes Nina Silber, "southern men seemed to be permanently cast in a military mold."[5] Likewise, the Highland-er, once defeated, is perpetually dressed for battle with claymore in hand. These male icons, prominent in both southern and Scottish mythologies stemming from defeat, are isomorphic in southern Scottish-heritage celebration.

Military professionals comprise a significant portion of the Scottish-heritage community in the South. They merge pride in career and American patriotism with pride in "family" heritage by combining military shirts, badges, and medals with a kilt of their clan tartan. They may also choose from tartans designed for each branch of the U.S. military or opt for a general "U.S. Forces Tartan." Occasionally, event attire incorporates Confederate colors or even portions of Confederate uniforms.

Military members of the southern Scottish community tend to be not just the rank and file, but members of the Army's Special Forces, the Navy SEALs, and officers from various branches. By invitation, war veterans may join the national Scottish-American Military Society founded in 1980 in North Carolina and headquartered in Charlotte. Members often credit their career paths and success to their Scottish and southern ancestry, which in heritage lore entails genetic and cultural tendencies to the "martial spirit." Heritage celebration compares and combines the legacies of these "war-like" but "noble and righteous" ancestors.

Romanticization praises, yet tempers, southern and Highland bellicosity by directing it to the service of lost causes. Southern slave owners have transformed into gallant, chivalrous gentlemen, and Highlanders, once known to the outside world only as feuding bandits, are now "Prince Charlie's own loyal and gallant men," possessors of exemplary, noble virtues. The male ideal of southern Scottish heritage has developed as an alloy of the southern cavalier and the Highland warrior.

The southern cavalier is important in southern visions of Scottish heritage, a descendant, literally and spiritually, of the Highland clansmen. Scottish heritage enthusiasts celebrate this link as newly discovered, yet it actually appears in an earlier period of southern myth-making. Heritage lore posits the eclipse of Scottish identity in the South by the Civil War, yet D. W. Griffith's 1915 *Birth of a Nation* demonstrates the survival of its less palatable associations. Eulogizing the Old South and describing the origins of the Ku Klux Klan (KKK), Griffith originally titled his film *The Clansman* after its inspiration, a 1905 novel by the Reverend Thomas Dixon. The film links the KKK's use of a flaming cross to a similar device used by Highland chiefs for summoning clansmen to battle.

Griffith's derivation argument is not well known within the Scottish American community; it is only the older members who indicate concern about the recent popularization of a public ritual incorporating the fiery cross at southern Highland games. In a ritual gathering of the clans on the evening before the games, representatives of each participating clan society symbolically answer the "summons" to their heritage. Positioned on the games field in the shape of a St. Andrew's Cross, they carry flaming torches to be tossed onto a central bonfire as they announce their clan's presence at the games. Participants seem unaware of the implications such an event might have had in Griffith's day. In fact, heritage lore leaves a gap in southern-Scottish awareness between the Civil War and the "revival" of the latter twentieth century. However, today's Scottish heritage participants do explicitly distinguish clan from "klan" and link southerner and Highlander predominantly through ideal male virtues.

Iconography: Tartan and the Confederate Flag

Material expressions of identity, lost causes, and the whole mythologies of Highlandism and the Old South meld in the combination of tartan and the Confederate flag. As markers of cultural identity, these icons visually reference the Highland and Old South legends, the concept of clan as family, and regional heritage. Both have come to symbolize "eras" that met with dramatic ends and "forgotten" parts of the American experience. Tartan and flag combine at Scottish-heritage events in the reclaiming of identities once suppressed "for the greater good." As descendants of Scottish settlers replaced Scottish with southern identities, their descendants supplanted both identities with a reaffirmed sense of American patriotism during the world wars. Post–World War II heritage revivals developed in the new high of American superpower status and evidence the resurgence of regionalism following the unifying experience of that war. Today, those claiming a Scottish identity or displaying a Confederate flag do not consider themselves unpatriotic. Rather, the identities represented by the flag and the tartan embody those values that participants now feel make them "better" Americans.

Commonly called plaid by most Americans, tartan is a badge of membership within the Scottish community, and one's choice of tartan signifies both clan affiliation and knowledge of clan and Scottish history. The link between clan name and tartan pattern, or *sett*, is largely a nineteenth-century innovation. Originally an effective merchandising strategy in the Balmoralism craze and in tourism, the association between clan name and sett has nonetheless *become* traditional. Tartan is omnipresent at heritage events, and in this context, it symbolically evokes the whole history and mythology of the eighteenth-century Highlanders' experience, the loss of this heritage, and its reclaiming.

Each clan tartan has come to represent a unique clan story, and telling and debating these stories is part of wearing the tartan. After discovering their clan tartan, many participants first learn about things-Scottish through the history of the clan with which they share a surname and, by enthusiastic extension, "a kinship." Southern Scottish-heritage events evidence a greater emphasis on clan and kinship than do those in the North or West. The Scottish American community is organized into general heritage societies and specific clan societies. Membership in the latter allows one to "rediscover" one's "cousins." Participants join clan societies that bear their surname or that of an ancestor. Members often assume that even those sharing names derived from occupations such as "Smith" or "Forrester" are necessarily kin. Actually, the large numbers of MacDonalds or MacNeils stem not from remarkable ancestral fecundity, but from the progenitors of today's MacDonalds or MacNeils allying themselves with a clan chief of that name at a time when most people did not need last names. Though the clan system was historically Highland, those with surnames of Lowland origin now form clan societies—something which, along with the wearing of tartan, would dismay their revered ancestors.

At southern Highland games, clan tents overshadow the actual athletic competitions. These tents display artifacts, books, and interpretation related to clan history. They also serve to recruit new members. First-time visitors to the games locate relevant tents to learn about their "family" history, and clan society members stop by their tents to visit with their "cousins" and chat about genealogy. At large southern games such as those held at Stone Mountain near Atlanta or the South's premier games at Grandfather Mountain in Linville, North Carolina, well over one hundred clans represent themselves on the games fields. Even at small southern games, clan tents are the central focus. In contrast, northern games may field fewer than a dozen clan tents, and in Scotland, clan tents are not a part of Highland games. The southern emphasis on "blood kinship" within the clan is a further elaboration of Highlandism: not only does each clan have a specific tartan, but all who wear the tartan are "kin."

Pedigree-conscious southerners may obtain one through Scottish heritage. Simply by having a Scottish last name one acquires new "kin" through clan membership, an ancient and illustrious past, and a new sense of place in a "homeland" one may never visit— the historic landscapes of the clan lands. As southern mythologizing supplies an elite, planter background and great house for those whose ancestral greatness is no longer apparent "because of the War," Scottish heritage lore enhances the "backgrounds" of those planters with chieftains in the "family" tree and castles in the "family" lands.

Associating clan with kin means that tartan operates as a type of heraldry. By donning a tartan one claims the heroic deeds of clans-folk as one's own heritage and the aristocrats of the clan as one's own "cousins." Within the community, tartan immediately distinguishes one not only as a Scottish American but as a Buchannan, Campbell, or Cameron. The wearer of tartan becomes a bearer of the clan reputation. Consciousness of clan history leads to awareness of "traditional" clan enemies—also identifiable by the tartans they sport. As clan feuds are researched and discussed by participants, they are born again, in a more playful way, on the Scottish Highland games field.

The large-scale Scottish-heritage movement in the American South is such a relatively new thing that being the first of one's family to rediscover the family Scottish heritage elicits congratulations rather than condescension as might be expected. Newly reborn Scots tend to place a special emphasis on the long loss of tradition and on ancestral grievances. Those claiming Scottish origins after discovering a Scottish surname in their genealogies also tend to display tartan with more enthusiasm than those with a transgenerational awareness of their Scottish ancestry. Southerners come to their Scottish roots in different ways, but what they share is a lifetime awareness of their southern identity—a kind of primary ethnic identity upon which the Scottish identity layers.

The familiar Confederate battle flag is also present at Highland games and heritage events on T-shirts or lapel pins, on bumper stickers, and side-by-side with American and Scottish flags in clan society tents and in Highland games campgrounds. Believing their southern heritage to be an extension of their Scottish heritage, members of the southern-oriented Heritage Preservation Association describe their flag-bearing association T-shirts as appropriate attire for Scottish events. They emphasize the flag's incorporation of the Scottish flag's St. Andrew's Cross, which is also a symbol, for many, of the Confederate states.

Both tartan and the Confederate flag encode beliefs about ancestry, but a difference in their symbolic power is obvious. Though proscribed for nearly forty years, tartan regained acceptance through the British army's efforts to recruit Highlanders. In that context, tartan was transformed from the garb of rebels to that of valorous Highland soldiers loyal to the Crown. The meaning of the Confederate flag, in contrast, is still a source of contention. Those who fly the flag at Scottish events speak of the South in romanticized terms:

of the cult of chivalry and southern belles, "aristocratic" southern manners, and Bonnie Robert E. For them the Confederate flag symbolizes something quite different from what its detractors perceive; it symbolizes the Old South as the product of their idealized Scottish ancestors' further idealized accomplishments and the loss of both Scottish and southern traditions. Likewise, tartan, gussied up in the nineteenth century, symbolizes the vision of Highland life from the Victorian period. Although those Highland Scots who came to the South adjusted their attire for the climate, the Scottish American adoption of Highland dress and distinctive tartan setts provides an iconography to a generalized—and more easily assumable—heritage. Southern states initiated the development of state tartans, the first being North Carolina, Georgia, and Texas. In 1997 the interweaving of Scottish and southern heritage found both literal and symbolic expression with the Alabama introduction of a Confederate Memorial Tartan featuring a sett of Confederate gray and battle-flag red. In this way, through costume and imagery, simplified visions of both "Highlandness" and "southernness" are comparable and blended by those raised on the latter. Southernness becomes an unproblematic outgrowth of ancestral proclivities.

Heritage and the "Faith of the Fathers"

Charles Reagan Wilson has called the ritual commemoration of the Lost Cause a civil religion.[6] Southern Scottish-heritage celebration might well be similarly labeled. The remembrance of both southern and Jacobite lost causes employs religious metaphors in commemoration of secular events and artifacts that have acquired a sacred sense as heritage.

Wilson notes that Civil War artifacts have a "sacred aura"; similarly, those of the Jacobite period (locks of Bonnie Prince Charlie's hair, sheets on which he had slept, crystal glasses or jewelry with his image) are venerated as "relics" today.[7] Contemporary images of Charlie and Flora MacDonald, the woman who helped him escape Hanoverian clutches, abound not only in Scottish representations of national identity (from touristic advertising to shortbread packaging), but also in heritage paraphernalia (in pictorial images "for the home," on desk sets and stationery, on CD jackets of "traditional" tunes, on tableware, and, of course, T-shirts). Like tartan and the

Confederate flag, these images instantly invoke the whole of their respective heritage lores.

The reverence and devotion accorded such symbols find more explicit expression in actual worship services focused on the heritage of faith. Scottish heritage events in the South often have religious, especially Presbyterian, portions that affirm the importance of faith in a secular age and link faithfulness to ancestral virtues. Such events show the influence of southern Protestantism in the use of evangelical language and references to "finding" or "coming to" the heritage. Celebrants often speak of this discovery as a conversion experience. Community members claim "converts" and like to be acknowledged for "shepherding" new members into "the Scottish fold." Just as responding to God's will is answering, heeding, or hearing "the call," so too does one "hear the call" to one's own heritage.

Heritage language also mixes military with religious metaphors. The emphases on Presbyterianism and military prowess combine in the virtuous service of noble causes. The southern knight is a Christian soldier, and the Scottish Highlander of heritage lore becomes both the ideal warrior *and* Presbyterian. Actually, Highlanders originally opposed Presbyterianism by fighting on the Crown's behalf against the Lowlander Covenanters. The history behind the heritage metamorphoses, however, in the southern construction of Scottish ethnicity.

Southern Scottish-heritage events celebrate Covenanter-style Presbyterianism with new rituals of Highlandism. Outlawed in the seventeenth century, Covenanters' religious meetings, called "conventicles," took place illicitly, out-of-doors and surrounded by armed guards. Today, a worship service honoring Scottish ancestors, called a Kirkin' O' the Tartan, often takes place in an open field to emulate conventicles. Interestingly, the "guards" for these services are reenactors in the stereotyped tartan dress of Highland soldiers, who actually attacked Covenanters, and the Kirkin' concludes with a blessing of the tartan—the fabric Lowland Covenanters associated with enmity. A further convolution involves the stressed link between religious faith and faithful labors for lost causes. Fidelity to Prince Charlie made heroes of the Highlanders, but Prince Charlie was loyal to Catholicism, an attachment that had denied his father the crown.

When history becomes heritage, Highland/Lowland and religious divisions vanish in the face of the more emotive Culloden. As nineteenth-century southerners perceived themselves loyal to their faith despite the moral issues involved in their lost cause, their descendants likewise hold religion very dear and very flexible. Celebrations of the past often blend exactly what forebears found most divisive. In southern Scottish-heritage celebration, participants fuse portions of the past into a unified heritage built on collective, rather than specific, grievances; on a particular faith, rather than historic diversity; and upon warrior ethics that also suit "gentlemen."

REVITALIZATION AND THE SOUTHERN VIEW OF SCOTTISH HERITAGE

Just as their creation originally served social needs, the revival and elaboration of both Highlandism and the southern myths in conjunction show that the new South is not so done with the old. The movement to revive a "heritage lost" and efforts to maintain the grievance identities themselves reveal a basic dissatisfaction with the order of things. The Scottish-heritage movement, as expressed in the American South, corresponds with what anthropologists call a revitalization movement: an intentional and organized attempt to create a more satisfying state of existence.

In their conscious attempts to recreate community and retrieve a sense of identity or ethnicity that participants feel to be lost, heritage celebrations may be considered a response to post-modernity. But here Anthony Wallace's distinction between a revitalization movement and revivalism proves relevant. He defines the aim of the latter to be the "return to a former era of happiness, to restore a golden age, to revive a previous condition of social virtue."[8] Celebrating the past and wanting to be in the past are vastly different phenomena. Scottish-heritage celebration calls for a return only to ancestral "values" and the security that predecessors are presumed to have had in their identity—the type of security born in moments of societal drama. Today's drama comes from within and plays out in culture change rather than lost causes. Southern Scottish-heritage enthusiasts do not claim the South or the Jacobites will rise again, but they do commemorate what they perceive to be southern and Scottish virtues as instructive for the present and as secure moorings at a point in history in which change seems more rapid.

By definition, mythologizing processes construct contrasts to the present. As a revitalization movement, the celebration of Scottish heritage in the South reflects what participants feel is happening to their own society, especially with regard to kin ties, faith, and gender identities. According to heritage tradition, Culloden dispersed the clans; delocalization of the American labor force, which southerners resisted for so long, distances families from each other and from southerners' peculiar attachment to place. Heritage pilgrims join clan ("family") societies and visit places made sacred by their historic ancestral associations—both in the South and in the ultimate pilgrimage to the Scottish clan lands.

The shape of heritage lore also echoes recent, dramatic changes in American gender roles. A central grievance of clan societies is the legendary demise of the clan chief's paternal role and unquestioned authority following Culloden. The heritage movement's emphasis on southern and Scottish military traditions and on patriarchically structured clan societies portrays such masculine roles as both ancient and proper. Within the context of Scottish heritage, male identities are secure and their celebration is the most expressive. It is the men who wear tartan costumes and who are on display. Women, for whom true kilts are off-limits, have fewer options for exhibiting tartan in the Scottish style. However, southern women are blending traditions to develop new strategies for heritage dress. In Georgia, Alabama, and Mississippi, hostesses of antebellum home tours are increasingly incorporating their clan tartans in the costume of the hoopskirted belle.

Stirred by the wake of Alex Haley's *Roots* and the post–civil rights movement emphasis on diversity, contemporary interests in ethnicity and in genealogical hobbies figure significantly in celebrations of all alternative American identities. Scottish and southern identities do not mingle alone at southern Scottish heritage events. John Reed notes that "southerners are more likely to claim Indian ancestry than are nonsoutherners," and Scottish-heritage events in the South are more likely to reference Native American heritage and ancestry than similar events in the North.[9] Southern Scottish Americans might send their children to both Highland dancing competitions at Scottish games and Native American dancing competitions at southern Pow Wows. Native American trading, social, and kin links with Scots find recognition in dress, reenactment, and story at southern Scottish gatherings. Scottish heritage is absorbed into the southern identity on the Old South model, but in the 1990s, even old mythologies can be further romanticized in a multicultural form.

Focusing on the Highlandism and romanticization that underpin the southern Scottish-heritage movement serves not to explode myths or deconstruct invented traditions, but rather to emphasize how perceptions of the past influence not only celebration but also conceptions of identity and the present. Far from being escapist, romanticization of past failures and hardships secures a sense of self in times of change. The celebrated past, refined and polished, sets precedents for today in the guise of "heritage."

In the southern celebration of Scottish heritage we see the synthesis of two similar romantic traditions. Highlandism transformed the impoverished Scottish Highlands from a land of treacherous insurgents into one of the last bastions of true chivalry, gracious hospitality, and religious fortitude—something of the ideal that southerners claimed as their own after the Sir Walter model. The celebration of Scottish heritage in the South may overlook the Scottish Highland/Lowland cultural divide, but the division between the American North and South still plays a powerful role in the claiming of identity.

NOTES

1. Figures are based on Games listings annually compiled by Jim Finegan of the Clan MacLachlan Association of North America. I include the following twelve states under the rubric of "southern": Alabama, Arkansas, Florida, Georgia, Kentucky, Louisiana, Mississippi, North Carolina, South Carolina, Tennessee, Texas, and Virginia.

2. John Shelton Reed, *The Social Psychology of Sectionalism* (Chapel Hill: University of North Carolina Press, 1983), 83.

3. James MacDonald, "Cultural Retention and Adaptation among Highland Scots" (Ph.D. diss., University of Edinburgh, 1993), University of Edinburgh Library.

4. See Grady McWhiney, *Cracker Culture: Celtic Ways in the Old South* (University of Alabama Press, 1988); Grady McWhiney and Perry D. Jamieson, *Attack and Die: Civil War Military Tactics and the Southern Heritage* (Tuscaloosa: University of Alabama Press, 1982); James Michael Hill, *Celtic Warfare* (Edinburgh: John Donald, 1986).

5. Nina Silber, *The Romance of Reunion: Northerners and the South, 1865–1900* (Chapel Hill: University of North Carolina Press, 1993), 173.

6. Charles Reagan Wilson, *Baptized in Blood: The Religion of the Lost Cause* (Athens: University of Georgia Press, 1980), 170.

7. Ibid., 26.

8. Anthony Wallace, "Nativism and Revivalism," in *Magic, Witchcraft, and Religion,* ed. Arthur Clehmann (London: Mayfield, 1985), 319–24.

9. John Shelton Reed, "The Cherokee Princess in the Family Tree," *Southern Cultures* 3 (Spring 1997): 111–13.

"THESE UNTUTORED MASSES"

The Campaign for Respectability among
White and Black Evangelicals in
the American South, 1870–1930

PAUL HARVEY

Examining the efforts of denominational modernizers to import Victorian middle-class decorum to an area still characterized by rural folklife and traditional worship, Paul Harvey takes the reader into the late nineteenth-century world of black and white Baptists and Methodists. Probing the dynamics and patterns of conversion experiences and singing practices, Harvey illuminates cultural conflicts in the post–Civil War South and suggests their influence on subsequent twentieth-century developments.

Historians of white and black religious culture in the post–Civil War American South have heretofore focused on the rebuilding of white southern churches, the religion of the Lost Cause, and the rise of African American denominations. Scholars have ignored the ways in which leaders of regional religious organizations of both races lumped together ordinary white and black believers, thus creating (and condemning) the concept of southern "folk religion." In the twentieth century, anthropologists, folklorists, and intellectuals transformed these pejorative categories into scholarly work on folk culture in the American South. Much of this analysis arose from antimodernist reveries of simple rusticity. The early anthropological impulse inverted the modernizing monoculturalism of the denominational reformers. Yet both of them envisioned a static southern folk, living in an ahistorical present, and both failed to account for the adaptability or evangelical expressive culture among ordinary white and black southern Baptist and Methodist congregants.[1]

The well-chronicled debate between the schools of the sociologist E. Franklin Frazier and the anthropologist Melville Herskovits illuminated the variety of influences on black American religious expressions, arising both from the African past (Herskovits's argument) and the American present, as Frazier insisted. More recently, historians such as John Boles, Mechal Sobel, and Erskine Clarke have argued for the institutions and practices linking white and black believers, while studies such as those of Margaret Washington-Creel have resurrected the Herskovits tradition.[2] This debate, however, has not adequately informed scholarship on southern Protestantism *after* the American Civil War. The consensus on white southern religion remains imprisoned in the "cultural captivity" thesis, while African American religious history continues to rehearse "protest versus accommodation" dichotomies.[3] American religious historians should employ the tools of social history and cultural studies to better understand regional religious expressions.

In the late nineteenth century, arbiters of American middle-class behavior cordoned off venues of high culture, defined a canon of Western classics, and depicted the rural South as a hopelessly backward, albeit appealingly romantic, region of ignorant whites and primitive Negroes. Meanwhile, visionaries of the "New South" and southern progressive movements, usually comprised of well-educated urban men and women who grew up after the turmoil of the Civil War and Reconstruction, envisioned a region humming with industry and progress. Southern progressives sought state mandates to improve educational standards, fight diseases, and combat abuse of labor. Denominational leaders, many of whom were affiliated with (or were themselves) progressive reformers, preached the middle-class virtues necessary to the building of this new southern social order: piety, sobriety, and the systematic accumulation of wealth. They built bureaucracies of benevolence and conceived of "intelligent worship" as a means of uplifting and educating their plain-folk constituents. Southern Baptist and Methodist leaders, who headed organizations representing some 90 percent of the South's churchgoers, preached a "politics of respectability" to a constituency living and worshipping in ways considered backward and primitive.[4]

While preaching of a "new" South, these denominational progressives faced, and attempted to tame, older racial realities. From the 1880s through the 1920s, a torrent of racial violence swept the region, while regional lawmakers created and enforced an American system of virtual apartheid popularly dubbed the Jim Crow laws. Early in this period, the agrarian protest movement of Populism challenged the one-party system of elite Democratic rule, which enforced the manifestly inequitable social order of the South. Progressive leaders feared the possibilities both of political cooperation and of racial violence emanating from the meeting of the "lower element" of both races. In response, southern legislatures mandated racial segregation in public settings, disfranchised white and (especially) black voters of the poorer classes, and maintained a peonage system legendary for its harshness.[5]

Many southern progressives argued that segregation and disfranchisement were the necessary means of setting the stage for forward-minded laws—Prohibition, mandatory school terms, women's suffrage, and child-labor legislation—that had been blocked by conservatives fearful of "splitting" the white vote and opening a path for renewed "Negro domination" (as allegedly had been the case during Reconstruction). White and black progressives allied with denominational leaders to support progressive political measures and teach plain-folk Christians norms for public decorum in the New South. But these planters of bourgeois economies and restrained spirituality worked in rocky soil. Despite the rapid urbanization of the South in the period from 1880 to 1930, the vast majority of southern churches were in rural areas. Throughout the region, farmer-preachers of little formal education exhorted from oral traditions in small, scattered rural churches. Congregants narrated meaningful conversion experiences in emotional public testimonies. Physical tactility (hugging, foot washing) and kinetic spiritual expressions (ring shouts, spiritual dancing) characterized worship gatherings. In short, public spiritual expressiveness derived from the interaction of whites and blacks in churches, camp meetings, and revivals remained a vital part of southern religious life. Nevertheless, white and black believers did adopt certain forms suggested by the advocates of respectable religion, leading to worship rituals that drew from both their rural southern past and the modernizing present.[6]

Southern Baptist and Methodist denominational leaders fought one another constantly on specific controversies internal to denominational politics. But on the critical importance of enforcing a standard of "intelligent worship" and connecting spirituality to bourgeois morality, progressive denominationalists, white and black, spoke in strikingly similar cadences. Thus, while church leaders should not be lumped together any more than should plain-folk congregants, this essay will consider the efforts of denominationalists as part of a broader, relatively unified effort to implant a Victorian middle-class decorum in a region still dominated by rural plain-folk living and worshipping in relatively traditional ways. The relation of the denominational leaders to the folk in the pews mirrored the larger themes of progressivism in the American South. Like the denominational programs for "intelligent worship," the larger strains of progressivism in the South advocated democracy while relying increasingly on bureaucracies to enforce the notions of "progress" that they wished ordinary folk to practice voluntarily.

"The churches throughout the rural districts were dilapidated in the extreme, and frequently . . . inhabited by hogs, sheep and other animals," remembered Solomon Conser, a Methodist cleric, of religious institutions in Virginia after the American Civil War. Conser described the "extravagant devotions" of the freed people, how they fell "into trances and cataleptic fits and professed to see visions of angels and demons." Such "spasmodic excesses" punctuated worship services among believers of both races. This religious "fanaticism" was "encouraged by a class of zealots and divines of limited physical learning," he commented acidly.[7] Mary Allan-Olney, a contemporary of Conser, expressed disgust that both blacks and whites expected religious experience to be "ushered in by a good, strong, unmistakable fit of hysterics."[8] Similar observations in the late nineteenth and the twentieth century suggest the continuity of southern religious expressive culture. At a camp meeting in Augusta, Georgia, in 1885, a visiting minister discovered that "southern people think nothing is done unless there is a gale of excitement, and they do not think they can seek pardon or purity without this."[9] In the 1930s, an ex-slave witnessed "both white and colored people responding to preaching in much the same way as in [the witness's] early life," with preachers appealing "to the emotions of their flock."[10]

Missionaries and traveling correspondents in the late nineteenth century observed the impact of class division on southern churches and optimistically described the spread of bourgeois public decorum. Walter Hines Page, an educational administrator in North Carolina, remembered black religious meetings in 1866 in which "mourners" would fall into trances and be carried off by ushers. To find similar customs decades later, he said, "one must now go to remote regions where the religious habits of the whites are of a similar kind."[11] When some ex-slaves raised a shout at one service in 1891, a Baptist missionary witnessed them being "sternly and promptly suppressed by a stout black matron, a leader in their church."[12] Upon hearing a "powerful good sermon" one Sunday in the early twentieth century, an elderly black congregant commented that "it most killed me to hold in them shouts." Her exertions attest to the internalization of public decorum among ordinary evangelicals. As the decades progressed, worship reformers grew hopeful. Despite the "wide-working leaven of old-time shouters," one minister suggested, younger black clerics were delivering quiet sermons "without any long agonizing or shouting." He explained to his northern readership, "this may not mean much to New England, but it means everything in the New South."[13]

Influenced by bourgeois conceptions of the good citizen drawn from political progressivism, Baptist and Methodist churchmen depicted plain-folk whites in the American South as descended from "sturdy" stock but degraded and indolent. With 18 million "undrilled, undeveloped, uninstructed, raw recruits of civilization, who do not know the rules of the march and who easily riot among themselves," wrote the prominent Atlanta minister John E. White, progressive southern citizens faced a huge trial.[14] "To take these untutored masses and culture them and organize them for the world's greatest battle" was, a Southern Baptist Convention (SBC) spokesman proclaimed, the "grandest duty" of regional religious leaders.[15]

Black Baptists and Methodists also articulated many of these same concerns. For them, the inculcation of respectability was a political imperative, not just a cultural crusade. Proper public behavior, a signifier of the uplift of the race, would lead to recognition and political rights—or so they naively hoped.[16] A black Baptist worker in the 1880s told Texas denominational leaders of how he met "with some strange customs and teaching not warranted by the word of God" in his mission travels. "These I deal with gently," he said, "but earnestly and pointedly." His congregants had not learned "to bring the movements of the world and the doings of the day into the churches."[17]

As mission efforts spread to the southern countryside, where the vast majority of southerners lived, ordinary congregants and unlettered ministers defended a religious culture that valued local autonomy over denominational direction and prized spontaneously emotional spirituality over dictated decorum. As a northern Baptist discovered in the 1880s, country pastors and church members were "as tenacious of their rights and prerogatives as the most intelligent churches in the land."[18] Workers for the northern American Baptist Home Mission Society encountered such powerful sentiments at one meeting in New Orleans in 1886. They were "delighted" in the "progress" they perceived, as congregational leaders calmed ecstatic worshippers. But the sermon at the gathering induced pandemonium. At the Pentecost, the minister thundered, the disciples were shouting. "Some folks preaches style and says 'keep still, stop that shoutin,' but I doesn't preach style. Who dares to say to a soul filled with the spirit, 'stop shoutin'?" he asked.[19] The powerful African Methodist Episcopal (AME) bishop Daniel Payne complained that his efforts to enforce more acculturated worship practices "invariably met" the response that the pastor "could not succeed in restraining" the congregants, and that "an attempt to compel them to cease would simply drive them away from our Church."[20] An ex-slave named Cordelia Jackson explained the meaning of African American expressions of piety for her life. "I stays independent of what white folks tells me when I shouts," she told an interviewer. "De Spirit moves me every day, dat's how I stays in. White folks don't feel sech as I does; so dey stays out. . . . Dey tries me and den I suddenly draps back to serving de Holy God."[21]

Among whites, churches in Appalachia and the southern up-country best preserved customs derived from the camp-meeting era of the early nineteenth century, the time of a democratic explosion of Protestant plain-folk fervor. Antimission traditions deeply rooted in these areas resisted the modernizing efforts of denominationalists. Not coincidentally, these regions, heavily populated by poorer white farmers, historically were strongholds of unionism, Republicanism, and agrarian radicalism. Analogously, believers in heavily black-populated counties, such as in the low country of South Carolina and Georgia, preserved African-derived rituals.[22] Under

sustained exhortation from missionaries to adopt a more acculturated worship style, they often saved their deepest expressions for
informal services held at night. In the churches of coastal South
Carolina, a respected black minister explained in 1913, "dignity,
decorum and quietness" characterized Sunday mornings precisely
because worshippers found other outlets for kinetic spirituality,
especially in the praise houses on the nearby Sea Islands. "In the
churches they act like 'white folks,'" he concluded, "but in 'praise
houses' they are 'cake walkers.'"[23]

The practice of religion at local levels in the United States has
often eluded the control of religious specialists and official theolo-
gies.[24] This contrast between the rural past and the modernizing
present took an especially dramatic form in the post–Civil War
South. Conversion experiences and singing practices illustrate the
emerging divisions between popular piety and the prescriptions of
southern denominationalists, white and black.

The conversion moment—a sacred instant in which God's Spirit
infused the soul—remained a central rite of religious expression in
the region, one that transcended denomination, class, gender, and
race. Converts expected that crying, screaming, and physical struggle heralded the working of God's Spirit in the individual soul. But
divines in the late nineteenth century preached that salvation was
a growth of grace, the culmination of a carefully controlled process
rather than a spectacular transformation. They offered their own life
stories as normative narratives of properly channeled spirituality.

Jeremiah Jeter, editor of a denominational newspaper in Virginia, narrated in his autobiography a prototypical conversion and
summons to the ministry for the southern evangelical establishment. Born poor on a plantation where his father was an overseer,
Jeter attended primary school in Bedford, Virginia. After a period of
struggle following his attendance at revival meetings in the 1820s,
the "burden of guilt and anxiety" that he had long felt "instantly
departed." He enjoyed an inner peace that was "inexplicable" and
that he was "not careful to analyze," and never lost control of his
physical self. Later, after cultivating the demeanor of a gentleman
theologian, he pastored prominent congregations in the state capital
and frowned on those who succumbed to religious theatrics. Baptists should honor their unlettered spiritual fathers, he wrote, "but it
would be absurd for us to regard them as infallible religious guides,"

particularly for Christians in a New South alive with industry and progress.[25]

Men of poor rural backgrounds who sought camp-meeting style conversion dramas struggled to comprehend their own surprisingly staid awakenings. The spiritual metamorphosis of George Blount, an obscure pastor in Georgia in the late nineteenth century, failed to induce the expected holy fervor. Though feeling a "calmness of mind" on the evening of his salvation, he remained dissatisfied: "I worked myself to feel fearful lest I should quench the Holy Spirit from my Breast and thus the whole of my experience at first was one of trying to feel." He admitted to falling into "many errors while my mind was worked to such a point."[26] Otis Webster Yates experienced conversion at a revival in rural North Carolina. A deacon told him of the great light he should see at salvation. "I looked for that wonderful light," Yates later wrote, "but have never seen it to this day."[27] George Richard Browder, a well-known Methodist minister in Kentucky, concluded that "regeneration is sanctification, perfect in its degree . . . and we must 'work out our own salvation' by improving the grace given," conclusions mirroring those of the evangelical establishment by the 1880s.[28]

Such teachings, however, did not penetrate the "cake of custom" thick in rural churches. Many congregations, as one minister lamented, still expected from a candidate for a call to ministry "some sort of special revelation, some articulate voice, some overwhelming and phenomenal experience, which he is unable to relate to ordinary causes." They were supposed to be moved by some "extraordinary tide of conviction from which [they] cannot disentangle." The further southern believers moved away from such anachronistic folkways, he argued, the nearer they would "accord with truth, Scripture, and common sense."[29] Attempts by denominationalists to reduce reliance on special spiritual moments simply drove congregants into Holiness movements and other unsanctioned ways of defending traditional spiritual understandings. The Methodist cleric Simon Peter Richardson witnessed with dismay the rise of the "second blessing brethren," Holiness advocates who denied that "the possibility of sin is an inhering possibility in the reason, conscience, and freedom of all moral beings." By insisting on complete sanctification, he argued, Holiness preachers threatened to infect southern evangelical belief with the virus of antinomianism.[30]

With even more vehemence, black denominational leaders also condemned the "erroneous, impious, and irreligious doctrine, which has been heeded as one should the truth."[31] They worried that a reliance on supernatural occurrences as evidence for salvation disgraced black Christians. A minister in Savannah emphasized the necessity of an "intelligent Christian experience." For his refusal to countenance local spiritual customs, he was "cast out as an evil" among those who trusted in "dreams, visions, and root-work superstition."[32]

Such dutiful rhetoric, however, seemed bland fare compared to the spiritual food provided by the public conversion narratives told by generations of slaves and their free descendants. "Mourners" or "seekers" struck by the Spirit removed themselves from daily life. Some candidates donned special clothes to signify their transitional status; others would tie cloths around their heads and "drop all work and look very woebegone" while struggling to make it to the other side. In the praise houses of the Gullah people, "raw souls" gained admission into church after proving the sincerity of their "striving," depicted by a local missionary as a "long process of self-examination and solitary prayer 'in the bush,'" with nothing interfering with the "action of the Spirit."[33]

The personal transformation of African Americans followed prescribed narrative patterns, which invoked a rich imagery of devils and "hellhounds" pursuing them as they "ran for salvation." Zora Neale Hurston was a minister's daughter in a Florida town where churchgoers, she soon learned, "plowed, chopped wood, went possum-hunting, washed clothes, raked up back yards and cooked collard greens like anybody else." Their very ordinariness made the oral artistry of their salvation narratives even more remarkable. Sometimes straying from the scripted narrative expected of them, they extemporaneously created variations of the time-honored narrative: "These visions are traditional. I knew them by heart as did the rest of the congregation. Some of them made up new details. Some of them would forget a part and improvise clumsily or fill up the gap with shouting. The audience knew, but everybody acted as if every word of it was new."[34] Converts added individual touches to preordained tales of redemption: "The individual may hang as many new ornaments upon the traditional form as he likes," she wrote, "but the audience would be disagreeably surprised if the form were abandoned."[35] W. E. B. DuBois described the tenacious hold of the "Frenzy" on worshippers, "when the Spirit of the Lord passed by, and, seizing the devotee, made him mad with supernatural joy."[36] Charley White, one of the devotees, explained that visions were "not anything you can touch, of course, but you know it's there." As a longtime Baptist and Holiness preacher in southeastern Texas, White understood on a personal level the "supernatural joy" that DuBois depicted from an intellectual remove: "When God gives you a vision your whole body kind of soaks up the message, like a biscuit soaks up red-eye gravy. And sometimes you can hear the message as well as feel it. And sometimes you can see it."[37]

Candidates for conversion often received the help of local spiritual elders, who reinforced the customs most derided by denominational leaders. Rossa Cooley, a missionary in the Sea Islands in the early twentieth century, described how young "seekers" had to "'see visions and dream dreams,' which are interpreted to [them] by a 'spiritual father' or a 'spiritual mother,' who is closer after having been seen in a dream."[38] Charles Satchell, a black missionary in New Orleans (a city with a tradition of older black women renowned for their esoteric spiritual powers), discovered that gospel mothers gained control over church members "on the ground of being sent to them by the Spirit." The consequences of crossing their will could be severe: "If a member can keep the right side of these officials he need have no fear of church displeasure; they can gain access to the church. But woe to that disciple who is so unfortunate as to be out of their favor." He saw "no way these things can be overcome but by a more enlightened ministry." Congregants were eager to free themselves from shackling superstition, he assured his northern supporters, and "unite with the friends of reform and progress."[39]

Yet church records from the period document that progressive ministers remained "troubled by the Deacons and so-called Shepherds assuming authority over and controlling the pastor in the discharge of his duties."[40] Church members routinely challenged the validity of conversion experiences, frustrating the advocates of systematic spirituality. Candidates were "'sent back to seek further,' until they can come with the usual stranger visions and physical demonstrations," a northern Baptist discovered on his tour of black southern churches after the Civil War.[41] The Gillfield Baptist Church in Petersburg, Virginia, one of the oldest black congregations in the South, pronounced one self-proclaimed convert "not to understand her self or the Principles of Christ's dealings with his people." It voted to send her back "to the Throne of God's Grace which is able to make her wise unto devotion."[42] Pastors came and went, but the mothers, the deacons, and other laypeople preserved local Afro-evangelical practices. They exerted considerable influence in passing on spiritual practices drawn from slavery times into a new era.

The evolution of singing practices and hymnology also illustrates cultural conflicts in post–Civil War southern religion. In this case, the denominational "modernizer," ironically, championed older hymns dating from the eighteenth century, while ordinary congregants enthusiastically responded both to their traditional styles (such as the black spirituals and white shape-note singing) and to the newer currents of gospel music coming from northern revivalists. The development of musical practices among southern Baptists and Methodists demonstrates the success of rank-and-file congregants in adapting distinctive regional forms to new technologies of print and publication.

Denominationalists started music-training programs, encouraging the use of professional music ministers in churches wealthy enough to afford them and promoting revivals with skilled song leaders. They discouraged lining-out hymns (that is, having a leader sing the line, and the congregants then repeat and follow the leader's line) and straight a cappella singing, both trademarks of rural southern style especially common in upcountry and mountain churches. They ridiculed the slow, seemingly discordant style of singing characteristic of country congregations. Those who raised the tunes in many rural churches often had "no idea either of harmony or of time," according to a South Carolina Baptist. The result was "an inharmonious jingling of nasal sounds—all is discord from beginning to end."[43]

Regularly notated hymnbooks and musical instruments gradually found their way into more churches, and lined-out a cappella singing began to sound antiquated. Congregations gradually adapted styles that absorbed sentimental Victorianism into rural southern culture. But this rapid assimilation of nineteenth-century gospel hymnology provided another example of resistance to the tastes of the middle-class denominational leaders. Recognizing that "the influence of songs is perhaps next to that of reading," the Mississippi

Baptist State Convention worried that "the Church that sings error, or caters to 'rag time' music is as far from right as the one that deals in mere sensational reading and preaching."[44] A member of a Baptist church in North Carolina sardonically suggested that if the gospel hymns, "these pious jigs," were slightly quicker in tempo, the congregations could "dance them beautifully."[45] Guardians of denominational orthodoxy warned of the theological and emotional traps contained in the lyrics of these evangelical songs: "The glow of sentiment in these hymns is inspiring. The lively or pathetic music with which they are associated, has given them popularity in the house and the street as well as in the Sunday-school and the church. Yet, in many instances, there is no substance in the productions, and in many they encourage a diversion of thought and feeling from the practical duties of Christian life."[46] Hymns should be selected "by the more spiritual and at the same time the more intelligent of the church, with careful consideration of what is good for all classes," denominationalists insisted.[47]

In response to their dissatisfaction both with old-time singing practices and new gospel hymns, white Baptists and Methodists produced hymnbooks for their own churches, intending to guide singing in proper ways. Southern Baptist Convention leader Basil Manly Jr. edited *The Choice* (1891), an anthology emphasizing older standards. The "rage for novelties in singing," he argued, was "driving out of use the old precious standard hymns."[48] Lansing Burrows, a prominent minister in the Southern Baptist Convention, edited the *Baptist Praise Book* (1904). It was to be, he explained, a "book of praise to Almighty God" rather than a simple compilation "in convenient form [of] a number of pleasing songs."[49] These denominationalists championed the stately cadences of hymns such as "How Firm a Foundation," an eighteenth-century classic:

> How Firm a foundation, ye Saints of the Lord,
> Is Laid for your faith, in His excellent Word.
> What more can he say, than to you He hath said?
> To you who for refuge to Jesus hath fled?

This contrasted starkly to the dominant image of the gospel hymns, that of a benign heavenly father looking after his children, as expressed in the popular gospel tune "Love Lifted Me":

I was sinking, deep in sin, far from the peaceful shore,
Very safely deep within, sinking to rise no more,
Then the master of the sea, heard my despairing cry,
From the waters lifted me, now safe am I!

Publishers responded to the market opportunity provided by congregational demands for readily accessible gospel lyrics and tunes. Gradually, hymns intended for limited use in Sunday schools and revivals came to dominate white southern church services, with older standards relegated to special formal occasions. Evangelical leaders once resistant to gospel hymnology reluctantly advised prospective ministers to adapt hymn singing to congregational needs, as in this instruction from a ministerial manual in 1913: "One of the severest tests of the devotion and adaptability of the cultured minister is his ability and willingness to lay aside the fringes and adornments of culture and so come at the heart of realities as to hold and help the plain man in his worship. . . . Popular gospel hymns, sung with verve and vigour, may not satisfy the artistic taste of the cultured, but they serve the purpose of worship for the common man far better than more elevated efforts."[50]

A new generation of twentieth-century gospel hymns, epitomized by the 1930s classic "I'll Fly Away," captured the hearts of ordinary evangelicals. The influence of professional music ministers, the trend toward paid choirs, and the spread of hymnbooks with standard notation and classics could not block the rise of an evangelical singing culture that would deeply influence American popular music through figures such as Elvis Presley. Americans came to know "southern" music not through the standards of worship leaders but through the complex melding of musical styles achieved in the singing practices of ordinary congregations.[51]

Contention over "proper" music for black congregations proved just as enduring. Sources as disparate as the Harvard-educated intellectual W. E. B. DuBois and a retired domestic servant from Texas named Vinnie Brunson eloquently relate the meaning of historically black sacred music in African American religious life. DuBois recognized the deep emotion rooted in black folk sacred music, whether it came through the quiet, intricately structured but intensely felt spirituals or in the impassioned shouts of celebratory song rocking a congregation deep in the expression of collective religious joy.

The movement of the spirit could vary from the "silent rapt countenance or the low murmur and moan to the mad abandon of physical fervor—the stamping, shrieking, and shouting, the rushing to and fro and wild waving of arms, the weeping the laughing, the vision and the trance. . . . Many generations firmly believed that without this visible manifestation of the God there could be no true communion with the Invisible."[52] In Vinnie Brunson's church building, which doubled as a schoolhouse, congregants removed the benches after preaching and enacted the scenario described by DuBois: "If de spirit moves dem dey jus up and dances to de tune of de song and sings and de crowd keeps de time pattin de feet and de hands." Singing "spressed his [the Negro's] feelin's an hit made him relieved, if he wuz happy, hit made him happy, if he wuz sad hit made him feel better."[53]

Northern missionaries in the South, and southern black church leaders, attempted to align black singing styles with American Protestant practices. With northern financial assistance, Charles Satchell's flagship congregation in New Orleans bought an organ and recruited a "reasonably fair choir of singers." Satchell forecast a finer style of worship for his church: "I think when we get fairly on the way, with the improvements in singing, order in worship &c., the people who may attend will see the advantages of an enlightened state of things, and it will be the leaven that will work until old fogyism and the tyranny of the old churches, with the popish idea of old shepherds and gospel mothers, lords over God's heritage, will be unknown."[54] AME bishop Levi Coppin, who taught a Sunday school in Maryland as a young man, instructed the choir in his boyhood church to sing "scientifically and correctly."[55] The AME hymnal reinforced these lessons, with staples of Euro-American hymnals such as "Whiter than Snow" taking precedence over traditional Negro tunes. The famous Fisk Jubilee Singers, the college choir that successfully toured the nation to raise money for the school, were acceptable mainly because they performed the spirituals in a classical style.[56]

Black American sacred music in the late nineteenth century grew more diverse, as congregations absorbed musical influences from missionaries, popular secular tunes, and white gospel hymnists. The "strange, wild songs" (the spirituals) were "coming to be regarded as relics and badges of the old conditions of slavery and heathenism, and the young men and women are ashamed to sing them," a correspondent wrote in 1882.[57] Revival musicians attracted crowds who traveled twenty or thirty miles in a day to hear the latest songs. Congregants returned with "music enough in their heads and hearts to stock the plantations, and a new era in their church music has been inaugurated," a missionary reported.[58] Churches with trained choirs and instrumentalists were "scornful of old fashioned people" who "sang the lines given out by the preacher, or improvised as they went along."[59] Older members who lived through this transition lamented "the way they have messed up our songs with classical music," as did one ex-slave interviewed in the 1930s.[60]

But black congregations held on to the religious music of their tradition more than such descriptions might suggest. At services for Alabama sharecroppers in 1894, Henry Morehouse, a northern Baptist educator, heard plantation songs, standard hymns, and gospel songs, all of which were "deaconed out," or lined out. Morehouse approved of musical modernization but realized that "nothing so alters their souls like the plaintive, weird, old plantation songs born of their bitter experiences, old slave songs of supplication to God for deliverance from their woes." He maintained that "no one thing can be a greater blessing than to get those songs and relics of the past barbarism out of the way, and displace them even by the ordinary Sabbath school songs."[61] But the way in which worshippers responded to such treasured forms appears clearly in Daniel Payne's account of his encounter with a "Praying Band" engaged in a ring shout in the 1880s. Payne demanded that the congregants "sit down and sing in a rational manner" and told them that their musical expressions were a "heathenish way to worship and disgraceful to themselves, the race, and the Christian name." After Payne demanded that parishioners cease their sacred dancing, the crowd "walked sullenly away" and the leader informed him, "Sinners won't get converted unless there is a ring."[62] Payne saw this as evidence of continued barbarism among the freed people of the South, but the freed people themselves kept alive a tradition which eventually won out over Payne's strictures. Black worshippers altered tunes from varied sources to match the cadences of their own rituals and improvised within the formulaic structure of Sunday school songs. Melville Herskovits documented the way in which ordinary gospel hymns of the late nineteenth century would be converted "into a song typically African in accompaniment of clapping hands and foot-patting, and in its basic singing style. All that is left of the original hymn is the basic melody which, as a constant undercurrent to the variations that play about it, constitutes the unifying element in this amazingly illuminating music."[63] And the spirituals were so successful at offering times that their continued life in African American churches was guaranteed. A New England woman witnessed the practice of waiting until the end of offerings to raise "some sweet wild melody" that inspired a final surge of almsgiving: "The music faculty of the Africans fails them when they attempt the congregational rendering of church music," she believed, but "when the audience becomes excited and ceases to struggle with these alien harmonies, it will . . . burst into a wild song whose musical and emotional qualities are fascinating."[64] The spirituals, the ring shouts, and the altering of gospel hymns with African-derived cadences thus survived every attempt by denominationalists to train black Christians to sing in standard evangelical (white) ways. "It will no doubt be a long time," conceded a white missionary in 1911, "before the negroes are developed to a point when they shall in their worship prefer a type of song that does not consist so much in repeating the same doggerel line over and over."[65]

Black denominationalists, at first opponents of black sacred song, eventually learned to respond to the market opportunities of preserving this music in hymnals and gospel song collections. In 1903, Richard Boyd, owner and manager of the National Baptist Publishing Board, the largest black publishing enterprise in the United States, compiled the *National Baptist Hymnal,* which soon found its way into thousands of black churches. "The books containing the old-established hymns are the best," he said of his initial effort. "Adopt those, and hold to them. Do not be carried away by 'catchy' tunes adapted to words that may be either destitute of all sentiment or full of that which would be positively injurious." Recognizing that nineteenth-century black sacred music was not disappearing, Boyd produced the *National Jubilee Melodies,* a collection of spirituals that, he hoped, would "show the rising generation who may yet become a great and educated people that they sprang from a deep and prayerful religious race." Congregational demands for historically black tunes and musical innovations eventually influenced hymnals intended to push the "classical" hymnology encouraged by denominational leaders.[66]

African Methodist Episcopal bishop Henry McNeal Turner was a champion of popular singing styles and revival songs. Editor of the 1876 official hymnbook of the denomination, Turner took the opportunity to reintroduce "the old Zion songs"—Methodist gospel hymns—that he felt had been unjustly neglected. He was, however, no champion of the spirituals, which he believed were commonly "devoid of both sense and reason; and some are absolutely false and vulgar." Unlike his fellow bishop and opponent in church politics Daniel Payne, Turner was also "not ashamed to say" that he loved nineteenth-century evangelical hymns "a thousand fold more than I do these later day operatio songs." A hymn and tune book published in 1898 strengthened Turner's work by setting his choice of words to music. The hymnbook of the AME Zion Church, a group strong in the eastern seaboard states, relied heavily on white Methodist revival songs. In 1909, filling the void in black hymnology, a cross-denominational group of black Methodists published *Soul Echoes: A Collection of Songs for Religious Meetings.* The compositions of the pioneering gospel tune writer Charles Albert Tindley dominated this book. The first edition of the hymnal sold out, with the publishers soon releasing a second edition with words set to music. Again, congregational demand for music in the black vernacular would remain strong despite the penchant of hymnists for "classical" Protestant music.[67]

In the 1920s the incorporation of music from the slave tradition as well as from early black gospel hymnists into the African American church repertoire culminated with the publication of *Gospel Pearls.* Produced under the direction of the Nashville physician, publisher, and hymnologist Arthur Melvin Townsend, it turned black hymnody away from an almost exclusive reliance on the white hymns of the eighteenth century and gospel songs of the Victorian era. During these same years, Charles Albert Tindley, Lucie E. Campbell, and, especially, Thomas Dorsey were improvising twentieth-century black gospel song styles that would permanently infuse American religious and secular music. "Sanctified" (Holiness-Pentecostal) congregations took the tradition into new realms, adding organs, tambourines, and drums to induce bodily spiritual expressions, precisely the practices that a generation of denominational reformers had attempted to stamp out.[68]

Later in the twentieth century, ordinary white and black southerners seized new opportunities elsewhere, moving out of the South to northern and western cities. Southern religious cultures accompanied them and readapted to new settings. Radio, professional gospel publishing companies, and television supplied the means to transmit adapted traditions to a new generation, despite the homogenizing efforts of denominational reformers and the scorn of national elites. This religious culture, however, was decidedly not the insular and backward folk religion perceived by mainstream leaders. Later in the 1950s and 1960s, black southern religious cultures energized the civil rights movement. Today, white southern religious expressions pervade the New Religious Political Right. In the nineteenth century, denominational reformers engaged in the invention (and disparagement) of tradition. In the twentieth and twenty-first centuries, southern congregants politicized this tradition, deeply influencing American cultural and political life in the process.

NOTES

All minutes for Baptist conventions and proceedings listed in the notes were consulted at the Southern Baptist Historical Library and Archives, Nashville, which keeps a complete record of all Baptist records from the most local to the national and international.

1. For a classic example of a romanticized anthropological account of southern music, for example, see Newbell Niles Puckett, *Folk Beliefs of the Southern Negro* (Chapel Hill: University of North Carolina Press, 1926). For an analysis of the perception of the uplands South by national elites, local color writers, and missionaries, see Henry Shapiro, *Appalachia on Our Mind: The Southern Mountains and Mountaineers in the American Consciousness, 1870–1920* (Chapel Hill: University of North Carolina Press, 1978). For antimodernism, see T. J. Jackson-Lears, *No Place of Grace: Antimodernism and the Transformation of American Culture, 1880–1920* (New York: Pantheon, 1981).

2. See E. Franklin Frazier, *The Negro Church in America* (Chicago: University of Chicago Press, 1954); Melville Herskovits, *The Myth of the Negro Past* (Boston: Beacon, 1941); Margaret Washington-Creel, *"A Peculiar People": Religion and Community-Culture among the Gullahs* (New York: New York University Press, 1988); Sterling Stuckey, *Slave Culture: Nationalist Theory and the Foundations of Black America* (New York: Oxford University Press, 1987); John Boles, *The Great Revival: The Origins of the Southern*

Evangelical Mind, 1787–1805 (Lexington: University Press of Kentucky, 1972); Mechal Sobel, *The World They Made Together: Black and White Values in Eighteenth-Century Virginia* (Princeton, N.J.: Princeton University Press, 1987); and Erskine Clarke, *Our Southern Zion: A History of Calvinism in the South Carolina Low Country, 1690–1990* (Tuscaloosa: University of Alabama Press, 1996).

3. The phrase "cultural captivity" comes from John Lee Eighmy, *Churches in Cultural Captivity: A History of the Social Attitudes of Southern Baptists* (Knoxville: University of Tennessee Press, 1971). The "culture-religion" thesis, however, receives its best explication in Samuel S. Hill, *Southern Churches in Crisis* (New York: Harper and Row, 1967).

4. See, especially, Lawrence Levine, *Highbow/Lowbrow: The Emergence of Cultural Hierarchy in America* (Cambridge, Mass., Harvard University Press, 1988).

5. For a beautifully written summary of the South during this period, see Edward Ayers, *The Promise of the New South: Life after Reconstruction* (New York: Oxford University Press, 1992).

6. For New South ideologists, see Paul Gaston, *The New South Creed: A Study in Southern Mythmaking* (New York: Knopf, 1970). The two essential works on southern progressivism are Dewey Grantham, *Southern Progressivism: The Reconciliation of Progress and Tradition* (Baton Rouge: Louisiana State University Press, 1983); and William Link Jr., *The Paradox of Southern Progressivism* (Chapel Hill: University of North Carolina Press, 1992).

7. Solomon L. M. Conser, *Virginia after the War: An Account of Three Years' Experience in Reorganizing the Methodist Episcopal Church in Virginia at the Close of the Civil War* (Indianapolis: Baker-Randolph, 1891), 39–40.

8. Myrta L. Avary, *Dixie after the War: An Exposition of the Social Conditions Existing in the South, during the Twelve Years Succeeding the Fall of Richmond* (1906; repr., New York: Negro Universities Press, 1969), 203–5.

9. Quoted in Briane Keith Turley, "A Wheel within a Wheel: Southern Methodism and the Georgia Holiness Association" (Ph.D. diss., University of Virginia, 1994), 283.

10. Interview with Willis Williams, in Federal Writers' Project, *The American Slave: A Composite Autobiography*, 2 ser., 41 vols., ed. George Rawick (Westport, Conn.: Greenwood, 1972–1977), vol. 17, *Florida Narratives*, 353. Hereafter citations from *The American Slave*, the collection of interviews done with ex-slaves by Federal Writers' Project workers in the United States in the 1930s, will be given by state, volume, and page.

11. Walter Hines Page, "Religious Progress of the Negroes," *Independent*, September 1, 1881, 6–7.

12. Orra Langhorne, "Southern Sketches," *Southern Workman*, October 1891, 34.

13. H. T. Kealing, "A Race Rich in Spiritual Content," *Southern Workman*, January 1904, 41–44.

14. John E. White, "The Backward People in the South," *Our Home Field*, May 1909, 15–17.

15. Southern Baptist Convention (SBC), Report of the Home Mission Board, in *Proceedings* (1885), appendix A, pp. xii–xiii. See also Joseph E. Campbell, *The Pentecostal Holiness Church, 1898–1945: Its Background and History* (Franklin Springs, Ga.: Publishing House of the Pentecostal Holiness Church, 1951), 217. The best analysis of the "politics of respectability" in the black American religious community may be found in Evelyn Crooks Higginbotham, *Righteous Discontent: The Women's Movement in the Black Baptist Church, 1880–1920* (Cambridge, Mass.: Harvard University Press, 1993), 185–230; and James Campbell, *Songs of Zion: The African Methodist Episcopal Church in the United States and South Africa* (New York: Oxford University Press, 1995), 32–64.

16. For a polemical critique of the rhetoric of "uplift," see Kevin Gaines, *Uplifting the Race: Black Leadership, Politics, and Culture in the Twentieth Century* (Chapel Hill: University of North Carolina Press, 1996).

17. Missionary Baptist Convention of Texas, *Proceedings* (1882), n.p.

18. *Baptist Home Mission Monthly*, July 1884, 174.

19. Ibid., April 1886, 90–91.

20. Daniel Payne, *Recollections of Seventy Years* (1888; repr., New York: Arno, 1968), 255.

21. *South Carolina Narratives*, orig. ser., vol. 3, part 3, p. 5.

22. For examples of how early missionaries viewed African-derived rituals such as ring shouts, see Laura Towne, *Letters and Diaries of Laura M. Towne, Written from the Sea Islands of South Carolina, 1862–1884*, ed. Rupert Sargent Holland (1912; repr., New York: Negro Universities Press, 1969). Later missionaries such as Rossa Cooley, however, wrote lovingly of rituals such as ring shouts that the earlier missionaries disparaged: *School Acres: An Adventure in Rural Education* (Westport, Conn.: Greenwood, 1970), 253–55. For whites, see Deborah Vansau McCauley, *Appalachian Mountain Religion: A History* (Urbana: University of Illinois Press, 1995).

23. Richard Carroll, "Negroes on the Coast of South Carolina," *Savannah Tribune*, April 22, 1911.

24. See, e.g., David Hall, *Worlds of Wonder, Days of Judgment: Popular Religious Belief in Early New England* (New York: Oxford University Press, 1989); and Jon Butler, *Awash in a Sea of Faith: Christianizing the American People* (Cambridge, Mass.: Harvard University Press, 1990).

25. Jeremiah B. Jeter, *Recollection of a Long Life* (1891; repr., New York: Arno, 1980), 52–54. See also Beth Barton Schweiger, "The Transformation

of Southern Religion: Clergy and Congregations in Virginia, 1830–1895" (Ph.D. diss., University of Virginia, 1994), 77–80.

26. George Blount diary, entry for July 26, 1868, in George Blount Papers, folder 4, Southern Baptist Historical Library and Archives, Nashville.

27. Otis Webster Yates, *A Country Boy Used by the Lord* (Nashville: Sunday School Board of the Southern Baptist Convention, 1938), 25.

28. George Richard Browder, *The Heavens Are Weeping: The Diaries of George Richard Browder, 1852–1886*, ed. Richard Troutman (Grand Rapids, Mich.: Eerdmans, 1987), 397.

29. "Call to Ministry," *Religious Herald*, October 6, 1910.

30. Simon Peter Richardson, *The Lights and Shadows of Itinerant Life: An Autobiography of Rev. Simon Peter Richardson, D.D., of the North Georgia Conference* (Nashville: Publishing House of the Methodist Episcopal Church, South, 1900), 197. For more on Holiness-Pentecostalism, see Edith Blumhofer, *Restoring the Faith: The Assemblies of God and American Culture* (Urbana: University of Illinois Press, 1993); and Robert Mapes Anderson, *Vision of the Disinherited: The Making of American Pentecostalism* (New York: Oxford University Press, 1979).

31. *Baptist Home Mission Monthly*, February 1881, 27–29.

32. *Savannah Tribune*, May 14, 1898.

33. W. D. Siegfried, *A Winter in the South, and Work among the Freedmen* (New York: Arno, 1970).

34. Zora Neale Hurston, *Dust Tracks on a Road* (New York: Arno, 1969), 275, 280.

35. Zora Neale Hurston, *The Sanctified Church* (Berkeley: Turtle Island, 1981), 83.

36. W. E. B. DuBois, *Souls of Black Folk* (1903; repr., New York: Bantam, 1989), 135.

37. Charley White, *No Quittin Sense* (Austin: University of Texas Press, 1971), 134. See also *Texas Narratives*, supp. ser. 2, vol. 3, part 2, pp. 860–61 (Preely Coleman).

38. Cooley, *School Acres*, 151.

39. *American Baptist*, February 15, August 4, August 18, 1868.

40. Missionary Baptist Convention of Louisiana and Mississippi, *Minutes* (1877), 34.

41. *Baptist Home Mission Monthly*, February 1881, 27–29.

42. Minutes of the Gillfield Baptist Church, Petersburg, Va., September 20, 1869, consulted at Southern Baptist Historical Library and Archives.

43. *South Carolina Baptist*, August 22, 1867.

44. Mississippi Baptist State Convention, *Minutes* (1905), 44–45.

45. *Biblical Recorder,* June 9, 1886.

46. *Alabama Baptist,* June 7, 1877.

47. John A. Broadus, "Syllabus as to Hymnology," typescript, C. M. Thompson Papers, Southern Baptist Historical Library and Archives, Nashville.

48. Basil Manly Jr., *The Choice: A New Selection of Approved Hymns for Baptist Churches* (Louisville, 1891), 2.

49. Quoted in Harry Eskew, "Use and Influence of Hymnals in Southern Baptist Churches up to 1915," *Baptist History and Heritage,* vol. 21, 1986, pp. 21–34.

50. W. J. McGlothlin, *A Vital Ministry: The Pastor of Today in the Service of Man* (New York: Fleming Revell, 1913), 136.

51. Bill Malone, *Southern Music, American Music* (Austin: University of Texas Press, 1979); James Gregory, *American Exodus: The Dust Bowl Migration and Okie Culture in California* (New York: Oxford University Press, 1989), 191–221.

52. DuBois, *Souls of Black Folk,* 135.

53. *Texas Narratives,* supp. ser. 2, vol. 3, part 2, p. 515.

54. *American Baptist,* June 25, 1867.

55. Levi Coppin, *Unwritten History* (Philadelphia: A.M.E. Book Concern, 1919), 119–20.

56. Louis D. Silveri, "The Singing Tours of the Fisk Jubilee Singers, 1871–74," in *Feel the Spirit: Studies in Nineteenth-Century Afro-American Music,* ed. George Kick and Sherrill V. Martin (Westport, Conn.: Greenwood, 1988), 105–15.

57. "Studies in the South," *Atlantic,* October 1882, 479.

58. "A Summer on a Southern Plantation," *Independent,* December 11, 1879, 3–4.

59. Langhorne, "Southern Sketches," 34.

60. *North Carolina Narratives,* orig. ser., vol. 14, part 1, p. 269.

61. H. L. Morehouse, "Plantation Life of the Colored People," *Baptist Home Mission Monthly,* March 1894, 95.

62. Payne, *Recollections of Seventy Years,* 254–55.

63. Herskovits, *Myth of the Negro Past,* 223.

64. Lillie Chace Wyman, "Colored Churches and Schools in the South," *New England Magazine,* February 1891, 787.

65. D. L. Gore, "The Negro Race," *Home Field,* July 1911, 21.

66. Jon Michael Spencer, *Black Hymnody: A Hymnological History of the African-American Church* (Knoxville: University of Tennessee Press, 1992), 80, 84.

67. Ibid., 3–43.

68. For twentieth-century gospel, see Bernice Johnson Reagon, *We'll*

Understand It Better By and By: Pioneering African American Gospel Composers (Washington, D.C.: Smithsonian Institution Press, 1992); Eileen Southern, *The Music of Black Americans: A History* (New York: Oxford University Press, 1971). For the revival and development of ecstatic worship among Sanctified congregations in the twentieth century, see Cheryl J. Sanders, *Saints in Exile: The Holiness-Pentecostal Experience in African American Religion and Culture* (New York: Oxford University Press, 1996). Walter Pitts, *Old Ship of Zion: The Afro-Baptist Ritual in the African Diaspora* (New York: Oxford University Press, 1993), concludes that contemporary black worship is an amalgam of a "devotional" period dominated by slower, restrained "classical" singing followed by a faster, more kinetic section that was characteristic of black vernacular worship.

RELIGION AND
MARKERS OF IDENTITY

Purgatory in the Carolinas

Catholic Devotionalism in Nineteenth-Century South Carolina

Diana Pasulka

Ritual experience, often codified in liturgy and intensified through an assortment of sights and sounds, is pervasive in the history of religions. In this essay, Diana Pasulka explores Roman Catholic devotional practices concerning purgatory through an analysis of religious societies, diocesan publications, and material culture. Where many southern Protestants championed a privatized interior relationship with the sacred, southern Catholics engaged in a comprehensive ensemble of actions and beliefs that stressed external and material values in the context of an extended spiritual, as opposed to physical, community. In this way, Pasulka contends, though Catholics may have been a numerical minority in the South, they understood themselves as part of a spiritual majority in the Church Universal.

During the nineteenth century, Charleston, South Carolina, was a major site of Catholic activity in the South. The Diocese of Charleston served the states of South Carolina, North Carolina, and Georgia, and although throughout most of these states Catholics lacked churches and other forms of centralized locations for devotion, the Charleston diocese promoted a uniformity of religious practice through publications, societies, and material culture. An analysis of two forms of source material reveals a similar conclusion. The evidence of diocesan and church publications such as prayer manuals, catechisms, and society guides, as well as material culture like stained-glass windows, church diptychs, and memorials, reveal that contrary to the trend followed by American Protestants, Carolinian Catholics did not espouse an interior style of devotion. The European Enlightenment, which stressed personal piety and de-emphasized the material and ornamental aspects of religion, had wide-ranging cultural influences in the United States that extended into the realm of religion. Jay Dolan and others have successfully argued that Enlightenment values permeated the faith of upper-class Catholics in the late eighteenth- and early and mid-nineteenth-century United States.[1] This form of *republican Catholicism* fit well within the early American ethos—rationalism trumped emotionalism, and the material aspects of religion were thought to be lesser forms of piety compared to textual religious forms like treatises and sermons. Although this may have characterized upper-class Catholics in the Northeast and the West, Catholics in South Carolina, of every class, defied this trend. They formed lay societies that encompassed Catholics everywhere, from the United States to Europe—even extending into the realm of the supernatural—stressing a radical sense of community. The first bishop of South Carolina, John England, wrote eloquent sermons and preached about the importance of art, icons, and the material aspects of sacred presence. Memorials to the dead were etched into the physical structures of churches, narrated in publications, enacted on holy days, and expressed through ornate public ceremonies. These elements served to remind southern Catholics that even though they were a minority within the culture of southern American Protestantism and upper-class northern Catholicism, they were actually a spiritual majority.

The Catholic Church in South Carolina's Antebellum Period

The rumored presence of a few Spanish Catholic priests prior to 1750 notwithstanding, the history of Roman Catholicism in South Carolina begins in the mid-eighteenth century with the arrival of a small population of English and Irish Catholic immigrants. According to the writings of John England, the first bishop of the Diocese of Charleston (established in 1820), around the year 1786 "a vessel bound to South America put into the port of Charleston. There was a priest on board . . . the few Catholics, who now began in the city to be acquainted with each other . . . invited him to celebrate Mass, which he did in the house of an Irish Catholic for a congregation of about twelve persons."[2] The few Catholics who did live in South Carolina in the mid-eighteenth century faced a hostile environment. Cultural Protestantism dominated the social and political lives of southern citizens, as did a fervent nationalism emerging out of the Revolutionary War. Catholics, viewed with suspicion due to their religious allegiance to the Roman pope, were the objects of derision and often violence. "In 1775 a mob tarred and feathered 'two acknowledged Roman Catholics' accused of plotting to distribute weapons to slaves, Indians, and Catholics intent on rebellion."[3] The real or perceived alliance between Catholics, Indians, and slaves was perhaps cultivated by the fact that many Catholics who lived in South Carolina in the late eighteenth century were Irish indentured servants who were now ensconced within a society that derived from English Protestantism. In any case, the majority of white Protestants in South Carolina viewed Catholics with suspicion and often outright hostility. "At one public rally in Charleston in 1775, for example, 'Liberty men' arranged effigies of the Pope, Satan, and [prime ministers] Lords Grenville and North on a platform so that they seemed to move in concert with one another."[4] This hostile scenario, however, was destined to change.

Due to a significant presence of southern Catholics in the Continental regiments, the social climate for Catholics changed significantly. The suspicion that Catholics were potentially subversive to the dominant racial and political order waned, and by 1790 the South Carolina constitution allowed Catholics to own property and run for public office.

For their part, Catholics were quick to support and claim the patriotism and individualism of the new Republic. If in the eighteenth century South Carolina Catholics were characterized, justifiably or not, as a fringe minority plotting against a hostile majority, just the opposite proved to be the case in the early nineteenth century. Several factors facilitated this change.

First, Catholics established a physical presence in Charleston through the building of churches and the establishment of a central diocese whose jurisdiction was South Carolina, North Carolina, and Georgia. St. Mary's Church in Charleston, built in 1789 and the first Catholic church to be built in these states, was well established by the early 1800s and before the arrival of the bishop John England. The presence of a Catholic church alongside those of Protestant denominations contributed to the perception of Catholics as citizens and owners of property, rather than as servants. Second, due to the lack of priests, lay Catholics had to maintain the rites, devotional practices, and sacraments that were the basis of their religion, and they funded these through their own efforts. This financial freedom gave them, in their own minds, some authority and distinguished them as independent from Roman jurisdiction. It also contributed to a struggle with ecclesial authority that lasted well into the nineteenth century. However, this type of Catholicism, distinguished by an autonomous body of lay practitioners who cultivated a distant relationship to the pope and the Vatican, suited the ethos of South Carolina Protestants. This "republican Catholicism" only intensified with the arrival of the first bishop in 1820.

After settling into his post as bishop, John England, from County Cork, Ireland, established a constitution for the Charleston diocese that was modeled after the American political system. Such constitutions had already been adopted by Catholic communities in the Northeast from the beginning of the nineteenth century. Pertaining to Catholics who resided within the three states that constituted diocesan jurisdiction, the constitution outlined a form of Catholicism that was specifically nationalistic yet retained its uniqueness from Protestantism. England stressed certain American values, such as ecumenicalism and American nationalism, yet beside these he also defended the nature of Catholic devotional practices. Whereas many Protestant religions in the South advocated a privatized, interior relationship with the sacred, Catholic devotional practices were just the opposite. Prayer societies and material objects like sacramentals and the bones of saints were physical signs of the presence of the sacred among Catholics, who participated in elaborate ceremonies of which these were the focus. Despite his fervent republicanism, John England was an ardent defender of these devotions.

The articles of belief contained in the constitution reveal the republican and independent character of southern Catholicism:

> Article 14. We are not required by our Faith to believe that the
> Pope is infallible; nor do we believe that he is impeccable, for it is

not a consequence of his being vested with great authority that he should be exempt from the frailties of human nature;

And Article 15. We do not believe that by virtue of this spiritual or ecclesiastical authority, the Pope hath any power or right to interfere with the allegiance that we owe to our state; nor to interfere in or with the concerns of civil policy or the temporal government of the State of South Carolina, or the United States of America.[5]

Rules for membership in the church resembled the criteria for state citizenship. Only members could vote, and to be a member one had to be a man over the age of twenty-one and one had to assent to the constitution. Women, although considered in "spiritual communion," could not be members of the church.[6]

Yet despite this insistence on a uniquely American Catholic identity, which drew considerable criticism from Catholic Europe, England was perfectly clear regarding belief in the dogmas that generated controversy among non-Catholics, such as purgatory, prayers for the dead, and associated practices. According to England, these beliefs and practices were to be maintained, fostered, and respected, as outlined in the constitution. The Mass is a sacrifice "for the living *and* the dead," and

> We constantly hold that there is a Purgatory, and that the souls therein detained are helped by the suffrages of the faithful. Likewise, that the Saints reigning together with Christ are to be honored and invoked; and that they offer prayers to God for us, and that their relics are to be respected.
>
> We most firmly assert that the images of Christ, of the Mother of God, ever Virgin, and also of other Saints, may be had and retained, and that due honor and veneration is to be given to them.
>
> We also affirm that the power of indulgences was left by Christ in the Church, and that the use of them is most wholesome to Christian people.[7]

It has been argued that the republican form of American Catholicism that dominated the late eighteenth and early nineteenth century fostered a personal piety or privatized sense of religion, as opposed to one centered on communal and baroque devotional practices.[8] However, this was not the case in South Carolina. Prior to the arrival of John England, and during and after his tenure as bishop, the devotional practices of South Carolina Catholics were characterized by uniformity, emphasizing the external and material within an extended community that defied physical limits. This is most clearly revealed by devotional practices for the dead. Republican Catholics in South Carolina may have adopted the political structure of the American political system and thus redistributed authority in a more democratic fashion than did their European counterparts, but the forms of their devotional practices reveal a piety that was very public in nature and extended into the communities of Europe, South America, and the hereafter.

South Carolina's Catholic Community: An Emphasis on Exterior and Public Devotion

The public and ornate nature of Catholic devotional practices elicited curiosity and often derision among non-Catholics. If England's intentions in establishing the diocesan constitution were strategic, that is, an effort to adapt Catholicism to the political climate of the United States and to quell anti-Catholic sentiment, then it would seem likely that he might also have de-emphasized the devotional practices that elicited much anti-Catholic rhetoric, such as the more public displays associated with All Souls' Day and other holidays devoted to the dead. However, this was not the case. There are several indications that ornate and "alien" devotional practices met with a friendly reception by non-Catholics. Bishop England found himself the object of much curiosity among the Protestant elite of Charleston and other southern cities. He was often invited to speak to large crowds about the nature of the Catholic religion.[9] Perhaps part of the reason that the more controversial devotional practices of Catholicism, such as those of praying to the saints or their images, Masses for souls of the dead, and so on, were not de-emphasized by England, a republican Catholic, was that they presented an opportunity to educate the non-Catholic public about Catholicism. In any case, devotional practices pertaining to the dead flourished and were fostered by ecclesial authority.

Prior to England's arrival, South Carolina was part of the Archdiocese of Baltimore, under the jurisdiction of John Carroll, its first bishop. Faced with a southern situation characterized by a lack of priests and a weak ecclesial presence, Carroll sought to unify the faithful through fostering a uniformity of devotional practices that emphasized a protocol of physical behaviors and devotions to sacred objects. He accomplished this through the written word—catechisms, tracts, and manuals that outlined specifically how to conduct ceremonies and prayers. His hope was to unify the faithful in the United States, but also to unify American Catholicism with that of Rome.[10] In order to ensure that devotions would be carried out in conformity with the church, they were "indulgenced," such that one could receive their benefit only if one conformed to proper ritual procedure. If one did practice according to the proper procedure, one obtained an "indulgence," an official spiritual benefit.

Rather than fostering a private, interior reflection upon God and spirituality, these manuals promote the physical and communal components of Catholic devotional practices. A manual that had wide circulation in the Charleston diocese before and during the early years of its formation, was *The Externals of the Catholic Church: Her Government, Ceremonies, Festivals, Sacramentals, and Devotions.* The manual stresses the communal nature of the physical devotions: "Our Church, like every society that has work to be done, knows full well that 'in union there is strength.'" The work that is to be done, however, is both physical and spiritual, in that it binds the immortal and the mortal worlds together, as the manual emphasizes: "Individual energy, even in spiritual things, is apt to be misdirected; or, at least, it is likely to be of benefit only to him who makes it, and to produce little or no good result in others. But when the religious efforts of individuals are combined with similar zeal on the part of others . . . great good is accomplished, both in the individual member and in the whole society. God's glory is promoted, and the members are sanctified to a degree that would not be possible except as a result of united effort." Specific devotions and the observance of holy days is work that is linked with the deceased. The community means members of the church, the living as well as those who have died. The festival of All Saints, which the manual reminds its readers is a day of holy obligation, must be attended in order to "give greater help to the suffering souls," and it recommends that priests celebrate three Masses on that day to ensure that many deceased souls find repose from their suffering.[11]

The communal aspects of the South Carolina church, encompassing Catholics living and dead, is further reflected in the manual's promotion of prayer societies or confraternities, which functioned to extend the community globally as well as supernaturally. Confraternities, voluntary societies that emerged in the medieval era, were formed within common geographical locations and were primarily intended to oversee the funeral rites of and prayers for deceased members. Founded by the laity, they often employed their own clergy and were associated with independent foundations. In the sixteenth century they slowly began to come under the jurisdiction of ecclesial authority. However, they still maintained relative autonomy, and evidence suggests that they often developed a parallel form of worship that was in competition with the parish Mass.[12] Archconfraternities are confraternities that have been given the right to align themselves with sodalities or groups of Catholics in other locations, in order to give them the spiritual benefits they accrue through prayer. An archconfraternity in Italy can assume a small society in Charleston, and all of the spiritual merits the archconfraternity earns are also transferred to the group in Charleston.

The Externals of the Catholic Church encouraged the formation of these societies and stressed outreach to well-established archconfraternities in Europe. According to the manual, the oldest societies were those devoted to the souls in purgatory, called "purgatorian societies." The universal nature of this society was made clear in the beginning of its formation: "Churches and monastic houses, even of different orders, enter[ed] into an agreement to pray and offer Masses mutually for the souls of all who were enrolled in a 'register of brotherhood.'"[13] Therefore, the society linked parishes, convents, and monasteries from diverse locations through prayer, including as well as members who had passed away. Joseph Chinnici's assessment of Catholicism in this era reflects meaningfully on these developments. He states that a set of "definite Christian values emerged in this process: a strong awareness of the communal dimension of prayer, witness to a universal Church, and a definite incarnationalism which refused to reduce the Christian life to strictly internal conviction."[14] The emphasis on the formation of confraternities and archconfraternities stressed the public nature of Catholic devotional worship as well as an extended sense of community.

The incarnationalism to which Joseph Chinnici alludes is reflected in the manuals and publications of Bishop England. After assuming the position of bishop, England began to publish manuals clarifying and explaining the "externals" of the Mass, as well as catechisms and pamphlets promoting devotions to the dead. His *Explanation of the Construction, Furniture, and Ornaments of a Church, of the Vestments of the Clergy, and of the Nature and Ceremonies of the Mass* was somewhat of an apology for the more misunderstood tenets of the faith, such as prayers to the saints during Mass, yet England was careful to note that it was not to function as such. "In the doctrinal explanations scattered through this little compilation, there is neither opportunity nor room for spreading out the evidence by which they are sustained. The reader must not therefore imagine them to be vindications, for they scarcely even deserve the name of brief and imperfect expositions of the doctrine of the Catholic Church." Despite the warning, he explains in detail the history and scriptural justification for praying to the saints, as well as retaining their relics and praying for those deceased—for whom there is "hope, but not assurance" of salvation. The manual is structured such that an explanation of belief is paired with a physical space within the church. In regard to prayers to the dead, part of the dogma "communion of saints," England is detailed: "Calling then to mind the saints, who, released from their bodies, are in celestial glory with the Lord, he brings before the divine view, that we not only communicate with them in the doctrine to which they adhered, but that we hold their names, their virtues and their memorials or relics in veneration, and trust much to the aid which we expect from their prayers and merits, through Christ, their Lord and ours." England connects this belief with a physical structure/space within the church. There are "church dyptics; that is, parchments or tablets with two folds, so as to make three columns; and the names of three classes of persons were inscribed upon these tablets. First, the apostles and martyrs. . . . Upon another column were inscribed the names of those who had died in peace or communion of the church, but yet, as they might be liable to temporal punishment, though released from the guilt of sin and freed from the danger of eternal pain, might be aided by prayers. The third column contained the names of the living."[15] In this way England's Catholicism connects the interior lives of practitioners with the exterior, physical space of the church as well as with the mortal and immortal realms. The living and the dead exist simultaneously in real time. This is not a symbolic representation. The prayers to the saints and their presence in the form of relics and images are efficacious and are characteristic of, in Chinnici's words, a sense of "incarnationalism."

Each of the catechisms published by England, one in 1826 and one in 1830, contains a lesson on the doctrines of purgatory and limbo. As in the aforementioned manuals, England connects an explanation of the Catholic belief in purgatory with something exterior and physical, in this case, works. Under the title "Lesson XV: On Purgatory, and Works," England explains how souls that are detained in the place of temporary punishment, or purgatory, due to venial or mortal sin, may be helped by the prayers and works of practitioners:

> Q. Can the souls in Purgatory be relieved by our prayers and other good works?
> A. Yes; being children of God, and still members of the Church, they share in the Communion of Saints; and the Scripture says, *It is a holy and wholesome thought, to pray for the dead, that they may be loosed from their sins. 2 Macc. Xii.46*
> Q. What means the Communion of Saints?
> A. It means that all who belong to the true Church, by their prayers and good works, assist each other.[16]

Lesson XV in the children's catechism is also devoted to an explanation of purgatory and the communion of saints but is less sophisticated in its explanations—England does not cite scripture. However, the relationship between the spiritual and the physical world is made explicit. Whereas the adult catechism assumes knowledge of the intricate connections between the physical and the material, for example, between the image of a saint and the actual saint, England utilizes the children's catechism to make these connections very clear. Interestingly, in the children's catechism England reduces the relationship to one of representation.

> Q. May we ask Saints to pray for us?
> A. Certainly; and since God loves them he willingly hears them, and often grants what they ask.
> Q. Is God in any of the pictures or images in churches?

A. Not at all. These were made by men, and God was not
   made by any person.
Q. Are any Angels or Saints in pictures or images?
A. No.—the pictures and images are made by men, and put in
   Churches to show us that we ought to think of God, of his
   law and of his Angels and Saints, and strive to keep his law
   as they do.[17]

There is a discrepancy regarding the relationship between the
image and the actual saint found in each catechism. England mentions the correctness of the veneration of relics and images in the
adult catechism, yet never clarifies the relationship, while in the
children's catechism he advocates for the apparent separation of the
spiritual and material realms. The earlier references suggest that the
realms are intermingled, yet the children's catechism is anomalous
regarding this issue. One of England's later manuals, the *Explanation of the Ceremonies of the Holy Week in the Chapels of the Vatican, and
of Those of Easter Sunday in the Church of Saint Peter,* addresses this
connection in detail.

England's explanation of the connections between the material
artifacts of the church and its interior meanings is framed within
an apologetic discourse. The overt physicality and materiality of
Catholic practice was a problem for the South Carolina church, as
evidenced by England's defensive position. "As an impression frequently exists in the minds of some well disposed persons, that the
multitude of ceremonies during this week is little consonant to the
spirit of religion; and really is superstition; it might not be amiss to
premise a few general observations before entering upon the special
explanation of the several parts." England faults a plain and rational
style of religion: "Men have written polished sentences, they have
constructed rounded periods, and called them by the name of religious philosophy, and philosophical religion and rational devotion,
merely to deprive religion herself of those natural aids, which under
the auspices of heaven, and frequently by the express command of
God himself, were used for the promotion of his service amongst
his people." His explanation of the physical components of Catholic devotional practice delves into aesthetics, as he conveys that the
physical is not reducible to mere materiality but contains something
spiritual as well.

The lessons which are calculated to produce so much benefit, might be conveyed not only by the voice of the preacher, but by the exhibition of the printed page: words whether spoken or written, are merely conventional signs for the purpose of exciting ideas, and the ear or the eye might be equally well impressed by other means, as by the sermon or the book. Music can affect the soul through the one, as painting can, through the other. How often has he to whom the most eloquent orator addressed himself in vain, been vanquished by the charms of melodious sound? How often has the painter or the sculptor riveted the attention of him, who has read description after description with complete indifference? To how many generations has Lacoon proclaimed his anguish? Can you count the multitudes that have hung round the transfiguration? Who will describe the sensations produced by the Miserere? He who would thus endeavor by the abstract semblance of philosophy, to argue against what is thus testified by nature through the voices of myriads, may well be expected to bid you hold fire in your hand.[18]

Exactly what it is that obtains in the physical components of the church is not stated, but what is clarified is the capacity of the material to evoke sincere religious sentiment, much more so than just scripture or religious treatise.

According to Joseph Chinnici's analysis of American Catholicism in the antebellum era, the laity and ecclesial authorities were united in a rejection of "the more interior approach to Christian life which had characterized the Enlightenment view of the person." The Laity's Directory of 1822 cited an earlier tract (1786) that stated "The use of ceremonies is to maintain order, decency, and uniformity in the exterior acts of religion, to raise and elevate the mind to a proper contemplation of our mysteries, and to inspire respect and awe for the supreme majesty of God."[19] The emphasis on the externals of the church, revealed by England's literature, confirms this assessment for South Carolina. The focus on exterior forms and community, as well as the lack of ecclesial presence, also gave rise to the formation of sodalities and prayer societies. Although sodalities and confraternities were encouraged by the ecclesial authorities, the identifiable presence of sodalities and prayer guilds in South Carolina was not significant until after the war.

IMMORTAL SPACE: POSTBELLUM CATHOLIC GUILDS AND SODALITIES

The formation of prayer guilds, sodalities, and confraternities in the United States began in 1806 and gradually grew with the arrival of Catholic immigrants from Europe.[20] The case in South Carolina differs from this in that the presence of prayer societies is not evident until the late nineteenth and early twentieth centuries. This is most likely due to few Catholic practitioners, little cohesive ecclesial presence, and the great distance between Catholic communities. The first prominent prayer guild in South Carolina, the St. Anthony Guild, attests to these circumstances: "The Mission of Saint Anthony comprises an area of 7,635 square miles. A population of 128,000 white, with 152,000 colored people, and have but one resident priest." The Catholic Church in South Carolina was devastated financially by the Civil War, the effects of which are frequently mentioned in the guild's quarterly publication: "Priests and Sisters are anxious and willing to come South and work for the needs and advancement of our Holy Faith, at present so desolate and barren in the Southland. But even the comparatively small burden of their support causes the good Bishop of the Diocese to refrain from accepting priests for mission work, so slight are the financial resources of the Diocese of Charleston."[21] Despite the barren financial resources characteristic of this era, the publications of the prayer societies attest to a rich devotional life focused on the dead. The dissemination of the *Saint Anthony Guild Publication* exemplifies this in that it functions as a public site for the recording of how the dead continued to live in the structures, physical and spiritual, of South Carolina churches. As it was expressed in the periodical itself, "The Dead are Not Absent, They are only Invisible."[22]

The St. Anthony Guild, the prayer society and confraternity devoted to the mission churches associated with the St. Anthony Church, was established in 1899 in Florence, South Carolina, with ecclesiastical approbation.[23] The stated aim of the guild was to solicit aid, monetary and spiritual, for the poor Catholic missions of South Carolina. However, there were other, implicit aims, which are made clear through attention to the amount of space devoted to discussion of dead members, prayers to and for dead members, and notation of the money associated with the costs of keeping the dead "alive" to living members. In this sense the St. Anthony confraternity resembled its medieval counterparts in its focus on dead members. More than half of the printed discussion of the "aims" of the guild is spent on matters regarding the dead. In reference to admission, it is stated that "persons desiring to be enrolled may obtain admission at any time of the year. Deceased persons can be made members and enjoy the spiritual benefits of the Guild."[24] Money was an inextricable component of membership and the benefits of membership. There was a tier of members, from regular members, who paid the lowest fees and derived the least benefit; to promoters, who paid for perpetual membership and obtained the benefit of a High Mass celebrated in their honor; to benefactors, who were given a physical presence in the church by having their names placed on the altar to the shrine each Tuesday. These options were also available to dead members. Prayers offered also followed the same financial tier system—more prayers were offered for those who contributed the most money. For example, for a certain family who donated the rectory, where were housed the children who attended the mission school and the sisters who taught them, there was a constant stream of prayers. "For the special intention of a deceased member of the family, and each Wednesday, for as long as the Guild endures, the children and the Sisters offer up Holy Communion and recite the Rosary at the Shrine of St. Anthony for the benefit and intention of the living and dead members of this family."[25]

The longest paragraph contained in the section outlining the guild's "aims" deals with purgatory, the Catholic doctrine that maintains that there is a state of suffering reserved for those who die in grace, yet are not sinless enough to attain heaven. The doctrine holds that prayers said by living practitioners help to alleviate the torments of purgatory for these souls.[26] Interestingly, although the publication received official approbation and sanction, the devotions to the souls in purgatory outlined by the guild are not in accordance with those officially sanctioned by the Vatican. Although the prayers and works of the living, when dedicated to these souls, can ameliorate the pain and suffering they endure in purgatory, the living, according to official doctrine, should not pray to the souls in purgatory for help on earth or try to contact these spirits. The guild, however, specifically recommends its members to pray for their help and active intercession. "Special Masses will be offered up for the dead; the holy souls of Purgatory are the objects of prayer and devotion to the 'Guild,' and we need their help in our mission work. The holy souls of Purgatory are powerful intercessors at the great throne of God."[27] In a later edition of the *Publication*, this aspect of intersession with the dead is further elaborated. "If the memory of the dead is so sweet, if it strengthens us so much in well-doing, what must be the efficacy of the more intimate thought of our intercourse with the dead? The Catholic doctrine opens the most consoling perspective in this sweet and tender communion with souls of the elect, which begins beyond the tomb and is continued in a happy eternity." Additionally, "there should be reciprocity between the members of one body; as the living of the Church help the dead, the dead should succor the living, each after their own manner."[28] The actual practices of South Carolina's Catholics exceeded the official doctrines outlined by the Vatican for prayers to those in purgatory.

Within the guild's publication, much space is devoted to discussion of the existence of the souls in purgatory: how they live, what they think, and so on. These narratives are often contradictory. While the narrative descriptions portray them as happy, affable intercessors, accompanying pictures show them as prisoners in torment. Medieval and early modern representations and iconography of souls in purgatory depict them as suffering painful torments, most often amid flames and behind bars. The agony reflected in their faces does not suggest that they are capable of providing help to others. The publication's narrative depiction of purgatory is not as a place of suffering but as a way station for loved ones who now have the benefit of a superior spiritual sense, of which those on earth are the beneficiaries. "He [the deceased] sees us, and procures us real assistance; he whose own infirmities have vanished sees ours more clearly than we do ourselves, and he pleads for the remedies necessary for our cure."[29] Yet the pictures that accompany the text reveal something quite contrary to this portrayal (see fig. 1). Perhaps the incongruity between the text and the picture is best explained by a shift that occurred during the nineteenth century with respect to images of immortality. Prior to this time, images of the afterlife revealed a stagnant heaven populated by those awaiting the Resurrection, often shown reverently contemplating God, and images of hell and purgatory that revealed souls suffering horrible torments. During the nineteenth century a more domestic vision emerged:

heaven was portrayed as a reuniting of family members with loved ones, and the sufferings associated with sin were de-emphasized.[30] This ubiquitous notion no doubt influenced the Catholics of South Carolina and contributed to this paradoxical portrayal.

Many Catholics served as Confederate soldiers during the Civil War, and there are memorials dedicated to their memory and devotion. An All Souls' edition of the *Saint Anthony Guild Publication* dedicated a whole page to the Confederate dead and published pic-

Fig. 1. "A Holy Mass of Requiem being offered for the Souls in Purgatory (*From an Ancient Painting of the 14th Century*)." *Saint Anthony Guild Publication* 9, no. 32 (1908), 3.

tures of the funeral ceremonies of one soldier (see figs. 2 and 3). Catholic funeral ceremonies, pictured alongside military ceremonies, reflect the unique amalgamation of Catholic devotion with southern regionalism. A typical memorial, which serves to remind

(*Above*) Fig. 2. "The Last Volley over a Grave of a Soldier: 'Remember O Man! thou art dust, and unto dust thou shalt return.'" *Saint Anthony Guild Publication* 9, no. 32 (1908), 9. (*Below*) Fig. 3. "The Comrades' Tribute: Praying for the repose of the soul of one fallen in battle." *Saint Anthony Guild Publication* 9, no. 32 (1908), 9.

family, friends, and others of the life of the deceased but also names him as a member of the guild and deserving of prayer, is the insert memorial, which is a type of floating obituary (see fig. 4). These are scattered throughout every issue of the *Saint Anthony Guild Publication* and are a special benefit of perpetual membership. Several of these memorialize Confederate soldiers, and literally hundreds

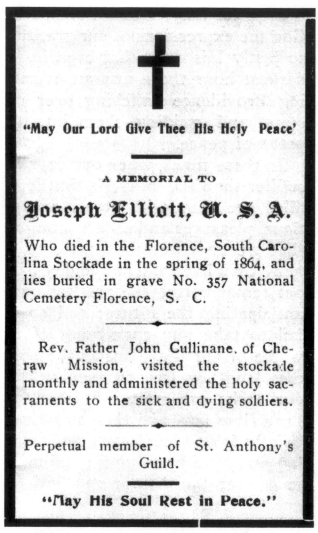

"May Our Lord Give Thee His Holy Peace'

A MEMORIAL TO

Joseph Elliott, U. S. A.

Who died in the Florence, South Carolina Stockade in the spring of 1864, and lies buried in grave No. 357 National Cemetery Florence, S. C.

Rev. Father John Cullinane, of Cheraw Mission, visited the stockade monthly and administered the holy sacraments to the sick and dying soldiers.

Perpetual member of St. Anthony's Guild.

"May His Soul Rest in Peace."

Fig. 4. Memorial obituary. *Saint Anthony Guild Publication* 9, no. 32 (1908), 9.

memorialize civilian members. These memorials serve several functions. They remind readers of the deceased and are therefore typical memorials. Their presence alongside the general mission news additionally serves to bring together the present with the past and bridge the mortal and immortal worlds by inserting the sacred into profane, day-to-day life. Unlike contemporary obituaries, which occupy the back pages of newspapers and are therefore relegated to a discreet space, these floating obituaries are read alongside the latest parish news and are a testament to the presence of the dead among Southern Catholics. The dead, as it were, are not absent, but present in a very literal way.

The dead are present in spatial ways, as well. St. Anne's Church, in Sumter, South Carolina, contains a rare display of stained-glass windows dedicated to deceased Confederate soldiers, and more generally to the southern defeat. The four corner windows of the transept are artworks of unique interest. The right-side window is dedicated "to the Confederate dead" and displays the battle flags of the Lost Cause. It is inscribed as follows: "Sacred to the Memory of Our Soldiers who fell in the War of 1861–'65." Window dedications to the dead are a significant part of how the deceased are made present to South Carolina Catholics. Deceased such as these soldiers, but more commonly civilians, are literally inscribed into the structures of the church and are linked, physically and metaphorically, to vision. Dedications are inscribed on the lower areas of the windows, and when an inscription is made, there is an accompanying note in the church bulletin, guild newspaper, or church archive to record the event. Both the narrative descriptions and the windows themselves are rich elaborations connecting a scene from sacred history with a particular deceased person. Windows are multidetermined symbols, especially those within sacred space. They represent a permeable barrier between two worlds, most literally between the outside and the inside but also between the sacred world and the profane. When one enters a Catholic church, one's vision is blocked to the outside, profane world and is instead confronted with beautiful scenes of sacred space and sacred history—saints in heaven, angels, or the souls in purgatory. To be inscribed into this space is significant, as it places the deceased within the sacred reality evoked by and through the windows. The stained-glass window effectively prevents one from seeing the outside, only allowing light to enter into the sacred space of the church. As part of a window, the deceased is also part of this space.

Nowhere is the incarnational aspect of Catholic devotionalism more evident than in the rituals and beliefs associated with saints' relics. The Catholics of South Carolina were lucky to have an "authenticated" arm bone of Anthony of Padua, the patron saint of the guild, which made the rounds among various South Carolina churches and was eventually probably sent back to Padua, Italy (see fig. 5).[31] The relic was a popular draw for Catholics and non-Catholics alike and inspired a lively discourse of "miracle letters," which attested to the efficacious intercession of the saint and which became a regular feature of South Carolina's Catholic publications. Additionally, articles describing the Catholic doctrine associated with saints' relics were popular features. As defined by one article in the guild publication, relics are "the bodies or portions of bodies of the servants of God who now stand as saints before the throne of God, or anything that belonged immediately to them, anything that touched their bodies, and things that were used by them."[32] These were not just parts of bodies, mere physical items, they shared in the holiness of God: "The bodies of the saints are, as it were, the temples of their souls, and the souls are, as it were, the temples of God Himself." To have a first-class relic, that is, an actual body part of a saint, was a matter of great spiritual significance, tantamount to having the presence of the sacred itself. The rituals surrounding the relic corresponded to its importance. South Carolina Catholics, like Catholic practitioners universally, were "bound to venerate, respect, and honor" the relics of saints. St. Anthony's arm bone had its own veneration once a month and was exposed during all novenas. (Novenas are prayers that are said consecutively for nine days and are usually accompanied by a "petition," or specific request from the practitioner to the saint for whom the novena is directed.) The exposure of the arm bone during novenas was significant in that the only other item in Catholic devotionalism that undergoes the ritual of exposure is the Eucharist, the wafer that for practitioners *is* the body of Jesus. The exposure of the Eucharist, called Eucharistic Adoration, is the exposure of the presence of the sacred, as it does not merely *represent* the sacred, it *embodies* it. The arm bone, being exposed in a similar manner, shares in the same ritualistic significance, to an extent. The sacred is being made present, physically, in the church. Accordingly, practitioners and the church ambiance were to conform to the occasion. "No relics are to be exposed without a certain amount of respect, hence lights are supposed to be burning before the altar when relics are exposed."[33] The faithful were exhorted to maintain the decorum of respect and silence when in the presence of the relic.

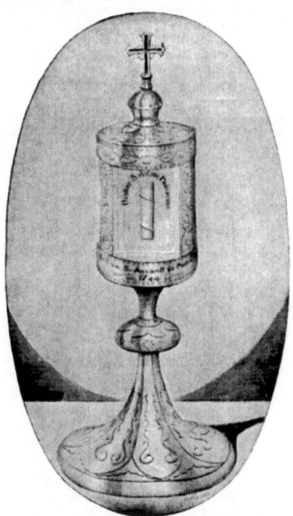

Fig. 5. "The Holy Relic of St. Anthony: An authenticated piece of the ulna, or arm bone, taken from the body of St. Anthony at Padua. The largest relic of St. Anthony in the United States, temporally [sic] loaned to the Guild."

This particular relic was perhaps one of the most popular objects of South Carolina Catholic devotionalism in the late nineteenth and early twentieth centuries. The popularity of relics is in no small way due to the miracles attributed to them, and practitioners who touch, venerate, and respect the relic, as well as ask for specific favors and cures, are apparently not disappointed. Miracle letters attest to the efficacious power of St. Anthony's relic and also served the function of providing positive press to the mission Church of St. Anthony as well as the guild, and, perhaps most important, helped to raise needed money. The letters, a semiregular feature in the guild *Publication*, reveals much about the relationships between practitioners and the saints they prayed to. A number of letters make monetary offerings contingent upon the granting of the favor requested of the saint, and most send in money once the favor is granted. One practitioner waited six years to have his favor granted. Others were luckier.

> Dear Father Wood—Your favor received, and many thanks for the same. I enclose $—— to help the St. Anthony Guild as a thank-offering for a favor granted. I will ask you to have the children offer again a novena for my intention.
>
> > I remain, yours sincerely, J. M. C.

> Dear Rev. Father Wood—Herewith we send you a money order for —— dollars; by so doing, we hope to throw a little ray of sunshine into the lives of some of your poor mission children, and at the same time gain the benefit of their prayers and the Holy Masses of your Guild for the good of our souls, and two temporal favors we want very much this coming winter. Should God hear our prayer, we will not forget St. Anthony's Churches and Chapels.
>
> > Yours sincerely in the Guild,
> > Mr. and Mrs. J. A. M.[34]

The connection between petitions granted and money paid, a long-controversial aspect of Catholic devotionalism and a significant contribution to the conflicts of the Protestant Reformation, can be viewed within the framework of the belief in the "communion of saints." Within Catholic doctrine, the communion of saints is linked to a similar doctrine called the mystical body of Christ.

The communion of saints is a supernatural society that combines together the faithful on earth, the souls in purgatory, and the saints in heaven in a unity that has as its head Christ. This community is also called the mystical body of Christ, which calls to mind its corporeal nature. According to Ann Taves, analysis of the language associated with the petitions of prayers and money from practitioners to their saints reveals that corporeal and economic metaphors predominate, and "merits and prayers are interchanged 'just as the blood circulates from and to the heart all over the body.'"[35] A treasury of "sacred goods" is thought to be exchanged between practitioner and saint, with the practitioner accruing merit or satisfaction through several means—prayers, works, or money. Money is just another form of the substance that links together the universal body of the church. The unself-conscious manner in which money was offered by the living to the saints for favors was not unusual within this framework.

Another devotional practice associated specifically with St. Anthony was the publication, once or twice a year, of hagiographic material relating to his life. Hagiographies, or biographies of saints' lives, have been a persistent genre within Catholic history. They serve many functions, one of which is prescriptive. A hagiography reveals why a saint becomes a saint—or, in other words, summarizes in narrative fashion the virtues that contributed to the subject's holy status. Practitioners read the stories and hoped to exemplify the virtues exhibited by the saints. The hagiographies of St. Anthony that appear in the guild's publication, however, were not likely intended to be prescriptive. First, due to the lack of education brought about by the poverty of South Carolina's church, Catholics were in need of basic information regarding their own churches. The hagiographies appear to have had educational goals in that they provide a lot of material regarding the history of St. Anthony, why he is venerated as a saint, as well as information about Italy and the church in Padua that is St. Anthony's namesake. Additionally, the narratives portray St. Anthony heroically, so they serve to entertain while providing this vital information. He carries on with his holy duties while under the duress of illness, but more miraculously he fights Satan hand to hand and finally defeats him by making the sign of the cross and invoking the Virgin Mary. These portrayals are so unlike the ordinary lives of practitioners that any prescriptive value is nullified by the sheer distance in time and conceptual space between them and their saint. However, the faithful were still encouraged to imitate the virtues of the saints in order to "obtain the protection and intercession of St. Anthony the more readily."[36] This was most likely to take place within the parameters of the annual shared novena occurring on the date of St. Anthony's feast day.

The year 1909 was a difficult one for South Carolina Catholics, who were still suffering from both the poverty that was a consequence of the Civil War and a general anti-Catholic ethos among non-Catholic southerners. The hope and fortitude to endure these trials was provided by active participation in the annual novena to St. Anthony, June 13–June 21. By joining their prayers and actions with the prayers and actions of all who participated in novenas to St. Anthony on his feast day worldwide, they believed the efficacy of their petitions would be more powerful. "It has been a trying year to many members of the Guild. We feel assured better times are in store, and meanwhile we will join the united force of our prayers. God will not fail but bless many fervent petitions."[37] The main objective of the guild, which is revealed in all of its devotional practices but most particularly in the feast day novena, was active participation in the communion of saints. The nature of this participation crossed boundaries between the material and the spiritual.

The special novena to St. Anthony linked practitioners directly to the communion of saints. The mystical body of Christ is nourished by the sacraments, especially the food of the Eucharist, and just as all parts of a body are interdependent and do not act as separate individuals, so, too, are the parts of the mystical body. For example, saints in heaven can pray to change the circumstances of those on earth, and those on earth, by their prayers and works, can change the circumstances of those in purgatory. A novena to a saint is one way to benefit from the shared power of all of those who belong to the communion of saints. When a Catholic practitioner in South Carolina participates in the novena to St. Anthony, he or she benefits from the prayers of all of those on earth, in purgatory, and in heaven who are also praying to St. Anthony during this time. In this way the novena connects the American Catholic to the European Catholic and forms a global—or, in Catholic terms, a universal—community that defies space and time. This is not just a spiritual or supernatural community; it is physical as well, as works and the performance of virtue are just as important to the effectiveness of the novenas as prayer.

A supplemental edition of the regular guild publication outlines the correct procedures for participating in the novena. First, guild members are assured of the united prayers of those who participate in the guild, not only those in South Carolina but also those in the societies in Italy that are aligned with the guild. Additionally, only members can participate. "Pious Practices" are outlined for each day of the novena, and members are encouraged to imitate these practices: "True devotion to the saints consists in the imitation of their virtues: we therefore subjoin for every day of the Novena some pious practice, which is to be performed in addition to the prayers, in order to obtain the protection and intercession of St. Anthony the more readily." The practices are focused on relationships with others, but also on one's relationship to oneself. Of the nine practices, two are directed toward others—one's neighbor and the souls in purgatory. "Practice charity. For example: be friendly toward those against whom you feel aversion"; "Offer up all good works during this day for the souls in Purgatory." The majority of the practices, six of them, exhort practitioners to purify their characters in a number of punitive ways: "Practice some sort of slight mortification of your appetite"; "Strive to know and to amend your predominant fault." The ninth practice is enacted for the benefit of the church and the pope: "Offer up prayers and good works of this day for the Church, the Holy Father, the bishops and priest. 'Pray for one another, that you may be saved.' (James 5. 16)."[38] The exercises outlined reflect how the material and spiritual nature of the devotion are inextricably linked. Practice is wedded to prayer, and physical location is obviated through linking into a supernatural corporate body. Another material component of the devotion that commingles with the spiritual is, again, money.

Money acts as an organizational force with respect to the novena. Members are the only ones who can officially participate in the novena and receive its benefits. This functions to secure the boundaries of the guild, but more important it guarantees that the guild will continue to receive money for its various missions and activities. Petitions are granted, according to the guild, only if one is a member and follows correct protocol regarding the devotion. In this way the guild secures loyalty through a contractual arrangement. A petition or prayer request costs $1 The more one requests, the more money one will give to the guild. The petitions sold are designed to be attractive. Children, sisters, and priests will be praying for those who submit petitions. "Every night at 8 o'clock there will be public prayer, Litany and Benediction for each intention recommended for the Novena. Our mission children will pray for your INTENTIONS AND PETITIONS." [39] Again, within the framework of the "treasury of sacred goods," money acts as a conduit for spiritual or temporal favors, granted by those who are able to provide them. However, it is money and not works or prayers that guarantees that a member is incorporated into the society of the novena. Money is the limit that defines the boundaries of the society and secures its benefits.

CONCLUSION

Evidence suggests that the attribution of an Enlightenment ethos to the South Carolina Catholicism inspired by Bishop John England should be reconsidered. England's promotion and eloquent advocacy of forms of religious devotion centered on the material aspects of Catholicism set the stage for a type of religion that was very different from the forms that contemporaneously developed in the Northeast. Rather than an interior, private piety, South Carolina Catholics focused their religious energies on devotions that promoted a radical sense of community and exteriority that transcended physical and temporal boundaries. Lack of financial means, dearth of ecclesial presence, and the scarcity of centralized sites of worship contributed to a community that stressed the virtual nature of the church. The actual physical presence of churches and practitioners was not so important when placed within the context of a universal membership that was accessed through prayers and devotions. In this way South Carolina Catholics kept the fire of faith alive amid less than ideal conditions.

NOTES

I wish to thank archivist Brian Fahey and Heather Walsh for their assistance with my research.

1. Jay Dolan used the term "republican" Catholicism to describe eighteenth- and early nineteenth-century American Catholics. See Jay Dolan, *In Search of an American Catholicism: A History of Religion and Culture in Ten-*

sion (New York: Oxford University Press, 2002); and Joseph P. Chinnici, *Living Stones: The History and Structure of Catholic Spiritual Life in the United States* (New York: Macmillan, 1989).

2. John England, *The Works of the Right Reverend John England, First Bishop of Charleston*, 5 vols., ed. Ignatius Reynolds (Baltimore: John Murphy, 1849), 3:250.

3. Randall Miller, "Roman Catholicism in South Carolina," in *Religion in South Carolina*, ed. Charles H. Lippy (Columbia: University of South Carolina Press, 1993), 83.

4. Ibid.

5. John England, *Diocese of Charleston, Constitution of 1826*, art. XV, archives of the Catholic Diocese of Charleston.

6. Ibid, art. XXII.

7. Ibid, 4.

8. Dolan, *In Search of an American Catholicism*, 24.

9. John England, *Diary of the Right Reverend John England, Records of the American Catholic Historical Society of Philadelphia* 6 (1895): 29–224.

10. "In October 1791, on the eve of the First National Synod, John Carroll wrote to Charles Plowden, a friend in England, that before he could divide the Baltimore Diocese, he needed to establish uniform discipline, 'that as little danger as possible may remain with a disunion with the Holy See.'" As reported by Joseph Chinnici, "Organization of the Spiritual Life: American Catholic Devotional Works, 1791–1866," *Theological Studies* 40, no. 2 (1979): 229.

11. Rev. John F. Sullivan, *The Externals of the Catholic Church: Her Government, Ceremonies, Festivals, Sacramentals, and Devotions*, 3rd ed. (New York: P. J. Kenedy and Sons, 1918), 345, 129.

12. Ann Taves, *The Household of Faith: Catholic Devotions in Mid Nineteenth Century America* (Notre Dame: Indiana University of Notre Dame Press, 1986), 96.

13. Sullivan, *The Externals of the Catholic Church*, 351.

14. Chinnici, "Organization of the Spiritual Life," 235.

15. John England, *Explanation of the Construction, Furniture, and Ornaments of a Church, of the Vestments of the Clergy, and of the Nature and Ceremonies of the Mass* (Baltimore, c. 1820–1822), 99, 94, 95.

16. John England, *A Catechism of the Roman Catholic Faith* (New York: A. Chandler, 1826), 31.

17. John England, *A Catechism of the Roman Catholic Faith, Published for the Use of Young Children* (Baltimore: F. Lucas Jr., 1830), 57.

18. John England, *Explanation of the Ceremonies of the Holy Week in the Chapels of the Vatican, and of Those of Easter Sunday in the Church of Saint Peter*, 2nd ed. (Rome, 1847), 4, 6, 5.

19. Chinnici, "Organization of the Spiritual Life," 233, 244.

20. Ibid., 249.

21. *Saint Anthony Guild Publication*. 2, no. 7 (1901): 1, 10.

22. Ibid., 9, no. 32 (1908): 1.

23. For a discussion of the emergence of parish missions in the nineteenth century, see Taves, *The Household of Faith*, 10–14; and Jay Dolan, ed., *The American Catholic Parish: a History from 1850 to the Present* (New York: Paulist, 1987).

24. *Saint Anthony Guild Publication* 2, no. 7 (1910): 1.

25. Ibid., 2.

26. Catholic Church, *The Catechism of the Catholic Church*, 2nd ed. (New York: Doubleday, 2003), 1030–32.

27. *Saint Anthony Guild Publication* 2, no. 7 (1901).

28. Ibid., 9, no. 32 (1908).

29. Ibid., 2.

30. For the shift that occurred in nineteenth-century representations of heaven and immortality, see: Ann Douglas, "Heaven Our Home: Consolation Literature in the Northern United States, 1830–1880," in "Death in America," special issue, *American Quarterly* 26, no. 5 (1974): 496–515; Gary Laderman, *The Sacred Remains: American Attitudes toward Death, 1799–1833* (New Haven, Conn.: Yale University Press, 1999); Colleen McDannell and Bernhard Lang, *Heaven: A History* (New Haven, Conn.: Yale University Press, 2001).

31. The relic may have traveled back to Italy, although there is no official record of this.

32. *Saint Anthony Guild Publication* 6, no. 22 (1905).

33. Ibid.

34. Ibid.

35. Taves, *The Household of Faith*, 50.

36. *Saint Anthony Guild Publication* 10, no. 35 (1909), feast day edition, supplement page.

37. Ibid.

38. Ibid.

39. Ibid.

Baptist Women and the South

From the "Woman's Sphere" to the Pulpit

Bill J. Leonard

The social construction of being masculine or feminine—in other words, the roles, expectations, and styles that make up the category of gender—has been significant in southern religion as elsewhere. Baptists in the South, in all their variety, have grappled with this issue as publicly as any other group. In this essay, Bill Leonard examines the hermeneutical and cultural backgrounds to arguments for and against female ordination. He discusses the development of the "woman's sphere"—a context that permitted females to exercise certain functions related to missions, the nurture of children, and homemaking while keeping them from more explicit ecclesiastical activities related to ordination and pastoral ministry—and concludes with a set of predictions for the future of Baptist women in ministry.

We believe that men and women are spiritually equal in position before God but that God has ordained distinct and separate spiritual functions of men and women in the home and in the church. The husband is to be the leader of the home and men are to hold the leadership positions (pastors and deacons) in the church. Accordingly, only men are eligible of licensure and ordination for pastor by the church.

—Baptist Bible Fellowship International,
"Of the Church," in *Statement of Faith*

This article from the *Statement of Faith* of the Baptist Bible Fellowship International, an organization of Independent Baptist churches, summarizes the twofold approach of many, perhaps most, Baptist groups regarding the role of women in the church. On one hand, it acknowledges spiritual equality of men and women "before God" and recognizes that each have specific "spiritual functions" that are ordained by God in the world. On the other hand, the statement closes the door to any consideration of females as pastors or deacons of Baptist congregations. In this way Independent Baptists perpetuate what is sometimes known as the "woman's sphere," a willingness to assign Baptist women roles in the church and the home while setting boundaries that limit their leadership and calling to wider participation in church offices and ordained ministries. Inside the woman's sphere, church women may develop significant leadership and even power in specific congregations—teaching children and other women, funding programs, engaging in various missionary and benevolent activities, and often serving as the largest segment of the Sunday and weekday life of the church. If they step out of those boundaries, however, women may experience sanctions or even de facto expulsion from a congregation that rejects their public leadership of worship or does not allow them to provide biblical instruction to men and boys.

Such a position is echoed, formally or informally, by most Baptist subdenominations in the United States, a list of which would surely include Independent Baptists, the Southern Baptist Convention, Primitive Baptists, National Baptists, Conservative Baptists, and innumerable local Baptist congregations. Baptist churches associated with the American Baptist Churches, USA—the Alliance of Baptists, the Cooperative Baptist Fellowship, Free-Will Baptists, Seventh-Day Baptists, the Progressive National Baptist Convention—and a wide variety of local churches in multiple Baptist groups are among those subdenominations that have affirmed the role of women as ministers, leaving the decision as to ordination and hiring to the individual congregation. Indeed, even those Baptist groups that accept or encourage the ordination of women and their presence on ministerial staffs of churches continue to be extremely hesitant to call women as senior pastors.

This essay suggests that women have always played vital roles in Baptist life and in fact to this day represent the largest constituency in most Baptist congregations. Nonetheless, Baptists, like other Christian communions, have generally bowed to particular herme- neutical and cultural methods for defining the role of women in the church, the family, and the larger society. A literalist herme- neutic led Baptist men (and many women) to believe that females were excluded from ordained ministry, "subject" to the authority of their husbands (or fathers) in matters spiritual and familial, and (in many cases) forbidden to teach males beyond the age of twelve. Bible proof-texts included the following:

> Let the woman learn in silence with all subjection. But I suffer not a woman to teach, nor to usurp authority over the man, but to be in silence. For Adam was first formed, then Eve. And Adam was not deceived, but the woman being deceived was in the transgres- sion. (1 Tim. 2:11–14, KJV)

> Wives, submit yourselves unto your own husbands, as unto the Lord. For the husband is the head of the wife, even as Christ is head of the church: and he is the saviour of the body, Therefore as the church is subject unto Christ, so let the wives be to their own husbands in everything. (Eph. 5:22–24, KJV)

> A bishop [pastor] then must be blameless, the husband of one wife, vigilant, sober, of good behaviour, given to hospitality, apt to teach. (1 Tim. 3:2, KJV)[1]

Twentieth-century Independent Baptist leader John R. Rice was among the most literal of the biblical literalists in asserting the essential maleness of the divine and the church. In a sermon ad- dressed "to men only," Rice declared that "God is a masculine God. A man, then, is nearer like God than a woman, and in a sense, man is in the image of God. . . . The Bible plainly says that Eve was de- ceived but that Adam was not deceived. He knew better. He knew it would not make him wise. God never intended women to lead men around by their noses. . . . Men are to lead out in music, in Bible teaching in the church, in personal soul winning in the church . . . God has reserved the main place in the church for men."[2] These words, though extreme, generally characterize the way in which many Baptists understand the role of women in Baptist churches.

Other Baptists suggest that the New Testament describes multiple possibilities for considering women as full participants in the ordained leadership of churches. Some note that the sweeping statement of St. Paul in Romans, chapter 8 applies to all persons who are "in Christ": "There is therefore now no condemnation for those who are in Christ Jesus. For the law of the Spirit of life in Christ Jesus has set you free from the law of sin and of death" (Rom. 8:1–2, NRSV). In those words all curses die; thus, if women are too cursed to be called, they may be too cursed to be saved![3] Likewise, at Pentecost the Holy Spirit is "poured out upon all flesh," thereby enabling men and women to "prophesy" and declare the good news. Thus St. Paul also concludes that "there is no longer Jew or Greek, slave or free, there is no longer male or female; for all of you are one in Christ Jesus" (Gal. 3:27, NRSV). In short, on this issue, like others, Baptists must debate the way they read and use biblical materials.

THE "WOMAN'S SPHERE" IN BAPTIST LIFE

Such divisions shaped the kind of "woman's sphere" that developed among Baptists and other Protestants in American religious life. Donald Mathews notes that, especially in the South, the "woman's sphere" was "a model of behavior and ideals which was peculiarly the possession of women and was based on their unique contribution to the ideal community."[4] Women were thus assigned or otherwise encouraged to exercise their spiritual gifts in ways that did not challenge the literal interpretation of certain New Testament texts. They were the models of virtue, nurture, and a special kind of spirituality not given to males. Mathews observes: "It was almost as if men willingly conceded the moral superiority of women in order to prevent active female participation in worldly [and churchly] affairs."[5] As new generations of women moved toward ordination and the ministry, they challenged this reading of scripture and its accompanying "sphere" in ways that brought them into conflict with men and other women who refused to relinquish what they felt to be absolute biblical teaching.

In a sense the evolution of Baptist women to the ordained ministry came as women moved from the "sphere" to a broader understanding of the nature of God's call upon all human beings. It actually began rather early in American history, with certain colonial women, such as Margaret Meuse Clay (1770), charged with "unlicensed preaching" in Virginia.[6] Participation in the frontier revivals also led many to exercise gifts of proclamation and religious fervor. Christine Leigh Heyrman wrote that early in the awakenings, Baptist and Methodist preachers supported the idea "that women of all ages and races might exercise their gifts by speaking before public, sexually mixed, religious gatherings. Thereby the clergy endorsed the view that acceptable forms of female spiritual expression went beyond fulfilling their private roles as dutiful wives, mothers, and sisters."[7] In other words, there was acceptance for the idea of women participating beyond the "woman's sphere." However, Heyrman's research led her to conclude that many ministers came to reject this larger role for females in Protestant churches, fearing that the churches would become the near-exclusive domain of women and men would turn away in droves.[8]

Nineteenth-century Free Will Baptists were perhaps the first to move women along toward a more formal participation in the ministry. Ruby Knapp Bixby was licensed as a Free Will Baptist minister in 1846. She married a minister and they apparently shared ministerial duties. Her 1877 obituary suggested that she was "an independent, self-reliant preacher. Her discourses were characteristically persuasive, and she was more than ordinarily successful. She preached much with churches as pastor, and much as an evangelist."[9] By the late nineteenth century, Free Will Baptists had ordained several women to the ministry. Likewise, Northern and Seventh-Day Baptists also ordained women in the 1880s and 1890s.[10]

THE MISSIONARY MOVEMENT

By the twentieth century, women's rights and later feminist movements no doubt had a significant impact on Baptist women who decided that ministry was part of their calling. Equally important, perhaps, was the communal rhetoric and personal piety that long shaped Baptist spirituality. Baptist rhetoric in revival meetings, Sunday school classes, and summer camps led youth, both males and females, to conclude that they were to "do whatever God told them to do" and "surrender for full-time Christian service." The rhetoric of the call and the duty to respond to the guidance of the Holy Spirit was heard by women as well as men; they simply took the preachers at their word. Likewise, the piety of Baptist life influenced women and men with a sense of call to ministry that did not know gender distinctions. If conversion—a radical transformation of grace—was for all persons, then surely it broke down all the walls that would obstruct genuine ministry and calling to "preach the gospel to all nations" (Matt. 28:19).

In a real sense, the power of rhetoric and piety in Baptist life was evident early in the nineteenth century with the decision to send out Baptist missionaries throughout the world. While these women were not ordained, and their activities were carefully curtailed by the missionary-sending agencies, it was inevitable that they would have multiple experiences in church leadership on "foreign fields." There is no doubt that the early female missionaries had a strong sense of call, even though they went out as wives or single women charged to carry out "women's work with women" only. In 1810 Ann Hasseltine received Adoniram Judson's proposal of marriage knowing that her positive response would send her with him to the mission field in India. Her language is clearly that of Baptist piety and ministerial calling. She wrote: "An opportunity has been presented to me, of spending my days among the heathen, attempting to persuade them to receive the Gospel. Were I convinced of its being a call from God, and that it would be more pleasing to him, for me to spend my life in this way than in any other, I think I should be willing to relinquish every earthly object, and, in full view of dangers and hardships, give myself up to the great work."[11] Hasseltine accepted "the call" from God and Adoniram Judson, departing with him for India in 1812 as a Congregational missionary—both accepting Baptist views on the voyage over—and moving with him to begin a Baptist work in Burma. A teacher, linguist, homemaker, and spiritual guide, she nursed her husband back to health after a debilitating disease only to die in childbirth in 1826 at the age of thirty-six. The stories of Ann Hasseltine Judson and hundreds of other women who went out as missionaries shaped a sense of call in generations of Baptist females, many of whom sought full acceptance into all aspects of Christian mission and ministry. In a sense, the women's missionary movement in Baptist life was kept within the woman's sphere. Women were encouraged to raise money for missionary efforts and were even permitted to go as missionaries, although they were constrained within clearly defined activities. Yet their leadership skills and gifts for ministry were cultivated through these missionary agencies at home and abroad. In short, the missionary movements kept women "in their place" while it also extended their influence and offered them an outlet for ministry.

WOMEN AS DEACONS

Another way in which women came to various aspects of Baptist ministry was through ordination (or election) to the office of deacon in Baptist churches. Their congregational polity has generally meant that Baptists accepted two basic offices of leadership in their churches, pastor and deacon, the latter being a lay leadership office in the church. Some Baptists ordain deacons with the laying on of hands while others simply install them by virtue of congregational election. Some Baptists welcomed women into the diaconate as early as the nineteenth century, but in many Baptist groups the addition of women deacons has been difficult or forbidden. Debates continue to rage in many Baptist churches regarding the ordination of women as deacons. Other churches settled it long ago in favor of males and females in the diaconate. Similar debates and decisions regarding the ordination are evident in a variety of Baptist subdenominations.

BAPTIST SUBDENOMINATIONS AND WOMEN'S ORDINATION

American Baptist Churches, USA

As early as 1964 American Baptist Churches, USA (ABC) approved a statement affirming that "there should be no differential treatment of men and women in the church, family or society and that there should be equal opportunity for full participation in the work of our God." It also called for "full participation of women in the life and work of the church (including pastorates) in all countries."[12] A woman's task force was established in 1974 to encourage the inclusion of women in all denominational boards and agencies as well as to support their becoming pastors and other church staff members. In 2003 the ABC reported 1,392 women on the "professional registry mailing list" of American Baptist Women in Ministry. It noted that 9 percent of all ABC pastors were female, with women representing 32 percent of all associate pastors.[13] In 2005 the American Baptist Women in Ministry reported 403 women serving as pastors or copastors in ABC-related churches, a 13 percent increase from 2004. The report noted that 374 were pastors and 29 were copastors.[14] The ABC probably has more ordained women as senior pastors than any other Baptist subdenomination in America.

The Southern Baptist Convention

The Southern Baptist Convention (SBC) is the largest Baptist subdenomination in the United States, claiming some 16 million members. It is also one of the most publicly troubled, having been involved in what seems an unending controversy with groups inside and outside its ranks for over two decades. Questions over the role of women in ministry, particularly the ordination of women as pastors, was one of the early issues that divided so-called conservatives and moderates in the battle for control of the denomination. With the success of the conservatives in gaining control of the national denominational boards and agencies and the general departure of the moderates, the SBC moved to revise its confession of faith, *The Baptist Faith and Message,* in 2000. The revision included a statement that recognizes the significant role that women play in all SBC churches but repudiates the ordination of women for the pastoral office. It reads: "While both men and women are gifted for service in the church, the office of pastor is limited to men as qualified by Scripture."[15]

What was once a local church decision thus became a denominational article of faith. Before this tightening of theological and congregational restrictions, numerous Southern Baptist churches had ordained women, with the first such event occurring in August 1964 with the ordination of Addie Davis by Watts Street Baptist Church in Durham, North Carolina. Unable to secure a pastorate in the South, Davis served churches in Vermont and Rhode Island.[16] Ordinations increased during the 1970s and 1980s, not without controversy in Baptist associations and state conventions across the South. Women in Ministry, SBC, was founded in June 1983 to "provide support for the woman whose call from God defines her vocation as that of minister or that of woman in ministry within the SBC and affirm her call to be a servant of God."[17] A 1984 (nonbinding) resolution passed by messengers to the annual meeting of the

SBC cited a variety of biblical texts, including the reference to the "Edenic fall" in 1 Timothy, chapter 2. It concluded, "We encourage the service of women in all aspects of church life and work other than pastoral functions and leadership roles entailing ordination."[18] Officially, therefore, the Southern Baptist Convention has rejected the ordination of women and the calling of women to pastorates in SBC churches. This is not to suggest, however, that churches previously affiliated with the SBC have ceased to encourage women's ordination.

Newer Baptist Subdenominations

A number of Baptist groups have been formed or reconfigured as a result of controversies related to the SBC. These include the Alliance of Baptists and the Cooperative Baptist Fellowship, coalitions of Baptist congregations and individuals formed, at least initially, in response to the rightward tilt of the SBC. The Baptist General Association of Virginia and the Baptist General Convention of Texas are two state Baptist conventions that have tended to separate themselves more intentionally from previous connections with the SBC. All these groups affirm women in ministry and generally leave the decision of ordination to the local congregation. In 2005 Baptist Women in Ministry approved a new survey regarding the role of women in churches affiliated with those four organizations. It found that in 2005 "102 Baptist women served as pastor, co-pastor or church planter in churches affiliated with the four groups listed above." "Of these women, 66 served as pastors, 34 as co-pastors, and 2 as church planters." The four largest configurations came from Virginia (16), North Carolina (12), Texas (11), and Georgia (11). The other states numbered 6 or below.[19]

These rather small numbers led Albert Mohler, president of the Southern Baptist Theological Seminary, Louisville, Kentucky, and an outspoken conservative, to suggest that even moderate to liberal Baptists are "virtually as reluctant as conservative churches to call a woman as pastor." Moderates, many of whom criticized and departed from the Southern Baptist Convention because of such issues as the ordination of women, may have a public commitment to women's ordination yet, as Mohler concluded, "at the congregational level . . ., the reality appears to be dramatically at odds with this public commitment." He asserted that support for female pastors "appears to be hypothetical, not real." Mohler also suggested that this did not bode well for the large number of Baptist women attending moderate Baptist seminaries, noting, "Will the feminization of these schools force a disconnect between these institutions and their supporting churches? Where are the men?"[20] Mohler's observations reflect the difficulties that churches related to more liberal Baptist groups face between their willingness to ordain women and their hesitancy to call them as senior pastors.

There are exceptions, however. During the early 2000s members of two moderate Baptist churches in Waco, Texas (a relatively traditional town), voted to call women as their senior pastors. Julie Pennington-Russell was called as pastor of Calvary Baptist Church and Doris Ann Cooper was called as pastor of Lakeside Baptist Church. They are the first women to serve in that role in either of the churches. In some respects, they and their churches now serve as models to other moderate congregations that might be willing to "take a chance" on women in the pastoral role and discover the benefits. Ironically, however, Albert Mohler's conclusions reflect those of Nancy Hastings Sehested, one of the earliest female pastors in moderate Baptist life in the South. After several years as a Baptist pastor in Tennessee, Sehested left the pastorate for a prison chaplaincy, noting: "The moderates might as well have a statement against women pastors. Even in moderate churches where they say they're open to women pastors, it's still difficult. The doors are not open."[21]

Independent Baptists

As noted at the beginning of this essay, Independent Baptists are among the most outspoken opponents of Baptist women in ministry. Independent Baptists are a collection of extremely autonomous churches, linked together in ministers' "fellowships" or conferences but rejecting all "hierarchical" alliances associated with denominationalism. They are also unashamedly fundamentalist in their theological orientation, with emphasis on clearly defined doctrinal views including the inerrancy of scripture, the virgin birth of Jesus Christ, his substitutionary atonement on the cross, his bodily Resurrection and his literal Second Coming. Many remain "separatist fundamentalists," meaning that they reject any association with those who are tainted by or associated with liberalism in any form. Some of the earliest Independent Baptists separated themselves from the Southern Baptist Convention in the 1920s and 1930s in the belief that the SBC had become corrupted by liberalism and that the "sacred cow" of denominational loyalty compromised the autonomy of local congregations, a nonnegotiable Baptist tenet. Independent Baptist groups include the Baptist Bible Fellowship, the Southwide Baptist Fellowship, and the General Association of Regular Baptist Churches.

Generally, Independent Baptists place the issue of women in ministry within the context of women's subjection to God and males, especially fathers and husbands. From their perspective, women's roles in church and family are clearly prescribed in scripture. Feminism, women's work outside the home, ordination of women, and other efforts to step outside the "sphere" are seen by some as evidence of the "last days," a prelude to the immediate return of Jesus Christ. One Independent Baptist church notes in a statement on the matter: "It is exceedingly dangerous for a woman to get out of her orbit. God never created woman to rule man. His whole Word is against it. Because of this broken law the curse of God is on the home, church, society, and nation."[22] Many Independent Baptists, men and women alike, feel strongly that the mandated role of each of the sexes must not be violated. They understand that women's attempts to usurp the power of men in the pulpit represent a direct challenge to the divinely ordained authority and order of the church.

African American Baptists

While African American denominations and churches use the language of liberation in their worship and ministry, many, perhaps most, continue to maintain the tradition of the woman's sphere. Indeed, in many African American Baptist churches, that sphere has long been defined in very specific ways, with extensive use of women's organizations that draw on sources of both formal and informal power. Women's guilds, deaconess organizations, mission groups, nursing sisters, and "mothers of the church" are the outlets for ministry and influence for women in many African American Baptist congregations. But the walls blocking women in ministry and ordination—the ability to stand "behind the sacred desk" (pulpit)—remain strong. Women have been ordained in churches related to the

National Baptist Convention of America, the National Baptist Convention, U.S.A., and the Progressive National Baptist Convention, but only in the latter denomination is it done with some consistency. Congregational autonomy allows churches to offer ordination of women but often involves controversy inside the church and the parent denomination. Surveys conducted by sociologists C. Eric Lincoln and Lawrence Mamiya among the three leading African American Baptist denominations indicated that majorities in each group opposed the idea of ordination for women, although it does occur. [23]

Many African American women have left the Baptist fold for those denominations that are more willing to call or appoint women to pastoral ministries. Others have attempted to start their own churches rather than wait for changes in Baptist traditionalism. Many ordained African American Baptist women such as Carolyn Knight (Interdenominational Theological Center), Veronice Miles (Wake Forest University), and Teresa Fry Brown (Emory University) have found greater acceptance for their ordination and their scholarship in academic institutions, from which they have had occasions to preach in multiple congregations. Alton B. Pollard III, director of black church studies at Candler School of Theology, Emory University, commented on the situation for women in African American (and Anglo) churches in 2006, noting: "It's a combination of age-old customs and democratic myopia: that in the marketplace of ideas and values, men matter most and that by definition, women have to take a back seat."[24]

BAPTIST WOMEN IN MINISTRY: LOOKING TO THE FUTURE

What does the future hold for Baptist women in ministry? The possibilities are as follows. First, it is clear that Baptist denominations and congregations will remain divided over the very nature of ordination and pastoral ministry for women. For many Baptists, acceptance of women as ordained pastors would require a change in biblical interpretation that they are unwilling or unable to make. It would require a reevaluation of their entire hermeneutical method, with implications for many other doctrines and practices. For these groups, the woman's sphere is grounded in the divine order of creation in the church and the world.

Second, if recent surveys and studies are any indication, the road to a senior pastorate remains extremely difficult for ordained Baptist women. While there are signs that a growing number of churches are revisiting the issue through their pastoral search committees, the willingness of churches even to consider female candidates for a pastorate remains the exception and not the rule.

Third, moderate/liberal Baptist churches now face a dilemma. After decades of encouraging, even ordaining, women to ministry, these churches have to decide what to do about them as full-fledged ministers. Are they willing to call them out and then watch them depart for other denominations or nondenominational congregations where the possibilities for ministry are more readily available?

Fourth, if it is true that a new generation of seminarians seems less interested in pastoral ministry in general, where will Baptists go to find younger ministers?[25] Will the initial entry of increased numbers of women into senior pastorates be due primarily to the shortage of men? Might this be a way in which women secure their first pastorates and by which churches learn that women are indeed gifted pastoral ministers? Are women willing to wait for the churches until demographics, if not spiritual inspiration, lead churches to consider them?

Finally, the presence of significant numbers of women in divinity schools and seminaries who are often drawn there by an expressed intent to go into pastoral ministry, means that churches will continue to confront the issue, especially related to females from their own ranks who have heard and responded to the church's call to "do whatever God calls you to do." Baptists who do not wish to accept women as fully called, fully accepted pastoral ministers in their churches would do well to stop ordaining them and to change the rhetoric of openness to that of spiritual restriction toward one entire gender of the human race.

NOTES

1. Many Baptists interpret this verse to mean that only men can be ordained since they alone can have wives. Others say this is a reference to polygamy, not about the inherent maleness of ordination.

2. Rosemary Radford Ruether and Rosemary Skinner Keller, *Women and Religion in America*, vol. 3, *1900–1968* (San Francisco: Harper and Row, 1986), 260–61.

3. Bill J. Leonard, "Forgiving Eve," *Pulpit Digest* 75, no. 473 (1985): 155–63.

4. Donald G. Mathews, *Religion in the Old South* (Chicago: University of Chicago Press, 1977), 111; and Bill J. Leonard, *Baptists in America* (New York: Columbia University Press, 2005), 204.

5. Leonard, *Baptists in America*, 113.

6. Ibid., 208.

7. Christine Leigh Heyrman, *Southern Cross: The Beginnings of the Bible Belt* (New York: Knopf, 1997), 166.

8. Ibid., 177.

9. James R. Lynch, "Baptist Women in Ministry through 1920," *American Baptist Quarterly* 13 (December 1994): 311.

10. Leonard, *Baptists in America*, 209–10. Licensing was and remains an entry stage for Baptist ministers. It was a way in which ministers were monitored and affirmed by a particular congregation as possessing ministerial gifts that could lead to ordination.

11. Dana L. Robert, *American Women in Mission: A Social History of Their Thought and Practice* (Macon, Ga.: Mercer University Press, 1996), 18.

12. American Baptist Convention, "Status of Women" (1965), *American Baptist Quarterly* 5 (June–September 1986): 320. In 1965 the denomination was known as the American Baptist Convention; later it became the American Baptist Churches, USA.

13. Leonard, *Baptists in America*, 217.

14. Eileen R. Campbell-Reed and Pamela R. Durso, "Assessing the State of Women in Baptist Life—2005," 2, Commissioned by Baptist Women in Ministry, Baptist Historical Society, Rochester, New York. This is not to suggest that all ABC-related churches have or would ordain women, simply that the denomination has taken a public position encouraging women in ministry. As in all Baptist subdenominations, ordination remains essentially in the jurisdiction of local churches.

15. Bob Allen, "Southern Baptist Leader Questions Moderates' Credibility on Women's Ordination," www.ethicsdaily.com (accessed August 22, 2006).

16. Ibid.

17. Leonard, *Baptists in America*, 218.

18. Ibid., 220.

19. Campbell-Reed and Durso, "Assessing the State of Women," 3.

20. Allen, "Southern Baptist Leader Questions Moderates' Credibility."

21. David T. Morgan, *Southern Baptist Sisters* (Macon, Ga.: Mercer University Press, 2003), 81.

22. "Eve Is Again Listening to the Voice of the Serpent," Landmark

Independent Baptist Church Homepage, users.aol.com/libcfl/woman.htm; and Leonard, *Baptists in America*, 222.

23. C. Eric Lincoln and Lawrence H. Mamiya, "The Black Denominations and the Ordination of Women," in *Down by the Riverside: Readings in African American Religion*, ed. Larry G. Murphy (New York: New York University Press, 2000), 368.

24. Neela Banerjee, "Clergywomen Find Hard Path to Bigger Pulpit," *New York Times*, August 26, 2006, nytimes.com. The *Times* article traces the difficulty women face in securing senior pastorates in all major denominations in America. It notes that many women, African American and Anglo-Saxon alike, have found the nondenominational movement more conducive to their ministries.

25. Neela Banerjee, "Students Flock to Seminaries, but Fewer See Pulpit in Future," *New York Times*, March 17, 2006, nytimes.com.

LYNCHING RELIGION

Why the Old Man Shouted "Glory!"

DONALD G. MATHEWS

Religion has been expressed in the communion of fellowship but also in the ecstasy of violence and revenge. In this essay, historian Donald Mathews examines "lynching religion," with its themes of blood sacrifice, atonement, and moral satisfaction as "licensed transgression." He interrogates the connection to the evangelical Protestant ethos of individualism, subjectivism, and purity that is so dominant in the South. Southern evangelical Protestantism did not cause lynching, Mathews concludes; however, it did help to justify it.

On an April Sunday afternoon in 1899, a crowd of five hundred men and boys in Coweta County, Georgia, seized by an "intense feeling of right and justice," forced a black day laborer to the outskirts of the county seat of Newnan and burned him alive.[1]

Newspaper reports never effectively captured the moment that they had helped to ignite. Fantasized rumor fed by folk myth and alarmist stories printed during a manhunt of over ten days sustained a widespread belief among citizens in the area southwest of Atlanta that an aroused manhood had sufficient cause to blend carnival, brutality, and pain into an act of what perpetrators understood as primal justice. Thomas Wilkes, whom the crowd knew as Sam Hose, had been justly suspected of homicide and unjustly accused of rape; but he was neither indicted nor tried in a court of law. Whether or not his burning evoked what an essayist much later called an "orgy of emotion," it was based upon a *provocation* that apologists believed justified the surrendering of reason to *passion* in a way that validated anything the crowd did.[2] Participants in the burning shouted taunts to the dying man, torturing him with knives and inhaling the stench of burning flesh in a brutal communion.[3] Finally, one white-haired man could contain himself no longer. "*Glory be to God!*" he screamed, jumping up and down. "God bless every man who had a hand in this. Thank *God* for vengeance."[4] From the crowd's total absorption in the burning black man, who uttered no sound—save the name "*Jesus*"—came this scream of religious celebration. Such spontaneous expressions were familiar to religious folk over the past century and not unprecedented at public killings. In 1888, for example, as a woman watched the hanging of a man by a Colorado mob, she had shouted, "*Praise the Lord!*"[5] But more subdued religious responses also occurred. When outlaw white Georgia Christians in Marietta hanged a Jewish businessman, Leo Frank of Atlanta, in 1915, reporters noted that the event was almost "like some religious rite"; for there was a "curiously reverent manner" and sense of "grave satisfaction" among the actors.[6] A Christian editor could be said to have confirmed the implications of such incidents as these when, after the killing of Hose and before the murder of Frank, he had written: "The spirit, which upholds lynch law . . . is the principal virtue which differentiates the civilization of the South from that of the North and West. It is *part of the religion of our people.*"[7]

These responses to a few of the more than five thousand lynchings in which a religious ambience is noticeable invite us to imagine others. Reading *Without Sanctuary*—published in 2000 but based on photographs of lynchings taken a century earlier—it is possible to conjecture about other reactions engraved into the imagination by such killings.[8] In compelling pictures, one sees a few children smiling in shyness or embarrassment; some appear somber, others confused by the actions of adults who have presented to their children something so strange that they do not know how to respond. Someone, who as a child was perplexed by the nonviolent rites of baptism and consecration, and transfixed by the mystery of the cross, can see in these photographs a similar awe in children confronted with the ultimate strangeness of dead humans hoisted high as a symbol of community. Complementing these representations of children having witnessed a communal butchery are snatched images of adults, who, too, are frequently smiling—even laughing, but not so much in mirth, perhaps, as in self-consciousness at being observed in such pageantry of death—a public event in which life and death were enacted in stark ritualistic ways—the ritual and the act it symbolized becoming, ironically, one. Such moments were and are not commonplace. Life and death, violence and camera came together in a flash of light against the darkness of *satisfaction* at such terrible punishment. Others stare out of curiosity and perhaps from fascination, gazing at the corpse(s) newly sculpted from living flesh by others in the crowd—or perhaps by themselves. Facing the camera to be identified with a killing implied a willingness to link oneself with such an act. Simply being there, simply *gazing* meant participation. *I'm "frozen,"* we can imagine someone thinking; *I'm caught with these people who did this "thing" to "that"—why? I had to come; I have to go! Pictures—damn! No—but, yes: Good! I've seen Something! A nigger! A Negro! A man! God! God! God!* We can imagine such words, unsaid, perhaps, but representing feelings aroused for a furtive moment. *That thing! That body—This doesn't happen; but it did. God—what a mess; what a time! God! Damn! God! Goddamn!* We can imagine one wondering about this exotic but utterly human moment in which human actions enact a transcendent moment of Life and Death. That moment could impose silence in contemplating death and punishment, or draw a troubled and troubling gaze, or elicit a smile, or explode unexpectedly in an excited exclamation of *transcendent* awe: *"Glory be to God!"*

Even in *denying* a sacred aura to such an event, a lynch mob could affirm a holy purpose to shedding blood, as once Aztec priests had done in ripping a beating heart from the breast of a sacrificial subject in sacred ceremony.[9] Blood stained Aztecs' altars not because they were hideous and inhuman practitioners of savage rites but because they understood the value of human life and the sublimity achieved in sacrificing it unto Transcendence. If the Lord spared Abraham the terror of sacrificing his son, Isaac, the patriarch nonetheless knew from the wisdom of the ancient ones that sacrifice was demanded of humans who would follow the ways of the Most High and who had heard their liege lord's call to sacrifice for a higher purpose. He knew that blood was demanded of those who would act supremely. Centuries later, Christians kneeling before the crucifix or receiving the blood of divine sacrifice in the Eucharist knew, too, that religion and blood and sacrifice could not be separated in contemplating the sacred. And so, it happened that in storming a Statesboro, Georgia, courtroom to seize and kill two convicted criminals, an anonymous man from among the crowd of self-appointed priests could shout at a Presbyterian minister who was trying vainly to hold back the tide of vengeance, "*We don't want religion, we want blood.*"[10]

But the polarity, exclaimed almost as a profane curse, was false. The desire for *blood* to be shed in vengeance as an act of justice was a desire for *religion* because the shedding of blood in sacrifice was familiar to even nominal Christians in the South of 1904; they had heard it in sermons based on Old Testament texts; they had heard it in sermons based on the Crucifixion, when blood and religion were one. Moderns too prissily renounce a religious affect in violence and blood because they do not reflect on the meanings of two thousand years of Christian fascination with the cross as an engine of killing, bloodletting, and divine action. The man who pushed aside the Calvinist cleric renounced a polite religion of appropriate behavior and Sunday school sentiment, to be sure, and the momentary confrontation with one who represented a caution *not* to do what he wanted (needed) to do seemed to intensify his righteous fury; he affirmed instead the religion of blood sacrifice; he wanted *blood*. And he may have sung about it in camp meeting or revival in Christian celebration of "power (power), power (power) wonder-working power in the blood (in the blood) of the Lamb (of the Lamb)."[11] The fusion of blood and power in religious verse was common, even if both minister and lyncher forgot it in the trauma and confusion of mob action. The blood of the "Lamb" was now of course lost to consciousness among those who wanted the blood of offenders to be shed on a more contemporary gallows than the cross, because in the shedding of that blood lay the community's own immediate salvation. The obsessive focus of the voice—and of the crowd whence it erupted—was on shedding the blood of black men who had burned a white family to death. These men's blood, when it erupted from burst arteries and curdled from the flames, would *end* the (white) community's anguish and grief; it would *pay for* terrible and grisly murders; it would *set aright* the imbalance of the moral universe; it would *foil* those who lay in wait amid the shadows of white people's fearful imaginations; it would somehow displace all the terrible accidents of life with a *perfect* death imposed by *perfect* men.[12] "*Glory be to God!*"

Such shedding of blood is always with a purpose. It is always justified from within the community of those who enact it. The people who killed or gazed or applauded both during and after the act had a purpose, and they did what they did because they believed themselves to be absolutely justified—or were drawn to a ceremony that was its own confirmation of being absolutely justified. The executioners would not have done what they did (or approved) had they not had *God's* permission to kill even as they renounced "religion" for "blood," for they believed that this killing was a good killing, and that shedding the blood of those humans at the compelling gravitational core of the crowd's consciousness would somehow *pay for* a vicious crime and calm the turbulence within the community. Ray Stannard Baker, a northern reporter who recalled the scene at Statesboro, in Bulloch County, thought the mob at first purposeless and capable of being broken by determined action, which authorities had refused to take. Only a few men had tried to assume the role that the religion of most southerners should have prepared Christians to claim before an angry self-righteous crowd, as Jesus did when presented with a woman taken in adultery. Jesus had challenged the crowd with the authoritative demand of sinlessness as a precondition for being enabled to cast the first stone.[13] In that narrative of Christian mercy a crowd had been deflected from vengeance, and the heroic Presbyterian minister in the Bulloch County courtroom undoubtedly believed that he was acting from similar motives by pleading for the mob to let justice take its course. The crowd in Statesboro, however, was determined—through an elemental ritual act—to assign the two black men divine status, an observation that may surprise not a few people.

Divinity is not to be mistaken for the sweetness and "light" of Victorian sentimentality or the sickly self-righteousness of narcissistic piety, for it is the Power to transform the moral universe. The white community in Statesboro had made the black men divinely powerful by making their deaths the *focus* or *subject* of all the evil then obsessing the (white) community. This made the black men, through their deaths, the solution to the intractable problem of good and evil in Bulloch County, insofar as white people understood it in their own power-defined and self-intoxicated way. Bulloch County whites changed guilty men into something more than simply "guilty men"; and such ritualistic transformation is not unique. Robert Jay

Lifton and Greg Mitchell, in discussing the death penalty in modern America, point out: "*A condemned man can be criminally guilty and at the same time an object of human sacrifice.*" The offender's crime and execution make him a target for all "the pain, guilt, and rage having to do with all crime—and beyond that, for the overall violence in our society." This "foster[s]," they continue, "the illusion that we are taking bold steps to combat evil."[14] And in such sacrifice we have an approach to the divine, through a collectively confirmed action that transcends human justice. The mob at Statesboro believed that the deaths they caused had the power to change the moral cosmos for the better, that is, in language evangelical Christians would recognize, to bring *salvation*—the goal of all executions, whether legal or illegal. The language associated with executions, whereby the offender *pays* for his crime or *atones*, is reminiscent of language Christians associate with the death of Christ, who is thought by some to have *paid* or *atoned* for human sin vicariously in his own death. Such theology focuses on the presumed moral *necessity* for the punishment of death because the sins of humanity are so heinous in their affront to divinity. Anyone exposed to the preaching of nineteenth-century Christians would have known that the *blood of Christ shed for them could save.*[15] This familiar mantra assumed that justice meant punishment, and that when punishment demanded death it was because the moral economy of the universe demanded it; that is, even the clergyman who tried vainly to stop the mob believed that the legal killing of the offenders would actually effect justice and heal the universe. In doing so, he and others like him elevated the subjects of these deaths, legal or illegal, beyond the quotidian profane into the realm of the sacred. The "peoples of the earth do not invent their gods," writes a student of religion. "They deify their victims."[16]

Within the terror of acts overwhelming in their impact upon the whole community, some blacks could even concede afterward to a curious white man that *justice* had been *served*—believing that was what he wanted to hear. But after the embers had cooled and people of goodwill hoped that peace had finally damped white terror, the demonic flared again, punishing black people not for specific acts but for the crime of being black, as stipulated by the sacred precepts of white supremacy. Secular logic dictated continuing violence, to be sure, but assumptions sanctified by the purity of human "whiteness" clashed with a continuing black presence to permit further cleansing by certain mobsters who flogged and shot black people until prevented by volunteer marshals. It was significant that in the holocaust of lynching and terror, *legal* authorities could not act. In the aftermath, the local white Methodist church expelled two members for participating in the mob; in reply, twenty-five others left the church in protest. The sheriff who had conceded authority to the mob was reelected; the white grand jury failed to indict any of the executioners; and "everyone" knew that no petit jury would have convicted anyway.[17] The moral sanction of the community was clear: religion *and* blood had fused in unmistakable clarity. Something terrifying, yet sacred within the dread of holiness, had happened. Thus, one caught up in the drama of punishment and death could very well feel—through the excitement of participation, no matter how far from the center of the crowd and the victims—that lynching *was* religion. He could very easily shout words he had heard in camp meetings and revivals all his life: "Glory be to God!" Or—if one could not shout "*Glory*," perhaps she could whisper in awe and wonder: "*O God!*"[18]

That lynching could be religion did not necessarily occur to the man who cried, "*We want blood.*" The religion that he did not want was one of rules and regulations, procedures and rubrics by which people lived ordered and respectable lives in peace. Ironically, a court—the local embodiment of law and limits upon human behavior—by announcing the magic word "*Guilty,*" had released this man in communion with others to transcend the limits protecting life and plunge themselves and community into *blood* through the mediation of two black men so that "justice" would be "served." This was transgression! Contempt for limits and law seemed in that moment of realization to reveal something transcendentally awe-inspiring and elemental—not merely retributive justice (which is a form of limits) but a *transcending* of limits (not their mere negation) that had ignited similar ecstatic expressiveness in camp meetings and revivals, which the crowd had known or known of when those touched by the divine had moaned and danced and fallen senseless to the ground.[19] The memories of evangelical Christians meeting in intense moments of sacred anticipation call up images of people acting as if they had been stricken by a Transcendent Power with such force that all limits and rubrics were shattered. Some black people remembered the moment as having been "struck dead."[20] Most people experiencing the moment remembered it as the means of entry into a new life, but the moment was also a moment of complete negativity in that it removed the stricken one from all limits, and thus transgressed them. Such moments of transgression, wrote Michel Foucault, may be "a flash of lightening in the night which, from the beginning of time, gives a dense and black intensity to the night it denies, which lights up the night from the inside, from top to bottom, and yet owes to the dark the stark clarity of its manifestation, its harrowing and poised singularity; the flash loses itself in this space it marks with its sovereignty and becomes silent now that it has given a name to obscurity."[21] The man shouting *blood* plunged into a time and space where the ordinary rules of the world did not apply, indeed, *could not even be conceived*. He was, perhaps, acting according to the logic of white supremacy, but logic does not dictate the cry of "blood!" There was an ecstatic excitement in his realization that by uttering the words that denied religion, he was uttering the words that denied God to a man of God, which was to deny all that he had ever heard about the source of morality, order, decency, and limits and to find a joyous freedom from these by acting out the insight of a German philosopher he never heard of: that *God is dead!*[22]

He was leaving behind the world of traditional procedures and legal safeguards, and had in effect been encouraged to do so by authorities who made no effort to prevent him. Thus he was negating all the things that made it possible for life to have been ordinary for him before and which would be ordinary for him again after he emerged from the spontaneously created realm of no prohibitions. He was a changed man, as were his fellows, who with him now became engrossed in what Michael Taussig calls a "period involving an enclosed, set-apart, theatrical-like space of make-believe for the representation and visceral realization of sacred force." Taussig points out that many students have "bleached out" the "erotic, obscene, sadistic, cruel, and licentious features" of the liminal rites popularized by anthropologists. Taussig calls attention to the "licensed transgression," which Mikhail Bakhtin disclosed in his great work, and reminds us that "transgression necessarily finds terrible application in the study of the sacred dimensions of violence in our time, as with the Holocaust and the ever increasing ethnic conflicts of the late twentieth century." Social historians resist calling attention to the nonrational in lynching probably because they have been schooled by students of collective action to affirm the logic of mobs and crowds in response to the previous dismissal of collective action as emotional and irrational. And to be sure, to say that crowds are driven by emotion tells us nothing; but engaging the Holocaust with its logic, ethnic cleansing with its purification, and lynching with its obscene brutality in the desire for "*blood!*" forces us to see the challenge accepted by some scholars of religion in the "representational pathos" of transgression. Viscerality, blood, and excess all collapse into the destruction of a body chosen as the vehicle for the transgressive. Taussig observes that the fact that transgressive phenomena "are seen as the antitheses of religion [*"We don't want religion, we want blood!"*] is testimony to the narrow moralism of organized religions today," which prevents us from understanding the compelling sacred attraction of violence, pain, and dread.[23] The many crowds and vigilantes who punished the violation of taboo in blood somehow understood in their solemn silence, or grim satisfaction, or in the ecstasy that demanded the shout of "glory," that when enacting their own theater of the sacred transgressive, they were engaging the Transcendent and entering the realm of the *sacred* abyss. That is, if an abyss—utter alienation, separation, and violation—could be *sacred*, so, too, lynching *was* religion.

Besides the Coweta and Bulloch lynchings, there have been thousands of other illegal American killings done in the name of community, justice, or despoiled innocence. The assumption behind each killing was that it was justified by a higher law than that inscribed in common law and statutes. White vigilantes in many different forms of collective action—posses and kinship groups, "Klansmen" and furtive clusters of neighbors and friends—killed people to "right" *wrongs* enacted by, attributed to, or inferred from something those people may have done. Lynching was a way to resolve confusion and ambiguity through stark action. William Fitzhugh Brundage has suggested at least four different kinds of collective action that resulted in illegal killings done in the name of a "higher" cause and distinguished by different kinds of spectators and participants—many and few; public and private; official (posses) and unofficial.[24] All of these engaged the sacred (in different ways, to be sure) by assuming prerogatives over the taking of life as an act of justice—the cliché has it that these were humans presuming to act as if they were gods. (Clichés are sometimes true.) One thinks of the night riders led by a Baptist preacher who took Mack Charles Parker from his cell in Poplarville, Mississippi, in 1959, or of the few who seized Emmett Till and beat him to death in 1955 for acting like the teenager he was, and one doubts that in these and thousands of other vigilante or small-group murders lay religious intent, substance, or mimesis. Killing a human being beyond the public gaze and for personal or private reasons with bullet, knife, bludgeon, rope, or hands seems quite *ir*religious because it treats a person as a thing to be discarded in as ordinary a way as any other disposable waste. We know, sadly enough, of killings every day in warfare, terrorism, illegal transactions, reckless bravado, idiosyncratic behavior, and accidents, and we fail to see the religious ambience of such action. But only accidental death is irreligious because only it is without purpose from which the killer can justify his (or her) actions according to a code within which he or she understands them before the compelling transgression of drawing blood. Dismissing the plea of justice in a death because it does not pass scrutiny by legal authority prevents understanding. Dismissing, moreover, as barbaric a death justified by vengeance ignores the fact that vengeance is a form of justice, however much one may disagree with that claim, and to understand actions identified with it we need to understand the values and reasoning of people who act on such assumptions. Since a human being is killed and *justice* is the claim by the killer within a discourse that "claims its concerns transcend the realm of the human, temporal, and contingent," the death has a religious meaning because it is thought to change the moral universe.[25] The fact that a human being, conscious of him- or herself as the subject of value and obligation within the community of other human beings, is killed by a purposeful act of other sentient beings confirms the religious character of the act.

The Presbyterian minister who tried to stop the lynching in Statesboro and the Methodist church that wrestled with how to treat those who had participated in it represented traditional religious institutions. But so did the laypeople who shouted "Glory" and "Praise the Lord." They had learned to do so within worship services of evangelical Protestant Christian churches at special times when song, preaching, and testimony combined to evoke a spontaneous combustible affirmation of "God!" The cries were primal expressions of recognition, but they would have been offensive to those frightened and angered at the violence. To have been thrust into a lynching as if it were a religious act would have been strange and dissonant—perhaps even demonic (but therefore "religious")—to those such as the frustrated Presbyterian cleric and his Methodist colleague, for they would have thought an illegal killing even in the name of community was inconsistent with justice, morality, and Christian commitment. Only a minority, however, could embrace such a position in Statesboro, Georgia, in 1904. Certainly the twenty-five Methodists who objected to the excommunication of their fellows believed that brutally killing convicted black criminals should not have disqualified anyone from the fellowship of Christian believers.

Such a conviction was profoundly disturbing to Arthur Raper twenty-five years later, when he wrote *The Tragedy of Lynching*. Investigating 21 lynchings that had occurred throughout the South in 1930 (down from over 240 in 1892), Raper discovered that he was studying mobs, fear, exploitation, xenophobia (localism), and racial contempt—that is, *culture*, in varied combustible combinations. "Mobs and lynchings," he wrote optimistically, "will ultimately fade from the scene with the general rise in the cultural level, which alone can provide the basis for the development of a public which will discard these crude methods of group expression." The culture would change when institutions and those who served them acted forcefully to suppress mobs and protect victims, but they could act only when white public opinion changed as the result of churches, schools, colleges, and universities teaching white people to embrace "fundamental human rights" for all citizens.[26] Raper seemed to believe mob violence happened in isolated communities where institutions were "least stable" and where churches were most likely to be "weak," as exemplified by Primitive Baptists, who were suspicious of any organization but the family and local church.[27] Instability and weakness for Raper meant the absence within local institutions of a powerful, educated, and responsible elite that could keep an ignorant and bigoted white democracy from doing what it wanted to do, heedless of the rights of African Americans. Instability and weakness were inherent, he believed, within a church that failed "to teach the sacredness and value of human personality." instead reinforcing what was in effect a tribal faith of narcissistic personal salvation and racial purity that attributed evil within the community not to self in honest confession but to others, dismissed as the unclean, shiftless, and licentious personification of sin.[28] This scapegoating mechanism, in which African Americans were reserved within whites' consciousness for blame when anything went awry, suggests the narrow limits of such moral imagination. Whites' contempt for black people was the cultural tinderbox that could easily explode into a spontaneous conflagration of hatred and violence when ignited by an incident that seemed to demand punishment. In such discussions, Raper did not analyze the role and nature of state and local power.

One of Raper's critics points out how carefully the scholar tried to present the contexts of lynching not by brilliant insight and accusation but through simple, matter-of-fact empiricism.[29] He was said to have forced readers to conclude for themselves the nature of a society in which institutions most associated with moral behavior were, in the face of illegal collective violence, silent. Raper went out of his way to report the silences of Christians and their congregations after each violent episode. Worshippers might hear repentance, salvation, and heaven from preachers, counting themselves therefore *religious*, perhaps even pious, and certainly respectable. They thought about things the religious ought to contemplate, but not lynching—it was a nonevent in the discourse of many, one infers *most*, faithful people after a lynching. Women's societies could be silent because their focus was missions. Men's Bible classes could be silent because their focus was the Bible. A county's population could be comprised of 80 percent to 95 percent church members, and their theology, such as it was, would have assured them that the only thing they needed to be concerned about was whether or not they personally were saved—which they would have been by throwing themselves on the mercies of Christ and being reassured that they were each blessed by being washed in his blood. But the blood of more immediate victims was ignored or suppressed or repressed—in silence. If during revival a man were lynched—the revivalist could justify his silence because he was not, after all, a policeman; he had to be true to his calling to lead people to eternal life; souls had to be saved! On other matters—Silence. Silence screamed its message, too, from the reticence of a Christian jurist who testified that there were "certain crimes" that ought to be punished by lynching, and from the reluctance of a Methodist minister to speak out on a murderous mob because he was new to the community and "knew so little of local conditions."[30] There were many matters upon which the minister could have commented in trying to gain the confidence of his new church, but he didn't believe that speaking about lynching was one of them. He was an outsider until confirmed as "all right" by the people who counted, and black people did not count in his sanctuary. When asked by Raper about his silence, the minister retreated to the apology upon which white southerners had relied since before the Civil War—the self-justifying excuse for violence in sustaining white supremacy: that is, "local conditions."

Raper did not comment on the nature of "local conditions," which his reporting made clear were the source of community violence, but he did sometimes reveal their power as, for example, when he wrote at length about mob violence and religion in Sherman, Texas. There, in May 1930, a black man by the name of George Hughes was brought to trial accused of raping the wife of a local white farmer. Before the trial could begin, and as the judge was in the process of changing venue, someone set fire to the courthouse. As officials fled the burning building, they allowed the prisoner to stay within a large fireproof vault, where it was thought he would be safest. The crowd prevented the fire company from fighting the fire and routed the militia ordered into Sherman to maintain order. After the courthouse was gutted, members of the mob used explosives to break open the vault and extract Hughes, who had been killed by the blast. They dangled his body from a cottonwood tree and roasted it over a pyre built from the furniture of African Americans whose ruined houses smoldered nearby. While Sherman's police directed traffic, the crowd began to destroy even more property owned by African Americans. Hotels, offices, homes, and shops were set ablaze until martial law was declared and the militia regained its morale and confidence. Invaders from the countryside and small towns of Grayson County had badly damaged the county seat and almost destroyed its black section of town. Before the riot, many villages in the county had over the years driven out black people, and the countryside had become a stronghold of the Ku Klux Klan until the Depression took its toll. It was later rumored that a former

Klansman had used the rape and trial to create a mob that could reenact the mythic glory of the KKK.[31]

In placing the riot in context, Raper pointed out that about 66 percent of the county's population held membership in churches, and that the city had sometimes been referred to as "the Athens of Texas" because of its several colleges. He imagined fumes from the burning courthouse and African American businesses drifting across the campuses, "mixed in with . . . the acrid smell of burning flesh," and he wondered what the "teachers and preachers" and Christian laity had done while the mob ruled. "They went to the scene," he wrote, with more indignation than usually expressed by a social scientist, "saw something revolting, and left without attempting to organize any opposition, perhaps not even considering the possibility of united resistance."[32] To Silence was now added Inaction; but then Raper added Caution and Confusion. He had been raised in a southern town where religious leaders were public spokesmen; he had been reared in a culture in which religion and Bible and Jesus were revered; and when he became a researcher he still believed that an essential part of every southern community was religion; he knew that lynching communities were religious communities. He believed this conjunction to be pathological. Churches were among the institutions that he thought should be strong enough to prevent community violence; but he was discovering that they were weak and timid. Ministers of the four largest churches in Sherman denounced the mob from their pulpits the Sunday after the Friday night conflagration. The Presbyterian congregation arose as one in standing confirmation of their pastor's statement. Ministers canvassed their congregations to help the African American community to rebuild; but then they stopped. The county attorney told them that such would prevent juries from convicting the rioters. Charity to black folk was anathema because it would send the message that some whites felt guilt at the mob's transgressions. Even a sentimental, almost meaningless, gesture of kindness was contrary to the popular canons of white supremacy.[33]

Raper relied on two commentators with a special interest in religion to raise questions about the role of popular Christianity in Sherman's conflagration. Will Alexander, a former Methodist minister associated with the Atlanta-based Commission on Inter-racial

Cooperation, observed as had Raper, that no ministers tried to stop the riot or tried to get others to stop it; he noted the cowardly timidity among professing white Christians, who thought it "was not safe" to raise a fund for African Americans dispossessed by the mob. Raper also printed a long letter written by a woman living in Sherman who castigated the cowardice of the town's ministry. She was livid: "Twelve good men and true could have quelled the mob—even one brave man could have organized a defense—but it was nobody's business." Religious leaders, she believed, had been responsible for allowing a "mob" *mentality* to have taken root deep in the cultural soil of the county. "I heard that the preachers in their pulpits today deplored the horrible tragedy, but," she emphasized by referring to the previous popularity of the Klan, "if they had lifted their voices against mob law when sheeted figures were sowing the seed, that ghastly fruit [of George Hughes's body] would never have hung from the court yard tree." The most outspoken critic of the mob, she pointed out, had once been a Klansman; and she thought to herself: "Your birds have come home to roost and you don't recognize them." As for the attempt to raise funds for Sherman's African American citizens, pastors of smaller white churches in the country simply refused to do so since their members were so "greatly in favor of the mob." She was discouraged. *"I wonder what the [white] churches have been teaching in the past twenty years—that their flock should be so savage."*[34]

Why, she wondered, could the churches not have prevented the violence? She knew the answer lay in the failure of their teachings and she knew that that failure had been with them for a long time. She shuddered at the thought of lynching as religion—*"so savage"*—for she wanted religion to prevent lynching. She knew that the reason for the failure of religion lay in history. What the (white) churches had been teaching for well over twenty years was personal salvation, and they could not have prevented the "savagery" loosed in Sherman because churches were the institutional expression of their flocks' self-consciousness. That is, the religion that had shaped her county, Grayson, as well as Coweta and Bullock, was the same religion that had grown with and eventually dominated the South after a history that insiders interpreted in mythic triumphalism. If that faith were complex enough to have many different expressions, it was, nonetheless, a kind of Protestantism that provided believers with a firm conviction of their own righteousness, confirmed by a subjective experience of God's grace effected through the work of Christ Jesus, who broke the power of sin over those who truly believed he had died upon the cross. This sense of being called out of the world unto righteousness was reinforced by being welcomed into a body of the like-minded who professed to submit themselves to the authority of the Protestant Bible (which was supposed to be read assiduously by all) and the community of faithful people (church) whose commitment to a practical Christianity was to be obeyed. The experience of receiving salvation was preceded by the experience of being convicted of sin so heinous that each individual realized he or she deserved punishment. This experience of sin and salvation could come to a Christian in one dramatic transformation or be enacted within private devotional life as two dramatic subjective events in which the self was exposed (in sin) and then transformed (to "glory") into a "child of God," one of the chosen, a saint, a justified "Christian" confirmed in his or her new status by the experience of grace.

The roots of evangelical southern Protestantism lay in the eighteenth-century southern colonies, where New Light Presbyterians and Baptists challenged the hegemony of the Church of England, which was less concerned with the conviction of sin and the dramatic awareness of grace than a reasonable and optimistic piety that allowed for a range of religious experiences. Soon within the church itself was birthed an evangelical party, some of whose members became Methodists. By the early 1800s, there was a distinct "evangelical" mood in a majority of fast-growing churches throughout the region, and after the Civil War that mood and its attendant ways of thinking, believing, and living dominated the religious life of southerners. There were few challengers to evangelicalism. The Roman Catholic Church was strong only in certain urban areas of the South; Jews were even fewer; and if antievangelical Protestants were scattered across the landscape, they often took on the protective coloration of a shared if conflicted Protestantism. Strict Calvinist Baptists were justly suspicious of the almost self-congratulatory and aggressive optimism of evangelicals but they, too, valued the ruling paradigm of the twice born and the importance of experiencing grace. The religious pluralism that intellectual ferment, industrialism, and immigration brought to the rest of the country did not affect the American South until after the Second World War. That the evangelical ethos suffused both black and white churches meant that the two peoples might share certain moods and styles at times and on certain things—such as an insistence on rebirth and an appreciation for evocative public oratory and the authority of the Bible, but the adversarial results of Emancipation and white southerners' resistance to its implications prevented cooperation and sympathy across what came to be understood as "the color line."

The *subjectivism* that would eventually prevent white evangelicalism from creating cultural space to thwart lynching (by making individual *experience* normative for evaluating civic order) also made that religious mood attractive. This was especially so in the early days of evangelical recruitment because it enabled individuals and groups marginalized by their race, estate, or gender to define themselves according to a "divine" power made available to them heedless of the invidious distinctions inherited within culture and society. A slave, a family, a woman, a young man, a group of men and women outside the local elite could think of self and similar selves as being valued more highly in the scheme of things (by God) than by the traditional rubrics of social-political structure. This transformation was confirmed within the new believers by their own *experience* of God as if they had been *born again*. The phrase, although rarely used in holy scriptures, became the guiding theme of evangelical transformation.[35] Life could be completely different, one heard, if *I*—not society, not other people, not my status, not my work, not my parents, not my spouse—but if *I* changed, through the power of a will freed from indecision by God's grace and the persuasiveness of the evocative promise that was at the core of most preaching. I could know life would be better by surrendering to God, whether in the company of believers or in the isolation of private prayer but always through accepting the offer to be born again—to be changed. The content of the change was not always clear until others provided the necessary Bible verses, perhaps, but the technique was. When you feel absolutely different from your old self through the grace of God and the sacrifice of Jesus Christ, you will have become a true Christian. This subjective experience of the holy Other assured the converts that, even if institutions and roles remained constant, they themselves could actually be changed if they really desired it. The dichotomy created by the experience of conversion emphasized in varying degrees (depending on individual idiosyncrasies) a radical sense of before and after, evil and good, unsaved and saved, alienation and intimacy. The hateful old self—sinful, clueless, ignorant, stupid—was contrasted with the holy, knowledgeable, alert, new self now empowered with ways of understanding that were foreign to the old self.[36]

For slaves and the otherwise dispossessed, this discovery of the *real me* inside (or transcendent to) the quotidian me could confound the logic of my social and political status and free me from it in my own mind—at least during moments of private prayer or collective celebration in expressive worship. The sense of being liberated for all who went through this process was reinforced by the intense *moral* drama of being saved from well-deserved condemnation to undeserved salvation. That is, within the intense subjectivity of conversion, especially for whites, God was imagined as a cosmic judge before whom all the unconverted should have quaked in terror because of their sins. But if the Father demanded punishment as the righteous judge, he allowed his own son to take upon himself the sins of all who believed in him and to die in an execution that satisfied divine justice through a retributive punishment that at the same time revealed divine mercy. "He died for me!" was the familiar mantra of evangelical Protestant Christianity. Even if believers did not quite understand the narrative of penal substitutionary atonement, as it was called, they did understand that before God, the guilty deserved death. The familiar story of orthodox Christianity became *evangelical* when the potential convert experienced a conscious radical transformation and the story told by others became, subjectively, *my* own story and *I* was made righteous and knew it because of *my* own experience of God. I felt it in *my* bones. In great relief and gratitude at escaping just punishment, I might very well blurt out the almost liturgical expletive I had heard from others in camp meetings and local churches, "Glory be to God!"

This celebration of a *new self* accounted for the popular appeal of evangelical preaching, which dismissed all ascriptive characteristics (such as race and sex) and man-made hierarchies (class, station, gender, beauty) as the definition of a person's worth and emphasized just one: *saved* or not. Then the preachers made immediate salvation plausible. One could be changed in the "twinkling of an eye." In appealing to their audience's sense of grief at who they were and their hope in whom they could become, preachers dismissed traditional invidious distinctions that enslaved the old self. The offer of a new self (perhaps the real *me*) could encourage African slaves, white women, and troubled men to participate in worship that resonated with their own needs and imaginations (and cultural baggage) and compensated for their sense of despair, powerlessness, and damaged self-consciousness. Both black and white could find resources to receive liberty in Christ through their own powers of self-exertion, no matter how feeble, because God would enable them. They could be saved from dysfunctional families, personal hurt, gendered humiliation, class distinctions, or racial exploitation and be made righteous in Christ. This change—with its mixed emotions of fear, hope, guilt, shame, and relief—happened within the shadow of condemnation and punishment. That is, converts may have escaped punishment, but they knew that they had once deserved it, and that all those who were unconverted and thus condemned still did. (If some converted women had received salvation in a softer paradigm of being empowered through grace to receive an ideal self, the harder, masculine [patriarchal] version of condemnation and punishment nonetheless ruled.) The ethic of the converted self demanded that those who had experienced the new birth share that experience with others still unconverted who, it was to be hoped, would accept the narrative told by evangelicals as normative for themselves and thus escape the punishment they so richly deserved. If converts did not take on this mission aggressively, the assumptions and discourse of evangelical Christianity nonetheless made the *converted righteous* the model by which to judge non-Christians as well as those Christians who resisted the conversionist norm.[37] Since conversion had a profoundly moral component, those other Christians were seen through the lens of one's own rejected and immoral preconversion self and therefore the unconverted were perceived to be immoral. Those enthralled by the miracle of their own conversion thus confronted the world in agonistic and moralistic terms. Life was a struggle between good and evil; conversion of the world to Christ was the goal of that struggle, and those already converted were the true exemplars of what it meant to be human.[38]

White evangelical Christians wanted other people to be like themselves—to embrace the same values, to think the same thoughts, and to behave the same way. This goal was, they believed, God's will. There were, however, limits. Religious conformity was not egalitarian. As much as preachers may have proclaimed an ideal of no invidious distinctions save those between the saved and damned, commitment to the ideal took root primarily within the minds of those who felt themselves diminished by human difference rather than those for whom recognizable difference remained a significant marker of individual distinctiveness and value. "God is no respecter of persons," for example, was the biblical watchword of Christian *blacks*, not whites. The white southern Christian defense of slavery in fact insisted that the Golden Rule, which the hated Yankee abolitionists had so mischievously misapplied, did not ban society's "*just* distinctions," but instead dictated that masters treat slaves as masters would wish to be treated if they themselves had been slaves. To be sure, a few masters here and there understood that conversion demanded emancipation, but most did not.[39] If social structure was in any way subverted by evangelical subjectivity, it was through strengthening the self-esteem of men, women, or youth *against* the logic of the context within which they lived—and suffered;[40] but it could also buttress the rule of the master. The subjectivity of the convert in each case ruled, and if a master's conversion reinforced his determination to make slaves behave as he thought they should, his faith could become a means of securing his authority. The converted slave and the converted master could perhaps do battle within the language of a "common" Christianity, but the master always had control of the dictionary, the thesaurus, and the lash, if not the Spirit. To strengthen that control, evangelical Christians called on Christian masters to support a mission to the enslaved, which would also function as a mission to masters because, publicists argued, the only legitimate defense of slavery was to make it Christian.[41] In this goal evangelicals did not mean to restructure slavery according to selfless Christian principles and the ethic of jubilee so much as to convert individuals, masters as well as slaves, to their status-restricted idea of a *purified* Christianity.[42] If achieved, this goal was supposed to raze the adversarial postures of master and slave by making the former less violent and the latter more submissive. In the end social structure would remain intact.

Critics of evangelicalism have pointed out that the flaw in this subjectivist way of understanding the Christian life was its focus upon the individual rather than the social. Salvation of the self, confirmed by an experience of transcendence within the self, made *self* central to the ethical life. Self-discipline within the traditional canons of gender, race, and class, rather than service to others in the community of Christ, was the first responsibility of the saved. Abstemiousness and sobriety ruled. Thus, the ideal Christian would be one who was aghast at memories of the sinful and rejected self because of the belief that that old and wicked self deserved punishment, and this would and did have an effect on how one understood others who conformed to the ideal image of the converted individual—they were suspect. And suspicion could invite an implicit hostility to the other, who was possibly very wicked; it could also elicit defensiveness when one was confronted with the frustration of living in a fallen world, even if one were separated from it in terms of behavior and goals. That separation rested on knowing the truth, and this meant that Christians could not learn anything significant from anyone unlike themselves, that is, others who did not share their views of the truth. The personal experience of God confirmed self-knowledge; no other confirmation was required. To be sure, evangelicals emphasized that their primary authority was the Protestant Christian Bible, and they could find selected texts from it to support their way of life and specific beliefs since they were after all supposed to read the scriptures for guidance and insight, but the subjectivity of their conversion illuminated how the Bible was to be understood.[43] The peril of pious narcissism was obvious and could encourage rudeness, as when an evangelical braggart observed at dinner that he had never known a "religious Episcopalian"—as he sat next to one.[44] Despite such foolishness, the evangelical ideal privileged the language of humility and deference to Christ while nourishing gratitude that one was unlike other people who could very easily be identified with the old, wicked, and stupid self. Evangelical self-consciousness could encourage a self-effacing arrogance.

It is possible to infer from such subjectivism that evangelicalism sustained no social ethic, but such a conclusion should be qualified. When early southern Baptists tried to create their ideal church in the wilds of the frontier, they monitored behavior to prevent violence and other forms of adversarial troublemaking among their members. The elders also investigated accusations of sexual misconduct, drunkenness, dancing, and breaking the Sabbath, behavior that Methodists and Presbyterians theoretically also shunned.

In some cases individual Christians would demonstrate remarkable acts of kindness and nurturance to slaves; and eventually, southern white evangelicals founded schools, colleges, orphanages, hospitals, settlement houses, and missions, though mostly for their own race (with a few exceptions). As an established community of Christians, white evangelicals never seriously challenged and only rarely questioned the ways in which society was ordered by gender, class, or race, even though in the first stages of the early movement they did so. The Christian proclamation of jubilee remained rooted in African American faith.[45] White evangelicals never thought much about how to engage people unlike themselves except as opponents or as subjects for conversion—a view that reinforced the perception of difference. White Christians' collective responsibilities within the slave system were to perfect the social role into which they had been born, but the Christian proslavery argument could in some cases be understood as a Christian social ethic. Evangelical writers might encourage white Christians to affirm slaves' rights to legal marriage and Christian education and sometimes to live free from brutality, but certainly not from the white authority that defined actions brutal and things punishable according to the masters' subjectively confirmed understanding of their Christian duty.[46]

The inferiority of blacks and their submissiveness to whites was a constant theme shaping white evangelical Protestants' attitude to black people, an attitude that would not change with passage of the Thirteenth, Fourteenth, and Fifteenth amendments to the U.S. Constitution. After Emancipation, only a few white southern Christians could accept freed people as citizens, much less equals, and the majority conceded to nonsouthern white Christians the roles of teacher and guide to blacks during the 1860s and 1870s. The resulting education of African Americans, together with their recruitment into politics by Republicans, frightened white southerners into clarifying and reinforcing wherever possible the increasingly important distinctions of racial difference. The process was aided by the pervasive, reassuring, and sacred distinctions between the old and new self and between the saved and the unsaved in southern white conversionist ideology, and lent an intense moralistic aura to racial difference. This was especially so with matters affected by sex and gender. Evangelical taboo was especially strict when it came to sex—even witty and lighthearted conversation between the sexes was under suspicion; and this was magnified into primal fears of pollution and danger when social difference was defined by race.[47] The fear of pollution demanded a separation of the two races, especially in educational facilities, in order to avoid danger from the "moral contamination" of "social equality" during childhood and youth, when people are especially vulnerable to fascination with the Other.[48] As Christian whites marginalized African Americans through segregation laws, the danger that blacks represented was intensified in whites' imaginations because social and cultural margins are always considered to be dangerous.[49] The overlay of color, wickedness, difference, and sex—illuminated by the evangelical polarities of good and evil, purity and danger, provided a social ethic that supported the ideology of white supremacy.

That is, evangelical Christianity could not prevent white people from seeing black people as the threatening antithesis to their own lives. Indeed, in the generation after Emancipation, white southerners used economic coercion, terror, and the state to restrict as radically as possible the rights of African Americans and in the process identified them as the adversaries (along with dangerous Yankees) of progress, civic consciousness, community morals, and public tranquility. Immediately after the abolition of slavery, southerners attempted to control the black workforce through laws that guaranteed an effective exploitation of black labor. When Radical congressional leaders responded by negating those laws and imposing Reconstruction upon the secessionist region, whites nonetheless continued to use the law as a way of maintaining control of the workforce, in conjunction with intimidation, coercion, and economic hardship.[50]

In the late 1860s and early 1870s, the Ku Klux Klan terrorized dissident whites and fractious blacks. Despite brief setbacks to using such tactics, whites throughout the South in the mid- to late 1870s used them to drive blacks further into submission. The blacks' death toll was high. When it was clear to southern legislatures that the federal government would no longer intervene in even a modest way on behalf of its black citizens, they began legally to prevent black men from voting after campaigns driven by blatantly hate-mongering racist rhetoric that described any black presence in local or state government, no matter how minor the role, as NEGRO DOMINATION! If white politicians were, however rarely, sometimes likely to consider the detrimental effects of public policy on African

American citizens, white demagogues cried NEGRO DOMINATION! If blacks tipped the balance to Prohibition in areas where a majority of whites might have opposed it, the cry was NEGRO DOMINATION! If blacks tipped the balance to free-flowing liquor in areas where a majority of whites might have supported Prohibition, the cry was NEGRO DOMINATION! Few southern white Christians objected to such shenanigans. Indeed, even though some Christian partisans may not have approved of the language of racial hatred, they nonetheless supported campaigns to "remove the negro [*sic*] from politics" to avoid his *corrupting* influence.[51]

I have argued elsewhere that segregation may be understood as a religious system, given the ways in which it used symbols and myth to establish powerful moods that could fashion what anthropologist Clifford Geertz calls "conceptions of a general order of existence" that established "such an aura of facticity" that the moods and motivations associated with them "seem[ed] uniquely realistic."[52] To be sure, politicians and industrialists used law and tradition to fabricate segregation for economic and political purposes, but the mood that enforced the system for white people was based on the emotional solidarity of group identity.[53] Religious feeling, a disciple of Emile Durkheim points out, is "the individual's awareness of the group."[54] And southern whites were taught by law, tradition, and the invidious distinctions of difference unleashed after Emancipation to be inexorably aware of the "white race" as the primary model of what it meant to be human. Local ordinances and practice had segregated southern public schools from their very beginning; and by 1884 nine of eleven southern legislatures had banned marriage between individuals of different "races."[55] Such laws and practices, since they were coupled in whites' minds with sex and gender as well as race, were of course reinforced by the taboos traditionally associated with sexuality among evangelicals. The sexual danger associated with the impurity of crossing "the color line" warned whites to avoid the "moral contamination" of painful "close physical contact" with blacks.[56] As the "pain" drove white legislatures to segregate, marginalize, and disfranchise African Americans, they were using the power of the state to transform black people into a threatening social presence whose existence could somehow explain the disappointments, failures, or crime that afflicted white people.[57] The major social problem of the South was "the Negro Problem," as far as whites were concerned, and this "problem," they believed, devolved from African Americans' poverty, sloth, ignorance, disease, immorality, lasciviousness, and crime.[58] Given the characteristics attributed to "the Negro" by whites, it would have been consistent for them to have required him to cry in unison with the lepers of the Christian Bible—"*Unclean!*"

Such a demand would not have surprised Lillian Smith, for she remembered segregation as based on the canons of purity. In *Killers of the Dream*, she analyzed how sin, sex, and segregation together had inundated the lives of southerners.[59] As children, she recalled, white southerners were taught to believe in the sanctity of their white skin as if it were essential to their reverence for God. They were guided by a religion "too narcissistic" to be concerned with anything except the ways in which a person's body became the "essence of morality" in such a way as to fortify the rubrics of segregation—no matter how often they might be compromised in practice—as a kind of practical theology to be lived with a greater attention to "orthodoxy" than were the abstractions of the pulpit. Both segregation and religion shaped the self by pushing "everything dark, dangerous, and evil" to "the rim of one's life," where danger hovered. As evil had been purged from the sin-distressed self, Smith believed, white southerners had become fascinated with other people's evil rather than their own—probably not unique to them—and had somehow been compelled to find personal salvation in the "death of Christ" without carrying their own cross on behalf of others.[60] The fusion of southern Protestantism with Prohibition, repressed sexuality, and the canonization of white women combined to blur distinctions between sacred and secular where race was concerned—such insights are by now a cliché, but they weren't in 1949 when Smith first made them. If the logic of market relations and the consumption of commodities by different races could ironically destabilize segregation in certain restricted ways, *true believers* of the segregationist faith could nonetheless regain stability by affirming racial orthodoxy in the face of such materialistic dissent.[61] Smith thought the Christian religion should have destabilized segregation, but it didn't; instead, southern whites learned Christianity and segregation from the catechism of everyday domestic life that warned of "everlasting flames" for disobeying the canons of both personal salvation and segregation.[62] Smith has been classified as part of a "shame and guilt" school of southern writers who have not appreciated the positive aspects of southern life, but heretics rarely embrace the orthodoxies that ignite the pyres constructed to punish their dissent.[63]

Smith gradually learned from her own personal pilgrimage, private musings, and public consciousness just how different she was from most other white people. Having been raised in a pious Christian household and become a missionary, she had been impressed by the exclusivist claims of Christianity to change people for the better. It seemed natural for her to have hoped that Christianity could have "destabilized segregation," but she was, of course, disappointed. The evangelical dichotomy of good and evil, new self and rejected self, white and black, converted and damned sustained whites' sense of moral superiority. The experience of conversion—even if it were primarily liturgical and not existentially transformational—certified a person as different from and thus superior to others unlike oneself.[64] How one defined significant difference would of course be idiosyncratic up to a point, but that point was always limited by the community within which one was "transformed." This subjectivity could not prevent a pervasive hostility toward blacks, which John Dollard found in Southerntown during the 1930s among all classes of white people, who knew that black people did not automatically accept their assigned inferiority; they had to be constantly challenged to defer to whites through daily reminders of their lower status.[65] Whites' religion could not make them address blacks as "Mr." or "Mrs." or receive them at the front door or shake their hands on introduction or eat with them; it could not make them provide equitable educational facilities or equal public utilities or the ballot. Nor could whites' religion and moral imagination diminish fears of African Americans' retaliation for the ways in which whites had treated them, even as whites denied they had done anything to deserve resentment. Ubiquitous white aggression against blacks in day-to-day rudeness, personal slight, dismissive contempt, and the status humiliations of public behavior, when reinforced by the sense of moral superiority that good white Christians *knew* they possessed, created an irresistible caste mentality. This way of thinking almost automatically forced whites, regardless of private sympathetic inclination, into personal disparagement of "the Negro," wrote Dollard, "and the expression of hostile pressure against him."[66] This pressure was promoted by an evangelical fear of difference, the moral superiority implied in responding to difference, and a feeling of sexual danger, heightened possibly by the guilty and pervasive knowledge of white sexual exploitation of black women. Such feelings were never far from consciousness and could erupt at any time, as in an offhand comment Dollard reports about the foolhardiness that had led a white female social worker to visit African American meetings at night. The conjunction of "night," "white woman," interracial proximity, and fears of retaliation birthed an immediate awareness of sexual danger among white people, who felt surrounded by a widespread and dangerous moral threat.[67] This *fear* was consistent with evangelical suspicion of difference, sex, and the rejected self. The knowledge of salvation by virtue of good intentions, even better manners (shaped by segregation), and the pervasive ambience of the white Christian religion sustained a culture in which all the best (white) people had been confirmed in their virtue by the subjectivity of their religious experience and the approval of their peers.

This sketch of southern evangelical Protestantism between 1820 and 1940 is meant to suggest how religion should be understood as a significant component of lynching in the American South. The sacred if moralistic polarity of unambiguous good and evil, so dear to revivalistic preachers, was a perfect fit with the mental foundations of white supremacy. If there was some flexibility in theological discourse that could find a place for paradox and inconsistency, and if the same was true when the color line was blurred by local custom, personal idiosyncrasies, and private action, the polarity inherent in saved and unsaved, the new and old self, and white and black was culturally confirmed by a religion of personal salvation that could not break the religious logic of purity and danger. The evangelical paradigm of conversion was affected not merely by the subjectivism of the "conversion experience," however, but also by the pervasive belief that sin must be punished—indeed, that in extraordinary cases it must be atoned for by the shedding of blood. A people confronted by generations of denunciatory rhetoric that insisted the evil self must be rejected and that evildoers must pay for their crimes lest the moral universe be compromised could easily believe that punishment was itself a religious act; indeed, the Crucifixion of God himself was part of the moral imagination of many—perhaps the most self-consciously religious—southerners.[68] Even God had to be held accountable to a moral and ethical system that demanded punishment in order to sustain the justice and majesty of the divine. But this understanding of violence as part of the human religious experience suggests, as we have seen in scholarly work on religion, further inquiry into the ways in which religion and violence become interfused—and not merely in punishment. A pervasive folk religion reinforced by a theology of personal salvation and experience that encouraged openness to the nonrational manifestations of the spirit (as well as a "commonsense" rationality) encouraged also an openness to the *transgressive*, which one can easily see—if not so easily understand—in the existential maw of lynching. A fuller investigation than the one attempted here is demanded if we are to explore the full dimensions of this insight, offered by Michael Taussig and Michel Foucault, among others; but it is clear that something more than mere punishment, sexual and gendered anxiety, and the logic of power was inherent in lynching.

To say that the moral and religious polarity sketched here could not prevent lynching is not to say that evangelical religion and segregation, linked as they were in the emotional life of white southerners, *caused* lynching; but they together did create ways of thinking that could justify it. The faith that together the two systems sustained was a compound of ideas, moods, and motivations that divided the world clearly into good and evil, pure and impure, safety and danger—white and black, both literally and figuratively. Segregation, with its commitment to white supremacy, relied as much on implied and illegal violence as upon manifest law to maintain social order. And evangelical religion, with a vaunted moral superiority supported by a *compelling subjectivity*, offered no inherent way for the saved, who felt the justice of *deserved* punishment, to stay the hand of the executioner, whether extended by the state or the democratic mob. As evangelicalism could not prevent racism and the scapegoating of an entire people by law, neither could it prevent the scapegoating of individuals. The churchgoing communities that supported revivalism for personal renewal could also support lynching for social cleansing. In both instances punishment was believed to be just; for Christians, punishment was deflected from the convert to Christ and thus sanctified; for lynching victims, there was no substitution, only a vengeful death. In both cases the *subject of execution* solved an intractable problem of evil by *compensating for it with a certain and specific death.* Yet we dare not leave the matter within the drama of scapegoating, for retributive justice was always the justification for lynching, as it is for legal executions. To be sure, it can be argued that retributive justice is inherently a scapegoating mechanism, but the actions that such justice requires are also actions that in themselves are thought to be worth doing. The significance of execution lies in its precision and "ritualization of killing," which distinguish it from the act(s) it punishes, just as in the dramas of lynching.[69] But there is something else that both executions and lynching share that seems contradictory to the claim that they are, according to the logic of retributive justice, absolutely justified. People enact them because both *transgress* the Ultimate command for which they are enacted. Executions and lynchings *kill* to punish killing.

At the present time, we have witnessed the compelling attraction of the transgressive more often than we may care to concede (in holocaust, ethnic cleansing, terrorism, torture, and elective warfare). In remembering our own history of violence, we are confronted with effects of the transgressive in the sober and sanctifying quietude enshrouding Leo Frank's lifeless body; and we are challenged by its imperative in the response of the lyncher who screamed in self-justifying fury, *"We don't want religion, we want blood!"* Such moments suggest an ecstatic seizure that excites humans to violence, which in itself somehow *justifies* them in *transgressing* justice. There may be a *logic* to such moments, to be sure, but there is also an absurdity to which some humans, overwhelmed by the enormity of what is happening, may respond in awed silence or "grave satisfaction." Others cry, *"Glory* be to *God!"*

NOTES

1. See press responses to the murder of "Sam Hose" by a mob in Newnan, Georgia, April 23, 1899, *Newnan Herald and Advertiser,* April 28, 1899, 6.

2. The quote is from Walter White, *Rope and Faggot: A Biography of Judge Lynch* (1929; repr., New York: Arno/New York Times, 1969), 43. This is not to say that there was no "logic" or "reason" to the mob's immolation of Wilkes; those who wish to infer logic from such action may do so. Indeed, I agree with them—as we shall see—but the public discourse surrounding the lynching of "Sam Hose" justified it on the ground that

white men who were faced with the terrible desecration of white woman-
hood were so provoked by the atrocity that they lost control of their reason
and submitted to the "logic" (perhaps) of their passions by enacting a justice beyond reason but nonetheless consistent with justice.

3. The cannibalism of inhaling the aroma of burning flesh is emphasized by Orlando Patterson, *Rituals of Blood: Consequences of Slavery in Two
American Centuries* (Washington, D.C.: Civitas Counterpoint, 1998), 194–
202.

4. "He Goes to Death without an Outcry," *Atlanta Journal*, April 24,
1899, 1.

5. Stephen J. Leonard, *Lynching in Colorado, 1859–1919* (Boulder: University Press of Colorado, 2002), 90.

6. Nancy MacLean, "Gender, Sexuality, and the Politics of Lynching:
The Leo Frank Case Revisited," in *Under Sentence of Death: Lynching in the
South*, ed. William Fitzhugh Brundage (Chapel Hill: University of North
Carolina Press, 1998), 175.

7. *Sparta Ishmaelite*, November 22, 1901 (emphasis added). This source
was discovered by Eric Tabor Millin in his research for a fine master's thesis at the University of Georgia, 2002: "Defending the Sacred Hearth: Religion, Politics, and Racial Violence in Georgia, 1904–1906," 60. It was
previously cited in Donald G. Mathews, "Lynching Is Part of the Religion
of Our People: Faith in the Christian South," in *Religion in the American
South: Protestants and Others in History and Culture*, ed. Beth Barton Schweiger and Donald G. Mathews (Chapel Hill: University of North Carolina
Press, 2004), 166. This current essay is a response to questions raised and
matters left ambiguous by my essay in the Schweiger-Mathews volume;
it is also confirmation of a critic's comment that my article was "disturbing." That original work was meant to be disturbing because the support of
lynching by Christians *is* disturbing—although many non-Christians may
find that support consistent with Christian pogroms of Jews as well as the
burning of heretics. One should study religion and lynching precisely because the conjunction of the two is indeed quite disturbing.

8. James Allen, Hilton Als, John Lewis, and Leon F. Litwack, eds.,
Without Sanctuary: Lynching Photography in America (Santa Fe, N.M.: Twin
Palms, 2000).

9. See David Carrasco, *City of Sacrifice: The Aztec Empire and the Role of
Violence in Civilization* (Boston: Beacon, 1999), 115–39, 188–210, especially
190–91.

10. Ray Stannard Baker, *Following the Color Line: An Account of Negro
Citizenship in the American Democracy* (1908; repr., Williamstown, Mass.:
Cortner House, 1973), 185.

11. Lewis E. Jones, "There Is Power in the Blood" (1899), written

for a camp meeting in Maryland, http://members.tripod.com/~Synergy_2/lyrics/power.html.

12. Baker, *Following the Color Line*, 180–90.

Brian K. Smith, "Capital Punishment and Human Sacrifice," *Journal of the American Academy of Religion* 68 (March 2000): 6, but also 3–25.

13. Rene Girard, *I See Satan Fall Like Lightening*, trans. with a foreword by James G. Williams (Maryknoll, N.Y.: Orbis, 2001), 58–60. See also the Gospel (KJV) according to St. John, 8:2–11.

14. Robert Jay Lifton and Greg Mitchell, *Who Owns Death? Capital Punishment, the American Conscience, and the End of Executions* (New York: HarperCollins, 2002), 230 (emphasis added). The authors write, "The death penalty is both a concrete policy—something we can do about killing and sin—and a highly abstract symbol. Behind it lies a mystical vision of total evil that can be extirpated to achieve total virtue. Our illusion becomes not only that of controlling crime and killing, but of controlling death itself. We resort to 'the most premeditated of murders,' as Camus wrote, in order to convert our moral and psychological confusion into an illusory certainty" (251).

15. Donald G. Mathews, "The Southern Rite of Human Sacrifice," *Journal of Southern Religion* 3 (2001), http://www.jsr.fsu.edu. Also printed in *Black History Bulletin* 65 (July–December 2002) and 66 (January–December 2003): 20–47.

16. Girard, *I See Satan Fall*, 66.

17. Baker, *Following the Color Line*, 188–90.

18. The word *God* elicits a broad range of meanings for the person who utters it, as well as for those who hear it. The imagined possible meanings for those who responded to horrendous acts by exclamations that evoke transcendence in popular culture begin with the immediate subjective response of wonder at something that simply surpasses previous experience and elicits fear and awe. For some this response may appear to be a curse, but the person who formulates the word knows better. To begin to understand the many meanings to be inferred from the word God, see Francis Schussler Fiorenza and Gordon D. Kaufman, "God," in *Critical Terms for Religious Studies*, ed. Mark C. Taylor (Chicago: University of Chicago Press, 1998), 136–59.

19. Catharine C. Cleveland, *The Great Revival in the West, 1797–1805* (Chicago: University of Chicago Press, 1916); Frederick Morgan Davenport, *Primitive Traits in Religious Revivals: A Study in Mental and Social Evolution* (New York: Macmillan, 1905); Sydney Dimond, *The Psychology of the Methodist Revival: An Empirical and Descriptive Study* (London: Oxford University Press, 1926).

20. Clifton H. Johnson, ed., *God Struck Me Dead: Religious Conversion*

Experiences and Autobiographies of Ex-Slaves (Nashville: Fisk University Social Science Institute, 1945).

21. Michel Foucault, "A Preface to Transgression," in *Religion and Culture*, ed. Jeremy R. Carrette (New York: Routledge, 1999), 61.

22. The phrase and aphorism is mentioned several times in the works of Friedrich Nietzsche. See Bernd Magnus and Kathleen M. Higgins, "Nietzsche's Works and Their Themes," in *The Cambridge Companion to Nietzsche*, ed. Bernd Magnus and Kathleen M. Higgins (New York: Cambridge University Press, 1996), 35–37. Michel Foucault would probably correct me here, for he writes: "Transgression is neither violence in a divided world (in an ethical world) nor a victory over limits (in a dialectical or revolutionary world); and, exactly for this reason, its role is to measure the excessive distance that it opens at the heart of the limit and to trace the flashing line that causes the limit to arise." "A Preface to Transgression," 61. But the violence and transgression inherent in lynching overlap; the boundaries do not hold even though they are eventually accepted as the normal.

23. Michael Taussig, "Transgression," in *Critical Terms for Religious Studies*, ed. Mark C. Taylor (Chicago: University of Chicago Press, 1998), 350, 352, 362.

24. William Fitzhugh Brundage, *Lynching in the New South: Georgia and Virginia, 1880–1930* (Urbana: University of Illinois Press, 1993), 17–48.

25. See Bruce Lincoln's definition in "Conflict," in *Critical Terms for Religious Studies*, ed. Mark C. Taylor (Chicago: University of Chicago Press, 1998), 65.

26. Arthur F. Raper, *The Tragedy of Lynching* (Chapel Hill: University of North Carolina Press, 1933), 51, 53.

27. Ibid., 1, 167–68; Daniel Joseph Singal, *The War Within: From Victorian to Modernist Thought in the South, 1919–1945* (Chapel Hill: University of North Carolina Press, 1982), 333.

28. Raper, *Tragedy of Lynching*, 49.

29. Singal, *The War Within*, 332.

30. Raper, *Tragedy of Lynching*, 19, 22, 23, 71–72, 81, 88, 91, 135, 146, 150, 152, 199, 229, 243–45, 278, 335.

31. Ibid., 319–55.

32. Ibid., 335.

33. Ibid., 334.

34. Ibid., 335, 337–39 (emphasis added).

35. Philip J. Lee points out that the phrase rarely appears in scripture in *Against the Protestant Gnostics* (New York: Oxford University Press), 117.

36. See ibid., 101–14.

37. Many Christians would object to the conversionist paradigm as privileging subjectivity over reason, tradition, and scripture (which evangelicals would protest since they believed themselves to be especially devoted to scriptural authority). Also objectionable would have been evangelicals' repudiation of liturgy as "empty formalism" even though the Eucharist is scriptural and presents the life-death-resurrection of Christ in action that appeals to the full range of human senses and functions as a corrective to subjectivist and idiosyncratic distortions.

38. The studies upon which this interpretation primarily rests are the critical analyses Dickson D. Bruce Jr., *And They All Sang Hallelujah: Plain-Folk Camp-Meeting Religion, 1800–1845* (Knoxville: University of Tennessee Press, 1974); John Boles, *The Great Revival, 1787–1805: The Origins of the Southern Evangelical Mind* (Lexington: University Press of Kentucky, 1972); Anne C. Loveland, *Southern Evangelicals and the Social Order, 1800–1860* (Baton Rouge: Louisiana State University Press, 1980); Donald G. Mathews, *Religion in the Old South* (Chicago: University of Chicago Press, 1977); Ted Ownby, *Subduing Satan: Religion, Recreation, and Manhood in the Rural South, 1865–1920* (Chapel Hill: University of North Carolina Press, 1990), 103–66.

39. Freeborn Garrettson, *The Experience and Travels of Mr. Freeborn Garrettson* (Philadelphia: Parry Hall, 1791), 36–37, 40, 76–77; Donald G. Mathews, *Slavery and Methodism: A Chapter in American Morality, 1780–1845* (Princeton, N.J.: Princeton University Press, 1965), chap. 1.

40. Paul Tillich, a twentieth-century theologian, called this "the courage to be" in his book of the same name (London: Nisbet, 1952).

41. Mathews, *Religion in the Old South*, 138–84.

42. See André Trocmé, *Jesus and the Nonviolent Revolution* (Maryknoll, N.Y.: Orbis, 2004), 13–41.

43. Samuel S. Hill, *Southern Churches in Crisis* (New York: Holt, Rinehart and Winston, 1967), 27–28. See also the statement by the anonymous Reverend John Doe, a Southern Baptist intellectual, as reported in Harold Bloom, *The American Religion* (New York: Simon and Schuster, 1992), 203–4: "Baptists conceive of the Christian life as an unmediated fellowship with God, and the Bible is indispensable for that fellowship; it is just that the Bible does not count as a true mediator. Instead, it is the immediacy of the Spirit which makes the Bible meaningful in the first place, though only to those with open hearts. You get the idea that the Bible is yours, personally, and not external to you as with Luther's sacraments. The Bible is internal to you with the Holy Spirit."

44. William Hooper Haigh, Diary, August 14, 18, 1844, Southern Historical Collection, University of North Carolina, Chapel Hill.

45. Trocmé, *Jesus and the Nonviolent Revolution*, 13–27. At the begin-

ning of his public ministry, Trocmé points out, Jesus announced through the words of the prophet Isaiah that he was proclaiming "freedom to the prisoners" and "the year of the Lord's favor." That is, he proclaimed jubilee out of the scripture available to him, and it is this sense of freedom that African Americans responded to when they heard Christian preaching in its messianic meaning.

46. See, for example, the discussion of masters' duties in William Andrew Smith, *Lectures on Slavery* (Nashville: Publishing House of the Methodist Episcopal Church, South, 1856).

47. See Mary Douglas, *Purity and Danger: An Analysis of Concepts of Pollution and Taboo* (1966; repr., Harmondsworth, U.K.: Pelican, 1970).

48. Philip Alexander Bruce, "Evolution of the Negro Problem," *Sewanee Review* 19 (October 1911): 385–99, reprinted as "In Defense of Southern Race Policies," in I. A. Newby, ed., *The Development of Segregationist Thought* (Homewood, Ill.: Dorsey, 1968), 70–78.

49. Douglas, *Purity and Danger,* 145.

50. William Cohen, *At Freedom's Edge: Black Mobility and the Southern White Quest for Racial Control, 1861–1915* (Baton Rouge: Louisiana State University Press, 1991).

51. See comments in *Raleigh (N.C.) News and Observer,* May 24, 1908. The Prohibition movements were ways of disciplining and controlling black men as well as white, and the racist expression of temperance campaigns implied the tactic of enlisting white "church people" in support of white supremacy; see Frederick A. Bode, *Protestantism and the New South: North Carolina Baptists and Methodists in Political Crisis, 1894–1903* (Charlottesville: University Press of Virginia, 1975). This conclusion was also suggested by conversations with Timothy Long, who has studied the white supremacist values of North Carolina Baptists. See Mrs. J. J. Ansley, *History of the Georgia Women's Christian Temperance Union from its Organization in 1883 to 1907* (Columbus: Gilbert, 1914); Paul Isaac, *Prohibition and Politics: Turbulent Decades in Tennessee, 1885–1920* (Knoxville: University of Tennessee Press, 1977); James Benson Sellers, *The Prohibition Movement in Alabama, 1702 to 1943* (Chapel Hill: University of North Carolina Press, 1943); Daniel Jay Whitener, *Prohibition in North Carolina, 1715–1945* (Chapel Hill: University of North Carolina Press, 1946).

52. Mathews, "Southern Rite of Human Sacrifice," 90; Clifford Geertz, *The Interpretation of Cultures* (New York: Basic), 89.

53. John W. Cell, *The Highest Stage of White Supremacy: The Origins of Segregation in South Africa and the American South* (New York: Cambridge University Press, 1982), 134; Cohen, *At Freedom's Edge;* C. Vann Woodward, *The Strange Career of Jim Crow* (New York: Oxford University Press, 1974).

54. Robert G. Hamerton-Kelly, *Sacred Violence: Paul's Hermeneutic of the Cross* (Minneapolis: Fortress, 1992), 15. See also James G. Williams, *The Bible, Violence, and the Sacred: Liberation from the Myth of Sanctioned Violence* (San Francisco: HarperSanFrancisco, 1991), 16–17.

55. Cohen, *At Freedom's Edge*, 214–15.

56. Bruce, "Evolution of the Negro Problem."

57. Woodward, *Strange Career*, 67–109; Edward L. Ayers, *The Promise of the New South: Life after Reconstruction* (New York: Oxford University Press, 1992), 52–54, 67–68, 121–27, 136–49, 175–78, 269, 289–90, 298–99, 304–9, 409–13, 429, 433–34.

58. Thomas Nelson Page, *The Negro: The Southerner's Problem* (New York: Charles Scribner's Sons, 1904); Philip Alexander Bruce, *The Plantation Negro as a Freeman: Observations on His Character, Condition, and Prospects in Virginia* (1889).

59. Lillian Smith, *Killers of the Dream* (1949; repr., New York: W. W. Norton, 1961). Smith's remembrance is in "A Report from Lillian Smith on Killers of the Dream," Lillian Smith Papers, 1283A, box 30, University of Georgia Library, Athens. An editorial in the *Atlanta Constitution* referred to Smith as "the ex-missionary who has made a profession of writing stuff that purposely sets out to debase the South, with a fury that continually overleaps itself." "Miss Smith," wrote Ralph McGill of the *Constitution*, "is a prisoner in the monastery of her own mind." See Lillian Smith Papers. Even recent critics find her too absorbed in race to be a worthy commentator on the South. See Fred Hobson, *Tell about the South: The Southern Rage to Explain* (Baton Rouge: Louisiana State University Press, 1983), 321: Because Smith focused on segregation, Hobson writes, she missed "much of what else the South was and had been."

60. Smith, *Killers of the Dream*, 83, 88–90, 101, 224–52.

61. Grace Elizabeth Hale, *Making Whiteness: The Culture of Segregation in the South, 1890–1940* (New York: Pantheon, 1998).

62. Smith, *Killers of the Dream*, 83, 85–86, 88–90.

63. Anne C. Loveland, *Lillian Smith: A Southerner Confronting the South* (Baton Rouge: Louisiana State University Press, 1986), 97–105; see also Hobson's evaluation in *Tell about the South*, 308–13.

64. The professed experience of conversion was so expected a part of growing up in an evangelical culture that one would be tempted by social and parental pressure to profess a conversion experience at the appropriate time in one's life even without an existential transformation.

65. Southerntown was the name John Dollard gave to the Mississippi town in which he studied segregation during the 1930s; he lived in the town doing fieldwork that included both black and white people. See Dollard, *Caste and Class in a Southern Town* (1936; repr., New York: Vintage, 1957).

66. Ibid., 350.

67. Ibid., 327. For a full range of observations that provided evidence for widespread white hostility and aggression against black people within the structure of segregation see especially ibid., 174–85, 316–59, 369–81.

68. Mathews, "Southern Rite of Human Sacrifice."

69. Smith, "Capital Punishment and Human Sacrifice," especially 12–16.

FUNDAMENTALISM IN RECENT SOUTHERN CULTURE

Has It Done What the Civil Rights Movement Couldn't Do?

SAMUEL S. HILL

In an appropriate closing essay, Sam Hill examines the interconnections between religious and cultural forms in the South. He suggests that contemporary popular fundamentalism (since the 1970s) has been instrumental in the disappearance of the South as a highly distinctive regional culture. Whereas early twentieth-century fundamentalism sat outside the familiar bounds of southern culture, the neofundamentalists of the late twentieth century nestled comfortably in the region, providing antidotes to anxiety but at the cost of pitting southerners against each other in crusades over "family values," "Christian" lifestyles, and "proper" understanding of the scriptures. In this way, the essay contends, contemporary fundamentalism has changed and challenged the region's historic correlation of church and culture far more than did the civil rights movement that immediately preceded it.

In fair weather and foul, the South is reputed; that is, it has reputation. Asking whether its reputation for this, that, or the other quality is justified has fascinated analysts—both Dixie admirers and detractors—for a very long time. One property long attributed to it, that it is religiously fundamentalist, has been incorrect until quite recently. In the same season that the South, in favor of becoming more like the rest of the country, was shedding some characterizations as too distinctive, the region has come to deserve description as fundamentalist, significantly if far from totally. Despite the South's reputation, the advent of fundamentalism into the region in recent decades has brought with it significant disruptions to the traditional religious order and has challenged the established southern culture as no other social movement in the twentieth century. In this essay, I propose to do two things. One aim is to characterize fundamentalism—what it stands for, what it opposes, and what its goals are—and in order to do that, we must glance briefly at the history of this movement both in the South and in the United States at large. I argue that for the first generation or two after fundamentalism gained a presence in the South, its place within the culture was marginal and its influence minimal. As much as its adherents may have wished that God would turn the society upside down, the movement came nowhere near destabilizing that society. Relegated to the fringes as it was, many thought it would go away or continue to be harmless, even if its presence was somewhat annoying. But fundamentalism did not fade away, and the second aim of this essay is to assess its influence on contemporary southern culture. If fundamentalism is not in keeping with the traditional religious and social forms of the South, then its recent advent and rapid acquisition of social power must mean that it has shaken conventional southern society in ways that the reputation of the South has obscured. To take a case in point, the civil rights movement, the other social force with which we are concerned here, arose as a powerful force in the years after World War II, and was soon to disturb everything. Both its intended and its actual effects were certainly destabilizing, but curiously, we may suggest, the civil rights movement did not overturn traditional regional life. All of the arrangements came to be different, but the building blocks of the emergent new order were in fact those that had composed it for centuries.

Beginning in the mid-1970s, fundamentalism attained an unprecedented prominence in the South. It disrupted two major denominations, the Presbyterian and the Southern Baptist, altering the place of each in the society. It also brought into being and prominence various new congregations, fellowships, media networks, and educational institutions that we will refer to here as a kind of "third force" among southern Protestants. Further, fundamentalism's ascent took place concurrently with the rise of the Republican Party as the white population's political home of choice, a political realignment that was clearly related to the religious one. Of course, the civil rights movement of the 1950s and 1960s contributed to these major changes that occurred in politics and religion, but my argument is that contemporary fundamentalism has wrought more changes in southern society and culture—along some lines, at any rate—than did the civil rights movement in its prime.

FUNDAMENTALISM: AN OVERVIEW

What is fundamentalism? It is a form of evangelical Protestantism, comprising perhaps 15 percent of the membership of that major national branch of Christianity, and, until recently, an even smaller percentage than that in the southern region. Like the larger company of evangelicals, fundamentalists are committed to evangelization and the cultivation of personal piety. But while fundamentalism affirms those activities in themselves, it is much more concerned with, and defined by, correct belief than practice. Christian doctrine is defined in the most precise and absolutist ways, and only a fractional degree of flexibility—or better, none at all—can be honored, regardless of one's experiential claims.

Fundamentalism is therefore exclusive; only those who preach and believe in line with the truth as the Bible presents it—*interpretation* is no issue here at all—are worthy to be called Christians. What identifies their faith, therefore, is of the head, and fundamentalists prize doctrinal exactitude and correct belief despite their attendant experiential claims. Further, fundamentalists are serial in their mode of thinking, not comprehensive or dialectic. In other words, fundamentalism identifies particular teachings and ranks them by importance. A fixed number may be held as constitutive of the true message, but they are arranged in a numerical series, not related to each other in a systematic pattern. Such a focus on the articulation of belief—in its most precise form—clearly identifies fundamentalism as a form of Christian rationalism in its approach to matters of faith, regardless of its reputation as anti-intellectual. Finally, fundamentalism may be understood as contrarian. Fundamentalists take their cues from the Bible and its teachings, honoring no other sources and reference points. They have no interest in consulting other authorities or opinions, nor do they entertain any interest in cooperation with other Christian groups. There is only one truth, and only one approved epistemic tool. All others are wrong, whatever they may claim about themselves; they are ultimately deceptive and evil, doomed to divine condemnation. Compromise is thus a vice, not a virtue, in the moral universe of the fundamentalist.

Such an attitude left little latitude for any type of cooperation, and classic fundamentalism, from its inception in the 1920s until the 1970s, took as an article of faith being withdrawn from society. The world was fallen, human public structures were evil—unless and until the Lord leads the righteous to establish a theocracy or, more likely, comes again. For fundamentalists, organizing politically was simply not an item in the divine calling. Thus, for a half century or more, the movement was separatist and contrarian. To most, there was no use, nor any faithfulness, in working to improve things; the Lord's second advent would take care of that. In a world gone horribly awry, only a position of full and complete separation from the larger society could provide the critical distance from which its condemnation could come.

At once we are struck by a historical anomaly. Since the 1970s, when fundamentalism once again came to command national attention, it has become politically active. It continues to preach a judgmental ideology, but in the process it has adopted a messianic spirit: not retreat but conquest. Classic American fundamentalism did its judging from a distance. Having neither ambition nor hope to take over the society, it took aim from long range, believing it to be unbiblical to participate in evil structures by joining forces with godless people. Such withdrawal was less tactical than strategic; the Lord's marching orders commanded the purity that can come about only through mingling with his obedient people and no others, shunning worldly folk and concerns.

The shift from withdrawal to involvement is a lengthy and complex story, and not central to this essay's argument. I will simply suggest two factors contributing to the shift: (1) the socioeconomic rise of many sectlike church people from social marginality to positions of social impact; and (2) the vacuum in public moral life that has resulted from radical polarization and the cultural conquest by relativist and secularist mentalities. Whatever the reasons, fundamentalism in America has become a political force and has taken an active voice in national public life. This condition is all but unprecedented in the American experience with fundamentalism, a fact that helps explain the fear that many citizens entertain over the effective political organizing conducted by conservative evangelicals (only some of them truly fundamentalist).

Fundamentalism in the South

In the South, Protestant evangelicalism has long been the largest Christian tradition, its most prominent and dominant religious form. But fundamentalism was rare before the 1970s, and the South's involvement in the movement bears its own marks (just as its historic forms of evangelicalism are somewhat regionally distinctive). The Churches of Christ, one prominent national fundamentalist group, have been in the South since the late antebellum period, and the Bob Jones heritage (an indigenous brand) dates back to the 1920s. Perhaps only the latter tradition and the Independent Baptists can claim to be part of the mostly northern fundamentalist movement that erupted in the early twentieth century. In the other cases, the varieties of fundamentalism that are present in the South are of mostly recent origin and sometimes comprise only one unit in a much larger fellowship. The Christian Coalition, the Southern Baptist Convention (SBC), the Baptist Bible Fellowship (BBF), and the Presbyterian Church in America (PCA) represent this second coming of fundamentalism to the region, although in some cases, notably with the Southern Baptist Convention, only some of the marks of the fundamentalist outlook are evident. Still, from the governing majority in the SBC to movements such as the Christian Coalition and the BBF—comprised mainly of Independent Baptist congregations such as Jerry Falwell's Thomas Road Church—fundamentalism has become both sizable and publicly influential. Thus, while some kinds and degrees of fundamentalism have been part of southern religious and cultural life for a century or so, the fundamentalist "reputation" of the South could have been acquired in fact only within the past quarter century—the same period that marks the emergence of fundamentalism into national and regional public life.

The response of the southern regional society to this recent religious-political innovation flies its own colors. That is, the involvement of southern evangelicals in public life is nothing new—except for that old and small fundamentalist sector that has been as strident and as world rejecting in the region as in the rest of the country. What makes the new phenomenon of southern fundamentalism distinctive is that its people have always been at home in the world. They are old-style southern evangelicals who have on certain issues shifted to align themselves with the recently emergent more conservative movements. Most of them, following their earlier counterparts, have voted and shown interest in politics, but typically without associating themselves directly with some organized Christian cause. Those who have come to see the Republican Party as alone taking the high moral road, or who have endorsed the advocacy program of the Moral Majority and the Christian Coalition and promoted such affiliations with messianic zeal, are people whose historic forebears would have manifested less interest in direct political activity. Now they are crying out against the moral vacuum fashioned by relativism and secularism and have centered their moral passion on family and sexual ethics, a natural course for them to take, as members of a "home, school, and church" localist culture.

Historian Will Glass has recently shown how largely region bound southern fundamentalism was in its early stages, from 1920 to 1960.[1] Upholders of the strictest doctrinal standards were making their appearance and their pronouncements; mostly they were Presbyterians and Baptists. Exercised over the emergence of liberal theology here and there in the southern churches, they were expressing a concern far better founded in the North, however. In the South fear of compromise was joined by other factors. One was resistance to cooperative Protestantism (proto-ecumenism), sometimes called "unionism," a fear that first surfaced in the Baptist ranks. Among Presbyterians, the continuing talks about reunion with northern Presbyterians also upset many—the two regional bodies having gone their separate ways over the sectional crisis of the mid-nineteenth century. A second factor further invaded Baptist thinking, namely, a fear of bureaucratization. Although Baptist heritage emphasized congregational self-government—"local autonomy" is their phrase—the church was becoming larger and larger, more and more organized, and yielding to forces of centralization. The tail was wagging the dog, as many saw it.

Noteworthy indeed is how conditioned by southern history, even how region bound, these currents of protests and warning were. Keenly aware of what had been happening within the northern denominations, southerners drew lurid pictures of how those bodies had abandoned sound doctrine. But they had scant interest in joining forces with orthodoxy's standard-bearers outside the region, notwithstanding the fact that the mistakes of the "mainline" Yankee churches stood as a model of what to avoid and prevent.

By the 1950s, the number of southern fundamentalists had increased slightly, and the shape of the movement in the region had been partially recast. One segment stayed within its denomination, seeking to stall or reverse liberal currents. A second cluster formed new separatist denominations and fellowships along its own denomination's lines, creating, in effect, southern versions of northern groups (or in some cases just allying with these like-minded groups). A third branch of southern fundamentalism was interdenominational in one of two ways: as fully separatist, or by its adherents leaving their denominational structures to join with others who nevertheless shared their own denominational heritage. As late as 1960, then, such fundamentalist development as there was stayed overwhelmingly within the region. That is an impressive datum. Not even a snug theological fit and a shared mission were sufficient to impel widespread interregional collaboration.

Although comparable forms existed earlier in the United States and even in the South, southern fundamentalism before the 1970s remained a breed apart. But the new condition of public activity that fundamentalism adopted in that decade became a mark of southern fundamentalism as well. No longer invisible within its own institutions, or dismissible as belonging to a sectarian mentality and a powerless fraction of the population, this fundamentalism has made its presence and influence felt. As part heir to the huge and culturally dominant evangelical community, activist fundamentalism has become a force in the South, and the southern version of fundamentalism is largely an extension of its traditional popular Protestant base. As such, its members, perhaps 10–15 million citizens, are anything but strangers to wide-ranging participation in public life—whether social, economic, or political. Far from being marginal, they are central recipients of and actors in the regional religious and cultural heritage. Lately they have "branched off" or "revolted" or insisted that they alone constitute true whatever-it-is; they are the authentic biblical people. But they are not novices at public involvement. In the most storied case, the white Baptist, they are simply the more conservative of the two sectors of the Southern Baptist Convention. Those who suspect, as I do, that their strength lies more in the clergy leadership than in the guiding sentiments of a massive number of churchmen and -women, are not blind to three facts: first, they engineered a "takeover" that could hardly have happened without a following; second, they hold firmly to the reins of the convention's leadership; and third, no alteration of the present deployment is in sight.

We might have seen this coming for the Baptists when in the early 1970s the Presbyterians battled their way to a rupture. A long record of distrust and disagreement shows up in southern Presbyterian annals, in this case statedly and actually over theology. But here, too, as with the SBC, we are dealing with a peculiarly southern form of evangelicalism. The people who created the Presbyterian Church in America (PCA) in 1973 are not fundamentalist in the classic American sense. They do not belong to the socially marginalized, therefore publicly inexperienced and isolationist, sector. Participation in ordinary society, including politics, has been natural and regular; these are not socially dissident people. What, then, has energized this company of Presbyterians? Are they even truly fundamentalist? It is not easy to characterize them when that is the question we pose. World rejecting they are not, nor society repudiating. Where the question becomes intelligible is in the area of beliefs. They hold convictions about what constitutes authentic and faithful theology, and they affirm particular doctrines defined in specified ways. Accordingly, they are exclusivist, with the criterion of inclusion being correct belief. But we cannot evade the datum that they are a blend of exclusive and inclusive. They are cooperative with like-minded right-minded fellow Protestants. Like their fellow rationalist believers, what they trust is not experience but propositions. The PCA does, however, regard Christian thought as systematic—the parts functioning in the setting of the whole—which distinguishes it from the serial approach of most American fundamentalist groups.

The realignment of the PCA and SBC was a precursor to the cultural changes that were to come. But even as southern fundamentalism made its way impressively onto the scene of the regional culture, it remained distinctive, peculiar in its own curious way. First, it was historically a rather small movement, perhaps because the conservative influence in the South was already so pervasive.

One had to look hard to find any more open space on the right. The contrast, one might say, was between the red-hot and the white-hot. Second, the early southern fundamentalists were aware of the movement in the northern states that had generated headlong confrontation in the Baptist and Presbyterian denominations and independent churches. They were in a position to take notes and learn from the attacks on liberalism led by these northern militants. But, although there was obviously some sharing of leadership and "fellowshipping" back and forth, by and large the founders and followers spread from Texas to Tennessee to Florida to South Carolina were people of and from Dixie. The heresies they exposed and the institutions they maligned belonged to the South. For them, the South was home, Zion, the area where they spoke the same language as everybody else. Finally, the third and most curious way in which early southern fundamentalism was culture specific lay in its *inability* to destabilize the society and culture. That it had impact on individuals, some congregations, and several locales is evident. It also waved ripples of dissent through southern Baptist and Presbyterian waters. But the movement and its spirit were only nuisances much more often than they were disturbances. And even though it did not affect denominational life greatly, its impact in the religious setting was far greater than it was on the civil order, much less on "the South" as a heritage, a way of life, and a biracial society. "The South" as a way of life hardly knew that the fundamentalists were around. All that would change in the 1980s.

THE CIVIL RIGHTS MOVEMENT

William R. Glass argues that a general fundamentalist subculture did not emerge in the South before the 1940s and 1950s.[2] Thus, the South's early generations of fundamentalists could not destabilize the society, much less the culture, before then. They were even unable for the most part to affect significantly the southern denominations. Fundamentalism was a minor minority movement, and little more than a nuisance in some particular locales and organizations. Its adherents were not easily ignored, but they were rather readily dismissed. Impotent insofar as being able to bring about any significant social change, southern fundamentalists were thus oblivious to any impetus to integrate regional society. If they did not devote much energy to defending segregation, neither did they feel called to challenge it. Informing this outlook was the fact that fundamentalist congregations, institutions, and orbits of influence remained overwhelmingly white. To the black citizens of the South, the fundamentalist message spoke not at all.

THE POWERFUL EFFECT OF FUNDAMENTALISM

The hypothesis that prompts this inquiry of what fundamentalism has achieved that the civil rights movement couldn't is this: At the deepest levels, the change in racial and biracial affairs brought about as a result of the civil rights movement was less disruptive of historic southern culture than the Baptist, Presbyterian, and "third-force" fundamentalist uprisings have turned out to be. If the reputation of the South as a hotbed of fundamentalist activity were true, then just the opposite would be the case; but in fact the fundamentalism of the past forty years or so has destabilized the traditional culture of the South in ways far beyond what the civil rights movement was able to accomplish.

First, it really is astonishing how little that was truly new was introduced into the South in consequence of the events of 1954, 1955, 1963, 1965, and so on. The citizen sector over which these violent and nonviolent battles were fought had been part of regional life for three and a half centuries by that time. As unavoidable, as central an ingredient as African Americans were to southern life, they had been put and held in "their place," denied their political and civil rights, doomed to educational and economic inferiority. One manner of describing what the civil rights movement brought about is this: the acknowledgment that a people and a culture, without either of which the historic South was unimaginable, were citizens in the communities of the region. That acknowledgment, far more than verbal, issued in major dislocations, disturbances, and realignments, to be sure. Yet, few new people were immigrating to the region, and few new institutions were making their appearance. Traditional southern culture was changed from the inside out, as it were, as what had been present all along found greater expression and acceptance. The civil rights movement might thus be termed a *conservative* revolution of the South's culture and society.

In contrast, the movement of fundamentalism into mainstream

southern life is turning out to be a *radical* revolution. Contemporary fundamentalism is contributing to the demise of southern culture as it has existed since the Old South period. Its orbit remains largely limited to the white population, dominantly in the traditional Baptist and Presbyterian denominations, but also in the once-fringe sectarian bodies that we are calling the "third force." It is hard to imagine more culturally central and influential institutions than the Baptists and Presbyterians have been in the historic South. Their economic prominence has been great, their political power so forceful as to oblige all people seeking public office to hail from their ranks or to assure the voters that they really think the same way. The triumph of fundamentalism in the South needs only one example. When Presbyterian conservatives created the PCA in the 1970s, they had to do so by withdrawing from a parent body, the Presbyterian Church in the United States, PCUS (Southern). By the 1980s, "fundamental conservatives" in the SBC mobilized themselves into a major force and acquired power in that massive organization. Theirs was a well-orchestrated takeover, not a defection, and they have successfully defended their domination through the intervening years. Indeed, any withdrawal from SBC ranks will probably be by a cadre of "moderate conservatives" who make up what is to date a nonschismatic group, the Cooperative Baptist Fellowship.

The civil rights movement had inclusion as its primary goal. In public policy it was democratic, in that it sought to identify and safeguard a place for everyone. The fundamentalist movement is differently disposed. Its passion is to promote the view that "truth" is absolute, with or without any acknowledgment that any absolutist position places truth ahead of people, in the sense that truth has its essence independent of people's existence. Individuals must come to the truth; it does not come to them. Instead of honoring inclusivity, then, fundamentalism propounds exclusivity. The infallibility of Christian truth and its attendant authority leave no other choice. This, of course, is not the view of fundamentalists themselves; after all, all people are invited to join the exclusive circle of truth believers. Christians of this persuasion do not desire to exclude anyone; their divinely ordained mission (as they understand it) is in fact to enlarge the true believers' circle to be congruent with the entire human race. But we must also be clear that what makes for a certain theology of inclusion proves to be an incompatible social policy when a democratic vision prevails. The fundamentalist Christian public policy is consistent with its theology: all, everyone, must own the truth. Those citizens who do not ought nevertheless to consider themselves blessed if their homeland lives by laws and customs that accord with the fundamentalist understanding of divine righteousness. By their own reasoning, fundamentalists have no right *not* to inform the recalcitrant what is best for them, no matter what that recalcitrant majority may think of them and the basis of their public policy.

Sketched out this way, we are afforded more than a hint into the interpretation that the fundamentalist movement is more disruptive than was the civil rights movement—or, it will have proven to be so if its effect is as comprehensive and enduring as was that of the earlier movement. The civil rights movement reconfigured all the existing parts of southern society and culture by insisting that all be considered equal partners, by law and, desirably, in informal practice. Fundamentalism insists on establishing public policy for the entire public whether most, many, or only a few subscribe to its tenets. That is the force of its inner authoritarian logic. It is perhaps too simplistic to label these competing views of public life as a contrast between democracy and theocracy, but their conflict is apparent.

The ultimate effects of such fundamentalist reasoning on national life remain to be seen. What can be said for certain is that fundamentalism's great achievement thus far has been to make southern religion less southern, that is, less culturally influenced or even less culturally captive. Fundamentalism has succeeded in the dissolution of two southern denominations as we have known them. No one ever had any reason to doubt that the PCUS or the SBC were southern. Both exhibited a strong alliance, or a neat fit, between church and culture in the American South: a fact affirmed by the incapacity of popular southern religion to be effectively exported to other American regions. But at home it has always been at home. No one could have imagined fifty years ago that southern bastions like the PCUS or the SBC would ever forfeit their identity and solidity. But something deemed more important than southernness intruded, namely, ideological correctness. Being sound, being right—theologically—toppled classic regional identity from its throne. A provincial spirit has continued, to be sure, but its dynamic has shifted from being an informal, strong cultural hegemony to being a crusade to conquer the region and the nation. From this angle of view, this radical revolution has certainly lived up to its prophetic vocation.

While the South never was an undifferentiated mass culture, there was for a long time an identifiable southern culture. What the fundamentalist-minded Baptists and Presbyterians and their third-force compatriots (the independent Bible churches and the charismatic and Pentecostal churches) have wrought is the supplanting of being true to the South. Now being the right sort of church person and citizen comes first. The old tribalism of southern life, a product of its history and its heritage, has been dissipated by the recent developments in these central and stalwart denominational organizations. It is being replaced by a new tribalism that represents a coalition of the right-thinking, the correct-minded, the doctrinally and ethically pure. Briefly stated, the old base on which unity and identity rested, which was social-cultural-historical, has given way to a new base that is ideological, theological, and ethical.

Cultural tribalism always carries with it boundaries of inclusivity and exclusivity. Before the religious revolution of the 1970s and the 1980s, those excluded in southern life were African Americans, Catholics, and northerners. With high ideals, the civil rights movement sought to expand these boundaries and succeeded in large degree. Since the revolution, the boundaries have again been redefined, but this time through restriction rather than expansion. The criterion for inclusion is now doctrinal belief, conformity to an orthodoxy that has been defined by those who think straight. Southern fundamentalists among the Presbyterians, the Baptists, and within the third-force institutions hold more in common with their coreligionists in other parts of the country than they do with many coregionalists within their own denominations. The end result is that many of those who were previously the cultural and religious "insiders" have been excluded by this new deployment. Theirs is perhaps the deepest pain, because they took so much for granted during the many generations that they participated in and led these bastion bodies of southern culture. Nor is their anguish lessened by acknowledging that they are getting a dose of their own medicine as the ones who had for so long regulated inclusion and exclusion. The aggrieved-become-aggressors in southern fundamentalism care not at all that they have scuttled hallowed heritages.

Conclusion

Economic or political historians slant all history toward economic or political explanations. As a religious historian, I am prey to the same kind of error by assuming that the religious life of a society is what really animates it. All of us as students of human behavior must do better than that. Yet, what is happening these days in the religious arena in the South and the nation is striking and demands our attention and analysis. In his book *Broken Churches, Broken Nation*, C. C. Goen argued that the breaking up along regional lines of the three largest denominations, the Methodist, the Baptist, and the Presbyterian, both presaged and helped cause the secession of the southern states to form an independent nation.[3] My contention here, more like a hypothesis, is that the southern religious sundering of our time bespeaks and furthers the disappearance of the South as a highly distinctive culture. The application, of course, is complex. These recent changes make the persistence of southern culture more tenuous. They have done so by forging new alliances between very conservative religious forces in the region and in the North and West. And by dividing and conquering, they have weakened the internal unity of the traditional denominations, prying them loose from their comfortable link with traditional southern culture. That in itself is an accomplishment that those who repute fundamentalism to traditional southern religion seem to miss.

Notes

1. William R. Glass, *Strangers in Zion: Fundamentalism in the South, 1900–1950* (Macon, Ga.: Mercer University Press, 2001), chaps. 3–5.

2. Ibid., esp. xvii–xvix.

3. C. C. Goen, *Broken Churches, Broken Nation: Denominational Schisms and the Coming of the Civil War* (Macon, Ga.: Mercer University Press, 1985).

Copyrights and Permissions

CONTRIBUTORS

WALTER H. CONSER JR. is professor of religion and professor of history at the University of North Carolina, Wilmington. His publications include *A Coat of Many Colors: Religion and Society along the Cape Fear River of North Carolina* and *God and the Natural World: Religion and Science in Antebellum America*.

JAMES R. CURTIS is professor of geography and urban studies at California State University, Long Beach. He is the author of several articles as well as the coauthor of *The Cuban American Experience* and *The Mexican Border Cities*.

MATTHEW DAY is assistant professor of religion at Florida State University. His current research focuses on religion and the natural sciences, and he has published several articles relating to this topic.

MARCIE COHEN FERRIS is assistant professor in the American studies curriculum at the University of North Carolina, Chapel Hill. Her publications include *Matzoh Ball Gumbo: Culinary Tales of the Jewish South*.

PAUL HARVEY is professor of history at the University of Colorado, Colorado Springs. His publications include *Freedom's Coming: How Religious Culture Shaped the South from the Civil War through the Civil Rights Era* and *Redeeming the South: Religious Cultures and Racial Identities among Southern Baptists, 1865–1925*.

SAMUEL S. HILL is emeritus professor of religion at the University of Florida. He is author and editor of a variety of publications on the subject of southern religion; his *The South and North in American Religion* and *Southern Churches in Crisis, Revisited* deserve special mention.

BARBARA LAU is director of Community Documentary Projects at the Center for Documentary Studies, Duke University. Her curatorial credits include *From Cambodia to Carolina: Tracing the Journeys of New Southerners* and *Durham Civil Rights Heritage Project*.

BILL J. LEONARD is professor of church history and dean of the Divinity

School at Wake Forest University. He is the author or editor of numerous books, including *Baptists in America* and *God's Last and Only Hope: The Fragmentation of the Southern Baptist Convention*.

WILLIAM MARTIN is Chavanne Senior Fellow for Religion and Public Policy at the James A. Baker III Institute for Public Policy and emeritus professor of sociology at Rice University. His books include *With God on Our Side: The Rise of the Religious Right in America* and *A Prophet with Honor: The Billy Graham Story*.

DONALD G. MATHEWS is professor emeritus of history at the University of North Carolina, Chapel Hill. His research interests center on the interrelationships of religion, violence, punishment, and lynching. His publications include *Slavery and Methodism* and *Religion in the Old South*.

WILLIAM D. MOORE is associate professor of history and director of public history at the University of North Carolina, Wilmington. He is the author of *Masonic Temples: Freemasonry, Ritual Architecture, and Masculine Archetypes*.

CHARLES E. ORSER JR., formerly Distinguished Professor of Anthropology at Illinois State University, serves as curator of Historical Archaeology at the New York State Museum. He is the author of *Race and the Archaeology of Identity* and *Historical Archaeology*.

DIANA PASULKA is assistant professor of religion at the University of North Carolina, Wilmington. She has published essays on the topics of religion and popular culture and is interested in representations of purgatory in American religion.

RODGER M. PAYNE, the former chair of the Department of Philosophy and Religious Studies at Louisiana State University, is now the chair of the Department of Religious Studies at the University of North Carolina, Asheville. He is the author of *The Self and the Sacred: Conversion and Autobiography in Early American Protestantism* as well as articles on southern religion and Catholic devotionalism in Louisiana.

CELESTE RAY is associate professor and chair of the Department of Anthropology at the University of the South. Her publications include *Highland Heritage: Scottish Americans in the American South* and *Southern Heritage on Display: Public Ritual and Ethnic Diversity within Southern Regionalism*.

RANDALL J. STEPHENS is assistant professor of history at Eastern Nazarene College. His research interests include the origins of the southern Holiness and Pentecostal movements.

CHARLES REAGAN WILSON is director of the Center for the Study of Southern Culture and professor of history and southern studies at the University of Mississippi. He is the author of *Baptized in Blood: The Religion of the Lost Cause, 1865–1920* and editor in chief of *The New Encyclopedia of Southern Culture*.

INDEX

African Americans, 93, 162–63,
363, 366; in Holiness
Pentecostalism, 195–97, 200–
204, 207–9, 211–13; lynching
and death of, 318–19, 321–24,
328–31, 336–37; migration
from South, 187–88, 266;
music, 10, 16–17, 20–21, 23,
71, 164, 182, 259–66; in "New
South," 249–55, 257–66; and
ordination of women, 313–14;
in paintings of McKendree
Robbins Long, 105, 111;
relations with Jews, 165–73,
177, 179–84, 186, 189; as
symbols of societal "pollution,"
339–41, 343–45. *See also* African
culture; slavery
African culture, 32–33, 48–50,
166; Africanisms debate, 41–43,
48, 250; Africanist literary
presence, 134–35; African
religions, 32–36, 43–49,
51–57, 254–55, 263–64; and
slavery, 39–44. *See also* African
Americans
African Methodist Episcopal
(AME) Church, 195, 254, 265;
AME Zion Church, 265
Alabama, 102, 177, 197, 199,
243, 246, 263; musicians
and singers from, 12, 14;
Pentecostal meetings in, 204,
208, 214; slave life in, 44. *See
also* Birmingham; Mobile;
Montgomery

Alabama, University of, 174
alcohol, 176, 179, 201;
consumption of, 95, 162, 236.
See also Prohibition
Anderson, Harry (artist), 98, 116,
120–22
Arkansas, 63, 206; Delta Jewish
culture in, 164–66, 178–80, 182,
184–85. *See also* Little Rock
art: in Catholic devotional culture,
276, 293–94; "outsider art,"
89–90, 93–98; southern art and
religion, 96–97, 124–25. *See also*
Long, McKendree Robbins
Assemblies of God, 15, 17, 18
Atlanta, 80, 96, 208, 211, 241,
253, 331; lynching near, 318;
lynching of Leo Frank in, 319,
346
Azusa Street revival, 195–97;
influence on southern
Pentecostalism, 206–9, 215;
and racial and gender equality,
211–13

Baltimore, 20, 90; Catholic
Diocese of, 280
Baptist churches/Baptists, 66–67,
74, 161, 327, 328, 333, 338;
Baptist Bible Fellowship,
303–4, 313, 358; Cooperative
Baptist Fellowship, 304,
311, 314; fundamentalism,
355, 358–67; and Holiness-
Pentecostal movement, 197,
202–5, 209–10, 213; influence